PUBLISHED ON THE FOUNDATION
ESTABLISHED IN MEMORY OF
HENRY WELDON BARNES
OF THE CLASS OF 1882
YALE COLLEGE

THE HENRY WELDON BARNES
MEMORIAL PUBLICATION FUND

The present volume is the thirteenth work published by the Yale University Press on the Henry Weldon Barnes Memorial Publication Fund. This Foundation was established June 16, 1913, by a gift made to Yale University by the late William Henry Barnes, Esq., of Philadelphia, in memory of his son, a member of the Class of 1882, Yale College, who died December 3, 1882. While a student at Yale, Henry Weldon Barnes was greatly interested in the study of literature and in the literary activities of the college of his day, contributing articles to some of the undergraduate papers and serving on the editorial board of the *Yale Record*. It had been his hope and expectation that he might in after life devote himself to literary work. His untimely death prevented the realization of his hopes; but by the establishment of the Henry Weldon Barnes Memorial Publication Fund his name will nevertheless be forever associated with the cause of scholarship and letters which he planned to serve and which he loved so well.

Edward FitzGerald as a Young Man

FROM A WATER-COLOR PORTRAIT BY WILLIAM MAKEPEACE THACKERAY

ORIGINAL OWNED BY ELEANOR FITZGERALD KERRICH

THE LIFE OF

Edward FitzGerald

TRANSLATOR OF

The Rubáiyát of Omar Khayyám

BY

Alfred McKinley Terhune

NEW HAVEN

Yale University Press

LONDON : GEOFFREY CUMBERLEGE : OXFORD UNIVERSITY PRESS

1947

To

Annabelle

who toiled that I might spin my yarn.

"I had no truer friend: he was one of the kindliest of men, and I have never known one of so fine and delicate a wit."

Foreword

"WRITE your biography if you will," Edward FitzGerald once advised his friend, Bernard Barton, "but think twice before you publish it."

I doubt that FitzGerald would have given even that much encouragement to anyone who proposed writing his life. His manner of living, molded by what he called "a talent for dullness," he would have insisted, provided scant material for a biographer. Not all would agree.

His lifelong friendships with Thackeray, Tennyson, and Carlyle are interesting enough in themselves to justify a biography. He generously helped both the novelist and the poet by giving freely from his ample means at times when they sorely needed funds, and he was directly responsible for Tennyson's breaking a silence of ten years to publish in 1842 the volumes which firmly established his reputation. "I had no truer friend," the poet declared. Thackeray named him when asked by his daughter whom, of all his friends, he loved most. At Cheyne Row FitzGerald was a welcome visitor, and Carlyle once even submitted to what he described in advance as a "mad, shrieking, and . . . quite horrible" railway journey to visit him in Suffolk.

But justification for his biography need not be sought in FitzGerald's relations with famous contemporaries. The merit of his translation of the *Rubáiyát of Omar Khayyám* would be sufficient reason for giving an account of his life. The poem has won an unassailable place among the masterpieces of English literature. The story of the translator's life, however, is still virtually unknown.

Aldis Wright, editor of FitzGerald's works, maintained that the correspondence which he published in the *Literary Remains* provided a satisfactory narrative of the poet's life; and he discouraged attempts to write a formal biography. Mr. Wright's selection of letters is an artistic achievement of unquestioned merit and discloses exceptional editorial acumen. However, ferreting out the story of a man's life from his correspondence is like reading a closely written manuscript by the light of a flickering candle. Only by intense application can so fragmentary a record of thoughts and occupations be pieced together into a coherent pattern. Despite one's pains it is impossible to find in letters all the items necessary to complete the design.

Correspondence reveals the man, but not the man's life; it whets but rarely satisfies the reader's curiosity. Mysterious names haunt the pages like unidentified characters in a play. Letters raise questions which they do not answer. The writer's interests, enthusiasms, and prejudices are apparent; but wherein they originated, by what steps they developed may never be revealed. How, for example, did FitzGerald become interested in Persian? When? To these and to many other questions his letters provide vague and unsatisfactory answers if any. And what lies behind Mr. Wright's footnote which identifies Bernard Barton as "the Quaker Poet of Woodbridge, whose daughter FitzGerald later married"? Thus did the editor dismiss the amazing story of FitzGerald's marriage, but his zeal in suppressing the details succeeded only in arousing the curiosity of readers.

I am sincerely grateful to Mr. Wright for his diligence in discouraging previous writers. He thereby reserved for me the privilege of undertaking the first biography to be written with the approval of the FitzGerald family. A wealth of manuscript material was made available to me. In my possession are copies of more than a thousand unpublished letters and portions of letters which I am now editing for a complete edition of FitzGerald's correspondence. Books from the poet's library, his commonplace and notebooks, diaries of friends, and numerous other manuscripts have been placed at my disposal. Only a small portion of this material was available to Thomas Wright,[1] the only previous author to attempt a complete account of FitzGerald's life. His book, although factually unreliable, has heretofore been accepted as the authority for information not found in the correspondence.

I am obligated to many who have helped me in my work, but few debts are as acceptable as those contracted in labor of this kind. To FitzGerald's grandnieces, Miss Mary Eleanor and Miss Olivia Kerrich of Beccles, Suffolk, for their hospitality, aid, and kindness, I am most grateful. The former is the poet's literary executrix. For the help given by Miss Madeleine de Soyres, another grandniece, and by Gerald Fitz-Gerald, Esq., a grandnephew, I am likewise indebted.

Without the approval and coöperation of the Council of Trinity College and the Syndics of the University Library at the University of Cambridge, England, this biography could not have been written. The permissions by which those authorities opened to me the manuscripts in their care made it possible to throw new light on virtually every portion of FitzGerald's life and work. The proposed edition of the correspondence could not have been attempted without their consent. To both the Council and the Syndics I wish to express my gratitude. To H. M.

[1] Thomas Wright was not related to Aldis Wright, FitzGerald's editor.

Adams, Esq., Librarian of Trinity College, and his aides, as well as to members of the University Library staff who helped me, I wish to express my thanks.

Specific acknowledgments to all who assisted me would be impossible, but a number must be mentioned. My debt to F. L. Lucas, Fellow of King's College, through whose experience as a writer and critic I benefited immeasurably, can never be repaid. Not only am I indebted to the Reverend Dr. H. F. Stewart, Dean of Trinity College, for assistance; but it is to his foresight that I owe E. B. Cowell's account of the genesis of FitzGerald's Persian studies. The noble character of Trinity's Dean goes far to restore one's faith in humanity. A. H. Hollond, Fellow and Dean of Trinity, gave unreservedly of his knowledge, advice, and support at a time when all were sorely needed. H. R. Creswick, generous and kindly Librarian of the Bodleian Library, Oxford, may be assured that his interest in this work and the counsel which he gave on many points will never be forgotten. Important manuscripts were placed at my disposal and invaluable aid was given to me by Mrs. Richard B. Fuller (Hester Thackeray Ritchie), granddaughter of William Makepeace Thackeray, and by Charles Tennyson, Esq., grandson of Alfred Lord Tennyson. I am indebted to both for their generosity and hospitality. I wish also to express my thanks to the trustees of the estate of the former Poet Laureate, whom Mr. Tennyson represents.

Although a complete list of those to whom my thanks are due would be too long to include here, I may at least name Vincent Redstone, Esq., antiquarian of Woodbridge, Suffolk, whose death robbed American writers and scholars of an unselfish and sympathetic adviser; Dr. A. Daly Briscoe and his delightful family, the present occupants of Little Grange; Mrs. Catharine B. Johnson, whose book, *William Bodham Donne and His Friends,* an entertaining memoir of her grandfather, is unfortunately little known to a public which would read it with delight; the Reverend Allan Wigham Price of Low Fell, Gateshead, and his gracious parents, Mr. and Mrs. Alex Price of Finchley; Gerald Spalding, Esq., son of one of FitzGerald's friends; Guy Maynard, Esq., Curator of the Ipswich and the Christchurch Mansion Museums; Keith Kennedy, Registrar of Syracuse University; Charles Ganz, Esq., editor of *A FitzGerald Medley;* Harry Goodwin, Esq., of Lowestoft; and the Omar Khayyám Club of London, through whose rare good fellowship the memories of Edward FitzGerald and Omar Khayyám are fittingly perpetuated. One of my keenest regrets is that the genial and kindly John Henderson, who for so long was secretary of the club and who took great interest in the progress of this book, did not live to see it completed. To these acknowledgments must be added those due to Sir Robert Eaton

White of Boulge Hall; H. H. Lachlan White, Esq., of Bredfield House; and Mrs. Janet White of Geldestone Hall. It is purely by chance that three of the homes about which so much of FitzGerald's life revolved are now occupied by owners bearing the same name. The three families are unrelated.

My task has been a long and arduous but by no means an unpleasant one. For several years I have lived with "Old Fitz." I have wandered about those portions of England where he wandered, trod footpaths which he trod, sailed on his beloved Deben, and visited homes in which he lived and visited. I have talked with the few surviving persons who knew him personally; and, through books, I have been a companion to his companions. His letters have been forwarded to me through devious channels. Mine has been a rare and fascinating adventure.

In writing my narrative, I have striven to be objective and impersonal, for I believe that, unless it is unavoidable, a biographer must not intrude between his subject and the reader. My zeal for objectivity has been supported by two remarks which haunted me as I wrote. The first, like an admonition from "Old Fitz" himself, I found in one of his commonplace books: "Truth, like Venison, is not only the best eating but the hardest hunting." The second was Othello's preface to his own brief biography: "I will a round unvarnish'd tale deliver."

Two or three technical practices, followed in writing the biography, call for a word of explanation. No uniform practice for the transliteration of Persian into English has ever been established. Considerable variety, therefore, will be observed in the spelling of Persian names and words. When quoting, I have, of course, followed the form used by the authorities from whom passages were taken. For the rest, I have adopted FitzGerald's transliteration. It might be pointed out here that the accent mark over the *a* in Persian words (Khayyám, for example) indicates a long *a*. The two sounds are differentiated by one translator by spelling the poet's name *Kheyyam*. Aldis Wright published four editions of FitzGerald's letters before issuing the *Letters and Literary Remains*. In that work was compiled all the correspondence which he had previously published. In order to avoid the confusion that might have resulted from the use of page references, I have given the correspondent and the date of the letter from which extracts were taken, when quoting from Mr. Wright's edition.

FitzGerald's use of capital letters has confused many readers. They have no significance whatever. "I love the old Capitals for Nouns," he once wrote.

East Rupert, Vermont

FIVE years have passed since this manuscript was completed. Complications resulting from the war have delayed the publication of the book. In the meantime, those to whom I am indebted have been joined by Dr. Emery E. Neff of Columbia University. Dr. Neff, the author of several books, among them an excellent biography of Thomas Carlyle, had the greatness of soul to read this manuscript while at work on one of his own.

SUFFOLK was the scene of considerable military activity during the war. A letter received from Miss Madeleine de Soyres as this book goes to press describes a recent visit to FitzGerald's homes. "Hardly any had changed," she writes, "except Bredfield House, which was badly damaged by blast. Its lodge had been demolished by a direct hit."

Syracuse University

Contents

Map of FitzGerald's Suffolk precedes the index.

THE LIFE OF EDWARD FITZGERALD
TRANSLATOR OF THE RUBÁIYÁT

I

Parentage and Early Life

> Into this Universe, and *Why* not knowing
> Nor *Whence,* like Water willy-nilly flowing;
> And out of it, as Wind along the Waste,
> I know not *Whither,* willy-nilly blowing.
>   FITZGERALD'S *Rubáiyát*

THE mood and charm of nineteenth-century rural England still pervade the countryside about Woodbridge in Suffolk. True, west of the town a modern highway cuts a raw gash across green fields, a path for noise and confusion where only tranquillity should be. Nevertheless, friendly byroads steal from the highway and lead to hidden villages and crossroad hamlets or, eastward, drop to the River Deben, one of the many lazy East Anglian streams which wander capriciously in search of outlets to the sea. Along these roads England of Victoria's time may still be found. Tracts of woodland dot the expanse of meadow and pasture. Stiles give access to alluring footpaths which thread the fields to kissing gates in the farther hedgerows. Here and there tower ancient trees in spacious parks. Roofs and chimneys, cushioned in foliage, are all that can be seen of dwellings except where openings in the trees reveal façades of stately halls.

In one of these, the White House, between Woodbridge and Bredfield Village, about seven miles northeast of Ipswich, Edward FitzGerald, poet, translator, letter writer, and intimate friend of Tennyson, Thackeray, and Carlyle, was born on March 31, 1809.[1] His birthplace [2] has changed little since the days of his childhood. The hall, a dignified Jacobean mansion, faces east to receive the

---

1. 1809 was also the birth year of Alfred Tennyson, Abraham Lincoln, William E. Gladstone, Charles Darwin, Felix Mendelssohn, Edgar Allan Poe, Oliver Wendell Holmes, Fanny Kemble, Richard Monckton Milnes, and Cyrus McCormick, inventor of the reaper.
2. The FitzGeralds did not own this home. The White House is now known as Bredfield House and is owned by Lachlan White, Esq. It is the subject of FitzGerald's poem, "Bredfield Hall."

first rays of the morning sun. To the south spread the gardens, bordered at the far end by a fish pond where, as a child, FitzGerald saw "many a tench caught." The tallest trees in the park were once visible from the sea, which lay eight miles to the southeast; and from the road before the house could be seen the topmasts of Nelson's men-of-war anchored in Hollesley Bay during the Napoleonic Wars.

FitzGerald's name at birth was Edward Purcell.[3] He was the son of John Purcell, gentleman, who in 1801 married his own first cousin, Mary Frances FitzGerald.[4] The marriage was one of several which united the two families. On the death of his father-in-law in 1818, Mr. Purcell assumed the FitzGerald name and arms. To avoid confusion, he will be referred to hereafter by his adopted name.

The Purcells were Anglo-Normans who had entered England in the army of William the Conqueror and crossed to Ireland with Henry II in 1172. Edward's father, a lineal descendant of the Barons of Loughmoe, was the eldest son of Dr. John Purcell, a wealthy physician of Richmond Hill, Dublin.[5] He entered Trinity College, Dublin, in 1790, took his degree in 1794, and enrolled in the Inner Temple, London. He never practiced law but, possessing considerable means, settled at Bredfield after his marriage, and devoted himself to politics and to his duties as squire. He served as High Sheriff in both Suffolk and County Cork, Ireland, and held a commission as lieutenant colonel in the East Suffolk Second Corps Volunteers. In 1826 he was elected to Parliament from Seaford, Sussex,[6] and sat in conjunction with George Canning until the latter's death in 1827. The borough was abolished by the Reform Bill of 1832, and Mr. FitzGerald's career as a legislator came to an end. He delegated the supervision of his estates to resident managers, one of whom absconded with several thousand pounds. During the 'twenties he began to mine coal on his wife's property at Manchester, an unlucky venture. An agent who marketed the coal cheated him of further sums and disappeared when his practices were discovered. Mining operations were beset by engineering

3. Accent on the first syllable.

4. Mr. and Mrs. FitzGerald's common grandfather was John FitzGerald of Williamstown, County Roscommon, Ireland. See genealogical table, p. 346.

5. FitzGerald's father was the eldest in a family of seven: John, Charles, Edward, Peter, Edward Carlton, Anne, and Isabella.

6. One of his grandsons has recorded, "Mr. FitzGerald desired to enter Parliament, and in the 1820's 'bought' the town of Seaford in Sussex. When a vacancy occurred, he was duly elected M.P. by his duteous tenants." Reminiscences of John de Soyres. MS. in possession of Miss Madeleine de Soyres, Edward FitzGerald's grandniece.

difficulties. After throwing his entire fortune into the shaft, Mr. FitzGerald died a bankrupt.

While living at Bredfield, however, his financial troubles lay hidden in the future. Tall, well built, and ruddy faced, he typified the English squire. He hunted and entertained as a country gentleman should, and was hearty, amiable, generous, and hospitable. "Draw closer, gentlemen," he would urge his guests, "and I will give you a glass of wine that never paid one farthing to his Majesty's customs—the King, God bless him!"

Mr. FitzGerald was overshadowed by his beautiful and imperious wife, who, on the death of her father, John FitzGerald of London and The Island, Waterford, Ireland, was reputed to be the wealthiest commoner in England. Descended from the fiery earls of Kildare, she inherited their temperament and bore herself like a queen.

The FitzGeralds were among the most illustrious of the Anglo-Norman families in Ireland. They traced their descent from the dukes of Tuscany through Otho Geraldino, a trusted commander under William the Conqueror when he invaded England. As a reward for his services, Otho was created a baron. Many Normans followed William across the Channel to gamble their lives against honor and fortune, particularly fortune. A century in England produced younger sons equally hungry for honor—and fortune— and equally daring. These responded eagerly when Dermod Mac-Murrogh, King of Leinster, appealed to Henry II in 1167 for aid to restore him to his lands from which he had been driven by Roderick O'Connor, the last Irish monarch. Maurice, great-grandson of Otho and the first of the family to assume the surname Fitzgerald,[7] was among the earliest volunteers. He crossed to Ireland in 1169, leading "10 gentlemen, 30 horsemen, and about 100 footsoldiers."[8] He landed near Waterford and joined his half-brother, Robert Fitz-Stephen, the first Anglo-Norman to invade the island, who had preceded him by a few months and taken Wexford. From the time of the landing of Maurice, the histories of Ireland and the Fitz-gerald family are inextricably woven.

Wherever English arms penetrated the Fitzgeralds were to be found. They were held in high esteem by their fellows—a doubtful commendation in the campaign of spoliation and pillage which is euphemistically called the Anglo-Norman invasion. After seven

7. The name was originally spelled with a small g.
8. Smyth, George Lewis, Ireland, Historical and Statistical (London, Whittaker & Co., 1844), I, 94–98. 2 vols. O'Hart, John, Irish Pedigrees (Dublin, McGlashan & Gill, 1876), p. 212.

years of campaigning, Maurice was named by Henry II one of the joint governors of Ireland. He died the following year in possession of vast territories in Cork, Wicklow, Kildare, and Sligo. Successive generations of Fitzgeralds ably maintained the eminence which he had gained. They were noted for their valor, rashness, disarming frankness, and utter contempt for any authority but their own. They waged almost constant warfare with the natives and with their own peers to add to their territories and to gain absolute dominion within them. By force of arms and personality and by advantageous marriages, they became one of the three great families which for almost five centuries controlled the unhappy destiny of Ireland.

The Fitzgerald annals contain legends, some possibly apocryphal, which rival romance. In the latter half of the thirteenth century John FitzThomas Fitzgerald, accompanied by his son, Maurice, left the Castle of Tralee on one of the periodic expeditions against a native tribe. They were ambushed, and every man in the force was killed. A messenger brought the news to Tralee and reported that the Irish were marching against the castle. The inhabitants prepared to flee. In the excitement Maurice's son and heir, an infant of nine months, was deserted by his nurse. A "pet monkey," legend states, seized the child and ascended with him to the battlements where it dandled him in its arms while the people below, forgetting their own danger, watched in horror. The monkey finally descended and replaced the baby in his cradle. The child was subsequently known as Thomas Nappagh—"Thomas of the Ape." The incident is said to be responsible for the monkeys which form the crest and supports of the armorial shield of the FitzGeralds of Kildare. Edward FitzGerald thought otherwise. "I suppose," he said in a letter written late in life, "that (after the manner of Myths) the Story gathered itself about the Crest which might have been adopted for no better reason than Lions, Bears, Eagles, and other Birds and Beasts in other Families. If Darwin be right, the Leinsters [9] chose the most noble animal of all, no less than Father Adam himself." [10] Sculptured monkeys still surmount the gateposts at Little Island, Waterford, the Irish seat of FitzGerald's family.

Thomas Nappagh is significant in FitzGerald history as the father of two sons, Maurice and John, from whom descended the two great branches of the family which were to control virtually the whole south of Ireland. Maurice established the house of Des-

9. The earldom of Kildare was later merged with the dukedom of Leinster.

10. Transcript of a letter to William Crowfoot of Beccles in Trinity College Library, Cambridge University.

mond, John that of Kildare. In 1315, when the Scots invaded Ireland under Edward Bruce, brother of Robert, the Fitzgeralds in Kildare offered the first successful resistance to his progress and turned the tide against the invaders. For his part in these wars John FitzThomas Fitzgerald was created Earl of Kildare by Edward II in 1316. It was from Maurice,[11] fourth Earl, that Edward FitzGerald's family was descended. The Kildares may be distinguished from the Desmonds by the presence of the capital G in the surname. After the Anglo-Norman invasion many of the new families in Ireland adopted Irish surnames, or modified the spellings of their own to resemble Irish names. In conformity with this practice, the Kildares adopted the capital G. The difference in spelling is retained for the most part by the two branches to the present day.

Some estimate of the part which the earls of Kildare played in Irish affairs is gained from the fact that nineteen of them served either as lords deputies or as lords justices of Ireland between 1371 and 1532. They were able administrators, yet so haughty and independent that they tried the patience of more than one monarch. They were frequently summoned to England to answer charges brought against them by their enemies. The first earl, in reply to a charge of treason, cut short his hearing by challenging his accuser, William de Vescey, the first lord justice of Ireland, to decide their dispute by combat. De Vescey fled to the Continent rather than face the challenger, and his lands were awarded to FitzGerald.

Gerald, eighth and greatest Earl of Kildare, held the position of lord deputy under five kings, from Edward IV to Henry VIII. He governed his island with the usual Geraldine disregard for laws not of his own making. Finally taken a prisoner to England, where charges of treason and sacrilege were brought against him, he insisted upon meeting his accusers in the presence of Henry VII and heard the complaints with haughty condescension. Among other crimes, he was accused of having burnt the cathedral of Cashel to the ground in one of his lawless expeditions. "Yea," he cried, interrupting the tedious evidence, "I did set fire to the church; but I thought the bishop had been in it."

"All Ireland could not govern this earl," one of his accusers was heard to complain.

"This earl, then, shall govern Ireland," the King is said to have responded, and FitzGerald was restored to his estates, honors, and office.[12]

11. Maurice, fourth Earl of Kildare, 1318–90.
12. Smyth, *Ireland*, I, 241–242.

Edward's immediate forebears were recognizable kin of the old earls of Kildare. His grandfather, John FitzGerald, married his first cousin, Mary, daughter of Keane FitzGerald of London and Hertfordshire. He was a man of great wealth, having inherited the ancient FitzGerald estate, Little Island, in the Waterford River near the town of Waterford, as well as properties in Suffolk, Lancashire, and Staffordshire. He lived in England and traveled frequently on the Continent, spending many years in Italy. "We used to hear," a friend of the family has recorded, "that her [Mrs. Fitz-Gerald's] father was a great patron of the arts." [13] This is supported by the fact that Daniel Steibelt, who, in his day, was considered a rival of Beethoven, dedicated a concerto which included "Storm Rondo," one of his most famous compositions, to Edward's mother. Edward once described his grandfather as "a rich and dissolute Irishman." He possessed a vigorous, though hardly a delicate, sense of humor. He "would play all sorts of pranks and practical jokes with old Jack Turner [an intimate, but miserly, friend] such as making him drunk with wine and sending him off shut up in a cab with a dissolute woman." [14] In later life he and his wife parted and established separate homes in London. Four times a year Mr. Fitz-Gerald called upon his wife at her dwelling near St. James's Park. He enjoyed the more constant companionship of an opera dancer.

Edward's mother, John FitzGerald's sole heir,[15] was described by a contemporary as a "very handsome, clever, and eccentric woman." Vain, proud, and ostentatious, she lived lavishly and entertained royally. Her town house was at 39 Portland Place, one of London's most pretentious residential thoroughfares. There she invariably spent "the season," indulging her passion for the theater and attending the Opera House, Haymarket, where she had a box in the third tier. One of her intimate friends was Mrs. Charles Kemble, wife of the actor-manager of Covent Garden. Fanny Kemble, who rose to fame in her father's theater, was profoundly impressed by the gold dessert service and ornaments with which Mrs. Fitz-Gerald decked her table. These were replaced by "a set of ground glass and dead and burnished silver, so exquisite, that the splendid gold service was pronounced infinitely less tasteful and beauti-

13. MS. notes of Mrs. Elizabeth Cowell, Trinity College Library, Cambridge University.

14. Diary of Frederick Spalding, one of FitzGerald's friends in later years. Oct. 13, 1867.

15. An older brother, John Charles, had died in 1807 without issue.

ful." [16] Fashionable Brighton, seaside haven of Victorian society, was one of her favorite resorts. "Yesterday I saw Mrs. FitzGerald arrive in great state," Thackeray once wrote from there, "four in hand, an army of flunkies and lady's maids and piles of mysterious imperials. There's a prospect of good dinners! The old woman's compliments are however overpowering to me: and to hear how the toadies who surround her compliment *her* is a good moral lesson." [17] Mrs. FitzGerald's vanity, austerity, and pride were redeemed somewhat by a lively sense of humor.

She is said to have sat for no fewer than twenty-three portraits and studies by Sir Thomas Lawrence, and there were at least two by Chalon, portrait painter in water colors to Queen Victoria, whose portraits in that medium were popular among ladies of the aristocracy. One of the Lawrence paintings, according to Edward, bore "a surprising resemblance to the Duke of Wellington . . . and though . . . too Wellingtonian, the only true likeness of her." [18] The portraits represent her with luxuriant black hair, bold dark eyes, straight, well-formed nose, thin, curved lips, and rounded chin. Her formal dress was usually of rich velvet, well calculated to set off her striking features. "Black velvet and diamonds," recalled one of FitzGerald's friends, describing Mrs. FitzGerald as he had seen her at the opera. Fanny Kemble said that she wore a bracelet of her husband's hair fastened by a heavy gold clasp on which was inscribed, *"Stesso sangue, stessa sorte."*

One writer has aptly described her beauty as "Junonian." With it was coupled an Olympian indifference to her children. She was often separated from her family, and even when at home did not much concern herself with them. The nursery at Bredfield was at the top of the house. "My Mother used to come up sometimes, and we Children were not much comforted," Edward said in later life. "She was a remarkable woman . . . and as I constantly believe in outward Beauty as an Index of a beautiful Soul within, I used sometimes to wonder what feature in her fine face betrayed what was not so good in her Character. I think (as usual) the Lips: there was a twist of Mischief about them now and then, like that in— the Tail of a Cat!—otherwise so smooth and amiable." [19] One of FitzGerald's sisters described their early life as "one of extreme dis-

16. Kemble, Frances Ann, *Record of a Girlhood* (London, Richard Bentley & Son, 1878), I, 135–136, 3 vols.
17. MS. letter in possession of Mrs. Richard B. Fuller, Thackeray's granddaughter.
18. Letter to Fanny Kemble, Mar. 26 [1880].
19. *Ibid.* [Feb. 27, 1872].

cipline and entire obedience." Mrs. FitzGerald, in fact, patterned
the regimen of her family after that described by Richardson in
Clarissa Harlowe. "My Mother read the novel assiduously," her
son remarked, "and imitated the Parents very effectually." [20] "My
dear," he once heard his Grandmother FitzGerald tell her daughter
during a severe scolding, "you are a very fine woman, but *a bad
Mother*." [21]

Edward was the seventh of eight children: Mary Frances,[22] John,
Andalusia, Mary Eleanor, Jane, Peter, Edward, and Isabella. Of
the boys, John and Edward were imaginative, while Peter made up
in vigor what he lacked in invention. Edward was particularly
sensitive. "Well I remember," wrote his sister Jane (Mrs. J. B.
Wilkinson) "when my Mother read to us anything interesting, he
used to creep under the table to *feed* on and enjoy what she read." [23]
He impressed an acquaintance, who knew him a few years later, as
"a clever, lively lad."

Onto the pages of FitzGerald's letters flash occasional pictures of
his life at Bredfield, each like "an almost obliterated slide of the
old Magic Lantern." From the nursery window, through which
floated the familiar peal of bells in the church of St. Mary the Vir-
gin in Woodbridge, he saw Squire Jenney, his father's friend and
landlord, crossing the stiles on the path leading from the Red
House at Hasketon. The FitzGeralds and Mr. Jenney, "a rather
refined Squire Western," entertained each other frequently. The
well-worn footpath to the Red House penetrated Hasketon Wood,
from the menacing shadows of which Edward always shrank in fear.
His active imagination peopled the spot with malevolent shapes
and forms which even the handclasp of an adult companion failed
to dispel.[24] From his nursery window, too, Edward often saw his
father and the Squire in scarlet hunting habits, whips in hand, as
they rode across the lawns, surrounded by their pack of restless
harriers.

Another family friend was Major Edward Moor of Bealings
House, Great Bealings, a retired officer of the Indian army and one
of Edward's boyhood heroes. While living at Bredfield, the Fitz-
Geralds took Christmas dinner each year at Bealings House, and

20. MS. letter to Stephen Spring Rice, Sept. 29, 1862.
21. Spalding diary, Oct. 13, 1867.
22. Mary Frances died in 1820. The others lived until well beyond the middle of
the century.
23. Mrs. Wilkinson's MS. notes, Trinity College Library, University of Cambridge.
24. Wright, Thomas, *The Life of Edward FitzGerald* (London, Grant Richards,
1904), I, 41. 2 vols.

the Moors returned the visit each New Year's Day. The Major, a county magistrate, was one of the most kindhearted of men. "Indeed," FitzGerald recorded, "one fault—and but one—did I ever hear this Major charged with; and that was by a very humane friend and fellow-magistrate of his; who told me that . . . 'You could scarce persuade him of a poor man's guilt.' " [25] The Major was a student of Oriental literature, but his enthusiasm for the subject had no direct influence on FitzGerald's later study of Persian.[26] However, a second avocation of the good man, that of publishing a dictionary of Suffolk provincialisms, eventually led FitzGerald to issue a similar vocabulary of terms peculiar to the Suffolk coast.

The shooting at Bredfield was the envy of the surrounding gentry, and Edward remembered that his spirited Grandfather Fitz-Gerald sometimes came to share in the sport. On mornings when his bed proved more magnetic than the field, the old gentleman would summon the boy to his room. To his last years FitzGerald recalled vividly the pervading odor of stale powder which hung about the chamber during these levees. The old man, propped among pillows, would have great battle pictures of the French wars lifted from the walls and set up at the foot of his bed and would point out the figures of Napoleon and Ney and have the boy observe the differently colored uniforms of various divisions of the French army.

FitzGerald always remembered, too, one particular occasion of his Bredfield years. On June 18, 1816, the family, dressed in their best summer clothes, crossed the fields, fragrant with newly cut hay, to Bredfield village to celebrate the first anniversary of Waterloo. Arriving at the scene of festivities, they found Napoleon hanged in effigy. The legs of the figure were formed by Wellington boots, lent to the village carpenter for the purpose by Mr. FitzGerald. Not content with hanging as an expression of their sentiments, the villagers discharged guns at the figure. Edward watched these activities from a tent where his family sat with the parson, eating beef and plum puddings and drinking loyal toasts. The clergyman was "one of the old sort with a jolly red nose caused by good cheer" who "used to lay his Hat on the Communion Table and gabble over the Service, running down the pulpit stairs not to lose the opportunity of being invited to a good dinner at the Hall." [27]

25. FitzGerald, Edward, "Sea Words and Phrases along the Suffolk Coast," *The East Anglian: or Notes and Queries on Subjects Connected with the Counties of Suffolk, Cambridge, and Essex*, III (December, 1868), 362–363.

26. See p. 171, n. 28.

27. Mrs. Wilkinson MS. notes.

Routine life at Bredfield was broken by summer holidays spent on the coast at Aldeburgh, thirteen miles to the northeast. There Edward "first saw, and first felt, the Sea." One experience he never forgot, for he was "ruthlessly ducked into the Wave that came like a devouring monster under the awning of the Bathing Machine— a Machine whose Inside I hate to this day." [28] At Aldeburgh Edward heard his elders tell stories of local smugglers, and the account of kegs of Hollands being found under the altar cloth at near-by Theberton Church was often repeated. These tales filled the children with awe for the revenue cutters which they saw offshore; and FitzGerald remembered one, *The Ranger,* which went down with all hands. It was at Aldeburgh, when he was about fifteen, that Edward first fell in love. His inamorata was a niece of Major Moor, the blithe, lighthearted Mary Lynn, with whom he played on the beach.

In 1816 the FitzGeralds went to France where they stayed for two years, the first at Saint-Germain-en-Laye, the second in Paris. At Saint-Germain they lived in a pleasant house overlooking a vineyard. Private tutors instructed the children in French and dancing. Mrs. Wilkinson recorded, "Edward was a beautiful dancer; grace and ease characterized all his movements." Dancing lessons were sometimes interrupted by their religiously inclined tutor, who would desert his pupils to join a church procession. A fencing master, one of Napoleon's Old Guard, was engaged for the boys. He wanted to make soldiers of all three; but Peter alone went into the army, and his term of service was short.

Saint-Germain was made memorable by glimpses of Louis XVIII and his entourage on their way to hunt in the near-by forest; and there another "lantern slide" was imprinted on FitzGerald's memory:

Louis XVIII first, with his *Gardes du Corps,* in blue and silver: then Monsieur (afterwards Charles X) with *his* Guard in green and gold— French horns blowing—"tra, tra, tra" (as Madame de Sévigné says), through the lines of chestnut and limes—in flower. And then *Madame* (of Angoulême) standing up in her carriage, blear-eyed, dressed in white with her waist at her neck—standing up in the carriage at a corner of the wood to curtsey to the English assembled there—my mother among them. This was in 1817 . . . I saw, and see it all.[29]

28. Letter to Frederick Tennyson, Sept. 9, 1882. Some of the machines are still to be seen at Aldeburgh.

29. *Tennyson and His Friends* (London, Macmillan, 1911), p. 127. Hallam Tennyson, ed.

At Paris the FitzGeralds lived in the Rue d'Angoulême, in a house which Robespierre had occupied. This environment stimulated the active imaginations of John and Edward. Whatever degrees of eccentricity these brothers developed in later years, they were perfectly normal boys and delighted in frightening their sisters with harrowing tales of the Revolution.

Many of FitzGerald's mature interests germinated during these impressionable years in France. Frequent visits to the Louvre, wrote Mrs. Wilkinson, fostered his love for art. Young as he was, he accompanied his mother to the theater and shared her enthusiasm for drama. The sensation caused by the murder of a magistrate at Rodez, one M. Fualdès, impressed him greatly; and he remembered being taken in 1818 to the Ambigu Comique to see the *Château de Paluzzi,* a play said to be founded on the crime. In 1875 he distinctly recalled one scene in which "some guilty Personage" came from a cupboard. His brother John assumed the leadership in improvising a small theater. He and Edward wrote plays on historic and imaginary themes, painted scenery, and coached the children in productions which were acted before their parents. Edward's characteristic humor was evident even at this early age. His father, writing to a friend, spoke of his keeping the whole family in good spirits by his unfailing fun and droll speeches.

FitzGerald never lost the attachment which he formed for France at this time. "I shall like to hear a word about my dear old France," he wrote to Fanny Kemble many years later, "dear to me from childish associations." [30]

On September 6, 1818, Mrs. FitzGerald's father died, and the family returned to England. Edward's mother came into her inheritance, and her husband adopted the FitzGerald name and arms. The chief properties bequeathed to her were Little Island, Waterford; Boulge, Suffolk; Castle Irwell, Pendleton, near Manchester; [31] and lands in Staffordshire, including St. Thomas' Priory. She had already inherited Naseby Wooleys in Northamptonshire and properties in Middlesex on the death of a great-aunt in 1810. [32]

30. Glyde, John. *The Life of Edward FitzGerald* (London, C. Arthur Pearson, 1900), p. 8.

31. The Castle Irwell race track at Manchester is located on a portion of the estate. Edward's brother John, who later inherited the property, did not approve of racing and repeatedly refused to sell to track operators, despite their liberal offers. The property was sold by John's heirs, and eventually it was acquired by the racing interests. The castle, then dilapidated, was torn down to make way for the track.

32. Sources: the will of John FitzGerald on file at Somerset House; and Burke, Sir Bernard, *A Genealogical and Heraldic Dictionary of the Landed Gentry of Great*

Little Island (now called The Island) is exactly that, an island of some three hundred acres in the Waterford River. It is an ancient seat, its location having been chosen in turbulent times more for ease of defense than for the beauty which surrounds it. To this day it is reached from the mainland by a small ferry. Boulge is little more than a mile from FitzGerald's birthplace at Bredfield. Naseby Wooleys embraced most of the battlefield of Naseby on which Cromwell overthrew Charles I. Castle Irwell, at Manchester, was on the battlefield of England's Industrial Revolution. It was there that Mr. FitzGerald dug the mine which devoured his fortune. Blessed with many estates, the FitzGeralds took possession of none but rented homes until 1835, when they occupied Boulge Hall.

Britain and Ireland (4th ed. London, Harrison, 1868), pp. 483–484. The great-aunt was Mrs. Jane Joye.

II

Bury St. Edmunds

"The danger of a polite and elegant education is that it separates feeling and acting; it teaches us to think, speak, and be affected aright, without forcing us to *do* what is right."
CARDINAL NEWMAN, quoted by FITZGERALD in *Polonius*

BEFORE he was taken to France, FitzGerald had attended a small private school in Woodbridge. In the autumn of 1818, after the family returned to Bredfield, the boys were sent to the King Edward VI Grammar School at Bury St. Edmunds, Suffolk.[1] John entered the sixth form, in which he remained for three years, preparing for entrance to Trinity College, Cambridge. Peter and Edward, who were enrolled in the first form, were pupils at Bury for seven and eight years respectively.

There was little resemblance between Bury and the many brutish schools which existed in fact as well as in Victorian fiction. The schoolroom, it must be admitted, was not unlike those described in the novels. To this day it is a cold, forbidding chamber with cheerless gray walls, heavily beamed ceiling, and bare platform. But there the similarity ended. The pupils were made to feel at home; the administration was benevolent, the discipline humane. For these features the character and policies of the headmaster, Dr. Benjamin Heath Malkin,[2] were responsible. He was broad minded, kindly, and humorous. By his nobility, integrity, and strength of will, he gained the respect of his pupils; by his thorough sympathy with their lives, his undisguised interest in their activities, and his unaffected respect for the qualities which boys respect in each other, he won their affection. When he met his charges socially, he laid the schoolmaster aside and treated them as equals. He sometimes took groups to the theater in Westgate Street or invited them to dinner. Naturally reserved, he had little faculty for entertaining; but he listened to the opinions of his guests with

1. In FitzGerald's day the school was located in Northgate Street in a building now used as a high school for girls.

2. Dr. Benjamin Heath Malkin, 1770–1842; headmaster of Bury St. Edmunds, 1809–28.

such benevolent interest that "to dine with the doctor" was a great privilege. "There was nothing of formality about him, or pedantry, or cant," James Spedding, a friend and contemporary of FitzGerald's at the school, has written.[3] Mrs. Malkin, by her sweetness of character, also contributed to the success of Bury. Her grace, kindliness, and vivacity won FitzGerald's heart. When, many years later, Fanny Kemble's sister Adelaide mentioned Mrs. Malkin's "charm," he replied, "Oh, but you can never know how charming she was; you were never a schoolboy under her care!" [4]

In the schoolyard the boys were granted the widest latitude consistent with order. There were no spikes on the gates nor broken glass on the walls, for Dr. Malkin believed that these merely tempted boys to climb over. Discipline was maintained by a few simple rules, the necessity of which the pupils themselves appreciated. Fagging and bullying were forbidden. Adopting a policy of noninterference, the master permitted his boys to administer justice among themselves. A fair fight in hot blood was never stopped except by the school bell. It was only when Dr. Malkin heard that a bout, so interrupted, was to be resumed after hours that he interfered to end hostilities. The master trusted his charges and assumed that his confidence in them would not be abused. There was no suspicion or watching, for he never doubted a boy's word.

When Dr. Malkin had become headmaster in 1809, the school governors enacted a new set of statutes. These stipulated that good manners, the Catechism, English grammar, literature, and "nothing . . . but the best Greek and Latin classics were to be taught, except that the headmaster might teach those who should desire it the rudiments of Hebrew.[5] One writer, himself a schoolmaster, said of Bury, "One of its features was the unusual amount of attention devoted to English literature, and the pains which Dr. Malkin took to make his pupils good English as well as good classical scholars. There was much essay-writing, and the essays that gained approbation were honored with a place in a series of large volumes entitled *Musae Burienses*." [6]

Judged strictly as a pedagogue, Dr. Malkin had his shortcomings. He assigned lessons and exercises according to an inflexible rule,

3. These facts pertaining to Dr. Malkin and the regimen of his school are derived from reminiscences supplied by James Spedding, editor of the works of Francis Bacon, for the *Record of the Tercentenary of the Foundation of the King Edward VI School at Bury St. Edmunds* (London, B. Fellowes, 1850), pp. 77–89.

4. Kemble, Frances Ann, *Further Records* (London, Richard Bentley & Sons, 1890), II, 179. 2 vols.

5. Governors' minutes, Bury St. Edmunds Grammar School.

6. Wright, Thomas, former headmaster of Olney School, *FitzGerald*, I, 60.

which sometimes unduly taxed his pupils. Once it was an entire book of Herodotus to be translated into English "in a preposterously short time." Nor was he entirely impartial. "An examiner from Cambridge," Spedding remarked, "would have made some confusion among our prizemen and classes." Spedding further observed that for training "verse-makers, medallists, and precocious professors," Bury was imperfect.

As a place for acquiring solid information even, and habits of rational and judicious study . . . it might have been improved. But for that which lies at the bottom of all education that deserves the name—that without which the whole super-structure of abilities and accomplishments is good for nothing—for laying the foundations and encouraging the growth of manly character and the independent mind—Bury School, under Dr. Malkin, was . . . one of the very best.

The school was recognized in England as one of the finest. A survey of winners of all classical prizes offered at Cambridge between 1806 and 1814 revealed that the greatest number was obtained by Bury School; the next, by Shrewsbury; and third, by Eton and Charterhouse equally.[7]

The enrollment was not large. It ranged from one hundred and sixty pupils when FitzGerald entered to ninety-six when he left in 1826. The decreased attendance resulted from straitened economic conditions during the post-Napoleonic period and not from any loss of prestige by Bury. Records reveal that other schools suffered loss of pupils during the same years. "Foreigners," as students from out of town were called, far outnumbered the "royalists," or local pupils. Some of the foreigners were quartered in small study-bedrooms in the school building. These accommodations, which had been added by Dr. Malkin, were another feature which distinguished Bury from the typical school of the day, for it was customary to lodge pupils of all ages in a single large room. Edward and Peter shared one of the studies, a room about nine feet square which looked "grand" to George Moor, a Woodbridge boy who attended a less select school in the town.

Although the regimen and course of study at Bury were ideally suited to his talents and inclinations, FitzGerald proved to be an erratic pupil. He started well, leading his class of twenty-one students in the first division of Form I at the end of his first year.

7. Donaldson, John W., headmaster of Bury School, 1841–55, quoting Samuel Butler, headmaster of Shrewsbury, in "A Retrospective Address Read at the Tercentenary Commemoration of King Edward's School," *Record of the Tercentenary*, p. 63.

Thereafter he coursed unpredictably up and down the scholastic scale.[8] Peter, on the other hand, after a surprising start proved to be a consistent pupil. At the end of his first year he was third in his class. From that time on, without fail, he hovered near the foot. His interests began at the schoolroom door—on the way out.

At Bury FitzGerald formed the first of many remarkable, lifelong friendships. One was with William Bodham Donne, son of a Norfolk gentleman and a descendant of John Donne. His mother was a collateral descendant of another poet, William Cowper. It was Donne's great-aunt, Mrs. Anne Bodham, who presented Cowper with the portrait which inspired "On Receipt of My Mother's Picture Out of Norfolk." Donne became librarian of the London Library and later Examiner of Plays for the Queen. He also wrote articles on a wide variety of subjects for periodicals and published several books, among them the *Correspondence of George III with Lord North*.[9] His biographer describes him as possessing "an extremely modest and retiring disposition" with a "power of fascinating all who came within his reach," [10] and one of his college friends said of him, "Many men are *liked*, but Donne is *loved*." The charm of his personality lay in its combination of gentle manner and genial humor. When his fourth child was born, he asked a friend,

Pray, how soon may Papas begin to calculate the number of their offspring? The first is, of course, mere and unmixed jubilation. The second is a godsend that the first may not be a spoilt child—so far so good—but the third? I had my doubts—and felt (did you?) a sort of wryness and constriction at the ends of my mouth when it amounted to a Holy Alliance! Moreover, our friends make their congratulations in a lower key, and do not keep up one's spirits as well as at first.[11]

In 1846 Donne moved to Bury St. Edmunds to place his sons in the school which he had attended. FitzGerald once wrote from the

8. FitzGerald's record, taken from the school records of 1819 to 1826, follows:
> Form I, 1818–19—first of 21 students.
> Form II, 1819–20—thirteenth of 21 students.
> Form III, 1820–21—third of 20 students.
> Form V, 1821–22—tenth of 19 students.
>   (Records for 1822–23 and 1823–24 missing.)
> Form VI, 1824–25—twelfth of 27 students.
> Form VI, 1825–26—fourth of 14 students.
9. Published in 1867 by John Murray.
10. Johnson, Catharine B., *William Bodham Donne and His Friends* (London, Methuen & Co., 1905), p. vii.
11. *Ibid.*, p. 15.

town, "I shall spend my time here wholly with my dear Donne; who shares with Spedding my oldest and deepest love."

James Spedding was the son of a prosperous farmer who lived at Mirehouse on Bassenthwaite Lake in Cumberland. Even as a boy he was distinguished for his exceptionally high and prominent forehead, the butt of many a joke. His brow, however, fulfilled the popular belief that an imposing forehead denotes exceptional intellectual powers. FitzGerald greatly admired Spedding's intellect, serenity of mind, and balance. "Spedding, you know, does not change," he said in 1845. "He is now the same that he was fourteen years old [sic] when I first knew him at school more than twenty years ago; wise, calm, bald, combining the best qualities of Youth and Age." [12] Spedding's boyishness is revealed in a letter written to FitzGerald in 1841 from Cumberland, where Spedding had gone on a holiday from his duties as under-secretary in the Colonial Office.

I have been occupied for the last week in trying whether I could sail the boat with a kite. It was necessary first to make one; and I had forgotten how. When I had made him to look like such kites as I have seen fly, it was necessary to teach him that art, about which I must say he was extremely awkward. And when I had partly brought him into order, we had three calm days. However this morning I succeeded in making him fly beautifully. He was more like an eagle than a kite; you would have thought it was only the string that prevented him from flying up to the 12 o'clock sun: but you would have been mistaken: for when the string broke and he might go where he would, his aspiration suddenly collapsed and he fell absurdly through flickering gyres upon the upper branch of an oak. Having recovered him (not undamaged) from his perilous position, I took him to the boat and got him up again, and succeeded in steering quite across the lake without oars,—I then wore; and was on my way to the other shore with a side wind; when he unfortunately dislocated his left wing in a gust, and after flying lame for some time at last came down head foremost into the lake like a seagull at a fish. I brought him home like the prodigal, "lean, rent, and beggared with the strumpet wind." I think of making a bigger.[13]

A brilliant scholar, entirely lacking in personal ambition, Spedding spent almost forty years editing the works of Francis Bacon and attempting to justify that worthy's manner of life to men. FitzGerald deeply regretted every hour that his friend devoted "to

12. Letter to Frederick Tennyson, June 12, 1845.
13. *Some New Letters of Edward FitzGerald to Bernard Barton* (London, Williams & Norgate, 1923), pp. 60–61. F. R. Barton, ed.

re-edit his [Bacon's] Works, which did not need such re-edition, and to vindicate his Character which could not be cleared." Fitz-Gerald often referred to the result as Spedding's "half-grilled Bacon" or as his "half-whitewashed" Bacon and repeatedly urged him to abandon the project and to devote his life to editing Shake-speare. Shakespearean criticism was, in fact, Spedding's avocation; and he took an active part in nineteenth-century interpretation and correction of the plays.[14] FitzGerald said that he had never heard Spedding read a page of Shakespeare without throwing new light on it. Spedding's forehead was another qualification recom-mending him as the Bard's editor, FitzGerald pointed out, because "one Frontispiece Portrait would have served for Author and Editor."

When Spedding died in 1881, FitzGerald wrote, "He was the wisest man I have ever known: not the less so for plenty of the Boy in him: a great sense of Humour, a Socrates in Life and in Death." [15]

Another Bury friend, as volatile as Spedding and Donne were stable, was John Mitchell Kemble, son of Charles Kemble, the actor, and brother of Fanny. He evidently shared the histrionic ability of his family, for FitzGerald frequently maintained that he "never heard such capital declamation as *his* Hotspur, and Alex-ander's Feast, when we were at Bury together, he about eighteen, and then with the profile of Alexander himself, as I have seen it on medals etc." [16] Kemble delivered "Alexander's Feast" on Speech Day, June 24, 1824, on which occasion FitzGerald gave "Mr. Bickerstaff—Swift." [17] But "Jacky's" inclinations ran counter to his heritage. After deciding in turn on the church and law for his career, he eventually became an editor, philologist, and Anglo-Saxon scholar, known thenceforward to his friends as "Anglo-Saxon" Kemble. In 1832 one of Donne's friends wrote, "Kemble is in town; he is reading law five hours a day . . . and besides this he finds time to write Articles in the Foreign Quarterly and a book on Anglo-Saxon, without which he says no one can understand Eng-lish and which he says no one can understand without understand-ing the other Teutonic dialects." [18]

A fourth schoolmate whose friendship FitzGerald kept through-out his life was William Airy, brother of the Astronomer Royal,

14. Spedding was an active member of *The Shakespeare Society* and was later active in the formation of *The New Shakespeare Society*.

15. Letter to Charles Eliot Norton, March 13 [1881].

16. Letter to Charles Merivale, Dean of Ely, Dec. 15 [1878].

17. Wright, *FitzGerald*, I, 61.

18. *Donne and His Friends*, p. 10.

Sir George Airy. William became vicar of Keysoe in Bedfordshire, and he and FitzGerald exchanged visits for many years. "Airy . . . came to see me here," FitzGerald wrote from Woodbridge in 1861, "and then we went together to Bury to ramble over our old School haunts."

FitzGerald's attachment for Bury St. Edmunds testifies to the happiness of his schoolday associations. He often visited the town, the St. Edmundsbury of Carlyle's *Past and Present,* during the middle years of his life, particularly while Donne was living there. In 1880 he advised W. W. Goodwin, Eliot Professor of Greek at Harvard, then traveling in England, to go to Bury "if only to look at the Abbey Gate there—Abbot Samson's, Abbey, though not *his* Gate—from the windows of the Angel Inn just opposite—with a Biscuit and a Pint of Sherry—as I have so often done: nay, did only six weeks ago on returning from Norfolk." [19]

As was the custom of students preparing for the University, FitzGerald spent two years in Form VI. In his last year, ending in May, 1826, he was fourth in his class, which was led by Spedding. Three months before, FitzGerald had been enrolled as a pensioner [20] at Trinity College, Cambridge.

19. MS. letter to Norton, July 26, 1880.
20. The majority of undergraduates at Cambridge enrolled as pensioners. The group included all but those who were granted special privileges and those who were "on the foundation," that is, who held scholarships. FitzGerald's brother John was a Fellow Commoner, one of the group given privileges. He took his degree the same month that Edward completed his work at Bury.

III

Cambridge

"Lycion, lying down on the grass, with his hat over his eyes,
composed himself to inattention."

FitzGerald's *Euphranor*

FITZGERALD was seventeen years old when he went into
residence at Cambridge in October. He took lodgings
with a Mrs. Perry at 19 King's Parade, near Great St.
Mary's Church, and there he lived throughout his college terms. The building, which still stands,[1] is almost opposite
King's College Chapel and overlooks the Senate House and Yard,
and the old University Library. Donne went up at the same time
to Gonville and Caius, where his father had been student and
Fellow; Kemble and Airy had entered Trinity the year before;
Spedding followed the year after.

Cambridge, of course, was much smaller than it now is. Two
streets beyond Hyde Park Corner and Lensfield Road to the south
were fields and farms. Queen's Road bordered the town on the
west, and Parker's Piece gave access to open country to the east.
Barnwell, haunt of Cyprians, extended about a mile out New-
market Road; and Castle End, "of equal fame with Barnwell,"
which terminated at the junction of the Histon and Huntington
Roads, marked the northernmost point of Cambridge. Both Newnham and Chesterton were separate villages.[2] Chesterton was a favorite resort of undergraduates, for it was "out of bounds"; and
there, at the inns, they could play billiards, a game permitted
"within bounds" to Masters of Arts only.

Contemporary sources provide intimate pictures of the routine
of university life during FitzGerald's time. One student recorded
the program of a reading man:

1. The building is marked by a plaque to commemorate FitzGerald's residence.
2. The approximate distances of these points from Great St. Mary's Church, as the
crow flies, are: Hyde Park Corner, one-half mile; Queen's Road, one-quarter mile;
Parker's Piece, three eighths of a mile; Barnwell Chapel, one and one-half miles;
junction of Histon and Huntington Roads, three quarters of a mile; Newnham, one-
half mile; Chesterton, one mile and one quarter.

You must rise to chapel, what indeed is chapel for but to make you get up? That will be at seven: at half past or a little earlier, provided the officiating minister (dean) knows his business, you will be let out; then go and take a constitutional till eight. . . . From eight to ten you will have lectures to attend: these miss on no account. You may pick up a good thought here and there, and that is better than picking a quarrel with your tutor, which you must, if you do not attend them. Besides, if the lectures were even of no use at all, how, my dear alumnus, can you with any conscience expect they should be? The poor man only has £2 10s. per quarter for giving them,—not a shilling a discourse that! The instant the lecturer closes his book, and makes his bow to you, snatch up your cap, hurry out, and make the best of your way home. Arrived there, take out your books, . . . there remain fixed and immovable, and never permit your eye to travel beyond the expanse of margin till the clock strikes two. . . . Two is the period for relaxation. You may make calls if you keep company: or if you keep none, stroll to Deighton's,[3] spell the daily prints, take down from the shelves any book which catches your eye . . . and when you have amused yourself sufficiently with it, put it up again; or if it be very entertaining, turn down a leaf to find a place when you come again. . . . At three you dine; after dinner you go to your own Rooms, or some one else's, as chance may direct . . . if you have anyone to talk to, talk of the Tripos; guess who will be spoon or wedge [4] . . . do anything, in fact, but read: this is a maxim,—"no man to read between hall and chapel." Vespers terminated, bitch—"O Fie!" bitch,—tea, that is. After bitch to work as before. At twelve, to bed.[5]

Rising for matins at seven o'clock was not always convenient, and under pressure of time students sometimes donned surplices over their night clothes to avoid being late. Neither was the early hour conducive to a pious frame of mind, and chapel could hardly be described as a devout ceremony. "The *bore* of chapel in my time," stated a Trinity man in 1827, "was so sensibly felt, that the Readers, or Chaplains, were afraid to do the full duty. Mr. S., a very conscientious man, being appointed, would read the Litany in the morning, and persevered for some time, amid the groans and stamping of the shivering audience. But at length, finding himself cannonaded on his way to and from chapel with snow-balls, he re-

3. Deighton's, now Deighton, Bell & Co., booksellers in Trinity Street.
4. Spoon: name given to the student lowest on the list of mathematical honors; so called from the custom of presenting him with a wooden spoon.
   Wedge: applied to the student occupying the corresponding place in classics.
   Tripos: the examinations given by the university to candidates for bachelors' degrees.
5. *Letters from Cambridge*, Anonymous (London, John Richardson, 1828), pp. 59–63.

signed the office." The writer further revealed that "the fastest readers have always been held in highest estimation." [6]

Nor, it must be confessed, did the conduct of the service foster reverence in the congregation. Three or four markers, lists of names in their hands, walked the aisles during a considerable part of the service, running a pin through the names of those present; one, named Anthony, was dubbed "Mark" by the students. A vigilant clerk patrolled the chapel, for the reverence, even of the devout, palled under the routine of daily services. Conversation or giggling would be interrupted by this official with the words, "Gentlemen, the Dean desires to speak with you after chapel." Penalties for such transgressions took the form of "impositions," the chief disciplinary measure of the time. An imposition was "having to get by heart a satire of Juvenal, a book of Homer, to give an analysis of Butler's Analogy," or some similar task.[7]

Students provided their own breakfasts and suppers, which they ate in their rooms. Dinner was served to them in mid-afternoon, but "dining in hall" was not popular. "The dinner . . . at Trinity at the undergraduates' tables," wrote Sir Frederick Pollock, one of FitzGerald's friends,

was all through my time, and for many years afterwards, scandalously bad. The joints were put on the table to be hacked and hewed at by young men who knew nothing of carving, and in this way alone great waste was incurred. Everything except the joints had to be "sized" for, or ordered separately and paid for as an extra, and the waiting was altogether insufficient for comfort. To dine in hall, in fact, involved much discomfort, until one got to the scholars' table, where things were fairly well managed. In consequence men who could afford it, as well as many who could not . . . only went to hall to get marked for attendance, and dined in their own rooms or in the town, which led to the running up of heavy cook's bills, so that it used to be said that the place of college cook [8] at Trinity was a more lucrative one than that of the master.[9]

Each college was a unit for the scholastic as well as for the religious life of its students. With the exception of a few lectures

6. *Alma Mater, or Seven Years at the University.* By a Trinity Man (London, Black, Young & Young, 1827), I, 82. 2 vols.

7. *Ibid.*, I, 32.

8. Common report had it that the cook at Trinity realized £2,000 from his position. The author of *Alma Mater* speaks of delicacies "decorated with all the devices . . . a cookship of two thousand pounds per annum could devise," I, 157. Other contemporary sources give the same figure.

9. *Personal Remembrances of Sir Frederick Pollock* (London, Macmillan & Co., 1887), I, 43–44. 2 vols.

delivered by University professors,[10] at which attendance was not compulsory, instruction was given by separate faculties in the seventeen foundations then established.[11] The work of each student preparing for the tripos was supervised by a college tutor. He met his charges individually once a week, except when the latter "cut" appointments. Upon entering the University, a student elected either to study for honors, for which competition was extremely keen, or for an ordinary, or "pass," degree. The former were known as reading men, the latter as the poll, a term explained by its derivation from *hoi polloi.*

FitzGerald became one of the poll and was assigned to George Peacock,[12] described by Pollock, who read under him shortly after FitzGerald's residence, as "unquestionably" the best of the Trinity tutors. "He was much liked by the men on his side," Pollock stated, "and was possessed of a sense of humor which tempered the strict exercise of his tutorial functions." [13]

FitzGerald's reasons for taking an ordinary degree are not difficult to determine. The private intellectual renaissance which had marked his final year at Bury did not survive the transfer to Cambridge. His natural interests lay in literature and the classics, tastes which had been developed under Dr. Malkin. At the University these subjects were secondary in importance to mathematics, for which he had no native enthusiasm. The curriculum when he entered was divided into three parts: "Natural Philosophy, Theology and Moral Philosophy, and the Belles Lettres." The first included Euclid's *Elements,* algebra, plane and spherical trigonometry, conic sections, mechanics, hydrostatics, optics, astronomy, fluxions, Newton's *Principia,* and related subjects: the second, Paley's *Natural Theology* and *Evidences of Christianity,* Butler's *Analogy of Religion,* Locke's *Essay on Human Understanding,* Duncan's *Logic,* and the Greek Testament; the third, "the most celebrated Greek and Latin Classics.[14] Two years before FitzGerald matriculated, the

10. The title "professor" in an English university is given only to those teachers who hold endowed chairs. They are well paid at Cambridge and Oxford, and ordinarily are required to give a few lectures only each year. Most of their time is spent in research and writing.

11. Instruction had originally been a function of the University, which the colleges had subsequently assumed. As a result of reforms during the nineteenth century it has again reverted to the University. For the rest, however, the system today is essentially the same as in FitzGerald's time.

12. Later, Dean Peacock.

13. Pollock, *Remembrances,* I, 27.

14. *The Cambridge University Calendar for the Year 1827* (Cambridge, J. Deighton & Sons), p. 142.

University had broadened its policy by establishing a classical tripos. However, only those students who had already won mathematical honors were permitted to take this examination; and "for a long time many colleges gave little or no encouragement to the reading of classics." [15]

The emphasis placed on mathematics was based on the conviction that the study fostered intellectual stability and provided what Cambridge educators of that day termed "practical education." Mathematics, they maintained, best developed students' minds for "future action." William Whewell, Master of Trinity College from 1841 to 1866, in a defense of "practical" Cambridge education as opposed to what he called the "speculative" German system, declared that "the lesson we learn from it [i.e., the 'experiment of education through the ages'] is this;—that so far as civilization is connected with the advance and diffusion of human knowledge, civilization flourishes when the prevalent education is mathematical, and fades when *philosophy* is the subject most preferred." After discussing the constant change and revolution of thought which takes place in a course of study based on speculative philosophy, he continued,

Now I conceive it cannot be doubted that the mind of a young man employed mainly in attending to teachers of this latter kind, must fail to acquire any steady and unhesitating conviction of the immutable and fixed nature of truth, such as the study of Mathematics gives. This constant change in the system of received doctrine must unsettle and enfeeble his apprehension of all truths . . . he cannot feel or relish old and familiar truths, such as mathematical sciences deal with.[16]

The rigid curriculum held no immediate terrors for FitzGerald. Neither economic pressure nor personal ambition spurred him to slave over his books. Studying only for a pass, he could do a minimum of work during the major portion of his residence and then, with the help of a private tutor, "cram," as it was called even in that day, for his examinations.

The poll included students with interests as varied as humanity. At one extreme were brilliant men who refused to submit to a course of study which required application to mathematics almost to the exclusion of other intellectual interests. Thomas Babington Macaulay and Charles Darwin, who were students about the same

15. Merivale, Charles, Dean of Ely, *Autobiography* (London, Edward Arnold & Co., 1899), p. 84. J. A. Merivale, ed.

16. Whewell, William, *On the Principles of English University Education* (London, John W. Parker & Son, 1837), pp. 47–53.

time as FitzGerald, took ordinary degrees. At the other extreme were "varmint men," as the "ultra-sporting or fast men" were called. They attended college to be amused rather than educated. "The Billiard Tables at Chesterton," stated a contemporary, "the Tennis Courts, the Races at New Market, the Balls at Huntingdon, Bury, Colchester, etc., the Hunts, Shooting, and other sports beguile much of the time that otherwise would be so dull, that, to make life tolerable, it would be necessary to seek occupation in study." [17] For excitement within town, the "varmint men" finished evenings of carousing in their rooms by sallying forth to engage townsmen or "bargees," as the river bargemen were called, in free-for-alls. Barnwell and Castle End provided them with less innocent diversions.[18]

FitzGerald can be classed neither with the best nor the worst of the undergraduates. An earnest, though not a zealous student, he combined a better than average intelligence with an average indifference to intellectual exertion and is best described as a "non-reading reading man." He read widely and voraciously, but not in the "set" books which his tutor recommended. That his qualities did not go unrecognized by his seniors is indicated in a letter which he wrote in 1881, after reading Bishop Connop Thirlwall's correspondence. "I remember him [Thirlwall] at Cambridge," he said, "he, Fellow and Tutor, and I undergraduate: and he took a little fancy to me, I think." [19]

One of his Cambridge friends described FitzGerald as "a very good fellow but of very retired habits." [20] Although an average, he was hardly a typical student. He was shy, stubbornly independent, and utterly erratic in observing social conventions. On one occasion his mother, who had driven to Cambridge, sent for him; but he returned word by the lackey that his boots were at the cobbler's and he could not leave his room until they were returned. Mrs. FitzGerald was insistent, and her son finally joined her, wearing borrowed boots.[21]

In spite of his reserve FitzGerald became a member of "Camus," a musical society composed of senior members of the colleges as well as undergraduates, all of whom took part in the club's programs.

17. *Alma Mater*, II, 125.
18. *Ibid.*, pp. 135–136.
19. Letter to Norton, March 7 [1882].
20. W. M. Thackeray, quoted by T. J. Mazzinghi in MS. letter to Aldis Wright, Trinity College Library.
21. Groome, Francis Hindes, *Two Suffolk Friends* (Edinburgh and London, William Blackwood & Sons, 1895), p. 72.

FitzGerald was one of the pianists. He was a creditable player in a day when piano playing was not a common male achievement. The society met in college rooms and five times each term gave vocal and instrumental concerts, each opening with an overture by Handel. One night as the recital began in Nevile's Court, Trinity, pandemonium broke out in rooms overhead. A rival "Camus" had been organized for the occasion, the "musicians" being provided with fire shovels and pokers.[22]

Spedding, Kemble, and Donne, in contrast to FitzGerald, entered wholeheartedly into undergraduate life. They were ambitious for University honors and engaged in extracurricular activities as well. Kemble was acknowledged one of the ablest speakers at the Union. Debating, however, proved an unsatisfactory preparation for the tripos; to the surprise and regret of his friends, he failed to win the high honors which he had set as his goal. All three became members of the Cambridge Conversazione Society, a group of undergraduate intellectuals popularly known as "The Apostles." The purpose of the society, an anonymous member has written, "was to make men study and think on all matters except mathematics and classics professionally considered." Literature and abstruse problems of philosophy and theology were usually discussed at their weekly meetings. Charles Merivale, Dean of Ely, remarked,

We soon grew, as such youthful coteries generally do, into immense self-conceit. We began to think that we had a mission to enlighten the world upon things intellectual and spiritual. . . . It was with a vague idea that it should be our function to interpret the oracles of transcendental wisdom to the world of Philistines, or Stumpfs, as we designated them . . . that . . . we piqued ourselves on the name of the "Apostles" a name given us, as we were sometimes told, by the envious and jeering vulgar, but to which we presumed that we had a legitimate claim, and gladly accepted it.[23]

In FitzGerald's time the twelve men whose names appeared at the foot of the poll list were called "apostles." This, and the fact that the Conversazione Society usually numbered about twelve members, may have suggested the name to "the envious and jeering vulgar." The Apostles considered life, themselves, and their education with astonishing gravity. "Hallam has gone back to Cambridge," wrote Joseph W. Blakesley, a member, in 1830. "He was not well while he was in London; moreover, he was submitting

22. Sources: *Rules and Regulations of Camus Musical Society*, 1829; and MS. letter to Aldis Wright from Archdeacon R. H. Groome, a member of the society.
23. Merivale, *Autobiography*, p. 80.

himself to the influence of the outer world more than (I think) a man of his genius ought to do." [24] Blakesley was twenty-two when the letter was written, and Hallam was nineteen.

No doubt the Apostles had an exaggerated opinion of their importance; that they were talented, keen, and sincere is equally beyond question. Most of Europe was rife with revolution or reform. In England itself the decade of the 1820's saw modification of the Corn Laws, Catholic Emancipation, and attempts at Parliamentarian reform, questions which shook the nation to its foundations. The Apostles considered themselves radicals. The revolutionary movements in Italy and Greece won their hearty moral support and the one in Spain their active support as well. They appreciated that they were part of a changing world and strove to become active in it.

FitzGerald made friends of many Apostles who were his contemporaries at Cambridge, but not until the years immediately after he had taken his degree. Alfred Tennyson; Richard Chenevix Trench, Archbishop of Dublin; Richard Monckton Milnes, Lord Houghton; Charles Merivale, Dean of Ely; J. W. Blakesley, Dean of Lincoln; and Robert Tennant were among the number. FitzGerald had many opportunities to meet these men while an undergraduate had he desired. He was present when Tennyson recited old English ballads "at some Cambridge gathering," but, he said in 1882, "I can tell you nothing of his College days; for I did not know him till *they* were over, though I had seen him two or three times before. I remember him well." [25] The turmoils of the world rarely won more than FitzGerald's indifferent attention, and undergraduates who became agitated over national and international problems did not attract him. Nor was he ever enthusiastic about metaphysical discussion. In a letter written shortly after he took his degree, he spoke disparagingly of "the common Cambridge run" with their "Farrago of College information." Simplicity, sincerity, and humor were qualities which he valued highly; and these were not apparent to him in many of the new friends whom Spedding, Kemble, and Donne made. With four Apostles, however, Douglas Heath, Senior Wrangler in 1832; [26] George Farish; William Hepworth Thompson, afterward Master of Trinity; and John Allen, later Archdeacon of Salop, FitzGerald became inti-

24. Tennyson, Hallam, *Alfred Lord Tennyson, a Memoir* (London and New York, Macmillan & Co., 1897), I, 69. 2 vols.

25. MS. letter to Anne Thackeray Ritchie, May 17, 1882.

26. A Senior Wrangler is one who has taken first-class honors in the mathematical tripos.

mate while still an undergraduate. The last two were close friends until the end of his life.

Thompson, a brilliant student, entered Trinity in 1828 as a sizar, a student holding a college scholarship,[27] and at the end of two years was made a scholar. He remained at Trinity after taking his degree in 1832, became Fellow in 1834, and Tutor ten years later. In 1853 he was appointed Regius Professor of Greek by the University and became Master of Trinity in 1866, a post which he held until his death in 1886. Thompson had a ready wit, and it was possibly this quality which first attracted FitzGerald. "We are none of us infallible," was an acknowledgment of his mature years, "not even the youngest of us."

FitzGerald's friendship with John Allen rivaled those with Donne and Spedding. Allen recorded their meeting in a diary which he kept as a student: "How vast and wondrous is the reflection on what little incidents depend the circumstances of our life [sic]. My intimacy with FitzGerald, the bright remembrance of which I shall look back on with delight till the day of my death, arose from being almost dragged by young Duncan to a breakfast party on a Sunday at his brother's which I had refused to go to." [28]

Doubts as to the propriety of attending a party on Sunday were responsible for Allen's hesitancy. The son of a clergyman at Burton-in-Rhos, Pembrokeshire, he had entered Trinity in 1828 to prepare for the Church. From a home in which his intellectual, moral, and spiritual training had been unbelievably severe, he took to Cambridge the conviction that anything pleasant was sinful. At college he found life a constant conflict between flesh and the soul. "Indolence, Evil, and Folly," vices into which he believed that he had fallen during the day, close his diary entries with routine regularity. Fidelity to the high purpose of his education demanded that he rise early and devote long and uninterrupted hours to his books. Flesh urged him to lie long abed, and flesh was usually victorious. Time after time he recorded a determination to reform; again and again he prayed for help to attain that end. "Oh, if I could get up in the morning and amend my life!" he wrote despairingly one day; and, two days later, "Through God's help I was enabled to get up to Chapel this morning." But the reformation was not permanent. Once he tried more practical means and "swapped" his um-

27. Originally sizars did menial tasks about the college and were held in low esteem, but by FitzGerald's day all opprobrium attached to the classification had disappeared. Sizar is apparently derived from the fact that these students were not required to pay for "sizings."

28. Allen diary, Sept. 22, 1830. Trinity College Library.

brella for an alarm clock, but the clock was no more efficacious than his prayers.

Food proved another snare. Allen had a natural fondness for food, a predilection which ill-fitted the asceticism of his theoretical code of conduct. Repeated determination to fast brought only rare victories. The environment of his home made the struggle easier and, during one vacation, he recorded, "At tea began course of amendment by leaving off butter." The conflict at college was more severe. "O what a wicked fickle character am I!" he wrote. "O my God have mercy! I had determined to fast this day and to have made it a day of humiliation. I could not keep even this resolution. I was up late and then was very idle. I must get up early or I shall do nothing. I fasted at breakfast time, drinking nothing, eating dry bread—went to FitzGerald's, eat with him some of Bedwell's bridecake and drank some Burton ale, walked with him." Having fallen from grace, Allen finished the day by going "to the feast in Hall." One's appreciation of the bitterness of his struggle is driven home by the entry. "Could not read because of bad headache although I did not touch anything at supper last night save one glass of ale and about twelve oysters."

The theater and cards likewise provided fuel for his burning remorse. Despite admitted pleasure in seeing Fanny Kemble and her father in a play in London, he was *"convinced* that going to the theatre is a *sin,* and I trust I shall never again be weak enough to go to see a play." This was another pledge which he was unable to keep. A few months later he stayed five days in London and spent every evening at the theater. The day after leaving town, however, he determined "with the help of God to lead a new life unto Him." And whist. "Made a determination to play cards no more. Neither won nor lost," he recorded one day and, less than a month later, "played cards till late." The innocent pleasure of reading was not entirely free from taint. "I must examine myself narrowly with God's help to discover if the delight I feel in Shakespeare etc. be from an unregenerate heart." Whom he meant by "etc." must be left to conjecture. Otway was one of the dramatists whose works he read.

Even in his devotions Allen could not shut out the distractions of the world in which he lived while meditating on the spiritual world for which he was so painstakingly preparing. "Splendid thunderstorm during Chapel," was one Sunday entry in the diary.

FitzGerald was attracted by John Allen's naïveté and earnestness. His character contrasted sharply and favorably with the students

marked, in FitzGerald's estimation, with "the Cambridge stamp."
Others, of course, also recognized his qualities. A reading man,
Allen was drawn naturally into friendships with university intellectuals. After becoming an Apostle, he conformed more to the
Cambridge type, which FitzGerald observed with regret. Always a
frank friend and outspoken critic, he wrote to Allen soon after
leaving the University:

You are now such a heterogeneous sort of animal that I scarcely know
how to talk to you. When you first came to College you were wrapped
up in old books and Theology: but now you are a little bitten with
Unions, and Quinquagents,[29] and aren't half so much "a whole" as you
used to be. I suppose after leaving College you will settle down: but
I think your principles, which were formerly strong enough, ooze away
through your fingers' ends. To me you look like a Quaker turned into
an Opera Dancer in a Pantomime. Is all this ill-natured? No, I swear it
is not: but first impressions are the strongest: and as my first impression
of you was a very pleasant one, I am angry that you are altered. For, before, you were very set apart from Cambridge men: and had a single
object in view: but now you are more made up [of] scraps, like them,
and get more of the Farrago of College information: so that you are
no longer John Allen: *but* I will not say but it is necessary that this
must take place in College: but do keep a look to yourself that you
mayn't get of the common Cambridge run. I will say that you are not
half so bad as I have made you out to be: but still, I think you will be
so, unless you look sharp. And all this I say because I love Johnny
Allen—[30]

To these strictures Allen recorded in his diary: "A letter of most
kind reproach from dear FitzGerald which I fully deserved."

FitzGerald, of course, made other friends at the University. One
was Francis Duncan, who had introduced him to Allen. "Together
did we roam the fields about Grantchester," FitzGerald wrote later,

discuss all things, thought ourselves fine fellows, and that one day we
should make a noise in the world. He is now a poor rector in one of
the most out-of-the-way villages in England [31]—has five children—fats
and kills his pigs—smokes his pipe—loves his home and cares not ever
to be seen or heard out of it. I was amused with his company; he much
pleased to see me: we had not met face to face for fifteen years—and
now both of us such very sedate unambitious people! [32]

29. A Cambridge debating society. Thackeray was also a member.
30. MS. letter to Allen [1831].
31. West Chelborough, Dorset.
32. Letter to Frederick Tennyson [Sept. 4, 1847].

Another friend was Francis Beaufort Edgeworth, half-brother of the novelist, Maria. His name immediately precedes FitzGerald's on the University matriculation books, and it is possible that their acquaintance began when, as awestruck freshmen, they sat on the benches of the Senate House at matriculation, waiting their turns to sign the rolls. However, the two seem not to have become intimate until after they left the University. In 1835, after calling on Edgeworth in London, FitzGerald said, "I think that he is a very remarkable man: and I like him more the more I see of him."

In letters which he sent to Cambridge after his graduation, FitzGerald frequently inquired about other men: Walford, Wilson, Sansum, Cameron, Chafey, W. Duncan, Francis Duncan's brother, and others. Most of them, however, soon drop out of his correspondence and apparently out of his life as well.

Although, as one of the poll, FitzGerald had considerably more freedom than his reading friends, all found time to participate in the busy social life which residence at the University involved. Organized sports played a small part in these activities, for they were only just developing. Boating had long been a favorite pastime; and in 1825, the year before FitzGerald matriculated, clubs at Trinity and St. John's [33] placed the first eight-oared boats on the Cam. The formation of crews followed naturally. The earliest crafts were built more for comfort than for speed, for they were liable at any time to be drafted into service to take club members down the river on picnics. The first "shell" of the Lady Margaret Boat Club at St. John's was thirty-eight feet long, five feet wide, and twenty-six inches deep. No attempt was made to obtain uniformity, even in so important a factor as seats. The first college race, which FitzGerald may have watched, was held on February 26, 1827. Four boats competed:

1. Jesus, six oar.
2. St. John's, eight oar.
3. Trinity, eight oar.
4. Trinity, ten oar.[34]

A few of the wealthier students played tennis, that is, the original indoor game; lawn tennis had not yet been evolved. Cricket had been moderately popular since 1820, and the first match with Ox-

33. First Trinity and the Lady Margaret Boat Clubs. The example of these colleges was soon followed by others. By 1827 the University Boat Club was organized and a regular system of racing was inaugurated.

34. *Aquatic Notes*, by a member of the Cambridge University Boat Club, 1825–50 (n.d.), p. 34.

ford was played in 1827. Rugby was not introduced until twenty-
five years later. Most students walked for exercise. Conscientious
reading men donned caps and gowns even when taking their "con-
stitutionals," but the majority wore them only in town, where
the attire was customary at all times.[35]

FitzGerald did not engage in any strenuous sport. True, he
tilted with singlesticks occasionally; but Allen, who, one gathers,
was not athletic, could beat him. With his companions he roamed
the fields or rowed, sometimes going to Chesterton to quaff home-
brewed ale at the Three Tuns Inn—when season permitted, in one
of the arbors cut into lilac bushes surrounding the bowling green.
Sometimes they would bowl a few games, have dinner in "the
little Parlour, very airy and pleasant," and return to Cambridge as
the sun dropped behind the towers of the colleges.

In strictly "social" pastimes with intimate friends, FitzGerald
was very active. As was customary, they entertained in their rooms
with breakfasts, suppers, or wine parties, equivalent of the modern
cocktail hour. Dinners were given infrequently, but breakfasts
rivaled the more formal meal in variety and bounty. One menu lists
"eggs, ham, beefsteaks, fowls, tongues, pies of all kinds, champagne,
porter, ale, tea, coffee, chocolate, tobacco, snuff." [36] Sunday was the
favorite morning for entertaining, the meal beginning about ten
and ending at one. Suppers, apparently, were simple and often
impromptu, consisting perhaps of soup or an omelette. Taking a
glass or two of wine quietly in a friend's room after dinner in hall
was a common practice; and Allen speaks of "wining about," that
is, going from friend to friend for a glass of wine and a chat. The
"wine party," given after hall, was, like the breakfast, an elaborate
repast. "Wines, white and red," runs a contemporary description,
"fruits, apples, grapes, oranges, French plums, almonds, and raisins,
filberts, preserves, a sponge cake, and cherry-brandy." [37]

It should be remembered that the period was the Georgian, when
"intemperance was the Englishman's everyday fault . . . the vice
of the nation from the highest to the lowest. . . . To be drunk
occasionally was no offence against good breeding." [38] Clergymen
tippled freely; and Mrs. FitzGerald was fond of recounting that the
vicar at Bredfield one night went to bed wearing his cocked hat

35. Gowns are now worn during the evening, but during the day only to College
and University appointments.
36. *Letters from Cambridge*, p. 176.
37. *Ibid.*, p. 182.
38. Walpole, Spencer, *History of England from 1815* (Revised ed., 1913, London,
Longmans, Green & Co.), I, 136. 6 vols.

and told her in the morning that "it was extraordinary, but he had found a remarkable difficulty in turning his head on the pillow all night." [39] Drinking was common at the University, and even John Allen kept a supply of wines and liquors on hand in order to acquit his responsibilities as host. Despite the occasional revelation in his diary that a friend had indulged too freely—that one, for example, became "a little elated," and that another was "rather bosky" at a meeting of his debating society—evidence indicates clearly that FitzGerald and his companions were temperate.[40] Milk punch was one of their favorite drinks; and Allen, after giving a party at which FitzGerald was a guest, stated that "although there were ten men, two bottles of wine were not drunk."

Evenings were spent in each others' rooms. While a fire blazed cheerily in the grate, FitzGerald and his friends filled the hours until bedtime with spirited debate or good-natured banter. Singing, or whist played for small stakes, sometimes provided diversion; and pipes, brimming mugs, glasses, or coffee cups added to the conviviality. They discussed, if not "shoes and ships and sealing wax and cabbages and kings," an assortment of topics equally diverse and provocative: books, opium, religion, Shakespeare, Sir Thomas Browne, pictures, and ghosts. Upon one occasion the conversation turned to nursery rhymes about London bells; and one of the group, whom FitzGerald identified no further than to say that he became a reverend dean, capped the discussion by improvising:

> "G— d— you all"
> Says the great bell of Paul.[41]

In the company of intimates FitzGerald lost his reserve and contributed liberally to the conversation, whether grave or gay. Once he irreverently dubbed Wordsworth, "Daddy," a name which the others gleefully adopted, for the poet was not held in high esteem by the University *literati*. FitzGerald probably caught occasional glimpses of Wordsworth at Cambridge, for the poet sometimes visited his brother Christopher, then Master of Trinity. Christopher was no more popular than his brother, "Like all Wordsworths (unless the drowned sailor) pompous and priggish," FitzGerald asserted. "He used to drawl out the Chapel responses so that we

39. MS. letter to Spring Rice, June 3, 1851.
40. FitzGerald drank moderately throughout his life, but felt only scorn for the man who drank to excess.
41. Spalding diary, May 19, 1872.

called him the 'Mēēserable Sinner' and his brother the 'Mēēserable Poet.' " [42]

The final term of FitzGerald's university career unfortunately brought examinations with it. To prepare for these, he engaged a private tutor, "one Williams," [43] to coach him during the October term of 1829. In his rooms one day Williams introduced Fitz-Gerald to a youthful, round-faced, cheery undergraduate with a misshapen nose. He was William Makepeace Thackeray.

Thackeray, in his second term of residence at Trinity, had traveled on the Continent the previous summer, accompanied by Williams as tutor. In the freshman, two years his junior, FitzGerald found a companion entirely to his liking; and their acquaintance quickly ripened into a close and hearty friendship. Thackeray became "Old Thack," and FitzGerald, "Yedward," "Ned," "Neddikens," or "Teddibus," for the younger student coined nicknames for everyone. The two were healthy, carefree youths, overflowing with fun and good humor and possessing infinite capacities for finding pleasure in life. Both believed in taking scholastic responsibilities merely as an item of life, possibly no more important, and probably much less so, than many others. The vagaries, not the order and purpose, of the world in which they lived attracted them and provided endless entertainment. Thackeray's keen wit, already edged with satire, neatly supplemented Fitz-Gerald's drollery. Both were imaginative; both were indolent.

With Thackeray as a companion, FitzGerald proceeded to close his University career with a term of glorious fun. The lures of Cambridge easily overcame the feeble attractions offered by mathematics and moral philosophy. The fresh green lawns and the checkered light and shade of the walks possessed a magnetic power which the two made little effort to resist. The Cam slipped coaxingly through the Backs and led tantalizingly into the open country. Byron's Pool was not far upstream; Chesterton and the Three Tuns Inn, with its good dinners and home-brew, were not far below. Nor was the return walk across the fields in the light of the setting sun apt to make them regret having forsaken their studies. And back at college Spedding, Kemble, Allen, and the rest were gathering; and the long evening awaited.

Whether in their rooms or abroad the two spent much time

42. Letter to Norton [Feb. 7, 1876].
43. William Williams, Corpus Christi College, was seventh Senior Optime in 1829. He became curate of West Tisted, Hants, in 1831; vicar of St. Bartholomew's, Hyde, Winchester, in 1833, and there he remained until his death in 1869.

drawing. In one of FitzGerald's scrapbooks is a pencil sketch of Thackeray with the legend, "W. M. T. 1829 Cambridge." Thackeray, a prolific cartoonist, made many drawings for FitzGerald's amusement. One is of an instrument designed to satisfy his friend's love for music. The sketch shows a row of young pigs lined up side by side in a small pen just a trifle longer, from front to back, than the pigs themselves. At the head is a swill trough at which the porkers are glutting themselves. A buxom and bucolic young woman sits at the contrivance with a sheet of music before her, playing the instrument by pulling the pigs' tails, which project through holes in the "keyboard." Thackeray labeled the device "The Hogmagundy." [44]

Singing, too, was a favored pastime. Thackeray liked to sing "The Friars of Orders Gray"; and they would join together in the rollicking cavalier song, "Troll, troll the bonny brown Bowl." Some years after Thackeray's death FitzGerald adapted the music to the novelist's poem, "Ho, Pretty Page," and distributed copies among his friends.

These diversions lured them from their studies but not altogether from their books. They read wherever curiosity led, an enjoyable, though hardly a methodical, procedure. Both loved the theater and the works of the old dramatists, from which they memorized passages. In a letter written in 1871, containing reminiscences of Charles Young, the actor, FitzGerald stated, "I remember his King John; and remember also how Thackeray, when I first knew him at Cambridge, would troll out some of that play in Young's roundly-modulated intonation; upon which I always thought Thackeray modell'd his own recitation of Verse.

> (And tell the Pope) 'that no Italian Priest
> Shall tithe or Tōll in our Dōminions—
>
> . . .
> Sō tell the Pōpe.' " [45]

Enjoying wit and drollery as they did, there is little doubt that the two laughed heartily and often at Thackeray's recitations of "Timbuctoo," a poem which he had contributed to *The Snob,* a humorous undergraduate magazine of which he was one of the editors. "Timbuctoo" had been the subject that year in the poetry competition for the Chancellor's medal, won, incidentally, by Alfred Tennyson. Thackeray submitted his verses to *The Snob* with

44. Thackeray, W. M., *The History of Pendennis* (Biographical ed. London, Smith, Elder & Co., 1899), II, xxxi. 13 vols. Anne Thackeray Ritchie, ed.
45. Letter to W. F. Pollock, May 11 [1871].

the explanation that although the composition "was unluckily not finished on the day appointed for delivery . . . I thought, Sir, it would be a pity that such a poem should be lost to the world; and . . . I have taken the liberty of submitting it."

The situation   In Africa (a quarter of the world)
Men's skins are black, their hair is crisp and curl'd;
And somewhere there, unknown to public view,
A mighty city lies, called Timbuctoo.

The natural   There stalks the tiger, there the lion roars   (5)
history   Who sometimes eats the luckless blackamoors;
All that he leaves of them the monster throws
To jackals, vultures, dogs, cats, kites, and crows.
His hunger thus the forest monarch gluts,
And then lies down 'neath trees called cocoa nuts.

After describing briefly a hunt in which the natives kill the marauding lion, the poet points to another danger in the lives of the aborigines, the danger of being captured and sold as slaves to

Reflections   . . . boil
on the fore-   Rack and molasses in Jamaica's isle!   (20)
going.   Desolate Afric! thou art lovely yet!!
One heart yet beats which ne'er shall thee forget.
What though thy maidens are a blackish brown,
Does virtue dwell in whiter breasts alone?
Oh no, oh no, oh no, oh no, oh no!   (25)
It shall not, must not, cannot, e'er be so.
The day shall come when Albion's self shall feel
Stern Afric's wrath, and writhe 'neath Afric's steel.
I see her tribes the hill of glory mount,
And sell their sugars on their own account;   (30)
While round her throne the prostrate nations come,
Sue for her rice, and barter for her rum.

There were also Thackeray's meticulous footnotes:

Lines 1 and 2. See Guthrie's Geography.
The enthusiasm which he [the poet] feels is beautifully expressed in lines 25, 26.

FitzGerald might frolic, but each day his examinations loomed more and more menacingly. He stayed in Cambridge during Christmas vacation to prepare for them. In January, 1830, three days before the ordeal in the Senate House began, Allen made a significant entry in his diary: "Called for FitzGerald's company to hall. His

temper is much soured by approach of degree. . . . FitzGerald
came in [that evening] ate biscuit and cheese and port wine, his
spirits revived." The examinations began on January 15 and continued for six days. On the last, Allen called on FitzGerald to ask
him how he had done and "found him melancholy over Paley's
Evidences." He was not at all hopeful of the results, but two days
later his anxieties came to an end. Allen recorded:

After dinner went to Duncan's and played whist with him, FitzGerald,
and Hilton. Won 8s.6d. off FitzGerald. Supped there at 9, went out at
1 o'clock and found Hilton a low Senior Opt.[46] Duncan 57 in poll. Fitz-
Gerald 106 in ditto. All delighted. Walked out Trumpington Road
making a great noise and very happy.[47]

46. Opt., optime. Senior and Junior Optimes were the two classes below the
Wranglers, or leading honors men, in the Cambridge tripos lists.
47. Allen diary, Jan. 22, 1830.

IV

The Genteel Gipsy

"You must know I . . . have got all sorts of Utopian ideas
into my head about society: these may all be very absurd, but I
try the experiment on myself, so I can do no great hurt."
                                        Letter to John Allen

FITZGERALD'S degree was conferred on February 23. Four
days later he went to visit his favorite sister, Eleanor, who,
in 1826, had married John Kerrich of Geldestone Hall,
Norfolk, just across the border from the little Suffolk town
of Beccles. A difference of opinion with his mother evidently
prompted him to go there. Mrs. FitzGerald had demanded some
course of action to which her son would not consent. Allen had
advised against rebellion, and at Geldestone FitzGerald received
a powerful admonition from his father, a threat to reduce his allowance from £300 to £200. "This wretched policy to induce me to
succumb to my Mother defeats its own end," he wrote indignantly,
"for it shows to what a stretch he is put to. I must certainly betake
myself to France and live there on what I have." Upon taking
counsel with his brother-in-law, however, he became more amena-
ble and wrote to make peace with his family. "I have received an
answer this morning from home," he told Allen a few days later,
"and we are all as before."

FitzGerald had expected to return to Cambridge from Norfolk;
but the prospect of a journey to France, once entertained, remained
alluring. Accordingly, he went to Paris in the spring and lodged at
the Hôtel de Douvres in the Rue de la Paix. Paris was gay; but,
without companions, he soon tired of the city. At the Louvre he
wished for the company of Roe, the Cambridge engraver; walking
in the parks "in this delicious weather," he longed for the companionship of Allen. By the middle of April he had determined
to return home when Thackeray arrived from Cambridge and
turned his "sorrow to joy."

Thackeray was a truant. Years later, while contributing the
Roundabout Papers to *Punch,* he recalled the excursion in an essay
on the Hotel Dessein at Calais.

How did I come to think of this escapade, which occurred in the Easter vacation of the year 1830? I always think of it when I am crossing to Calais. Guilt, sir, guilt remains stamped on the memory. . . . I met my college tutor [1] only yesterday. We were travelling, and stopped at the same hotel. He had the very next room to mine. After he had gone into his apartment, having shaken me quite kindly by the hand, I felt inclined to knock at his door and say, "Doctor Bentley, I beg your pardon, but do you remember, when I was going down at the Easter vacation in 1830, you asked me where I was going to spend my vacation? And I said, 'With my friend Slingsby, in Huntingdonshire.' Well, sir, I grieve to have to confess that I told you a fib. I had got £20 and was going for a lark to Paris, where my friend Edwards [2] was staying."

Thackeray's arrival transformed Paris for FitzGerald, and the two friends set about to make the most of the holiday. They visited the Louvre. "There are delightful portraits," FitzGerald reported to Allen, ". . . and statues so beautiful that you would forever prefer statues to pictures. There are as fine pictures in England: but not one statue so fine as any here. There is a lovely and very modest Venus: and the Gladiator: and a very majestic Demosthenes, sitting in a chair, with a roll of writing in his hands, and seemingly meditating just before rising to speak. It is quite awful." They roamed the streets and avenues and dined at boulevard restaurants, "talking nonsense of all kinds." Who knows? Perhaps with Fitz-Gerald Thackeray for the first time wandered into Terré's tavern and discovered his favorite *bouillabaisse:*

> A sort of soup or broth, or brew,
> Or hotchpotch of all sorts of fishes,
>   That Greenwich never could outdo;
> Green herbs, red peppers, mussels, saffron,
>   Soles, onions, garlic, reach, and dace;
> All these you eat in Terré's tavern
>   In that one dish of Bouillabaisse.

The evening before Thackeray's departure for England, they dined at the Palais Royal at two francs a head. Next morning the truant set out on a "long dreary guilty forty hours' journey" to Calais. Every jolt of the stagecoach agitated his restless conscience. At Dover, after paying his fare to London, he had but twelve shillings left of the £20 with which he had begun his holiday. Into the *Ship* he went and ordered for dinner "a whiting, a beefsteak, and a glass of negus; and the bill was, dinner 7s., glass of negus 2s.,

1. Thackeray's tutor at Cambridge was William Whewell, later Master of Trinity.
2. Edwards is FitzGerald.

waiter 6d." Alas, his extravagance served only to quicken his remorse, for it left him, as he "was a sinner," but half a crown for the
guard and coachman of the London stage.[3]

In Paris Thackeray left a happy, carefree FitzGerald. He had
ample funds. The truant had returned to Cambridge indebted
to him for £5. Allen collected this and an equal sum from Sansum
and forwarded the money to Paris. As insurance, he tore the bills
in half, taking care to jot down their numbers in his diary, and
enclosed the fragments in letters posted several days apart. Fitz-
Gerald wandered about the city, stimulated now by the bustle and
activity. France was on the brink of the revolution which was to
turn out despotic Charles X and put the popular Louis Philippe in
his place. FitzGerald did not see or, if he saw, did not mention the
unrest which preceded the revolt. Instead, he noted the happiness
of the people. He stopped one evening "by the Madeleine to listen
to a man who was singing to his Barrel-organ. Several passing
'Blouses' had stopped also: not only to listen, but to join in the
Songs, having bought little 'Libretti' of the words from the musician." [4] He bought one also and joined the singers, who repeated
the words first called out by the vender.

> Bons habitans de ce Village
>   Prêtez l'oreille un moment:
> Ma Morale douce et sage
>   Est faite de Sentiment:
> Vous saurez bien me comprendre
>   C'est mon coeur qui parlera.
> Quand vous pourrez venez m'entendre,
>   Et le bon Dieu vous bénira.
>
> Chorus: Quand vous pourrez m'entendre,
>   Et le bon Dieu vous bénira.

FitzGerald took his copy of the song, *"Le Bon Pasteur,"* back to England with him and copied it into a scrapbook to which he gave the
title, *Half Hours with the Worst Authors.* Many years later he recalled, "I suppose the Circumstances: the 'beau temps,' and the
pleasant Boulevards, the then so amiable People, all contributed to
the effect this Song had upon me; anyhow, it has constantly re-
visited my memory these forty-three years; and I was thinking the
other day, touched me more than any of Béranger's most beautiful
Things." [5]

3. "Desseins," Thackeray Biographical Edition, XII, 395.
4. Letter to Fanny Kemble, 1873.
5. *Loc. cit.*

Although he was but twenty-one years of age when he returned to England in June, FitzGerald began immediately to put into practice certain theories which he had formed about society and his place in it. "Tell Thackeray," he informed Allen, "that he is never to invite me to his house, as I intend never to go: not that I would not go out there rather than any place, perhaps, but I cannot stand seeing new faces in the polite circles. You must know that I am going to become a great bear: and have got all sorts of Utopian ideas into my head about society: these may all be very absurd, but I try the experiment on myself, so I can do no great hurt." [6] He left no exposition of his theories, so we know of them only through his manner of life. They applied, as he said, only to himself, and were based on a Wordsworthian principle of "plain living and high thinking," to which he remained constant throughout his life. In 1833 he adopted a diet in which bread and fruit were the staples, and after four months reported that he found no benefit except, he thought, in "more lightness of spirits." However, he persisted in his experiment until his life became "of an even gray paper character: needing no great excitement." Although he adhered to simple fare for the remainder of his life, FitzGerald never became a faddist. He served meat and fowl to his guests and never scrupled to partake of them himself. When alone, however, his diet normally consisted of bread, cheese, fresh fish (when it was available), vegetables, pudding, and fruit.

In view of his social background, FitzGerald's attitude toward society is surprising. Reared in a home directed by a woman fond of luxury and lavish entertainment, he entered manhood with a contempt for ostentation and an aversion for "polite society." His tastes were simple; his requirements, modest. Rather than live at the pretentious town house of his parents, he rented lodgings, usually in Soho, sometimes in Bloomsbury, for his frequent visits to London. He often complained of the dirt in his "upper rooms in Charlotte Street," but the squalor of lodgings never became so objectionable as to drive him to clean rooms in Portland Place. Nor did he entertain his friends at home, for each member of the family seems to have maintained his pursuits and associations rigidly independent of the rest. "We are different from other people," FitzGerald told Allen, "and I never have introduced any of my friends to my Father or Mother, as it is quite out of their way. We have absolutely no society whatever." [7]

6. MS. letter to Allen, May 21, 1830.
7. *Ibid.*, March 16, 1831.

Although he avoided social life at the home of his parents as far as possible, he could not entirely. Mr. FitzGerald's mining venture and other interests left him little time for the activities of society in which his wife participated. She, nevertheless, demanded the attendance of at least one male member of her family; and this duty, much to his distaste, fell to Edward. His obligations to his mother appear to have been threefold. He escorted her to theater and opera, attended her at dinner, both at Portland Place and abroad, and accompanied her when she went to Brighton. Going to theater and opera, happily, conformed to his own inclinations. "I think I love the Haymarket," he wrote in 1872, "as much as any part of London, because of the Little Theater where Vestris used to sing 'Cherry Ripe' in her prime." In 1880, having a free evening in London, he went into the pit of "my dear old Haymarket Opera, remembering the very corner of the Stage where Pasta stood when Jason's People came to tell her of his new Marriage . . . also when Rubini, feathered hat in hand, began that 'Ah te, oh Cara'—and Taglioni hovered over the Stage. There was the old Omnibus Box too where D'Orsay flourished in ample white Waistcoat and Wristbands: and Lady Blessington's: and Lady Jersey's on the Pit Tier: and my own Mother's, among the lesser Stars, on the third." [8] To another correspondent he referred to "the several Boxes in which sat the several Ranks and Beauties of forty and fifty years ago: my Mother's Box . . . in which I often figured as a specimen of both." Of formal dinners, however, he had no such pleasant recollections. "I feel the Dullness of that Dinner Party in Portland Place," he wrote to Fanny Kemble of one evening in 1831, "when Mrs. Frere sang . . . Pasta too, whom you then saw and heard." [9] Another, at the home of the Kembles, he described as "one of the very few delightful Dinner parties I was ever at." Brighton, where he was frequently required to go, became "the hatefullest of all places," with the "roaring unsophisticated ocean at one side, and four miles' length of idle, useless, ornamental population on the other." [10] Little as he enjoyed these obligations, FitzGerald performed them dutifully. "I have been ever wishing to get into the country," he confided to a friend in May, 1831, "but find that I am very useful to my Mother: and, as I wish to do all that may be good, I do not leave town: nor shall, till July." [11]

His father, too, required certain duties of him. The Manchester

8. Letter to Fanny Kemble, Dec. 6 [1880].
9. *Ibid.*, April 6 [1880].
10. Letter to Bernard Barton, Dec. 29, 1844.
11. MS. letter to Allen, Spring, 1831.

mine was Mr. FitzGerald's chief private interest and occupied much of his time. Moreover, the months from March, 1831, to June, 1832, were politically of great importance to him, for the battle over the Reform Bill was then raging in Parliament. Seaford, which he represented, was one of the "rotten boroughs." Edward took an active interest in the struggle, not only because his father was involved, but also because of his own sympathy with the liberal cause. "New converts are daily made to support the new Bill," he told Allen in March, 1831.

My father set out against it at first, but is coming over, I think. The question with him is, not whether the bill is a good one, for he thinks it is: but whether he ought to vote for the disenfranchisement of his own borough: wherein he certainly would not be its representative, because no borough would ever wish to be disfranchised. It is the general opinion now that it will be carried. At first bets were 3 to 1 against it: but on Friday or Thursday they were even. Nothing can equal the anxiety of the Members. I wish they had proposed universal suffrage: but I know that you wouldn't listen to my wherefore.[12]

A short time later he reported, "The Reform Bill is to be carried by 150 majority, they say."

His duties as a member of Parliament and his activities at Manchester left Mr. FitzGerald comparatively little time to devote to his properties. To Edward, after he went down from Cambridge, was delegated the task of collecting rents and sometimes of supervising work on the estates. In November, 1830, arriving at Naseby, presumably to collect rents, he found that the resident agent had absconded with more than £5,000 of his father's money. "Pleasant this, to hear of a November morning," he remarked. The theft did not diminish his admiration for the locality, however. "Do you know, Allen," he continued,

that this is a very curious place with odd fossils: and mixed with bones and bullets of the fight at Naseby; and the identical spot where King Charles stood to see the battle, whereon my dad has erected a *pillow* to commemorate it. . . . I do wish you and Sansum were here to see the curiosities. Can't you come? I am quite the King here, I promise you. . . . I am going to-day to dine with the Carpenter, a Mr. Ringrose, and to hear his daughter play on the piano-forte. Fact. My blue Surtout daily does wonders. At Church its effect is truly delightful.[13]

One other duty which devolved upon him was escorting his sisters about England to visit relatives or friends. "Edward FitzGerald

12. *Ibid.*, March, 1831.
13. *Ibid.*, November, 1830.

. . . staid a day or two with me," wrote Donne to Blakesley. ". . . He was, when he left me, under marching orders for Hastings to convoy certain sisters. He has some of the inconveniences of marriage even in his state of innocence—and among them I should reckon not the least that of accompanying Mrs. FitzGerald (his Mother) the round of the theatres to see the 'Demon Dwarf,' [14] and sometimes the melodramas." [15] FitzGerald was devoted to his sisters and appears always to have been willing to sacrifice his own desires and to abandon his own plans for their pleasures. "Our prospect of going down to Suffolk this year is on the wane," he informed a friend. "The Doctor has desired that Lusia should remain in town. Though I should like much to see you and others, yet I am on the whole glad that my sisters should stay here, where they are likely to be better off. I shall stay with them, as I am of use." [16]

When in London and not engaged by family duties, FitzGerald led a delightful existence. He read at the British Museum, browsed in bookshops, and visited picture galleries. His lodgings gave him a freedom which was as vital to him as breathing. There he could come and go as he chose. Although he disliked formal entertaining, he enjoyed the free camaraderie of bachelor friends; and in rooms in Charlotte Street, Southampton Row, or Russell Street, he could entertain when and as he wished. Many of his friends, on leaving Cambridge, gravitated to London. Thackeray and Thomas Mazzinghi, another Trinity friend, were often in town, and the mercurial Jacky Kemble would return from the most unexpected places and missions. He had left the University without taking a degree when he failed to win honors in 1829. For three years he moved about, now in Germany studying philology under the brothers Grimm, now back at Cambridge completing requirements for his degree and preparing for the Church, now in Spain with other Apostles supporting revolutionists under General Torrijos. After these adventures he often entertained FitzGerald and Thackeray in London lodgings by singing German airs or the more spirited revolutionary song, learned in Spain:

Si un E - li - o con-spi - ro a - le - vo - -

14. Probably Edmund Kean, whom FitzGerald described as "undersized."
15. *Donne and His Friends,* p. 47.
16. Letter to Bernard Barton, Nov. 27, 1841.

so contra el pueb-lo y   Su ·· li-ber-tad-·&c

In 1832 he went to London to study law, finally settling down in 1835 as editor of the *British and Foreign Review*. For diversion he edited Anglo-Saxon manuscripts. Spedding, Thompson, Heath, and others who were still at Cambridge frequently came down to spend their holidays. One day a number of them visited DeVille, a lampmaker and phrenologist, who kept a shop in the Strand. After examining Spedding's head, he said, "No wonder at this being a good man. There is nothing bad in his head to counteract." He diagnosed Heath, who later became a Wrangler at Cambridge, as a clever mathematician, and gave "a very true account" of FitzGerald but failed to mention his ability at drawing. Surprised at this, Thompson asked the phrenologist if he saw no indication of it. "Well, perhaps so," DeVille replied, "but he would always be puzzled about perpendiculars and trifles." [17] Spedding, writing to Donne, said that DeVille had predicted that FitzGerald "would be given to theology and 'Religion in the supernatural parts.' Was there ever so felicitous a mistake?" he asked. "Was there ever a stronger instance of the organs of marvelousness and veneration predominant, though driven so effectually out of their ordinary, if not their natural channel? I take this to be the secret of all that is strange and wayward in his judgments on matters of art: for very strange and wayward they appear to me, though so original and often so profound and luminous." [18]

FitzGerald, Spedding, and Thackeray were all avid theatergoers. "How I long for the sight of a dear green curtain!" Thackeray wrote to FitzGerald from Paris about this time. "After going three times a week to the play for a year, one misses it so. O the delight of seeing the baize slowly ascending, the spangled shoes which first appear, then as it draws up, legs, stomachs, heads, till finally it ends in all the glories of a party of 'musqueteers' drinking. . . . Yet another month and all this paradise will be in my reach. Really, London is to me only the place where the theatres are." [19] Fitz-Gerald and Spedding were in London together in October, 1833,

17. Spalding diary, Sept. 23, 1867, and Aug. 1, 1876.
18. Brookfield, F. M., *The Cambridge Apostles* (London, Sir Isaac Pitman & Sons, 1906), p. 267.
19. Thackeray Biographical Edition, IX, xxvii.

and "saw an awful Hamlet . . . a Mr. Serle," the former told Donne, "and a very good Wolsey, in Macready: and a very bad Queen Catherine, in Mrs. Sloman, whom you must remember. I am going tonight to see Macready in Macbeth: I have seen him before in it: and I go for the sake of his two last acts, which are amazingly fine, I think." [20]

In 1830 Fanny Kemble became a sensation on the London stage. The previous year her father, Charles Kemble, had gambled desperately to save himself from financial ruin, and Covent Garden from the hands of his creditors, by introducing another member of the family to London theatergoers. The successes of her parents, as well as those of her aunt, the popular Mrs. Siddons, and her uncle, John Philip Kemble, had prepared the way. Fanny, barely twenty years old, scored an immediate success in her debut in *Romeo and Juliet.* "Miss Kemble's 'Juliet' creates such a sensation in London," Donne reported, "that Drury Lane, I understand, is saved from emptiness, and blank cheques, by the *over-flowing* of Covent Garden." [21] FitzGerald, however, was not among those who were dazzled by his young friend's brilliance. "I did not see much of her acting," he wrote in 1878, "nor hear much of her reading,[22] for in truth I did not much admire either."

From time to time FitzGerald returned to his home in Suffolk, where his sisters usually stayed. A year or two before he entered Cambridge, his parents had moved from Bredfield to Wherstead, an estate two miles south of Ipswich at the rim of the highlands overlooking the River Orwell. Wherstead Lodge was the most attractive of the many beautiful FitzGerald homes. From without, the mansion possesses an ageless beauty derived from good line and proportion; within, it is imposing. The spacious, high-ceilinged rooms are entered from a palatial hallway, an open well extending from ground to roof. A broad staircase rises from the center of the reception hall to a landing from which the stairs split into two flights along the walls. Access to the rooms on the upper floors is gained from balconies supported by marble columns. Large windows overlook the gardens and command a view across rolling fields. To the east glitter the waters of the Orwell estuary; some two hundred yards to the north stands the manor church; and beyond rise the roofs and steeples of Ipswich.

FitzGerald loved Wherstead, which was, and is, an idyllic spot.

20. Letter to Donne [Oct. 25, 1833].
21. *Donne and His Friends,* p. 4.
22. After a residence of several years in America, where she had married, Fanny Kemble returned to England and was popular as a reader of Shakespearean plays.

He would wander off by himself to read, sometimes in the churchyard, where white violets grew in the spring, sometimes to a tiny
pond, containing the smallest dot of an island, which sparkled in
the fields below the church. There, while home for one of his vaca-
tions from Bury, he had pushed out in a little skiff to read *Redgauntlet,* published a short time before.[23] Occasionally the entire
family gathered at the Lodge. "You say sometimes how like things
are to dreams," FitzGerald wrote to Allen from Wherstead one
summer, "or, as I think, to the shifting scenes of a play. So does this
place seem to me. All our family, except my mother, are collected
here: all my brothers and sisters, with their wives, husbands, and
children: sitting at different occupations, or wandering about the
grounds or gardens, discoursing each their separate concerns, but
all united into one whole. The weather is delightful; and when I
see them passing to and fro, and hear their voices, it is like the scenes
of a play." [24] Elizabeth Charlesworth, daughter of an evangelical
rector at Flowton, near Ipswich, has given another glimpse of life
at Wherstead. "I used to be so much with his sisters there," she said.
"The Library was a most delightful room, and there he and we used
to [sit] every evening, listening . . . to his sisters practising the
new music he used to bring them. They played splendidly at
sight." [25]

When Mrs. FitzGerald was at Wherstead, house parties were frequent and elaborate. Bernard Barton, the genial, unsophisticated
bank clerk and Quaker poet of Woodbridge was sometimes a guest,
and once met Macready, the actor, there.

Attendance at Portland Place, time spent in London with his
friends or at Wherstead with his family still left FitzGerald many
free weeks in each year. These he spent roaming about from Sussex
to Cumberland, from Suffolk to Pembrokeshire. He visited relatives and friends, made pilgrimages to points of literary or historic
interest, went wherever his curiosity drew him, and led a genteel
gipsy life, keeping, as he said, "on the windy side of care." As he
wandered about, he tried to decide upon a locality in which to
establish country lodgings, independent of his family, as a supple-
ment to his London quarters. He wanted, merely, to have rooms
at some quiet farm or in an attractive town where he could return
from his London holidays and provincial journeys. Where should
it be—Suffolk? Norfolk? Pembrokeshire? The problem haunted

23. Spalding diary, Sept. 24, 1867. Scott's *Redgauntlet* was published in 1824.
24. Letter to Allen, July 4, 1835.
25. MS. letter of Mrs. E. B. Cowell, née Charlesworth, Trinity College Library.

him for seven years; its solution constantly evaded him. Meanwhile, he went round and round his beloved England like a restless dog about to lie down.

On his return from Paris in 1830, he spent most of the summer at Southampton. Williams, his Cambridge coach, had just been appointed to a living near by at West Tisted. FitzGerald "saw him installed in his parsonage, and eat of his meat and drank of his beer, and tasted all the produce of his glebe." Allen went to Portsmouth with a reading party from Cambridge that summer, but FitzGerald did not visit him because he had "such an arrant dislike to Portsmouth." In August, however, Allen went to see Williams and from West Tisted walked to Southampton. The morning after his arrival he called on FitzGerald, who "jumped and almost cried for joy to see me." They walked to Netley Abbey, chatting "about Apostles, Cambridge men, etc." The next day they crossed to the Isle of Wight, FitzGerald talking "all the time most delightfully of Shakespeare, the Tempest, etc." At Cowes they watched the regatta and saw the banished French royal family with the exception of Charles X. The next day Allen returned to Portsmouth.[26]

FitzGerald spent the remainder of the year in London, Suffolk, Geldestone, Cambridge, and Naseby. He was at Naseby again in March and April of 1831 and there wrote his first published poem, "The Meadows in Spring," an epitome of his life before he had lived it.

> 'Tis a dull sight
>   To see the year dying,
> When winter winds
>   Set the yellow wood sighing:
> Sighing, oh! sighing.
>
> When such a time cometh,
>   I do retire
> Into an old room
>   Beside a bright fire:
> Oh, pile a bright fire!
>
> I never look out
>   Nor attend to the blast;
> For all to be seen

26. MS. letter to Allen, July 26, 1830; and Allen diary, Aug. 20 and 21, 1830.

Is the leaves falling fast:
Falling, falling!

. . .

Then with an old friend
 I talk of our youth—
How 'twas gladsome, but often
 Foolish, forsooth:
But gladsome, gladsome!

Or to get merry
 We sing some old rhyme,
That made the wood ring again
 In summer time—
Sweet summer time!

Then go we to smoking,
 Silent and snug:
Nought passes between us,
 Save a brown jug—
Sometimes!

. . .

Thus, then, live I,
 Till, 'mid all the gloom,
By heaven! the bold sun
 Is with me in the room,
Shining, shining!

Then the clouds part,
 Swallows soaring between;
The spring is alive,
 And the meadows are green!

I jump up, like mad,
 Break the old pipe in twain,
And away to the meadows,
 The meadows again!

Few poets have been so successful as Fitzgerald in getting their early efforts into print. "The Meadows in Spring" was published in two magazines, Hone's *Year Book* and the *Athenaeum,* within the space of ten weeks. The poem appeared first in the *Year Book* on April 30 with an explanatory note which FitzGerald had sent to the editor:

These verses are in the old style; rather homely in expression; but I honestly profess to stick more to the simplicity of the old poets than the moderns, and to love the philosophical good humour of our old writers more than the sickly melancholy of the Byronian wits. If my verses be not good, they are good-humoured, and that is something.

The poem appeared again on July 9 in the *Athenaeum*. In a letter, which was also published, FitzGerald stated:

These verses are something in the old style, but not the worse for that: not that I mean to call them good: but I am sure they would have not been better, if dressed up in the newest Montgomery [27] fashion. If they are fitted for your paper, you are welcome to them.

To this the editor responded:

They are fitted for any paper, and most welcome to us. The writer must not imagine that the delay in their appearance was occasioned by any doubt. . . . His verses are not, indeed, in the Montgomery style, or the latest fashion—they are not all glare and glitter, patch and paint, and meretricious ornament—they are deep in feeling, and sweet in harmony; but we must not write commendations even on contributors. We have a suspicion that we could name the writer—if so, we are sure his name would grace our pages as much as his verses.

The explanation of the dual appearance of the poem may lie in the apology offered by the editor of the *Athenaeum* for delay in publishing the verses. It is possible that FitzGerald had first sent his poem to that magazine and, when it failed to appear, assumed that it had been rejected. William Hone, known for his political satires, published successively a series of miscellanies under the titles, *The Every Day Book, The Table Book,* and *The Year Book.* The publications differed in name only. All were collections of information on customs, folklore, ceremonies, dress, sports, and a thousand and one other topics. Each was intended to be a "perpetual almanac," its contents being arranged under calendar headings. The miscellanies appeared in weekly parts. At the beginning of each month the numbers of the preceding month were bound together and re-issued. At the end of the year all parts were published in book form. Poems appropriate to the various seasons appeared frequently; and FitzGerald's lines, submitted in the spring, were ideally suited for Hone's use.

Charles Lamb, whom the *Athenaeum* editors apparently believed to be the author of the poem, called the attention of Edward

27. Robert Montgomery (1807–55). His religious poems were popular at the time.

Moxon, the London publisher, to the previous appearance of the poem and paid the anonymous author a rare tribute:

The *Athenaeum* has been hoaxed with some exquisite poetry, that was, two or three months ago, in Hone's Book. . . . The poem I mean is in Hone's Book as far back as April. I do not know who wrote it; but 'tis a poem I envy—*that* and Montgomery's "Last Man": I envy the writers, because I feel I could have done something like them.[28]

During the first four years after leaving the University Fitz-Gerald often returned to Cambridge to visit friends. Allen, Spedding, and Thompson did not take their degrees until 1832; then only Allen went down. Spedding remained at Cambridge until 1834, the year that Thompson took his first step toward the mastership of Trinity by being elected a Fellow of the college.

Sometimes FitzGerald spent but a few days in Cambridge; at other times he remained for whole terms. When they were available, he rented his old rooms in King's Parade. He took them for the entire Michaelmas term of 1831, but his mother and Thackeray detained him in London until mid-November. Cambridge, however, was his home for the remainder of the year. His visits were projections of his student days. He spent his time reading, walking, boating, dining, and talking with friends, just as he had done as an undergraduate. Allen was his most constant companion in the autumn of 1831. Many were the walks they took, and varied were their conversations. "Talked with FitzGerald about Opium, Shakespeare, Sir Thomas Browne, and Pictures," Allen recorded in his diary on November 18. Another entry reads, "Walked with FitzGerald. . . . a very pleasant conversation about the miserable depravity of humanity, Chaucer, associations, etc." Sometimes their discussions were more personal. "We talked of Human Life Changes and Chances," Allen divulged. "He said he expected to live till 35 or 38. I thought I might die within a year or, if not, then live till 60 or 70." Allen escaped death "within a year" and fulfilled the remainder of his prediction by living until 1886. He took his degree at the end of the term and became a schoolmaster in London but soon transferred to King's College, established in the Strand in 1831, where he lectured on mathematics.

Cambridge held an irresistible charm for FitzGerald in the spring, and he returned for each May term from 1832 to 1834. He was there in February, 1833, as well, and wrote to Allen in London,

28. *Letters and Literary Remains of Edward FitzGerald* (London, Macmillan & Co., 1902), I, 6. 7 vols. Aldis Wright, ed.

"Last night I smoked for the first time: and came home merry, and played the Harmonious Blacksmith out of pure remembrance of you." During the May term of that year he joined a club which met once a week to read and discuss Shakespeare's plays. "It is good so far as that men may meet together pleasantly once a week under his noble name," he said. "We are also to have a dinner on his birthday, I believe, which I shall like well." It was in this group that he made the acquaintance of other Apostles, among them Merivale, Blakesley, Tennant, and Stephen Spring Rice, son of Lord Monteagle, described as "one of the most gifted and charming of men." [29] Spedding sketched a pencil portrait of each of the group, and FitzGerald wrote Allen in May, "I have been sitting to him this morning, and my phiz is impaled on Paper for ever."

Spedding's drawing was made as FitzGerald sat reading. The lower part of the sketch is unfinished, but the artist took considerable pains with the head. The face is a pleasant one, the most striking features being the mouth and chin. The lips are full, the chin rounded and deeply cleft. The flesh above the upper lip forms a singular lineament by curving out prominently to join the division between the nostrils. The nose is straight and the eyebrows are highly arched. The hair, parted wide at the forehead, is fairly long.[30]

FitzGerald was stimulated by his friends at Cambridge, and his letters from there are animated and enthusiastic. "I could wish you were here to talk [sic] a turn with me in the walks," reads a typical passage to Allen. "The Chestnut trees are in their usual glory at this season, crowned over with blossom; and I never saw the fields so rich. I have been laughing out of measure of late: by which learn that I am in good case—Bless thee, my boy, and farewell." [31] By 1834 most of FitzGerald's friends had left the University, and with the May term of that year his close association with Cambridge came to an end. He returned occasionally in later years, but for brief visits only.

During the summer of 1832 and again in the autumn of 1833, he visited Allen in Pembrokeshire. On both trips he stayed in lodgings at Tenby. Allen proposed a walking tour in 1832, but Fitz-Gerald demurred. "If [we] can reside together, let it be," he wrote,

29. Spring Rice's father, the Right Honorable Spring Rice, was Chancellor of the Exchequer in the Whig cabinet from 1835–39. In 1839 he resigned to enter the House of Lords as Lord Monteagle and become Comptroller of the Exchequer.

30. Spedding's sketch of FitzGerald is now in the Fitzwilliam Museum, Cambridge, Exhibit 674.

31. MS. letter to Allen, 1832.

"but I am too poor a walker to go over South Wales." They spent a few days with cousins of Allen's at Freestone, near Narberth, where FitzGerald found "by far the pleasantest family I ever was among." He returned alone to Tenby, and wrote to Allen, "I have taken a very nice lodging looking out on the sea, with two bed-rooms—I cannot have less. Pray come then and fill one of them, for a week, and live with me. I have arranged all matters." [32] Allen accepted. At this time FitzGerald must have shown Allen the first two stanzas of his poem, "To a Lady Singing," for he sent two more stanzas from London in December, to be added, he said, to those which Allen already knew. Both kept what they called "Paradise Books," commonplace books into which they copied favorite selections of poetry. Into his, FitzGerald admitted only such poems as "breathe content and virtue." He included "Back and syde go bare" because it breathed of "both of these, with a little good drink over."

When he went to Pembrokeshire in 1833, he again visited Freestone, and again Allen stayed with him at Tenby. Sitting on a rock which jutted into Tenby Harbor one day, they repeated passages from the poems of George Herbert. Years later, FitzGerald maintained that he did not remember a pleasanter place than Tenby. He returned to London by stagecoach, leaving at half-past nine one morning and reaching Bristol at midnight. He was on the road again at six o'clock the following morning and arrived in London at eight that evening. Soon afterward, he learned of the death of Anne Allen, a member of the Freestone family. Thereupon he wrote the following lines, which he sent to Allen:

> The wind blew keenly from the Western sea,
> And drove the dead leaves slanting from the tree—
>   Vanity of vanities, the Preacher saith—
> Heaping them up before her Father's door
> When I saw her whom I shall see no more—
>   We cannot bribe thee, Death.
>
>   • • •
>
> She bound her shining hair across her brow,
> She went into the garden fading now—
>   Vanity of vanity, the Preacher saith—
> And if one sigh'd to think that it was sere,
> She smiled to think that it would bloom next year:
>   She fear'd thee not, O Death.
>
>   • • •
>
> Her pleasant smile spread sunshine upon all;

32. *Ibid.*, 1832.

We heard her sweet clear laughter in the Hall;—
Vanity of vanities, the Preacher saith—
We heard her sometimes after evening prayer,
As she went singing softly up the stair—
No voice can charm thee, Death.[33]

33. "On Anne Allen"; stanzas 1, 4, 5.

V

Doubts and Perplexities

"I still vacillate like a fool between belief and disbelief, sometimes one, sometimes the other, for I have no strength of mind and very little perception."

Letter to Allen

FOR several years after leaving the University, FitzGerald experienced a *Sturm und Drang,* like so many of his contemporaries who found it impossible to accept without question the orthodox religion of their fathers. The reading of "Moral Philosophy and Theology" at Cambridge was designed to provide a sound foundation for Christian faith. Many students, however, completed their study of Paley's *Evidences* and related books with views on religion confused and faith shaken. FitzGerald was one of these; Spedding, Thackeray, and Mazzinghi, to mention only three of his friends, emerged from the University similarly disturbed. The more FitzGerald pondered the subject, the more uncertain and melancholy he became. His meditations strengthened a habit of moody introspection which was natural to his temperament. For several years he vacillated "like a fool between belief and disbelief."

The causes of the religious perplexities in which FitzGerald's generation floundered are apparent. Since the seventeenth century science had been making discoveries which were to revolutionize man's concepts of his place in the scheme of creation. At the opening of the nineteenth century the average layman accepted modern science as far as it had developed but still retained his belief in the validity of a literal interpretation of the Bible. However, the revelations of the new stratigraphical geology and of biology were providing further evidence that a reinterpretation of creation and the origin of life was imminent. The long battle between "fundamentalism" and "modernism" was about to open; the first skirmishes had hardly begun, but the lines of conflict were forming while men of FitzGerald's generation were at the universities. With the curiosity and enthusiasm of youth, they examined and discussed the revelations of science. Soon after he left Trinity in 1831,

Tennyson, in a letter to his friend, Arthur Hallam, suggested that the "development of the human body might possibly be traced from the radiated, vermicular, molluscous, and vertebrate organisms"; to which Hallam replied, "Do you mean that the human brain is at first like a madrepore's, then like a worm's, etc? but this cannot be for they have no brain." [1] FitzGerald's contemporaries were keenly aware of the bearing of such speculations on orthodox religion. Many found it impossible to accept the new thought and retain the literal interpretation of those portions of the Bible which conflicted with it. Naturally enough, uncertainties thus engendered stimulated questionings which involved the traditional foundations of religious faith.

FitzGerald's doubts were the source of considerable anguish for Allen, who labored to guide his friend to a perception of religious truth as he himself saw it. FitzGerald spent his last evening at Cambridge after receiving his degree, in Allen's rooms. When all other guests had left, Allen "talked . . . with FitzGerald on serious subjects and begged him to think about religion. Promised me he would . . . Gave him . . . Jeremy Taylor's Holy Living and Dying. Pray God that it might be of service to him." FitzGerald wrote from Paris that the book was "beautifully written," but added, "I want something more elementary and fundamental. However, it is always a great strengthening of belief to see great minds believing: to be sure a great many have not believed: but many have. When once belief is made, the way is plain, and the rest remains with oneself to do: but one has it not in one's power always to believe." [2] Despite waverings which were frequent and distressing, he thought for a time that he was "coming very quick *round to a* rooted belief in Christianity." But a path through his maze of doubts was not so easily discovered. When Allen joined him at Southampton in August, he again "tried to make him steady in his views on religion. God, I hope and trust, in his good time will turn his heart," reads Allen's diary.

FitzGerald sometimes attributed his despondency and periods of ill health during these years to his lack of faith. "Last week," he confided to Allen in 1832,

I was unhappy and in low spirits on account of the same turmoil in my head that I once had at Seaford. The other night when I lay in bed feeling my head get warmer and warmer, I felt that if I should pray to

1. Tennyson, *Memoir*, I, 44.
2. MS. letter to Allen, Spring, 1830.

some protector for relief, I should be relieved: but I have not yet learned the certainty of there being any. It is a melancholy thing that the want of happiness and security caused by scepticism is no proof of the truth of religion: for if a man is miserable because he has not a guinea, it may make him happy to believe he had a guinea, but still he has it not. So if one can delude oneself into a belief, it is a happiness; but some cannot help feeling all the time that it is a delusion.[3]

It should not be assumed that FitzGerald left Cambridge a morbid hypochondriac. In the company of those who, as he told Allen, were unconnected with his darker views, he was humorous, happy, and carefree. He realized, too, that his trouble lay partly in too much introspection. "I feel," he wrote, "that, being alone, one's thoughts and feelings, from want of communication, become heaped up and clotted together, as it were: and so lie like undigested food heavy upon the mind: but with a friend one *tosseth* them about, so that the air gets between them, and keeps them fresh and sweet." [4]

FitzGerald and Thackeray carried on a lively debate on theological questions in letters which passed between them. FitzGerald wrote in 1831:

I had got over all doubts as to Christianity . . . except the Miracles, but I think the evidence of them is to be doubted. But Paley is very clever about them. It is a case made out as by a lawyer, and he thoroughly answers Hume on the point of there being any likeness between Christ's miracles and the Abbé Paris. Religious people are very angry with one for doubting: and say, "You come to the question determined to doubt, not to be convinced." Certainly we do: having seen how many follow and have followed false religions, and having our reason utterly against many of the principal points of the Bible, we require the most perfect evidence of facts, before we can believe. If you can prove to me that one miracle took place, I will believe that he is a just God who damned us all because a woman eat an apple; and you can't expect greater complaisance than that, to be sure.

You are wrong, my dear Thackeray, in fancying that Christ does not call himself God. Every page of the Bible will shew you he did. There is one thing that goes some way with me: if Christ was not really God, he was either a fanatic, or an impostor: now his morals and advice are too consistent, and too simple and mild, for a fanatic; and an impostor, one fancies, would not have persevered in such a blameless life, nor held in his heart at once the blasphemous design of calling himself the

3. *Ibid.*, Nov. 21, 1832.
4. Letter to Allen, Feb. 24, 1833.

Son of God and a code of principles which the best and wisest of men never preached before. What do you say to this point? Think of it. I am in a quandary of doubts.[5]

FitzGerald's perplexities were those of a vitally inquisitive man in search of a faith. "I assure you, a slender pretence will make me throw myself upon Christianity," he told Allen in 1832.[6] At his friend's suggestion he read Isaac Barrow, Richard Hooker, and other theologians, in addition to Jeremy Taylor, and became an ardent admirer of the literature of the seventeenth-century divines. The Bible, too, he studied carefully. Nor did he question the value of religion to humanity. "I have always told you," he said to Allen, "that I knew a religion to be necessary for men." [7]

With all his doubts FitzGerald was a loyal member of the Church of England and attended services regularly until well past middle life. Paying one's devotions at Boulge, where he lived for many years, involved such mortification of the flesh as would satisfy an ascetic. The church was as damp as a tomb. Fungi grew "in great numbers" about the communion table, and in winter members of the congregation sat through the service bundled in their warmest clothing. Church customs, too, he observed. On Good Friday one year, a Woodbridge friend called unexpectedly and dined, he reported, on "boiled salt-fish and egg sauce, with a roast wild-duck. Edward, being orthodox, stuck to the salt-fish, I, more lax, attacking the wild-fowl." [8] The Boulge clergyman was sick the following Sunday; so FitzGerald walked the three miles to Woodbridge, feeling it a duty to go to church somewhere on Easter. The church at Woodbridge could be almost as uncomfortable as that at Boulge. "You are to know," FitzGerald told a friend one December, "that I slept at Woodbridge last night, went to church there this morning, where everyone sat with a purple nose, and heard a dismal well-meant sermon; and the organ blew us out with one grand idea at all events, one of old Handel's Coronation Anthems. . . ." He sometimes substituted for the Woodbridge organist, but confessed that he once began his performance with an unexpected "squawk."

FitzGerald's sympathies were with the Low Church group. While planning a visit to William Airy, vicar of Keysoe in Bedfordshire, he wrote, "I am not sure if he is not offended with his old school-

5. MS. letter to Thackeray, Oct. 11, 1831.
6. MS. letter to Allen, Nov. 28, 1832.
7. Loc. cit.
8. Donne and His Friends, p. 92.

fellow . . . partly because his High Church propensities perhaps resent my Low Church heresies." In the early 'forties he was attracted by the preaching of the Reverend Timothy R. Matthews,[9] a Nonconformist, whom he heard on visits to Bedford. Matthews was a zealous evangelist, for whom his congregation had built a spacious chapel in the Bromham Road. During the week he preached on the greens in surrounding villages, attracting worshipers by blowing a trumpet. FitzGerald first heard him in the streets of Bedford and was so impressed by his sincerity and earnestness that he often attended services in the chapel, which was always filled to overflowing. More than once he was deeply moved by Matthews' eloquence. "I heard a man preach at Bedford in a way that shook my soul," he said after hearing a sermon on Good Friday, 1844.

He described the crucifixion in a way that put the scene before his people—no fine words, and metaphors: but first one nail struck into one hand, and then into another, and one through both feet—the cross lifted up with God in man's image distended upon it. And the sneers of the priests below—"Look at that fellow there—look at him—he talked of saving others, etc." And then the sun veiled his face in Blood, etc. I certainly have heard oratory now—of the Lord Chatham kind, only Matthews has more faith in Christ than Pitt in his majority. I was almost as much taken aback as the poor folks all about me who sobbed. . . .[10]

After the sermon Matthews asked his congregation to say "that they believed Christ had redeemed them: and first one got up and in sobs declared she believed it: and then another, and then another . . . all poor people: how much richer than all who fill the London Churches. Theirs is the Kingdom of Heaven!" [11] FitzGerald believed that Matthews' influence would effectively counteract that of the Chartist leaders who were active during the 'forties. "I rather want to get him to Manchester," he wrote in 1842. Matthews died in September, 1845, after an illness brought on by overwork and neglect. "I would have given a great deal to save his life," FitzGerald stated.

Ritualism and other Romish tendencies, which were widely adopted by clergymen in the Established Church as a result of the Oxford Movement, so disturbed FitzGerald that in 1849 he drew up a petition advocating reform of liturgy and rubric. He printed

9. The Reverend T. R. Matthews was educated at Sidney Sussex College, Cambridge.
10. Letter to Barton [1844].
11. *Ibid.*, April 11, 1844.

copies of the paper, addressed to the Prime Minister, Lord John Russell, but it is doubtful if he ever submitted it. The document read, in part:

My Lord,

We, the undersigned, being deeply attached to the Protestant Faith, have seen with sorrow the Pope's recent creation of a Roman Hierarchy in England.

But, in tracing this act to its cause, we are compelled to admit,— first—That this advance of the Pope's results less from any unusual aggression on his part, than from some unusual invitation from ourselves; so many Ministers of the Church of England (encouraged by some Bishops) having been so long and so loudly proclaiming the essential Unity of the Church of England with that of Rome; practising some of Rome's vain ceremonies; . . . and, finally, by going themselves, and drawing many of their people, over to the Church to which they had striven to liken their own.

But—secondly—these persons have in many instances sheltered themselves from effectual reprehension under certain words in the Liturgy and Rubric of the Church of England, which seem to authorize such doctrines and practices; . . .

The evil being thus traced home to the Liturgy of the Church of England, we venture to suggest to your Lordship, that here the cure of the evil ought to begin; such words in the Liturgy or Rubric as have given countenance to these errors being removed, so as to prevent any like danger for the future from foolish or designing men. . . .

And believing, as we do, that the security of a Religion lies in its own purity, and in the sincerity of the People professing it, not in any legislative enactments against other Religions; we hope that no restrictions which the milder policy of late years has removed from the Roman Catholics will be reimposed upon them, at least until some more injurious effects follow this measure of the Pope's than the mere assumption of empty Titles.

And, considering besides that, while exclaiming against the Pope's invasion of her Hierarchic Titles, Protestant England has appropriated not only the Titles, but the Revenues, of Papal Ireland; we further beg to suggest to your Lordship if such Honours and Revenues may not be more equitably distributed, according to the claims of the Irish people; either by returning them in part to their original owners, or so disposing them in Protestant hands as better to secure the advance of a purer Faith.

FitzGerald sent a copy to Allen, then Archdeacon of Salop, who responded, "I think your petition very simply expressed, clear, and forcible, but I do not agree with you in thinking the Liturgy needs alteration. . . . I believe that every sentence honestly admits of a safe and sound interpretation . . ." [12] Allen continued with a defense of his position, to which FitzGerald replied:

(1) What! the Communication of the Holy Ghost in Ordination! the form of Absolution in the Visitation of the Sick—nay, of the rubrical law which confines the utterance of the Absolution in the form of Daily Prayer to *the Priest!*—*One* of the worst things in all this matter is that really honest and able men like yourself, feel obliged to *explain away* the plain and literal understanding of such passages in quite as unnatural a way as the Jesuitical party of the Church have explained away what militates against their views. If such passages are taken literally they *are* of Rome, and lead to Rome direct; if explained away they still, alas! are of Rome, and still lead to it by another road, fixing a character of insincerity on those who thus explain them. Besides, by persisting in leaving them there, you do leave the direct road to Rome open, as well as instructing [*sic*] a bye-path of your own; for it is by such passages that Newman, Pusey, Dodsworth, and BP. of London, have authorized doctrines which, as we have proved by the experience of fifteen years, have led multitudes to Rome.

(2) Of course, alterations are difficult and dangerous; but has not the thing *without alteration* been dangerous enough? Are not *any* schismatic disputes better than the high road to Popery?

(3) If what is said before be true, what becomes of the *perfect* human Wisdom of the Liturgy? O John Allen, you tell me not to address you as Archdeacon; but if I had not known that you always had the deepest Reverence, (on Religious, not on interested, grounds) for the Powers and Systems that be, I should have said that your shovel hat had partly overlaid and extinguished the Understanding and the Conscience within. I always say there is no man honest in his own calling: no man who does not let the "esprit de corps" and *conventional* conscience of his Cloth modify and pervert the free Divine Intuition within him. I think you are scarce exempt from my general proposition—woe is me that it is so—! though I most sincerely say that it is not a Shovel hat, and keeping bad company with Bishops, has done it, but your innate and old true Reverence for your Father's cloth!—So much divinely good is mixt up with what I think is poor and vulgar error—*mischievous* error, if so much of the evils we complain of in the shape of perversions to Rome, and the Pope's inroad here, be ascribable, (as no one seems to deny) to practices which are directly, and *justly,* founded on the words of a Liturgy you consider as perfect as Human wisdom can make it!—

Even granting that, as you say, "every sentence honestly admits of a safe and sound interpretation," yet if it also be so easy to put an *unsafe and unsound* interpretation upon it, (as has been proved by recent experiments) is not this sufficient reason for altering it?—

If I were a man of influence in any way, I would *leave the Church*

12. Undated MS. letter from Allen, Trinity College Library.

this year if measures were not taken by Queen, Parliament, or Bishops, to alter this Liturgy. As it is, I am nobody; and my secession would do more evil in creating ill-will in the small circle of my neighbours than good to the community to whom my influence and example cannot reach.[13]

Despite his loyalty to the Church, it cannot be said that Fitz-Gerald ever overcame all of his doubts; and his frank confessions of them largely account for his reputation as an irreligious man. Although his opinions were natural for any thinking man, they sounded like rank heresies to contemporaries who could not divorce logic from piety. One of his most intimate women friends,[14] for example, spoke of him in 1850 as a man "of the highest principles, as far as man can be, who doubts if Scripture be altogether the highest guide." Perhaps a reiteration of his skepticism about the miracles, revealed in a letter to Thackeray almost twenty years before, was responsible for his friend's reservations. Perhaps he had repeated what he told Allen in 1835, after reading Plato's dialogues: "I say there is no use in any new books: for if men won't listen to these, the human mind never can produce anything worth listening to. The best Christian must admit this: for Socrates says nearly all that Christ said: so much so that, as I dare say you know, Origen, Irenaeus, and other Platonical Fathers are blamed by some for declaring that the Logos was partially revealed to Plato." [15] Throughout his life he made observations which would have shocked the pious as well as the pietists. When Charles Eliot Norton of Harvard sent his photograph in 1880, FitzGerald replied that he had none to give in exchange; "and," he added, "the Ipswich Artist, who did mine, died, I am told, some months ago: his 'Negatives' all lost, I suppose: himself a Negative—to be reproduced hereafter, they say." [16]

No religion has ever existed which has not, in some points, challenged the credulity of the man of reason, no matter how conformable he may appear to be. Although FitzGerald questioned some articles of Christian dogma, he was no heretic. Orthodox views were just as characteristic of him as unorthodox, and his writings contain many statements which reveal reverence for religion in general and Christianity in particular. Shortly after leaving Cambridge, he commented on the books which Allen had given

13. MS. letter to Allen, January, 1850.
14. Mrs. Cowell. Cowell, George, *Life and Letters of Edward Byles Cowell* (London, Macmillan & Co., 1904), p. 92.
15. MS. letter to Allen, Oct. 31, 1835.
16. MS. letter to Norton, Feb. 22, 1880.

him: "I have not got on with Jeremy Taylor, as I don't like it much. I do not like subdivisions of virtue, making a separate article of each particular virtue or crime: I much more like the general, artless commands of our Saviour. Who can say anything new after him?" [17] While reading Spinoza in 1846, he remarked, "It is fine what he says of Christ—'*nempe*,' that God revealed himself in bits to other prophets, but he *was* the mind of Christ." The following year he wrote to Carlyle,

I also hope you will have some mercy now, and in future, on the "Hebrew rags" which are grown offensive to you; considering that it was these rags that really did bind together those virtues which have transmitted down to us all the good you noticed in Derbyshire. If the old creed was so commendably effective in the Generals and Counsellors of two hundred years ago, I think we may be well content to let it work still among the ploughmen and weavers of to-day; and even suffer some absurdities in the Form, if the Spirit does well upon the whole.[18]

Again, in commenting on Carlyle's *Cromwell,* he said, "I am very tired of these heroics; and I can worship no man who has but a square inch of brains more than myself. I think there is but one Hero: and that is the Maker of Heroes." [19] Finally, in his dialogue *Euphranor,* the character who expresses FitzGerald's views says of Raphael's "Sistine Madonna," "Well, however it may be with young Wordsworth, Raffaelle's child certainly *was* 'drawing Clouds of Glory' from *His* Home, and we may suppose him conscious of it—yes, and of his Mission to dispense that glory to the World."

FitzGerald's independence of thought and honesty of opinion had their repercussions among people who were acquainted with but did not know him; and the citizens of Woodbridge, where he spent the last years of his life, condemned the austere Nonconformist whom they could not understand. Robert Hindes Groome, Archdeacon of Suffolk, wrote at the time of FitzGerald's death,

He lived so retired a life that the outside world not only did not know our dear old friend, but spoke hard things of him, as he had been a .very heathen man. Some years ago—perhaps fourteen—the then Rector of Woodbridge called upon him and spoke, as it is termed, "faithfully" with him, for that he seldom if ever went to church. The sure result was that after that he never did go to church, at least at Woodbridge. So People said things of him which were not true.[20]

17. MS. letter to Allen, Feb. 3, 1830.
18. Letter to Carlyle [Sept. 20, 1847].
19. Letter to Pollock, Sept. 20, 1842.
20. MS. letter from Archdeacon Groome to W. H. Thompson, Master of Trinity, June 29, 1883.

It was doubtless on this occasion that FitzGerald dismissed his visitor with the words, "Sir, you might have conceived that a man has not come to my years of life without thinking much of these things. I believe I may say that I have reflected on them fully as much as yourself. You need not repeat this visit." [21]

The man of whom Woodbridge did not approve nevertheless retained the friendship and regard of many worthy clergymen, among them, besides John Allen and Archdeacon Groome, George Crabbe, vicar of Bredfield; George Crabbe, Jr., rector of Merton, Norfolk; [22] Charles Merivale, dean of Ely; R. C. Trench, Archbishop of Dublin: and others. "Would that many who go to Church regularly," said Crabbe of Merton after FitzGerald's death, "joined with it his own deep feeling for religious reverence and his respect for that feeling in others whenever he thought it sincere." [23]

In a final analysis FitzGerald is best classified, if he must be classified, as an agnostic. Although he could not personally find satisfactory answers to the problems of the soul and man's relations to his Creator, he respected others' solutions of these enigmas. Upon presenting some of his books to Mary Lynn, he said, "I shall not give you a copy of *Omar Khayyám,* you would not like it." "He was always careful," Miss Lynn assured an interviewer, "not to unsettle the religious opinions of others." [24]

In appraising FitzGerald's early religious perplexities, his acute sensitivity should be recognized. Beauty, whether of color, form, or sound, moved him deeply. He entertained himself during long evenings spent alone by playing the piano. In the country he was ever alert to the hue and form of flowers, to the harmony of colors in a landscape, to the song of a bird from a thicket. "The reign of primroses and cowslips is over," he wrote one spring, "and the oak now begins to take up the empire of the year and wears a budding garland about his brows. Over all this settles down the white cloud in the West, and the Morning and Evening draw toward Summer." One of his pleasantest and most vivid memories of Wherstead was the profusion of white violets in the churchyard. At Wherstead, too, he would sit for hours gazing at a solitary flower in a glass of water, watching it unfold, not from any botanical interest but from

21. *Two Suffolk Friends,* p. 76.

22. As there are three George Crabbes, grandfather, father, and son, who will be referred to frequently, I shall speak of them when necessary as Crabbe the poet, Crabbe of Bredfield, and Crabbe of Merton or Young Crabbe.

23. MS. letter to Archdeacon Groome, June 25, 1883.

24. Wright, *FitzGerald,* II, 202.

sheer appreciation of its beauty.[25] His pronounced sensitiveness is revealed in a letter which he wrote to Allen from Cambridge in 1833:

I, being filled with great kindness just now, turn again to you: who are a good subject to vent one's kindness upon. . . . I am filled with this kindness just now by having read Undine [26] at breakfast. I think I must be a very great fool, and it must look like vile affectation to talk of being moved by books, and childish books, in this manner: but I swear it is so (as to me). Nor is there any thing to affect in it, because it shews that one has a mind which lies ready to be swayed either way by good or bad: which is truly the case with me. So it happens that whenever I open Undine, I become very tender and loving: and in such a humour, I do not like to think that perhaps if I were to read a page of Voltaire I should feel inclined to scoff. When I am in these humours I cannot believe that I should so soon change again into their opposites. It is a great vanity to tell other folks of one's feelings, as if one were a great man: but I speak of them because I suppose you feel the same kind of thing. After having read Herbert or Jeremy Taylor, and become suffused with their spirit, do you not wonder that you ever go back to coldness and worldliness? Our good feelings are so entrancing while they last: but that is the reason they last so short a time: but our more paltry propensities are cold and rational, and so stay by us, and become part of our natures. When I came from Leicester the other day on the Coach, I am sure I felt like an Angel: it was a fine morning, the country richly tilled and full of promise, and here and there spires of churches, and little villages, over the face of the country. I felt tears in my eyes often, I could not tell why. Now I was not ashamed of feeling this: but I am ashamed now I tell you of it: it looks like foolish romance but it is not: however it requires an indulgent friend to confide it to.[27]

If FitzGerald had established clearly defined objectives in life, no doubt his spirits would not have fluctuated so erratically. But the wealth of his family made a vocation unnecessary; and until he became accustomed to an aimless life, his unquiet spirit gave him little peace. A preference for living alone nurtured his melancholia during the period of storm and stress. The personalities with whom he came in contact either stimulated or depressed him. The society of most of his family, unfortunately, was depressive. John Allen was an influence for both good and bad. Among FitzGerald's friends, however, were those who made him forget his doubts and, above all, forget himself. Such were Thackeray, Spedding, Donne, and

25. Mrs. Cowell's MS. notes.

26. *Undine*, supernatural romance, written by Baron de la Motte Fouqué, German novelist (1777–1843).

27. MS. letter to Allen, March 14, 1833.

Kemble. The letters which he wrote from Cambridge during the early 'thirties reveal an insouciance about disturbing religious questions. "I shall write you no more sad letters, if indeed they make you sad," he promised Allen in 1833, "but the great reason is that I am less sad myself: it is always so when I get among . . . those unconnected with some of my dark views." [28]

28. *Ibid.,* Feb. 5, 1833.

VI

Thackeray and Tennyson

"I see few people I care about, and so, oh, Willy, be constant to me."

Letter to Thackeray, 1831

"Many, many times, my dear Fitz, have I both thought of you and spoken of you, and quoted your sayings and doings, as those who live with me and know me can testify . . ."

Letter from Tennyson, 1835

AFTER returning from his Paris holiday with FitzGerald in 1830, Thackeray spent only one term at Cambridge and left without taking his degree. He believed that he was "wasting time upon studies, which, without more success than was possible to him, would be of no use in later life." [1] It was at that time that FitzGerald refused to visit Thackeray at his home, Larkbeare, near Ottery St. Mary in Devon, because mixing in polite circles did not harmonize with his "Utopian ideas" about society. From Larkbeare Thackeray sent him numerous letters, profusely illustrated. One sketch is of the house itself. Another shows the writer, seated in an armchair, draining a large goblet; below is written, "Now I have been making myself a glass of punch, and here is your health." A third shows him leaping into bed. "Here I go, gute Nacht, lieber Edward," is the caption. Pictures of pleasant rooms with easy chairs beside sparkling fires with kettles steaming on the hobs convey an atmosphere of luxurious ease and comfort. Perhaps Thackeray was trying to lure FitzGerald to Larkbeare; if so, he failed. [2]

While FitzGerald was wandering about England in 1831, the two engaged in an exchange of voluminous letters. FitzGerald later referred to the period as "that immortal summer of foolscap." [3] He kept each letter on his desk for a week or more, adding

1. Thackeray Biographical Edition, XIII, 693.

2. After Thackeray's death in 1863 FitzGerald made a scrapbook of these drawings, retaining only enough of the script to explain the illustrations. He sent the volume to Thackeray's daughter, Anne Thackeray Ritchie, who used the sketches to illustrate the prefaces of the Biographical Edition of her father's works.

3. MS. letter to Thackeray, July [29], 1835.

to it at odd moments, filling sheet after sheet. No sooner did he post one than he began another. One of these, written from Geldestone, has survived. Almost every square inch of four foolscap pages is filled with a riot of comment on his reading, reflections, and activities; and two poems which he dashed off are added for good measure. *Most* of the letter follows:

I have just come home from a walk of two hours or so, and put my letter to you in the post. It rained so hard in the morning that I could not get my early walk—so I lay in bed; for I think there is no difference, in the matter of wholesomeness, between lying in bed, or sitting up, provided one does not sleep, or have too much blanket. I gave you plenty of advice about health in my last, I think. I shall come to London, with some of my sisters, about the 20th of October—will you be there then? Do, if you can. . . . You are a genuine lover of the theatre. When we are in London we must go to the pit. Now, Thackeray, I lay you ten thousand pounds that you will be thoroughly disappointed when we come together—our letters have been so warm, that we shall expect each minute to contain a sentence like those in our letters. But in letters we are not always together: there are no blue devilish moments: one of us isn't kept waiting for the other: and above all in letters there is Expectation! I am thus foreboding because I have felt it—and put you on your guard very seriously about it, for the disappointment of such hopes has caused a flatness, then a disgust, and then a coldness betwixt many friends, I'll be bound. So think of meeting me not as I am in my letters (for they being written when in a good humour, and read when you have nothing better to do, make all seem alert and agreeable) but as you used to see me in London, Cambridge &c. If you come to think, you will see there is a great difference. Do not think I speak thus in a light-hearted way about the tenacity of our friendship, but with a very serious heart anxious lest we should disappoint each other, and so lessen our love a little—I hate this subject & to the devil with it. 7 at night. I always come up to my room after dinner, at which we are not more than an hour: my sisters go into the drawing room, and I, as I drink no wine, come up here, and generally "spin a yarn" with you. Swift, Bolingbroke, and Pope were three very clever men—Pope I admire more and more for his sense. As to his poetry, I don't know of much. But still it is prose more beautifully and tastefully dressed than any one has ever made it—and he has given even epigrams the appearance of poetry. I am angry with Hume for admiring the French so: and standing up so for polite manners to the ladies—a practice which turns Nature topsy turvy. I have got the character of being rather a brute in society—can't help it; I am worth more, I believe, than any young lady that ever was made, so I am more inclined to tell them to open the door for me, than for me to get up and do it for them. This is a most horrid sentence, on second thoughts—for millions of girls have existed a million times more virtuous than I am; and I am ashamed of having said it. I ought to scratch out the sentence—but why should you not see that I can say a silly thing? (i.e. because I so often say wise ones— N.B. sic cogitat vanitas) I never do write poetry now: and am sure you will make a much better hymn to God Save the Emperor than I could. 'Tis a noble air. I am elevated by my glass of port, & am looking round the table to see what I can be at. There is Byron—Hume—Helvetius— Diderot—Shakespeare. I have not read Shakespeare for a long time. I will tell you why. I found that *his manner* stuck so in my head that I was always trying to think in his way. I mean with his quaint words &c—this I don't wish. I don't think I've read him for a year. I expect a rich treat when I begin the old dear again. Your caricature of Death is a very good one indeed—don't exaggerate the faces, pray, but get them near to Nature—which will make it impressive—but excessive carica- ture will spoil it. I did not know that I had been so foreboding of Death in my last letter: I want to live long, and see everything. I am glad you have taken to Cowper: some of his little poems are affecting far beyond anything in the English language: not heroic, but they make me cry. The Poplar field, is one of the best: & Alexander Selkirk. Good Night— I am going to Hume—his Essays are the most clear I ever read. Thursday morn. "Greece, for her wisdom famed for ages, and always quoted in our schools, could only boast of seven sages—think of the number of her fools!" This is a translation of a French epigram, a very tolerable one, I think. ½ past one. What have I been doing the last hour? Behold these verses, they are the fruits; for they never came into my head before: but the wind was blowing hard at the windows & I somehow began to think of Will Thackeray: so the cockles of my heart were warmed, and up sprouted the following: I have drunk a glass of port, & so sit down to transcribe them.

1.

I cared not for life: for true friend I had none
I had heard 'twas a blessing not under the sun:
Some figures called friends, hollow, proud, or cold-hearted
Came to me like shadows—like shadows departed:
But a day came that turned all my sorrow to glee
When first I saw Willy, and Willy saw me!

2.

The thought of my Willy is always a cheerer;
My wine has new flavour—the fire burns clearer:
The sun ever shines—I am pleased with all things;—
And this crazy old world seems to go with new springs;—
And when we're together, (oh! soon may it be!)
The world may go kissing of comets for me!

3.

The chair that Will sat in, I sit in the best;
The tobacco is sweetest which Willy hath blest;
And I never found out that my wine tasted ill
When a tear would drop in it, for thinking of Will.

4.

And now on my window October blows chilly
I laugh at blue devils, & think of my Willy:
I think that our friendship will not drop away
Like the leaves from the trees, or our locks when they're grey:
I think that old age shall not freeze us, until
He creeps with Death's warrant to me and my Will.

5.

If I get to be fifty—may Willy get too:
And we'll laugh, Will, at all that grim sixty can do;
Old age?—let him do of what poets complain,
We'll thank him for making us children again;
Let him make us grey, gouty, blind, toothless, or silly,
Still old Ned shall be Ned—and old Willy be Willy!

6.

We may both get so old that our senses expire
And leave us to doze half-alive by the fire:
Age may chill the warm heart which I think so divine,
But what warmth it has, Willy, shall ever be thine!
And if our speech goes, we must pass the long hours
When the earth is laid bare with a Winter like ours,
Till Death finds us waiting him patiently still,
Willy looking at me, and I looking at Will!

There are my verses—I have polished them a little more, which has not done them any good. Take them, however, and may they tell no lies—I must go & get a walk—I am half blind with writing out these things. 5 o'clock. I have had a long walk, and have such a composing vein to-day that my head is in a swim of different thoughts. The metre of these verses has made me drunk; there is a rolling in it; or else this intoxication is a proof that I feel what I have said. I could do anything now—would you were here; I am just in the humour for a pipe. I desire you to make some lines to me as your Neddy. Wait your opportunity when a fit come on you. Never mind about the goodness: 7 same day I shall think these bad tomorrow when I am cool. 7 At night. p.p. (i.e. past port) My one glass is down—that descended upon a bed of boiled pork, which I had gorged before. Boiled leg of pork, parmesan cheese, & a glass of port maketh a dinner for a prince. What shall I be at?—I think I could versify enormously. I have more verses in my head about Willy: but you have enough, I think. Ye Gods! I am in a fit state of mind to sit with Willy in the Cigar Divan,* or the Sultan's Divan! I believe I am mad today. What hath made me mad? A great October wind which whistles at my window when I am indoors and blows me along when out of doors—I think I could drive four-in-hand just now. Lord Edward's death [4] I have read—I think it dull very—I think he is a poor creature as to mind—he had the valour of a brute. He gave in to Revolutionary principles without thought, but through Irish impulse. I have a wondrous inclination for to sing—A glass or two more of Port would make me rate myself above 20 Lord Edwards. No Hume, no nothing reasonable have I read for I wish now that all morality was impulse, and all the system of the world too. I keep hurrying on my spirits, not letting them stop—hurra—hurra—the dead can ride—i.e. those who are dead in heart. I don't pretend to have, like Mrs. Norton, a heart like a "withered nut that rattles in its shell" but I see few people I care about, & so, oh Willy, be constant to me. Don't suppose I am drunk—only my one poor glass of port—but like the hares in March, I have my seasons. Perhaps tomorrow I shall be like a fellow after a debauch. In my walk to-day I drew an old house near Beccles which I send. What a glorious tune the British Grenadiers is—nothing goes so near to make me cry as that song. There is great feeling in it. "When e'er they come to quarters in any country town, the lasses cry, 'Huzza, lads, the Grenadiers are come: The Grenadiers are come, my boys, their lovers' hearts to cheer—then hip, hurra, hurra boys, for the British Grenadiers!' " Capital stanza that is, isn't it? & the tune is noble. On Christianity, are you true, and, if you are, must we give up liking the British Grenadiers? Come to London—oh, come, my dearest boy, & we'll yet have a good meeting. My feeling of security is now so great that I believe the great comet will not touch us,[5] but hit the colure: which, in its turn, will fix on the

* Divans: in FitzGerald's time, public smoking rooms furnished with lounges.

4. Thomas Moore, *The Life and Death of Lord Edward Fitzgerald* (1831), 2 vols. Lord Edward Fitzgerald, an Irish patriot, born 1763, died June 4, 1798, from wounds received while resisting arrest.

5. FitzGerald referred to Biela's Comet, which had a period of six and three-quarters years. Its appearance had been predicted for late November, 1832, when it was to pass within 20,000 miles of the earth. Sir John Herschel wrote, when it was expected in 1866, "The orbit of the comet very nearly intersects that of the earth at the place which the earth occupies on or about November 30. If ever the earth is to be swallowed up by a comet, it will be on that day of the year. In the year 1832 we missed it by a month. . . . Had a meeting taken place, from what we know of comets, it is probable that no harm would have happened, and that nobody would have known anything about it."

Biela's Comet no longer exists. Upon its appearance in 1846, it was observed to split into two distinct comets. Because of the position of the sun, these were not visible in 1858; and they failed to appear in 1866. Instead, observers noted a shower of shooting stars. The same phenomenon was observed when the comet was due in 1872, at which time Yale astronomers counted 1,000 shooting stars in a single hour.

comet so as to freeze it to death in 24 hours!!! All we have to hope, in that case, is that the earth won't be the comet's for his freezings are assuredly fire. Good Night—I shall be in London on the 20th or probably before. Come you up then, and we will hunt for lodgings for thee and be merry. Hurra! hurra! God help you, my dear Boy: and may we never part! Here is a flight of crows to the right of the wish—a good omen. Friday. I think I made a fool of myself last night in my letter. There is no affectation however for I was in tip top spirits. To-day I am also very well. Do you know anything of a Court of Love which formerly was in Provence? It is mentioned in Hume's Essays. I should like to know something of it: my head is already at work cooking up some dramatic materials out of it. I am planning a play on it. I wonder where there is any account of it. However, I suppose it was a court where lovers pleaded their causes and their proposals and differences were judged. These are good materials for a play, and quite new. 7 at night. I have been thinking of this plot all day. Saturd. Morning. Did not write much to you yesterday, certainly. Last night I was seized all of a sudden with a tune I had heard Fanny Kemble sing to—the fit remained on me all the evening, and on coming up to bed I made some verses to it. I send you them and the tune, which you may get your Mammy to play for you. It is a pretty tune—the words tol de rol. To-day there is a most extraordinary heat in the atmosphere—quite unseasonable—something seems brewing, and we are all stupid. I will write out the words to the tune.

1.

Farewell to merry summertime—I hear the wintry gale
That bids me fill my pipe again, & tap the foaming ale.
The trees are dying fast without, & cheerless is the scene,
But tobacco leaves are sprouting, boys, and friendship's evergreen.

2.

In summer Friendship wanders out along the sunny plain,
But she swears she never feels so strong as o'er the fire again:
I hear the winds cry piping by:—let's tackle to our cheer,
And drink a merry stirrup-cup to the departing year.

3.

Old year full lusty hath thy youth, and summer manhood been,
Stretched out at ease beneath the sun, or in the forest green.
But now your pipe is cracked with age, & peevish you are grown,
While you chatter in the wood that you have starved to skin and bone!

4.

No matter, friends, kind Nature blows some good with every gale:
And if October kills the year, he brews our nutbrown ale,

Let's fill our glasses up & drink his health with hearty minds
In ale as yellow as his leaves, & stronger than his winds!

There you be—all done, no more fun. You can sing them an you please—They are rather of the Williams order on a re-perusal. Sat. Night. Shall be glad to see you, my boy. This letter shall up to post tomorrow. "Tomorrow to fresh Church & parsons new!" Twill be Sunday. Good Night. Sunday. I shall seal my letter. Shall I have one from you tomorrow? [6]

Thackeray's letters were equally enthusiastic and spirited:

I have been thinking of a walking trip for us two next year. . . . about this time say. We will go like the German Students in France or Germany wh. shall it be? I am really afraid of going to Italy because of the fleas. Really last year the whole pleasure of the Rhine was spoilt to me by these infernal animals. When we go to Italy together, we will I vote each take our own bed—how delightful an old calèche with one horse or two and a country servant! We need not travel faster than we like. It is written & then from Italy we will pass back through France into Spain. Fancy going to Spain the country of the THEED! Black-eyed donñas (mark the ∼) mules, robbers, segars. We will have an antique vehicle with pack in front to hold our books, 2 portmanteaux apiece (one for the bed which is indispensable), three brace of pistols each & a trusty Toledo to repel the attacks of the brigands, likewise a pair of seven-leagued boots to run away if necessary. Fancy a "combat of eight" in a lonely Sierra.

A sketch of the encounter illustrated the letter. The "calèche," drawn by two mules, is halted at the edge of a precipice. In the distant background towered cities perch on mountains, behind which the sun is setting. In the foreground are the combatants and written below is Thackeray's explanation:

The carriage, of a peculiar construction, is in the background; the mules are quietly gazing down the precipice; the faithless postilion (the miserable Pedro) has paid the price of his treachery—he is lying with his face cut in two by Captain FitzGerald who is seen in the act of stamping out the wind of one of the banditti, while he is running another through the chin. Hon the right hoff the picture Mr. Thackeray his to be hobserved; hafter the manner of a true Englishman he has fastened his fists on the vizzens of two of the robbers, and his a squeadging out hof their miserable souls. In the foreground to the left is a rude cross! Christian, pray for the wretch who fell at that spot without having the

6. MS. letter to Thackeray, Oct. 11, 1831.

good fortune, like Messrs. FitzG. & T., to save his life, or most likely the bravery to defend it.[7]

In the autumn of 1831 Thackeray began to study law under a special pleader in the Middle Temple; but when FitzGerald went to London for three weeks, books were neglected for museums, streets, taverns, and theaters. "I don't think my rooms will ever appear comfortable again," Thackeray wrote after his guest had left to visit Cambridge. "Here are your things lying in the exact place you left them. . . . The Kembles have called; John yesterday, Henry to-day . . . and we talk about nothing but you and the theatre." [8] Law proved even less attractive to Thackeray than had mathematics at Cambridge; and, upon inheriting his patrimony in July, 1832, he forsook the Middle Temple for France. "My dear Teddikin, will you come with me to Paris in a month?" he asked, writing from Plymouth. "We will first take a walk in Normandy, and then go for a fortnight or so to Paris. I have a strange idea that I shall be in Italy before the autumn is over, and if my dear old Teddibus would but come with me, we will be happy in a paradise of pictures. What say you, O my Teddibus?" "Teddibus," who was at Seaford, was inclined to say "Yes." He went to Southampton on July 24, expecting to hear further from Thackeray. While he waited, he visited the cathedral at Salisbury, and walked through the fields "alongside a pleasant stream with old-fashioned watermills beside" to George Herbert's church and parsonage at Bemerton. He drew sketches of the village and was disappointed to find no tablet commemorating the poet's residence. "I would gladly put up a plain stone if I could get the Rector's leave," he told Allen.

After spending a week at Southampton, FitzGerald finally heard from Thackeray. The latter wrote from France. He, too, had spent a fortnight in the vicinity of Southampton, and had finally sailed alone. "And thus have we played at bopeep together," said FitzGerald. He was on the point of following Thackeray when a letter arrived from Allen, urging him to come to Pembrokeshire; and he accepted.

Thackeray was not yet twenty-two when he returned to England in December, decidedly impressed by his own importance. He possessed a fortune estimated at £20,000, which he set about losing with the greatest dispatch. He purchased the recently established

7. Shorter, Clement, *William Makepeace Thackeray and Edward FitzGerald,* printed privately. A copy is in the British Museum.
8. Thackeray Biographical Edition, III, xvi.

National Standard and Journal of Literature, Science, Music, Theatricals, and the Fine Arts, a transaction which he later likened to Moses Primose's investment in green spectacles. He became editor and for a year was a very busy young man. He served as the paper's correspondent in Paris, making frequent trips to London where he labored with the editorial board on matters of policy and finance. Despite, perhaps with, Thackeray's help, *The National Standard* was hauled down just a year after he had purchased it; and the young journalist lost a large part of his fortune. The failure of an Indian bank took more of his capital, and he lost a considerable sum to professional gamblers at cards. In a letter written to his mother late in 1833, he revealed a philosophy, surprising for one of his years. He said that he ought to thank Heaven for making him a poor man, as he would be so much happier.

Concerned about his friend's reverses, FitzGerald attempted to find means to relieve his straitened circumstances. Despite his own skill, he commissioned Thackeray to illustrate his copy of *Undine* with sixteen water-color illustrations. The sketches were made in the spring of 1834 as the two sat talking together in the home of Thackeray's stepfather, Carmichael-Smyth, in Albion Street.[9] FitzGerald even considered venturing into publishing to help his friend. "I'll tell you what I have it in my head to do," he wrote to Allen in August,

and that is to publish all the Sir Roger de Coverley papers in the Spectator by themselves in one Volume: so making the life of a Country Gentleman of that time. I should like Thackeray to illustrate it, which he would do beautifully . . . don't you think this is a good plan? For Sir Roger is very fine: and a character worthy of all acceptation among Englishmen. When I go to London I shall see about this. The Volume would not be more than 120 Duodecimo pages: I should like to have it in a very small old Quarto.[10]

The project occupied FitzGerald's attention for several weeks, but the book was never published.

When Thackeray, deciding that he was better qualified for art than for journalism, went to France to study in 1834, FitzGerald

---

9. The volume sold at Sotheby's after FitzGerald's death for £17. On the fly-leaf FitzGerald had written, "The drawings in this volume were made by W. M. Thackeray, as we sat talking together two mornings in the spring of 1835 or 1836 at the house of his step-father, Carmichael-Smyth, in Albion Street, Hyde Park, London." However, FitzGerald refers to the illustrations in a letter to John Allen written on July 1, 1834. That the illustrations were made as a commission is indicated by Anne Thackeray Ritchie in her preface to the *Christmas Books,* Thackeray Biographical Edition, IX, xliii.

10. MS. letter to Allen, Aug. 28, 1834.

enthusiastically encouraged him. From Paris the aspiring artist sent many letters, telling of his work and of his diversions, which were numerous. Included in one letter was a proposal for another holiday in France.

Curzon has told me, âpropos of castles, that there is a château in Normandy, with an excellent garden, a wilderness, and some land, to let for £16 a year. Shall we take it, and be nothing to the world for a year? I have not made my château that paradise which might have been expected from my taste. We would fit it up in the old style, and live in it after the manner of Orestes and Pylades.

The suggestion was not carried out. FitzGerald received some of the earliest sketches of *Flore et Zephyr,* the burlesque drawings of ballet dancers, which Thackeray published in Paris in 1836, and numerous other packets of his friend's work. He responded with letters of praise and encouragement.

What has become of those Eastern plans? [he asked in July, 1835, after Thackeray had intimated that he considered going to Constantinople as correspondent for the *Morning Chronicle*.] For my part, I am glad that you stay at Paris, and work at your Art. . . . So you don't like Raphael! Well, I'm his inveterate admirer . . . "the mind, the mind, Master Shallow" . . . Raphael's are the only pictures that cannot be described: no one can get words to describe their perfection. Next to him, I retreat to the Gothic imagination, and love the mysteries of old chairs, Sir Rogers etc.—in which thou, my dear boy, art and shalt be a Raphael. To depict the true old English gentleman, is as great a work as to depict a Saint John—and I think in my heart I would rather have the former than the latter.[11]

In 1836 Thackeray's stepfather became chairman of a company formed to establish a liberal newspaper, the *Constitutional and Public Ledger*. Thackeray was appointed Paris correspondent at £400 a year and again shifted his interest to journalism. On the prospect of having a steady income, he married at Paris in April. "Do come and see me," he urged FitzGerald. "It would do your heart good to see how happy I am."[12] The career of the *Constitutional and Public Ledger* was even more brief than had been that of Thackeray's own paper. It failed in June, 1837; and its Paris correspondent was forced to return to London. Thereupon he began a new chapter in his life—his struggle for literary recognition. In this, also, FitzGerald was involved.

11. MS. letter to Thackeray, July, 1835.
12. *Letters of Anne Thackeray Ritchie* (London, John Murray, 1924), p. 3. Hester Thackeray Ritchie, ed.

During these same years FitzGerald became intimate with Alfred Tennyson, but it is impossible to determine positively the date of their first meeting. It appears most likely, however, that it took place in London in the autumn of 1833.

Tennyson had entered Trinity in February, 1828; so they had been contemporaries at the University for exactly two years. Had he wished, FitzGerald could have made the poet's acquaintance, for Tennyson associated with Spedding, Kemble, and others of his Apostolic friends. FitzGerald's shyness and his aversion to undergraduate intellectuals were probably responsible for their not meeting. He knew the poet by sight, however. " 'Clerke Sanders,' " he said in 1879, "has been familiar to me these fifty years almost, since Tennyson used to repeat it, and 'Helen of Kirkconnel' at some Cambridge gathering. At this time he looked something like the Hyperion shorn of his Beams in Keats' Poem: with a Pipe in his mouth. Afterwards he got a touch, I used to say, of Haydon's Lazarus." [13]

In the poet, had he but known it, FitzGerald would have discovered a kindred spirit at Cambridge, for Tennyson, also, was extremely independent and unconventional as an undergraduate. Gentlemen, if they smoked at all, smoked moderately in that day. Tennyson's pipe was his constant companion, to the dismay of some of the Apostles. Blakesley once complained that he smoked "the strongest and most stinking tobacco out of a small blackened old pipe on an average nine hours every day." In dress, too, Tennyson appears to have departed from the standards of the polite circles in which most of the Apostles moved. When Sunderland, a brilliant undergraduate of the time, was told that he had been caricatured by Tennyson in a poem, he asked, "Oh, really, and which Tennyson did you say wrote it? The slovenly one?" Heath once pointedly suggested that a clean shirt would be desirable. Tennyson looked at him for a moment, then replied, "H'm, yours would not be as clean as mine if you had worn it a fortnight." [14]

Although FitzGerald had been indifferent to meeting the poet at the University, he was not apathetic to his work. He revealed his first enthusiasm for Tennyson's poetry in 1831. "How good Mariana is!" reads the postscript of a letter written to Allen in May. While at Cambridge in the spring of 1832, FitzGerald read a manuscript copy of "The Lady of Shalott." He wrote to Allen on his return to London, "I forgot to tell you that when I came up on the

13. Letter to Fanny Kemble, Nov. 13, 1879.
14. *Cambridge Apostles*, pp. 310–311.

mail, and fell a-dozing in the morning, the sights of the pages in crimson and the funerals which the lady of Shalott saw and wove, floated before me: really, the poem has taken lodging in my poor head." [15]

References to Tennyson and his poetry in FitzGerald's letters for a time are impersonal but reveal a steadily developing interest in both the man and his work. "The next news is that a new volume of Tennyson is out," [16] he told a friend in the spring of 1833, "containing nothing more than you have in MS. except one or two things not worth having. I will give you a specimen—it is to Christopher North and you will judge if it will do much good." FitzGerald also copied the four opening stanzas of the 1832 version of "A Dream of Fair Women," a passage which Tennyson later deleted. "Have you got this beginning to your MS?" he asked. ". . . This is in his best style: no fretful epithet, nor a word too much." FitzGerald may have made the poet's acquaintance by this time or he may have copied the lines from a manuscript in the possession of one of his friends, for copies of the poems circulated freely among Tennyson's intimates before publication. The following October FitzGerald wrote to Donne.

Tennyson has been in town for some time: he has been making fresh poems, which are finer, they say, than any he has done. But I believe he is chiefly meditating on the purging and subliming of what he has already done: and repents that he has published at all yet. It is fine to see how in each succeeding poem the smaller ornaments and fancies drop away, and leave the grand ideas single.

This letter was written within a month after Tennyson had been plunged into despair by the death of his friend, Arthur Hallam, at Vienna on September 15. Spedding, likewise, was in London. "He and I have been theatricalizing lately," wrote FitzGerald. It is not unlikely that Spedding persuaded the poet to accompany him and FitzGerald to the theater one evening, or that he took FitzGerald to Tennyson's lodgings to divert the latter from gloomy reflections. Conditions, at least, were favorable for their becoming acquainted. Certain it is that the friendship was firmly established at the time of their first recorded meeting in 1835.

In April of that year they were Spedding's guests for three weeks at Mirehouse, his home on Bassenthwaite Lake in Cumberland. They climbed Dod Fell, one of the lesser peaks; but rain kept them

15. MS. letter to Allen, May 31, 1832.
16. *Poems*, published in 1832, dated 1833.

within doors much of the time. They amused themselves by sketching; and FitzGerald produced a rather inexpressive rear view of Tennyson in which his head, covered by a heavy thatch of long hair, tops a pair of massive shoulders which dwarf the chair in which he is sitting.[17] FitzGerald was delighted by the sight of daffodils which grew in profusion in the field before the house, but Tennyson could find no such consolation and tended to become morose in enforced confinement: "His little humours and grumpinesses were so droll" that FitzGerald was "always laughing."

Tennyson attributed his doldrums to the weather and to Spedding's salty banter. Probably the contrast between his lot and that of his friends aggravated the poet's gnawing dissatisfaction with life. Spedding had recently left Cambridge and was casting about for a congenial vocation. His family was well off, and he could take his own good time in choosing his life's work. FitzGerald was even more independent. Tennyson, on the contrary, was a poor man, to whom the future appeared anything but promising. His family attempted to persuade him to enter a profession, but that he doggedly refused to do. He was determined on a literary career, even though it entailed poverty; but the constraints and privations which his life imposed irked him. The splendor of the goal to which he aspired was not dazzling enough to blind him to the sacrifices and obstacles which beset his path.

Tennyson, to be sure, was not unsocial. He entertained his companions by reading poetry by Wordsworth, Keats, and Milton. From a little red book into which he had copied them, he read some of his own poems, "mouthing out his hollow oes and aes," FitzGerald said, "his voice very deep and deep-chested, but rather murmuring than mouthing, like the sound of a far sea or of a pine wood." [18] At Mirehouse FitzGerald heard for the first time the "Morte d'Arthur" and other poems not published until 1842.

With Spedding, Tennyson devoted many evening hours to analyzing and criticizing his verse, while FitzGerald played chess with Mrs. Spedding. Her husband, a wise, quiet man, "always courteous and quite content with any Company his Son might bring to the house as long as they let him go his way," felt some misgivings at "Jem's" interest in poetry. He hoped that his son would "turn his faculties to . . . public topics rather than to poets, of whom he had seen enough in Cumberland not to have much regard for: Shelley, for one, at one time stalking about the mountains, with Pistols,

17. The sketch appears opposite p. 153, Tennyson, *Memoir*, Vol. I.
18. Tennyson, *Memoir*, I, 194.

and other such Vagaries. . . . 'Well, Mr. FitzGerald,' he would
ask, 'and what is it? Mr. Tennyson reads and Jem criticizes:—is
that it?' " [19]

After leaving Mirehouse, FitzGerald and Tennyson spent a week
together at Ambleside. "Resting on our oars one calm day on Windermere," FitzGerald recalled later, ". . . and looking into the
lake quite unruffled and clear, Alfred quoted from the lines he had
lately read us from the MS of 'Morte d'Arthur' about the lonely
lady of the lake and Excalibur—

> Nine years she wrought it, sitting in the deeps
> Upon the hidden bases of the hills

'Not bad that, Fitz, is it?' Tennyson asked.[20] FitzGerald happened
to mention his brother-in-law, saying, "A Mr. Wilkinson, a clergyman." "Why, Fitz," said Tennyson, "that's a verse, and a very bad
one, too." Thereafter they would sometimes amuse themselves by
attempting to compose the weakest line of poetry in the language,
but none surpassed that which originated the game.

Spedding joined them for their last two days at Ambleside and
tried to persuade Tennyson to call upon Wordsworth at Rydal
Mount, but the young poet was too shy to obtrude himself on the
great man. Hartley Coleridge came from his cottage at the foot of
Nab Scar one day and took dinner with the three friends at their
inn. Spedding wrote that Coleridge, "after the fourth bottom of
gin, deliberately thanked Heaven (under me, I believe, or me under Heaven, I forget which) for having brought them acquainted."
FitzGerald recorded that their guest "did not sit three minutes in
his chair without getting up to walk about while he talked." [21]
Among other things Coleridge told them "how Professor Wilson
and some one else (H.C. himself perhaps) stole a Leg of Mutton
from Wordsworth's Larder for the fun of the Thing." [22]

In a letter to Allen, FitzGerald revealed the profound admiration which he felt for Tennyson after their visit to Cumberland.

I will say no more of Tennyson than that the more I have seen of him,
the more cause I have to think him great. . . . I felt what Charles
Lamb describes, a sense of depression at times from the overshadowing
of so much more lofty intellect than my own: this (though it may seem
vain to say so) I never experienced before, though I have often been
with much greater intellects: but I could not be mistaken in the uni-

19. Letter to Miss S. F. Spedding, July, 1881.
20. Tennyson, *Memoir*, I, 152–153.
21. MS. letter to Cowell, Aug. 31 [1880].
22. Letter to Norton [Feb. 7, 1876].

versality of his mind; and perhaps I have received some benefit in the now more distinct consciousness of my dwarfishness.[23]

From London, FitzGerald wrote to the poet on July 2:

. . . After leaving you at Ambleside, I stayed a fortnight at Manchester, and then went to Warwick, where I lived a king for a month. Warwickshire is a noble shire: and the Spring being so late, I had the benefit of it through most of the month of June. I sometimes wished for you, for I think you would have liked it well. . . . I have heard you sometimes say that you are bound by the want of such and such a sum, and I vow to the Lord that I could not have a greater pleasure than transferring it to you on such occasions; I should not dare to say such a thing to a small man: but you are not a small man assuredly: and even if you do not make use of my offer, you will not be offended but put it to the right account. It is very difficult to persuade people in this world that one can part with a banknote without a pang. It is one of the most simple things I have ever done to talk thus to you, I believe: but here is an end; and be charitable to me.[24]

Tennyson, a wretched correspondent, did not reply until Fitz-Gerald wrote a second time.

Many, many times, my dear Fitz, have I both thought of you and spoken of you, and quoted your sayings and doings, as those who live with me and know me can testify, and long ere this had I written to you and exprest my sincere repentance for not having answered on the instant your last kind letter . . . but unfortunately I mislaid your letter, and your direction escaped my memory. I am not such a beast, my dear fellow, as you take me for. Grumpy at receiving a warm-hearted brief from an honest man! I may have been sometimes grumpy in the North, for I was out of health, and the climate Arctic, and Spedding had a trick of quiet banter that sometimes deranged one's equilibrium; but grumpy to *you*—never, as I hope to be saved . . .

I have not forgotten our quiet sojourn at the end of Windermere, nor our rows on the lake, nor the crabs that I caught therein, nor your over-fastidiousness about the fine arts—how can I forget all these or thee
as just a man
As e'er my conversation coped withal—
and the sooner I see thee again the better . . .

But do not let me live for so long a time again without hearing from you . . . If you knew how warm a glow of gratitude pervaded me, when I saw your name at the bottom of the sheet, you would let your accusation of "grumpy" and "grumbler" sleep for ever and a day.[25]

23. Letter to Allen, May 23, 1835.
24. Tennyson, *Memoir*, I, 155.
25. MS. letter, "Somersby," 1835.

In London during the late 'thirties FitzGerald made the acquaintance of Frederick Tennyson,[26] Alfred's eldest brother, Savile Morton, Samuel Laurence, and Frederick Pollock, all of whom became intimate friends. Frederick Tennyson was likewise a poet; but, being sensitive to criticism, he published comparatively little until the last decade of his long life. His reputation among contemporaries was therefore limited. Alfred described his brother's poetry as "organ tunes echoing among the mountains," while FitzGerald spoke of it as "grand gloomy stuff." Frederick was a man of independent means with a passion for travel. Shunning the bleak English climate, he wandered about Italy and in 1851 settled at Florence. From time to time FitzGerald considered joining him but could never force himself to leave his homeland. "Well, say as you will," he asserted in 1840, "there is not, and never was, such a country as Old England—never were there such a Gentry as the English . . . I am sure no travel would carry me to any land so beautiful as the good sense, justice, and liberality of my countrymen make this. And I cling the closer to it, because I feel that we are going down the hill, and shall perhaps live ourselves to talk of all this independence as a thing that has been." [27] To Frederick, FitzGerald wrote some of his best letters: accounts of the activities of their friends, descriptions of his life at Boulge, and criticisms of art, music, and literature. Sometimes he twitted his correspondent on his efforts to determine "whether spirit can exist separately from matter," for Tennyson was intensely interested in spiritualism. Frederick occasionally returned to England, several times visiting FitzGerald in Suffolk; and they would quarrel, as FitzGerald called it, "in the sense of a good strenuous difference of opinion, supported on either side by occasional outbursts of spleen."

Tennyson was frequently accompanied on his Italian travels by Savile Morton, a young Irishman who had been an Apostle at Cambridge. He went to Italy to study art, but found traveling more to his taste. The letters which these two sent FitzGerald were "full of fine accounts of Italy, finer than any I ever read," he maintained.

They came all of a sudden on Cicero's villa—one of them at least, the Formian—with a mosaic pavement leading thro' lemon gardens down to the sea, and a little fountain as old as the Augustan Age bubbling up as fresh, Tennyson says "as when its silver sounds mixed with the deep voice of the orator as he sate there in the stillness of the noon day,

26. FitzGerald rarely used the *k* in writing Frederick Tennyson's name.
27. Letter to F. Tennyson, June 7, 1840.

devoting the siesta-hours to study." When I first read of these things I wish to see them; but, on reflection, I am sure I see them much better in such letters as these.[28]

FitzGerald described Morton as "a wild Irishman" and "an ill-starred man of genius." His family met with financial reverses and Morton returned to London where he lead a Bohemian existence. His moral standards were elastic. He considered every woman fair game for his amours, and, FitzGerald once said, "really felt *hurt* at my undue harshness in remonstrating with him on any such score." [29] In literary judgments the two were more harmonious, for Morton recognized Thackeray's merits when the novelist was still struggling for recognition. He wrote prophetically to FitzGerald in 1841,

His [Thackeray's] Critique on the French Painting is capital. . . . How great a distance between the Comic Almanacks, and the 9th and 10th Chapters of Catherine! He certainly has Genius, and a true and warm Love for what is natural, simple, and something of a hearty hatred of Humbug, and Quackery, besides a swashing stroke of his own when his mettle is up. We shall see our Ami a great man yet.[30]

FitzGerald thought so highly of Morton's letters that he once submitted a selection of extracts to *Blackwood's Magazine,* hoping, thereby, to put ten pounds in his friend's pocket. The article was not accepted, and FitzGerald's only reward was the loss of the manuscript. He admired Morton's conversational powers also. "The rogue bewitches me with his wit and honest speech," he said; and he once assured Frederick Tennyson, "I shall see your good physiognomy one of these days, and smoke one of your cigars and listen to Morton saying fine and wild things, 'startling the dull ear of night' with paradoxes." It was doubtless to Morton that Fitz-Gerald referred when he wrote from London in 1839, "A man has just come from Italy, and he stood on one of the Alps and saw at once the moon rising over the Adriatic while the sun sank into the Mediterranean. That was a neat sight." [31]

FitzGerald probably met Samuel Laurence through Spedding, who described him in 1842 as

a portrait painter of real genius, of whom during the last year I have seen a great deal and boldly pronounce him to be worthy of all good

28. Letter to Allen, Aug. 29, 1842.
29. MS. letter to Norton, May 19, 1877.
30. FitzGerald's transcript of Morton's letters in Trinity College Library.
31. Letter to Barton [Nov. 25, 1839].

men's love. He is one of the men of whom you feel certain that they will never tire you, and never do anything which you will wish they had not done. His advantages of education have been such as it has pleased God (who was never particular about giving his favourite children a good education) to send him. But he has sent him what really does as well or better—the clearest eye and the truest heart; and it may be said of him as of Sir Peter that

> Nature had but little clay
> Like that of which she moulded him.[32]

FitzGerald engaged the artist to make portraits of Alfred Tennyson, Thackeray, Allen, and Spedding. His portrait of Tennyson as a young man, now in the National Portrait Gallery, was painted for FitzGerald in the late 'thirties. The poet described the picture as "blubber-lipt"; but it was "the only one of the old days," FitzGerald said in 1871, "and still the best of all to my thinking." Carlyle, Donne, Thompson, Pollock, Anthony Trollope, James A. Froude, and many other Victorians sat for Laurence.

FitzGerald, keenly interested in promoting the artist's welfare, obtained many commissions for him and often sent advice and criticism. In one of his published letters, written when Laurence was about to go to the Lake Country, appears the warning, "If you paint—put him not only in a good light, but to leeward of you in a strong current of air." In a copy of an early edition of the correspondence a marginal note opposite the blank reads, "Hartley Coleridge." FitzGerald's advice, however, was usually more technical. After Laurence completed a portrait of the Reverend J. B. Wilkinson, he wrote,

It is very capital, and gives my sister and all her neighbours great satisfaction. I will say this, however, with my usual ignorance and presumption, that I think the last day's sitting made it a little heavier than when I left it unfinished. Was it that the final glazing was somewhat too thick? I only mention this as a very slight defect which I should not have observed had I not seen its penultimate state, and were I not a crotchety stickler for lightness and ease. But I hope and trust you will now do all your future sketches in oil in the same way in which this is done: the long brush, the wholesome distance between canvas, painter, and sitter, and the few sittings. For myself, I have always been sure of this: but I can assert it to you with more confidence now, seeing that every one else seems to agree with me, if I may judge by the general approval of this specimen of the long brush. Besides, such a method must shorten your labour, preserve the freshness of your eye and spirit,

32. Letter from Spedding to Thompson, quoted in FitzGerald's *Letters*, I, 89, n.

and also ensure the similitude of the sitter to himself by the very speediness of the operation. . . . Mind what I have told you, I may not be a good judge of painting, but I can judge of what people in general like.[33]

However Laurence, according to FitzGerald, was "the most obstinate little man—'incorrigible,' Richmond [34] called him; and so he wearies out those who wish most to serve and employ him; and so has spoiled his own Fortune." It was probably through Laurence that FitzGerald became acquainted with a number of artists whom he occasionally entertained in his London lodgings. He never identified his guests by name; but he appears to have known, although they were not among his intimate friends, Daniel Maclise, Charles Landseer, and Frank Stone.

Frederick Pollock, who later became Sir Frederick and Queen's Remembrancer, a legal post now abolished, entered Trinity in 1832 and proceeded to London in 1836 to study law. He was an anomaly among FitzGerald's friends, for he seems to have been the only one impressed either by his own or by others' importance. He was a man of culture, however, and published a blank verse translation of Dante, and the *Reminiscences and Diaries of Macready,* the actor. Pollock, Spedding, and FitzGerald were guests of Douglas Heath at his home, Kitlands, near Leith Hill, Surrey, on the day of Queen Victoria's coronation in 1837 and celebrated the event with an enthusiastic but wholly original display of patriotism.

"We went down the evening before," Pollock related,

and in the early afternoon of the 28th June, a beautiful warm day, we four assembled on the edges of a long open bath, which lay in the garden surrounded by thick bushes—a most tempting spot for the purpose. As the hour of the placing of the crown on the Queen's head in Westminster Abbey approached, we made ready for the plunge, and when the sound of the distant salutes of cannon reached us, we all took headers into the water, and swam about singing "God Save the Queen." [35]

33. Letter to Laurence, July 4, 1844.
34. George Richmond, Victorian portrait painter.
35. Pollock, *Remembrances,* I, 114.

VII

Boulge Cottage

"His tranquillity is like a pirated copy of the peace of God."
Spedding on FitzGerald, 1835

FITZGERALD spent a few days in London on his return from Warwickshire. Early in June he went to Wherstead, where most of his family had gathered, expecting to spend the summer there. His father, however, suddenly decided to occupy Boulge Hall, his estate about a mile from Bredfield and three from Woodbridge.[1] FitzGerald was reluctant to leave the Lodge, "this really beautiful place," he told Thackeray, because the new house had "no great merit." Nevertheless, he spent the remainder of the year at the Hall in company with two of his sisters who would otherwise have been alone.

A number of times since leaving Cambridge, he had thought of settling in Suffolk. Once he considered advertising "for room in some family, where there was cheerful society." At another time he proposed renting and furnishing a cottage, and even progressed so far in his designs as to search London for an ancient drinking cup "which I may use when I am in my house, in quality of a housekeeper." However, neither of these plans materialized. At Boulge his search ended. Just outside the park gates stood an attractive, rambling, one-story thatched cottage, built by a former mistress of the Hall. This woman, called by the natives "the Queen of Hell," found it impossible always to live harmoniously with her husband; and the dwelling had been her refuge when the two were estranged. FitzGerald took possession in the spring of 1837 and furnished two rooms at the front, one as a study, the other as a bedroom. The remainder of the house was given over to his housekeeper. The walls, FitzGerald said, were "as thin as sixpence," the windows wouldn't shut, and the thatch was "perforated by lascivious sparrows." For a few years he occupied the cottage only from spring until autumn, moving into the Hall for the winter.

---

1. Boulge Hall stands in a park about a mile west of the crossroads called Bredfield Pump and an equal distance south of Bredfield Village. The parish is called Boulge, but there is no village by that name.

In 1843 he added eave troughs and installed a new grate in his study, "a Register . . . a capital thing. When Peel said, 'Register —Register—Register!' I now see what he meant." He never did eliminate the draughts; but after making these repairs, he occupied the cottage the year round. His books on the study shelves did his heart good, he told Allen. A spinet stood in the room, Stothard's picture of the Canterbury Pilgrims hung over the mantelpiece, and a bust of Shakespeare surveyed the apartment from a recess. In the pantry he kept a barrel of beer which he tapped himself. "I really do like," he confessed, "to sit in this doleful place with a good fire, a cat and dog on the rug and an old woman in the kitchen. This is all my live stock." His dog, Bletsoe, a black retriever, was later replaced by a Skye terrier named Ginger; the cat has reached posterity nameless; the old woman was "red-armed" Mrs. Faiers, whose husband was a laborer on the estate. Later Beauty Bob, a parrot, was added to the ménage.

FitzGerald was not a fastidious bachelor, and the care with which he first arranged his possessions was short lived. "The chaos of the room is vividly in my mind," stated a woman who, as a young girl, had called at the cottage with her parents. "Large pictures standing against the walls. Portrait on an easel, books, boots, sticks, music scattered about on tables, chairs, and floor. An open piano with music, lumber everywhere, so that there was a difficulty in emptying a chair for my mother to sit on. He himself had let us in, in dressing-gown and slippers." [2]

For a Victorian gentleman to admit his guests himself was extraordinary enough; to receive them in dressing gown and slippers was shocking. How much the damsel's agitation colored her memory cannot be estimated. But although her description of the apartment may have been exaggerated, it was probably not unwarranted. The room was primarily for FitzGerald's convenience. Yet somewhere amid the confusion very likely could be found the touch of the artist. Perhaps in a bit of brilliant color. Perhaps in a flower. "On my table is a long-necked bottle with three flowers just now in it," he once told Laurence, ". . . a tuft of rhododendron, a tuft of scarlet geranium, and a tuft of white gilliflower. Do you see these in your mind's eye?"

The cottage was sheltered by Scotch firs and oaks. Casement windows looked out upon a garden in which he planted "anemone roots which in Spring shall blow Tyrian dyes, and Irises of a newer and more brilliant prism than Noah saw in the clouds." One June

2. Glyde, *FitzGerald*, p. 51.

he described his beds, "now gorgeous with large red poppies, and lilac irises—satisfactory colouring: and the trees murmur a continuous soft chorus to the solo which my soul discourses within."

At Boulge FitzGerald spent sixteen leisurely years. Sometimes, but not often, he tired of the monotony. "Day follows day with unvaried movement," he declared, "there is the same level meadow with geese upon it always lying before my eyes: the same pollard oaks: with now and then the butcher or the washerwoman trundling by in their carts." He rose early and spent his mornings reading and writing: walked with his dog in the afternoon; sometimes sketched; and passed his evenings smoking, and playing "some of Handel's great choruses" which, he said, "are the bravest music after all." This routine was frequently broken by the neighboring parsons and other friends who called to spend an evening, visits which FitzGerald sometimes repaid. "Here I sit, read, smoke, and become very wise, and am already quite beyond earthly things," he told Frederick Tennyson.

I must say to you, as Basil Montagu once said, in perfect charity, to his friends, "You see, my dear fellows, I like you very much, but I continue to advance, and you remain where you are (you see), and so I shall be obliged to leave you behind me. It is no fault of mine." You must begin to read Seneca, whose letters I have been reading: else, when you come back to England, you will be no companion to a man who despises wealth, death, etc.[3]

Leisure and philosophic serenity no doubt contributed to FitzGerald's gaining weight while living at Boulge. "I weigh 14 stone —fact," he announced in 1842. His diet, simple as it was, was hardly calculated to produce a slim figure. "We have had . . . new peas and young potatoes—fresh milk (how good!)," he once wrote. Bread and milk formed a staple meal. Although in 1846, he spoke of his "obese, ill-jointed carcase," he probably carried his weight well, for he was six feet tall and contemporary descriptions do not mention that he was corpulent. He aged in appearance while still comparatively young. In 1840, when only thirty-one, he reported that he was growing bald and four years later that he was becoming gray. George Crabbe, Jr., recorded his youthful impressions of FitzGerald at Boulge. "He seemed to me when I first saw him," he said, "much as he was when he died, only not stooping: always like a grave middle-aged man." At this stage of his life he began to reveal an indifference to niceties of dress observed by

3. Letter to F. Tennyson, Feb. 24, 1844.

typical Victorian gentlemen. His clothes were always of good quality and were made by reputable tailors; but comfort dictated his
choice of costume, and he never hesitated to wear a garment because it was old. "Edward FitzGerald . . . staid a day with me in
the autumn," Donne wrote. "He is more of a philosopher than ever,
and his proficiency appears in wearing a most venerable coat and
clouted shoon."

FitzGerald was not so idle at Boulge as he pretended to be. His
reading was that of a scholar; he wrote, even though he did not
publish; and, after settling in the cottage, he began to take a more
active part in the supervision of his father's estates. "Since I saw
you, I have entered into a decidedly agricultural course of conduct," he informed Thompson in February, 1841, "read books
about composts, etc. I walk about in the fields also where people
are at work, and the more dirt accumulates on my shoes, the more
I think I know. Is not this all funny?" [4] He complained to Pollock
of "these demnition snows and frosts; in fact, we can only thresh
in the barn, and hedge and ditch a little—all which, you know,
when you have set your men to work, requires but little supervision." But even when most deeply engrossed in agricultural pursuits, FitzGerald, like Burns, remained an artist at heart. To
Thompson he sent a passage from a book on the care of soils to
illustrate its "not unpleasing" style. The loaded wagons rolling to
the barns were an exhilarating sight. During leisure hours he took
long walks and made "such sketches," he told Laurence, "as will
make you throw down your brush in despair." He found time for
other diversions as well. "Can you shoot with a pistol, Pollock?"
he asked.

Can you hit an oak tree (they grow large in this part of the country) at
the distance of about ten yards? I tell you how it is with me: I generally
miss; and when I hit, the bullet returns with great violence back upon
me. So if you read of an inquest sitting upon me one of these days,
don't wonder: I think they'll find it hard to bring in a verdict, whether
Felo-de-se or Accidental Death. For I go on with my eyes open: though
to be sure I am taking the quickest course to put them both out. A worse
shot never existed.

Altruism marked FitzGerald's relations with the laborers on
the estates and his attitude toward the lower classes generally. His
whole family, in fact, accepted the paternal responsibilities of the
English gentry, which made rural society in Victorian England
function as well as it did despite many defects. "This parish is a

4. Letter to Thompson [Feb. 18, 1841].

very small one," FitzGerald wrote shortly after moving to Boulge, "it scarce contains fifty people: but that next to it, Bredfield, has more than four hundred: and some very poor indeed. We hope to be of some use."

Edward's views on the relations of the classes would have shocked the average Victorian. When the Speenhamland System of relief was replaced by the Poor Laws of 1834, which established workhouses for the unemployed, he wrote to Allen,

. . . the new Poor Laws have begun to be set afoot, and we don't know who is to stop in his cottage, or who is to go to the Workhouse. How much depends upon the issue of this measure! I am no politician: but I fear that no political measure will ever adjust matters well between rich and poor. I have always thought that the poor have been neglected: and, if the rich will not relieve necessity from their superfluity, believe that the poor have a right to demand it. I would not say this to a poor man: but say so to you, not in the radical spirit of the day, but according to the best of my reason and natural feelings.[5]

The hardships of the laboring classes never failed to quicken his sympathies.

"If we could but feed our poor!" he exclaimed in 1844,

It is now the 8th of December; it has blown a most desperate East wind, all razors; a wind like one of those knives one sees at shops in London, with 365 blades all drawn and pointed. . . . What are all the poor folks to do during the winter? And they persist in having the same enormous families they used to do; a woman came to me two days ago who had seventeen children! What farmers are to employ all these? What Landlord can find room for them? The law of Generation must be repealed. The London press does nothing but rail at us poor country folks for our cruelty. I am glad they do so; for there is much to be set right. But I want to know if the Editor of the Times is more attentive to his devils, their wives and families, than our squires and squiresses and parsons are to their fellow parishioners. Punch also assumes a tone of virtuous satire, from the mouth of Douglas Jerrold! It is easy to sit in arm chairs at a club in Pall Mall and rail on the stupidity and brutality of those in High Suffolk.[6]

It is very likely that the woman with seventeen children went to FitzGerald for help, for he was always ready to aid the needy poor. As a young man at Wherstead, he gave small weekly allowances to some of the poverty-stricken cottagers, a practice which he maintained and extended until his death. His contributions were al-

5. MS. letter to Allen, Oct. 31, 1835.
6. Letter to F. Tennyson, Dec. 8, 1844.

ways given unobtrusively; but the number of persons whom he helped was large, and the total sum of money which he gave to charities amounted to a small fortune. He was scornful of that portion of the gentry which refused to accept responsibilities toward the poor. In *Polonius,* his book of aphorisms, appears a paragraph which expresses his views and is undoubtedly original with him. After quoting Samuel Johnson's remark, "A decent provision for the poor is the true test of civilization," he states:

How often one hears an English gentleman (as good as any gentleman, however) mourning over the loss, as he calls it, of a hundred or two a year in farming his estate—so fine a business for an English gentleman! "It won't do—it won't pay—he must give it up," etc. Why, what do his fine houses, equipages, gardens, pictures, jewels, dinners, and operas *pay?* "Oh, but there he has something to show for his money." And is a population of honest, healthy, happy English labourers—honest, healthy, happy, because constantly employed by him, with proper wages, and not so much labour exacted of them as to turn a man into a brute —is not *this* something to show for your money? As good pictures, jewels, equipages, and music, as a man should desire?

Not, however, to be bought wholly by money wages.

He quotes, also, four lines from Goldsmith's *Deserted Village:*

> Princes and lords may flourish or may fade,
> A breath may make them, as a breath has made;
> But a bold Peasantry, their country's pride,
> When once destroy'd can never be supplied.[7]

A legend that FitzGerald became a recluse at Boulge has become established. Never was there a more sociable or mobile hermit. Throughout the years at the cottage his friends were always welcome; and Donne, Spedding, Allen, Frederick Tennyson, and many others were his guests.[8] He continued his peregrinations about England, haunting, Donne said, "the same places at similar seasons of the year with the regularity of a plant or a ghost." Boulge was his winter retreat and a refuge whenever he tired of nomadic life. During the 'forties, it is true, he developed an aversion to London with its "modern wits" and "d——d smutty atmosphere"

7. *Polonius,* "The Poor" and "Love Is the True Price of Love."
8. There is nothing to substantiate the statement made by Thomas Wright in his life of FitzGerald (I, 151) that Alfred Tennyson visited FitzGerald at Boulge in 1837. Wright, in fact, quotes FitzGerald as describing the poet as "very droll and wayward" on that occasion. These words are a paraphrase of a passage in a letter which FitzGerald sent to Bernard Barton from London in April, 1838, describing a meeting with Tennyson in town. The passage may be found in *Letters,* I, 53.

which "clings to you like a wet blanket." Nevertheless, the presence of friends was sufficient attraction to lure him to town. "I am just returned from London where I have been staying a month," reads a typical passage from his letters. "A joyful month it was, for I found all my friends there, unexpectedly, so that we had all kinds of delights, and smokings and sittings up." Few years of his life passed in which he failed to make at least one journey to the city to attend the theater, concerts, and the exhibition of the Royal Academy, for "a sup of music and painting," as he said. "Last night I appeared at the Opera," he wrote in 1845, "and shall do so twice a week till further notice." His enthusiasm for the theater was still vital.

"Last night," he told Frederick Tennyson,

I went to see Acis and Galatea brought out, with Handel's music, and Stanfield's scenery: really the best done thing I have seen for many a year. As I sat alone (alone in spirit) in the pit, I wished for you. . . . I tell you, you can't understand Macready without coming to London and seeing his revival of Acis and Galatea. You enter Drury Lane at a quarter to seven: the pit is already nearly full: but you find a seat, and a very pleasant one. Box doors open and shut: ladies take off their shawls and seat themselves: gentlemen twist their side curls: the musicians come up from under the stage one by one: 'tis just upon seven: Macready is very punctual: Mr. T. Cooke is in his place with his marshal's baton in hand: he lifts it up: and off they set with old Handel's noble overture. As it is playing, the red velvet curtain (which Macready has substituted, not wisely, for the old green one) draws apart: and you see a rich drop scene, all festooned and arabesqued with River Gods, Nymphs, and their emblems; and in the centre a delightful, large, good copy of Poussin's great landscape (of which I used to have a print in my rooms) where the Cyclops is seen seated on a mountain, looking over the sea-shore. The overture ends, the drop scene rises, and there is the sea-shore, a long curling bay: the sea heaving under the moon, and breaking upon the beach, and rolling the surf down—the stage! This is really capitally done. . . . The choruses were well sung, well acted, well dressed, and well grouped; and the whole thing creditable and pleasant.[9]

FitzGerald's customary rural haunts, other than Suffolk, were Bedford, where a young friend, William Kenworthy Browne, lived; Mattishall, Donne's home; and the home of the Kerriches at Geldestone. Occasionally he visited members of his father's family in Ireland.

He had made Browne's acquaintance on the steam packet to

9. Letter to F. Tennyson, Feb. 6, 1842.

Tenby when he visited Allen in 1833, and the two had lodged at the same inn. Browne, "quick to love and quick to fight—full of confidence, generosity, and the glorious spirit of Youth," although eight years FitzGerald's junior, captured his admiration and became one of his closest friends. FitzGerald paid frequent and prolonged visits to Goldington Hall and, later, Goldington Bury, Browne's homes at Bedford; and for many years the two annually visited London together. His young friend, FitzGerald thought, developed into the ideal citizen—the cultured man of action. Intellectuals, he pointed out, quoting Cardinal Newman, fell into the error of thinking and speaking aright, without *doing* what is right. Browne, on the contrary, fulfilled his duties as squire, became a captain in the militia, and was an ardent hunter and angler. He did not neglect books, and his interest in literature and art was greatly influenced by his older friend. Comparing him with Spedding, FitzGerald said that the one was representative of the "Vita Activa," the other of the "Vita Contemplativa." He might have drawn the same comparison between himself and Browne; it was this difference which attracted him. He strove valiantly to qualify as a suitable companion for his athletic friend. He kept a horse at Bedford and even accompanied Browne when he fished. The older man had little enthusiasm for angling, however; and on these expeditions usually carried, instead of rod and creel, a color-box and "poked about," making "horrible sketches." In the valley of the Ouse FitzGerald spent many idyllic holidays.

"Here I am again in the land of old Bunyan," he wrote from there in July, 1839,

better still in the land of the perennial Ouse, making many a fantastic winding and going much out of his direct way to fertilize and adorn. Fuller supposes that he lingers thus in the pleasant fields of Bedford, being in no hurry to enter the more barren fens of Lincolnshire. So he says. This house is just on the edge of town: a garden on one side skirted by the public road, which again is skirted by a row of such Poplars as only the Ouse knows how to rear—and pleasantly they rustle now —and the room in which I write is cool and opens into a greenhouse which opens into said garden: and it's all deuced pleasant. For in half an hour I shall seek my Piscator, and we shall go to a Village two miles off and fish, and have tea in a pot-house, and so walk home. For all which idle ease I think I must be damned.[10]

The village to which FitzGerald referred was probably Bletsoe, from which he wrote:

10. Letter to Barton, July 24, 1839.

The Inn is the cleanest, the sweetest, the civillest, the quietest, the live-liest, and the cheapest, that ever was built or conducted. Its name, the Falcon of Bletsoe. On one side it has a garden, then the meadows through which winds the Ouse: on the other, the public road, with its coaches hurrying on to London, its market people halting to drink, its farmers, horsemen, and foot travellers. So, as one's humour is, one can have whichever phase of life one pleases: quietude or bustle; solitude or the busy hum of men: one can sit in the principal room with a tankard and a pipe and see both these phases at once through the windows that open upon either. But through all these delightful places they talk of leading railroads: a sad thing, I am sure: quite impolitic. But Mam-mon is blind.[11]

FitzGerald found his Land of the Lotus in England itself, and his letters of this period contain many passages pervaded by the essence of sunny spring days or drowsy summer afternoons. His faith in the idyllic, however, was sometimes betrayed. "I have been suffering for these last four days," he informed a friend in 1843, "with an attack, which I partly attribute to my having walked to Thornby under a burning sun, then eaten unripe peaches, and then gone to sleep upon long wet grass! A pretty mixture—I have paid for it: and am even now in a state of water gruel, shiverings, headaches like a thundercloud over the eyes, etc." [12] Nor was his conscience entirely stifled. "I have been all my life apprentice to this heavy business of idleness," he stated, "and am not yet master of my craft; the Gods are too just to suffer that." Sometimes distrust of his aimless life became more poignant. "I am now returned to my dull home here after my usual pottering about in the midland counties of England," he once wrote to Frederick Tennyson, whose letters from Italy often left him with a keen sense of stagnation.

A little Bedfordshire—a little Northamptonshire—a little more fold-ing of the hands—the same faces—the same fields—the same thoughts occurring at the same turns of the road—this is all I have to tell of; nothing at all added—but summer gone. My garden is covered with yellow and brown leaves; and a man is digging up the garden beds before my window, and will plant some roots and bulbs for next year. My parsons come and smoke with me, etc. "The round of life from hour to hour"—alluding doubtless to a mill horse.[13]

Nevertheless, he was not convinced that his *dolce far niente,* as Carlyle called it, was necessarily a vice. "I begin to have dreadful suspicions," he confessed,

11. *Ibid.,* Aug. 31, 1840.
12. *Ibid.,* Sept. [12, 1843].
13. Letter to F. Tennyson, Oct. 10, 1844.

that this fruitless way of life is not looked upon with satisfaction by the open eyes above. One really ought to dip for a little misery: perhaps however all this ease is only intended to turn sour by and by, and so to poison one by the very nature of self-indulgence. Perhaps again as idleness is so very great a trial of virtue, the idle man who keeps himself tolerably chaste, etc., may deserve the highest reward; the more idle, the more deserving. Really I don't jest: but I don't propound these things as certain.[14]

In Donne, gentle, cultured, humorous, FitzGerald possessed an ideal companion for the "Vita Contemplativa." In 1828, after spending seven terms at Cambridge, Donne left without taking a degree, because of conscientious objections to signing the Thirty-nine Articles, an act required of every student proceeding to a degree. He returned to Mattishall, married in 1830, and settled down to the life of a country gentleman. Later, overcoming his scruples, he prepared to return to Cambridge in 1837; but his wife became ill, and he was forced to abandon the project. Meanwhile he had become a capable classical scholar and supplemented his income by writing on ancient history and antiquities. He possessed a talent for *vers de société,* the exercise of which he confined, for the most part, to his correspondence. His letters and conversation were delightful. One of his daughters, upon being asked why she always took off her gloves in church, replied, "I don't know—I can't pray in gloves." "It's lucky," observed her father, "that you can pray in stockings." When *Household Verses* by the Quaker poet, Bernard Barton, appeared, Donne wrote to the author, "Meanwhile I congratulate you on having published at all, which is always a relief. As Sheridan said when Mrs. Macaulay published her 'Loose Thoughts' that 'the sooner a Lady gets rid of such thoughts the better.' " [15]

With Donne, FitzGerald engaged in the good-natured banter and light-hearted nonsense that he so fully enjoyed. "We have suspended a portrait in our dining room that excites FitzGerald's indignation," Donne once related:

It is a respectable middle-aged man, not quite, but nearly large enough for a Town Hall . . . FitzGerald proposes his being altered into Moses, and given to some church in want of a legislator, especially, if at a London picture-broker's, we could pick up an old Aaron. I am of [the] opinion that by successive additions, judiciously made, he might represent, one after another, all the heroes in Plutarch.[16]

14. Letter to Barton, July 24, 1839.
15. *Donne and His Friends,* p. 96.
16. *Ibid.,* p. 61.

Donne's comments on family portraits were usually entertaining. When a dealer offered him a seventeenth-century painting of a lady and child, asserting that they had borne his name, Donne commented to Barton,

. . . abstractedly I have no reverence for what frequently constitutes family pictures, and though I might be tempted by a well-favoured progenitress, I will not have a stiff, awful, bilious, unpropitious looking dame with a dropsical boy in her arms. Nay, I have practised what I profess, and burned or buried some years ago, sundry of my forefathers and foremothers for their ugliness. I would much rather as a matter of taste have a gallery of my posterity than of my predecessors. There is some chance the former will never wear wigs or hair-powder, or buttons as big as muffins, or posys in their breasts, or flaps to their pockets or red heels to their shoes, and therefore an equal chance that they will look as they were created—with a slight addition of drapery.[17]

He once complained that FitzGerald had sent him "a screed of paper with six lines, and not sealed, and instead of the lines containing letters and words, as you might have concluded, there was something that looked like an exercise in punctuation, e.g., 'j:,:?:.-x.;' ". At another time Donne asked Barton, "Can you not put a little ratsbane in E. F. G.'s toasted cheese—not enough to make it fatal, but merely purgative? He has used me vilely. First he takes me to task for using long words, such as he says he does not understand: and then when I protest against being accused of affectation, he defends himself by saying that I am not so much affected as stupid."

FitzGerald was always welcome at Mattishall and frequently spent a few days there on his trips into Norfolk to visit the Kerriches. "He is a most agreeable person," Mrs. Donne said of him, "laughter-loving and ever suited to make holiday. The children think so too and spare him not." [18] He was fond of the children, calling them the "Goths and Vandals."

It was to the Kerrich home that FitzGerald went most often and stayed longest during his wanderings. "My brother-in-law and my sister," he told Allen, "are so kind to me that I am almost spoiled." He felt a deeper love for Mrs. Kerrich than for any other member of his family.

Geldestone was another of those idyllic spots in which FitzGerald spent so much of his life. The Hall, about two miles northwest of Beccles, overlooks the valley of the meandering Waveney River.

17. *Ibid.*, p. 50.
18. *Ibid.*, p. 28.

There, FitzGerald's room, with windows facing marsh and river and the distant tower of Beccles church, was always kept in readiness for his return. His visits were often unannounced. He would slip into the music room through French windows, and the first warning of his arrival would be the notes of some favorite selection which he would strike up on the piano.[19]

During a heat wave in August, 1834, he learned to swim in the Waveney at Geldestone. Usually, his occupations were less strenuous.

"Here I live with tolerable content," he informed Allen,

perhaps with as much as most people arrive at; and what, if one were properly grateful, one would perhaps call perfect happiness. Here is a glorious sunshiny day; all the morning I read about Nero in Tacitus, lying at full length on a bench in the garden: a nightingale singing, and some red anemones eyeing the sun manfully not far off. A funny mixture all this: Nero and the delicacy of Spring: all very human however. Then at half-past one lunch on Cambridge cream cheese: then a ride over hill and dale: then spudding up some weeds from the grass: and then coming in, I sit down to write to you, my sister winding red worsted from the back of a chair, and the most delightful little girl in the world chattering incessantly. So runs the world away. You think I live in Epicurean ease: but this happens to be a jolly day: one isn't always well, or tolerably good, the weather is not always clear, nor nightingales singing, nor Tacitus full of pleasant atrocity. But such as life is, I believe I have got hold of a good end of it.[20]

Evenings were spent in the same leisurely way. After late tea he read in the library or wrote letters, not always without distractions. "My brother-in-law is fallen asleep over Buckland's Bridgewater Treatise," he once complained, "his breathing approaches a snore. Now could I drink hot blood." After the Kerriches retired, Fitz-Gerald usually withdrew to the kitchen to enjoy his pipe, because, as in most Victorian homes, smoking was forbidden in the family apartments. He was at least spared the inconvenience of retiring to the stables to smoke, as many gentlemen in that day were compelled to do.

There were ten children, eight of them girls, in the Kerrich family, and it was largely their attraction which drew FitzGerald to Geldestone year after year. "The children here are most delightful: the best company in the world, to my mind," he said. "If you could see the little girl dance the Polka with her sisters! Not set up like

19. For these and other facts about FitzGerald's life at Geldestone I am indebted to his grandniece, Miss Eleanor FitzGerald Kerrich of Beccles.
20. Letter to Allen [April 28, 1839].

an Infant Terpsichore, but seriously inclined, with perfect steps in perfect time." His young companions were as fond of him as he was of them—and with good reason. "And now I must go out," he wrote during one visit, "for a covey of children with bonnets on are waiting for Uncle Edward to take them to a great gravel-pit in the middle of a fir-wood, where they may romp and slide down at pleasure. This is Saturday, and they may dirty stockings and frocks as much as they please." He also took them to Beccles to buy "bulls-eyes (dost thou remember them?) and other sweetmeats," a journey which was as impressive to them, they were so simply reared, he said, as an excursion to London would be to others. He liked to spend Christmas with the Kerriches and once observed that the children ate "as much as they could, and more than was good for them, and looked paler all next day in consequence." In 1848 he wrote from Geldestone, "Here I am like the Father of a delightful family, without the responsibilities attached. These girls are now all grown up, or growing up; *ladies* in the only true sense of the word: finding their luxury in going among the poor: and doing what good they can." He retained his affection for them until his death and was particularly solicitous of the welfare and happiness of his nieces.

Of all of his relatives in Ireland FitzGerald most frequently visited his uncle, Peter Purcell, at Halverstown, Kilcullen, County Kildare, and his own brother, Peter, who during the early 'forties lived at Ballysax. Mr. Purcell, with a partner, a Scotsman, controlled almost the entire stage-coach transportation in the southern counties and operated in the north as well. When the Dublin and Cashel Railroad was organized in 1844, he became chairman of that company and transferred his operations to the new form of transportation. He was a jolly, good-natured Irishman. Between him and his children existed a camaraderie which contrasted sharply with the amicable, though hardly buoyant, fellowship in FitzGerald's family. "Nothing but laughing and sunshine from morning till night," declared Thackeray after spending several days at Kilcullen.

Mr. Purcell was as successful a farmer as he was a business man, and his estate of four hundred acres was as carefully tilled as a well-ordered garden. In 1842 he conducted an experiment to determine the relative merits of bone dust, guano, and a commercial fertilizer, discovering that the first two produced by far the best crops. Between owner and the hundred and ten laborers on his land existed a regard and spirit of coöperation such as is uncommon today and was extremely rare in Ireland a century ago. Tenants occupied their homes rent free; each tilled his own little plot and kept a pig. Mr. Purcell was so careful to recognize the slightest improvements about the cottages that the laborers prided themselves on keeping their homes as neat as the rest of the estate. The owner's liberality and interest in these matters were typical of all his relations with employees. His very charity, it was said, was one of the causes of his good fortune.

FitzGerald went to Halverstown on alternate years from 1839 to 1845, and spent the entire summer in Ireland in 1841 and 1843. He visited his brother, Peter, in the latter year and one day picnicked with the family on the bank of the river Liffey at Pool-a-Phooka, "the Leap of the Goblin Horse." There they dabbled in the water, splashing one another, and forded the stream to climb among the rocks. Veal pies and champagne made up the lunch, and the party laughed and sang and returned home as the sun sank red behind the hills.

In 1841 and again in 1843 he went to Edgeworthstown, the home of his Cambridge friend, Francis Edgeworth, who had returned there after discovering that a talent for metaphysics was of comparatively little value in gaining a livelihood in England. Fitz-Gerald arrived in 1841 to learn that his friend had departed for England the previous day. The visitor found himself in a household of women, including Edgeworth's mother, seventy-four, and his half sister, the renowned Maria, seventy-two. All were so pleasant and kind that FitzGerald felt quite at home and stayed for more than a week. "I am now writing in the Library here," he informed Barton,

and the great Authoress is as busy as a bee making a catalogue of her books beside me, chattering away. We are great friends. She is as lively, active, and cheerful as if she were but twenty: really a very entertaining person. We talk about Walter Scott whom she adores, and are merry all the day long. . . . I have now begun to sketch heads on the blotting paper on which my paper rests—a sure sign, as Miss Edgeworth tells me, that I have said quite enough.[21]

FitzGerald returned to Edgeworthstown to spend a week in 1843, on that occasion finding his friend at home. "He farms and is a justice," the visitor reported, "and goes to sleep on the sofa of evenings. At odd moments he looks into Spinoza and Petrarch. People respect him very much in those parts. Old Miss Edgeworth

21. Letter to Barton, Sept. 2, 1841.

is wearing away: she has a capital bright soul which even now shines quite youthfully through her faded carcase." [22]

Even though he felt a deep attachment for Ireland, FitzGerald never returned there after 1845. "I love Ireland very much, I don't know why," he confessed. "The country and the people and all are very homogeneous: mournful and humorous somehow: just like their national music. Some of Tommy Moore's Irish Ballads (the airs, I mean) are the spirits of Waterford women made music of. . . . Don't you think that blue eyes with black hair, and especially with long black eyelashes, have a mystery about them?" Once when he and Browne were fishing in Bedfordshire, a band of Irish laborers who had walked all the way from County Mayo came to their inn and called for small beer. "We made their hearts merry with good Ale," FitzGerald revealed, "and they went off flourishing their sticks, hoping all things, enduring all things, and singing some loose things." [23]

His friends never knew, nor did FitzGerald always know, where his Wanderlust would lead him.

"How did I get here?" he asked, writing from Lowestoft in 1841.

Why I left Geldestone yesterday to go to Norwich: when I expected Donne to carry me back to Mattishall: no Donne came: so, after sitting 7 hours in the commercial Room, I got up on the Coach by which I had set out, and vowed in desperation that I would not descend from it till it stopped. It stopped here by the sea—I was satisfied: I felt that it could not reasonably be expected to go further—so here have I spent the day: and like a naughty boy won't go home to Geldestone quite yet. Such fine weather: such heaps of mackerel brought to shore: pleasant flippant Magazines at the Circulating Libraries—above all an Inn to live in! After living some time at my brother-in-law's expense, there is something very refreshing in launching out at one's own.[24]

His manner of life was a constant source of astonishment to his friends. "Fitz is on his way to Bedford," Spedding once informed Allen, "in a state of disgraceful indifference to everything, except grass and fresh air. What will become of him (in this world) ?" [25] And after FitzGerald visited Mirehouse, Spedding told Donne, "E. F. G. was here for about a month, and left us some three weeks ago. He is the Prince of Quietists. I reckon myself a quiet man, but

22. Maria Edgeworth died in 1849 at the age of eighty-two.
23. Letter to Pollock, Aug. 14 [1839].
24. Letter to Barton [June 17, 1841].
25. Grier, R. M., *John Allen, a Memoir* (London, Rivington's, 1889), p. 93.

that is nature, in him it is a principle. Half the self-sacrifice, the self-denial, the moral resolution, which he exercises to keep himself easy, would amply furnish forth a martyr or a missionary. His tranquillity is like a pirated copy of the peace of God. Truly he is a most comfortable companion. He would have everybody about him as tranquil as himself." [26] Donne described his life and conversation as "the most perfectly Philosophic of any I know. They approach in grand quiescence to some of the marvels in Plutarch. He is Diogenes without his dirt." [27] His friends often insisted, but Fitz-Gerald denied, that he was a philosopher. His life, he maintained, was merely patterned by "a talent for dullness."

From his wanderings FitzGerald returned to the cottage, glad to get back to his books and pictures, glad to return to the familiar countryside despite his description of Boulge as "one of the ugliest places in England—one of the dullest—it has not the merit of being bleak on a grand scale." But that was written in February. In May, which he considered the most delightful of all months, the burden of his descriptions was quite different.

I read of mornings; the same old books over and over again, having no command of new ones: walk with my great black dog of an afternoon, and at evening sit with open windows, up to which China roses climb, with my pipe, while the blackbirds and thrushes begin to rustle bedwards in the garden, and the nightingale to have the neighbourhood to herself. . . . And such verdure! white clouds moving over the new fledged tops of oak trees, and acres of grass striving with buttercups. How old to tell of, how new to see! [28]

26. *Cambridge Apostles*, p. 267.
27. *Donne and His Friends*, p. 24.
28. Letter to F. Tennyson, May 24, 1844.

VIII

The Woodbridge Wits

"We are the chief wits of Woodbridge."
Letter to Laurence, 1843

ON Saturday I give supper to Bernard Barton and Churchyard," FitzGerald wrote in 1843. "We are the chief
wits of Woodbridge. And one man has said that he
envies our conversations! So we flatter each other in the
country."

The "wits" eventually numbered four, George Crabbe, vicar of
Bredfield and eldest son of the poet, later being included in the
group. Sometimes they were joined by the dapper Captain F. C.
Brooke of near-by Ufford, owner of a library of more than 20,000
volumes, said to have been one of the finest private collections in
England.[1] Thomas Churchyard was a Woodbridge solicitor and
amateur artist, whose enthusiasm for painting was nicely adjusted
to an indifference to law.

Barton, the Quaker poet whom Mrs. FitzGerald had entertained
at Wherstead, was twenty-five years FitzGerald's senior. For forty
years he served as clerk in Alexander's bank in Woodbridge and
once considered abandoning that vocation for literature. From
this he was dissuaded by Byron and Lamb, with whom he corresponded. Writing verse was an avocation in which he engaged
with zeal, convinced that there could never be too much poetry
abroad. After gaining a modest recognition in 1822, he produced
five volumes within six years. "He wrote," FitzGerald stated, "always with great facility, almost unretarded by that worst labour of
correction; for he was not fastidious himself about exactness of
thought or of harmony of numbers." [2] He never deluded himself,
however, that he was a great poet. Cheerful, generous, improvident,
and humorous, Barton was good company in all companies. "His
literary talents, social amiability, and blameless character," said
FitzGerald,

1. *Two Suffolk Friends,* p. 69.
2. "Barton Memoir," *Literary Remains,* VII, 380.

made him respected, liked, and courted among his neighbours. Few, high or low, but were glad to see him at his customary place in the bank. . . . Few, high or low, but were glad to have him at their tables; where he was pleasant and equally pleased, whether with the fine folks at the Hall, or with the homely company at the Farm; carrying everywhere indifferently the same feeling, good spirits, and good manners; and by a happy frankness of nature, . . . checkering the conventional gentility of the drawing-room with some humours of humbler life, which in turn he refined with a little sprinkling of literature.[3]

Barton, a widower, lived in the Thoroughfare, Woodbridge, with his daughter, Lucy, a woman of FitzGerald's age. FitzGerald became intimate with him after moving to Boulge and was always welcome at the poet's home. He called whenever he was in the town and often walked from his cottage to take supper, usually of toasted cheese and ale, and spend the evening. Barton valued his company. "The skies do not drop such larks every day," he once said, quoting his friend, Lamb. When in 1840 he learned that a new ship was to be named *The Bernard Barton of Woodbridge,* he communicated the news, he informed Donne,[4]

too abruptly to poor Edward FitzGerald, just as he was going to sit down to dinner with me, and jumped up, chair and all, taking that and himself into the far corner of the room, professing he could not presume to sit at the same table with one about to have a ship named after him. . . . If my Bardship never gets me on the Muster-roll of Parnassus, it will into the Shipping-List. If I fail of being chronicled among the Poets of Great Britain by some future Cibber, I shall at any rate be registered at Lloyds along with the Spitfires, Amazons, Corsairs and what not.[5]

Honors came more slowly to FitzGerald. Two years later, however, he advised Barton from Geldestone,

I shall assuredly be down again by the latter part of February: when toasted cheese and ale shall again unite our souls. You need not however expect that I can return to such familiar intercourse as once (in former days) passed between us. New honours in society have devolved upon me the necessity of a more dignified deportment. A letter has been sent from the Secretary of the Ipswich Mechanics' Institution asking me to Lecture—any subject but Party Politics or Controversial Divinity. On my politely declining, another, a fuller, and a more press-

3. *Ibid.*, pp. 392–393.
4. FitzGerald had introduced Donne to Barton, who wished to see the Cowper relics in Donne's possession. An intimate friendship resulted.
5. *Donne and His Friends*, pp. 58–59.

ing, letter was sent urging me to comply with their demand: I answered to the same effect, but with accelerated dignity. I am now awaiting the third request in confidence: if you see no symptoms of its being mooted, perhaps you will kindly propose it. I have prepared an answer. Donne is mad with envy.[6]

George Crabbe, like Barton, was considerably older than Fitz-Gerald. He was fifty, twice FitzGerald's age, when appointed vicar of Bredfield in 1834. He closely resembled his father in features; but had no love for poetry, declaring that it was "a useless art" and that the world would have done better without it. He had two ardors besides religion—church architecture and trees. The destruction of an oak, however needful, caused him to complain that the squires "scandalously misused the globe." FitzGerald said of him,

To manhood's energy of mind, and great bodily strength, he united the boy's heart: as much a boy at seventy as boys need be at seventeen; as chivalrously hopeful, trustful, ardent, and courageous; as careless of riches, as intolerant of injustice and oppression, as incapable of all that is base, little, and mean. With this heroic temper were joined the errors of that over-much affection, rashness in judgment and act, liability to sudden and violent emotions, to sudden and sometimes unreasonable like and dislike.[7]

Crabbe was as sensitive as he was guileless. FitzGerald and Barton never knew when one of their pranks or an innocent difference of opinion would offend their "techy" friend. "He attacked me most furiously," FitzGerald once told the Quaker, "on the old score of *Pride,* on which the man is distracted: and so I told him. . . . I am dropped out of his Category of Heroes for ever! He shall always be right glad to see me, he says: but he never can be disappointed in me again! How much the best footing is this to be upon with all one's friends." [8] FitzGerald succeeded in mollifying the vicar but heartily hoped he would "never replace me on the pedestal from which he so lately took me down. . . . And so from my happy station on the common mortal ground I salute you and him." [9] The amiable Barton ignored Crabbe's temporary defections; but FitzGerald, himself sensitive, sometimes attached importance to tiffs which he should have disregarded. Thanks to the Quaker's wholesome common sense and good-natured chiding,

6. Letter to Barton, January, 1842.
7. *Literary Remains,* VII, 422–423.
8. Letter to Barton, Sept. 19, 1846.
9. *Ibid.,* September, 1846.

their differences were never of long duration. The poet wrote to Crabbe after the disagreement just referred to,

I am glad of thy frank admission that thou hast been a thought too captious toward that Cottager. You are both a trifle eccentric, but, despite your eccentricities, capable of cordially appreciating each other, and do so, bating brief moods, when like the two Knights in the old Story one will have it the Shield is all black, and the other maintain it is all white: when the truth is, that it is party-coloured. You have no right to be at variance and hardly a decent excuse for being so a whole day long. But I cannot say that your little differences of opinion have ever much discomposed me, for I always feel certain you will jumble together again. I would not have a serious quarrel between you for a good deal.[10]

The "wits" met whenever one of them chose to entertain, or whenever one decided to call on another. "Come by all means tomorrow, an thou wilt," FitzGerald once urged, replying to a note from Barton. ". . . I will ask Crabbe, who I have no doubt will come. . . . Bring up with thee a pound of Derby Cheese, for a toast: and some oysters, with knives; that thou mayst eat. And I will pay thee the cost—I have a fowl hanging up." [11] The "Cottager" appears to have been host most frequently, and an invitation which he once sent to the Vicar has survived.

> Dear Crabbe,
>> When from your walk you're rested
>> And your dinner's half digested,
>> Prithee, then set off again
>> Through the dirty roads and rain,
>> And win your way with courage here
>> To smoke cigars and drink small Beer.
>> Churchyard I expect, and Barton;
>> But should they fail—here's I for sartain;
>> Who, as e'en my foes do boast,
>> Am always in myself "a host."
>> And so expecting you to see
>> I'm your obedient E. F. G.[12]

The following, written by Crabbe, was doubtless his acceptance on this occasion:

>> As sure as a gun
>> I'll be in at the fun;
>> For I'm the old Vicar

10. MS. letter from Barton to Crabbe, Sept. 26, 1846, British Museum, Add. 36,756.
11. Letter to Barton [Boulge Cottage, 1845].
12. MS. letter to Crabbe, undated.

> As sticks to his liquor;
> And smokes a cigar
> Like a jolly Jack Tar:
> I've no time for more,
> For the Post's at the door;
> But I'll be there by seven,
> And stay 'till eleven,
> For Boulge is my Heaven! [13]

Barton usually referred to the meetings of the wits as symposiums, and such they were in the original sense of the word. He wrote:

Tom Churchyard drove me last night to a symposium given by Edward FitzGerald to us two and old Crabbe—lots of palaver, smoking, and laughing. Edward was in one of his drollest cues, and did the honours of his cottage with such gravity of humour that we roared again. It was the oddest *mélange*. Tea, porter, ale, wine, brandy, cigars, cold lamb, salad, cucumber, bread and cheese; no precise line of demarcation between tea and supper. It was one continuous spread, something coming on fresh every ten minutes till we wondered whence they came and whither they could be put. "Gentlemen, the resources of the cottage are exhaustless," shouted our host. "Mrs. Faiers, the salad there, the cucumber here, oil at that corner, vinegar and pepper yonder; there put the cream, and that glass of butter in the middle, push those wine and brandy bottles close together," Certes, it was rare fun.[14]

FitzGerald, Churchyard, and Crabbe enjoyed smoking; but Barton hated tobacco in any form except snuff. "The odour of that room after the first hour or two from the time of lighting up was really awful," he complained after an evening at the cottage. "Talk of my tippling Port! Marry the clouds such a trio as yours can and do blow would do more to make me drunk than all the Wine I could ever be induced to swallow." The odor, he maintained, flavored his tea at breakfast and his meat at dinner. "Have you ever tried the Guano?" he asked Crabbe. "Marry I smelt some the other day, and thought it wondrous like the residuary perfume left next morning by pipe, or cigar." [15]

Barton and Churchyard were zealous collectors of paintings, and

13. Barton sent the rhyme to Donne, adding, "I would not let every one see it, but I copy it for thy own private reading, because I am sure thou wilt read it with a liberal toleration, and wilt not suppose the good old Vicar to be a Bacchanalian, when he only meant, con amore, to express his hearty willingness to be social. But certain ill-disposed folks might take it literally, and quarrel with, and misconstrue its heartiness." *Donne and His Friends*, p. 129.

14. Letter from Bernard Barton to John Wodderspoon of Ipswich, author of *Memorials of Ipswich*, quoted in the *London Daily Chronicle*, May 7, 1900.

15. MS. letters to Crabbe, Feb. 1 and March 24, 1845. British Museum.

FitzGerald became infected with their enthusiasm. The three were continually buying, selling, and bartering canvases. FitzGerald was no connoisseur in matters of art, but he placed full confidence in his taste. "I suppose a visit to Rome," he remarked to Laurence, "or an exact technical knowledge of pictures, is very essential. I am sure I can understand the finest part of pictures without doing either." [16] Churchyard, according to FitzGerald, was a competent judge of works by Constable, Gainsborough, and John Crome, the Norwich artist.[17] Barton, though fond of paintings, had little critical knowledge of them and was the victim of every itinerant dealer who passed his door. "And then was B. B. to be seen," FitzGerald related, ". . . examining some picture set before him . . . the dealer recommending, and Barton wavering, until partly by money, and partly by exchange of some older favourites, with perhaps a snuff-box thrown in to turn the scale; a bargain was concluded— generally to B. B.'s great disadvantage and great content." [18]

FitzGerald found buying canvases far more exciting than viewing them in galleries. Moreover, having walls of his own to decorate stimulated his interest. Auction rooms and the shops of picture-dealers and pawnbrokers supplanted bookstalls as his favorite haunts during rambles in London. Their spell even invaded the privacy of his study. "Who can sit down to Plato," he wrote from London, "while his brains are roaming to Holborn, Christie's, Phillips's, etc.?" He did not have means to buy second or even third best canvases, he said, "but I can get the imitations of the best: and that is enough for me."

During the winter of 1841–42 he bought a number of pictures, among them a copy of a Raphael, and a Constable which was pronounced "Quite genuine by our great judge," Churchyard. "And now, Barton," he announced in the spring,

know that I really have made my last purchase in the picture line for the season—today at Phillips's I fell—my virtue fell under the Auctioneer's hammer—an early Venetian picture the seducer—a Holy Family—to think such Families should be painted to allure unwary youths into Sin! There they sit collected in a quiet group just outside the walls of Nazareth, or Bethlehem—sweet St. Catherine with the palm in her hand, her yellow hair encircled with a row of pearls. The child is an ugly swollen child:—but I skip him. . . . I bought the best picture in today's auction: and this over the dealers' heads. . . . I exult over the whole tribe.

16. Benson, A. C., *Edward FitzGerald* (London, Macmillan & Co., 1925), p. 149.
17. The elder Crome.
18. "Barton Memoir," *Literary Remains*, VII, 406–407.

But he was not so safe from temptation as he assumed. In a dealer's window hung a landscape which reminded him of a village near Cambridge, "a small bit of canvas," he wrote, "but well suggestive of the Spirit of the time: that is, of Twilight. . . . I don't know however, if I can yet pronounce myself safe: I walk insensibly *that* way: flutter round the shopwindow—there it is: meeting my gaze with a kind of ironical quiet." Within a fortnight he had bought the picture. He had greater success in resisting another, a "Battle Piece," offered by a Holborn dealer, which tempted him all spring. He did not buy that until September.

In the excitement of an auction he did not always deal wisely. "Never was a stupider purchase," he once admitted of a large painting of a fruit girl by Opie. He cut it down, borrowed Laurence's palette and brushes "and lay upon the floor two hours patching over and renovating. . . . It has now to be varnished: and then I hope some fool will be surprised into giving £4 for it, as I did." Kenworthy Browne's father took tea with him a few days later and praised the picture. "I said nothing then," he wrote, "but I hope to make him buy her for what I gave." But Mr. Browne demanded that other pictures, with which FitzGerald refused to part, be included in the sale; and the transaction fell through. The canvas was placed with a dealer, and seven months later, was still hanging in the shopwindow—"an unpleasant sight."

During the first weeks after receiving his quarterly funds, Fitz-Gerald bought with a free hand. As each quarter advanced, however, attendance at auctions involved nice calculations to determine which bargains were within his means. "I have bought no more pictures," he informed Barton one December. "Indeed, I have spent all my money: and I must wait till next quarter before I make a fresh plunge." The following March, after he had been particularly active in the picture market, he announced, ". . . a man at Bedford has offered to buy a picture I have there: good fellow: so he shall: and then I shan't have to borrow monies this quarter, shall I?—And as for the future, I utterly scorn it."

He bought not only for himself, but also for relatives and friends. Sometimes they commissioned him to buy; at other times he purchased canvases which he believed they would like. "What I gain by buying pictures for my friends," he said, "is the keeping those pictures for a time in my room, and then seeing them from time to time afterward. Besides, the pride of making a good purchase and shewing one's taste: all that contributes to health and long life."

Some of the pictures he kept in his London lodgings; others he sent to his cottage, the walls of which had been papered a "still green" to provide a proper background. When his quarters could hold no more, he called upon friends to keep canvases for him. "I bought a huge naked woman," he once informed Barton, "a copy of Raffaelle—as large as life down to the knees, which you will allow is quite enough of her. . . . Only, such exhibitions are not fit for Quakers' eyes. I have sent her to Laurence's house to preserve my reputation. He is a married man." [19] Cleaning and varnishing his pictures, reframing them, and touching up rubbed spots kept FitzGerald busy at times. "I have just got home a new coat for my Constable," he informed Barton after buying a new frame, "which coat cost 33 shillings: just the same price as I gave for a Chesterfield wrapper (as it is called) for myself some weeks ago. People told me I was not improved by my Chesterfield wrapper: and I am vext to see how little my Constable is improved by his coat of Cloth of Gold."

FitzGerald was not always certain of the paternity of his paintings. "I . . . also bought a picture of course," he once wrote, "a fine head, either by Georgione, or a Flemish copyist. But as I am not particular, I call it Georgione." In 1841 he purchased for Barton a painting which he thought was a Gainsborough, although Laurence did not agree with him.

"Whoever it may be painted by," he declared,

I pronounce it a very beautiful picture: tender, graceful, full of repose. I sit looking at it in my room and like it more and more. All this is independent of its paternity. But if I am asked about that, I should only answer on my own judgment (not a good one in such a matter, as I have told you) that it *is* decidedly by Gainsborough, and in his best way of conception. My argument would be of the Johnsonian kind: if it is not by G., who the devil is it by? There are some perhaps feeble touches here and there in the tree in the centre, though not in those autumnal leaves that shoot into the sky to the right: but who painted that clump of thick solemn trees to the left of the picture:—the light of evening rising like a low fire between their boles? The cattle too in the water, how they stand! . . . It is better painted far than the Market Cart in the National Gallery: but not better only equal (in a sketchy way) to the beautiful evening Watering Place. . . . Oh the comfort of independent self-confidence! [20]

The masterpiece of FitzGerald's collection, in his judgment, was a landscape, painted, he believed, by Titian. It has since been

19. Letter to Barton, January, 1842.
20. *Ibid.*, Nov. 27, 1841.

identified as the work of Ippolito Scarsella. He bought the picture on the recommendation of Morris Moore,[21] art critic for the *Times,* a friend whom he had met through Laurence. Moore was an ardent admirer of Titian and had persuaded the previous owner to buy the canvas. In 1847 he told FitzGerald that it was being offered for sixty guineas. FitzGerald made a bid by sending the owner "an immense packing case or two of Pictures he had grown tired of and Thirty Pounds, and down came the Titian." [22] The picture represents Abraham and Isaac on their way to the sacrifice. The patriarch holds a lighted torch in his left hand, and his right rests on the hilt of his sword; Isaac carries a bundle of faggots. The figures appear against a somber background of trees, a castellated promontory, and mountains. Until his death FitzGerald believed the picture to be a genuine Titian. He bequeathed it as such to the Fitzwilliam Museum in Cambridge, where it now hangs.[23]

21. Morris Moore was a critic of independent judgment and exceptional frankness. His letters on "The Abuses of the National Gallery" were published in the *Times* at the end of 1846 and the beginning of 1847. They led to a controversy with Charles Eastlake, the painter. Moore's letters, signed *Verax,* were published by Pickering in 1847. FitzGerald wrote in 1848, "Moore is turned picture-dealer: and that high Roman virtue in which he indulged is likely to suffer a picture-dealer's change, I think." Letter to F. Tennyson, May 4, 1848.

22. Barton MS. letter to Wodderspoon, July 7, 1847.

23. Exhibit 113, Fitzwilliam Museum. It bears the title, "Landscape with Abraham and Isaac."

IX

London during the 'Forties

"What bothered me about London was—all the Clever
People going wrong with such Clever Reasons for so doing
which I couldn't confute."

Letter to Charles Eliot Norton

IN 1837, the year that Thackeray returned to England to em-
bark on his literary career, Alfred Tennyson and his family
moved from Lincolnshire and settled at High Beech, Epping
Forest, twelve miles north of London. On visits to town thereafter FitzGerald saw much of his two friends. All three were guests
of Charles Dickens one day in 1842. They went driving during the
afternoon and returned to Dickens' home to dine. The evening
was spent playing cards and drinking mulled claret. FitzGerald observed that his host was "quite unaffected, and (after all his American triumph) [1] seeming to wish anyone to show off sooner than
himself."

Dickens alone at the time might have attracted attention on
a London Street. *Pickwick Papers* had taken the country by storm
five years before, and *Oliver Twist* and other stories had added to
his reputation. Thackeray was ambitious of rivaling the fame of
his host; Tennyson was hopeful of doing so. Not for five years was
Vanity Fair to win recognition for the novelist; not for eight years
was *In Memoriam* to fulfill the aspirations of the poet. FitzGerald
was merely an obscure friend who had been "taken there." He
had apparently abandoned the youthful literary ambitions, confided to his classmate, Duncan, as they roamed the fields at Cambridge more than a decade earlier. Not for many years, and never
in his lifetime, was the *Rubáiyát* to win a fame comparable to that
of *Pickwick Papers, Vanity Fair,* or *In Memoriam.*

Thackeray applied himself earnestly to writing after his return
from Paris. He did hack-work of all kinds: reviewed books, wrote
for the *Times* and the *Morning Chronicle,* and contributed to
various periodicals. His first stories were published in *Fraser's*

1. Dickens had been a popular success on a lecture tour in the United States in 1841.

Magazine; but, although he could satisfy editors, he could not please subscribers. None of his early efforts were popular.

FitzGerald was a frequent visitor at Thackeray's home, 13 Great Coram Street—"Jorum Street" as the young writer usually called it—in Bloomsbury; but his companionship was not an unmixed blessing for the busy author. "They say the town is very gay," he wrote to his wife, who was in the country, in 1839, "but I have almost left off going to operas and theatres, and come home early, when FitzGerald and I have a pipe together and so go quietly to bed. It is delightful to have him in the house, but I'm afraid his society makes me idle, we sit and talk too much about books and pictures and smoke too many cigars." [2] In December, however, he spoke of applying himself to "books, books, books all day until night, when to my great consolation FitzGerald has been here to smoke a cigar and keep me company until one or so." [3]

In the midst of Thackeray's struggles for recognition, his wife's health broke. After the birth of their third child in 1840, she failed to gain strength; and her mind became affected. For two years Thackeray sought a cure for her maladies, but all treatments failed. In 1842 he realized that the case was hopeless. He placed her in the care of a nurse and took his children to France to live with his mother.

FitzGerald proved himself a staunch friend during these troubles. He asked Thompson in 1841, "Have you read Thackeray's little book, 'The Second Funeral of Napoleon'? If not, pray do; and buy it, and ask others to buy it, as each copy puts 7½d. in T's pocket: which is very empty just now, I take it. I think this book is the best thing he has done." [4] When away from London, FitzGerald wrote long letters to cheer his friend; and when he returned to town, he stayed at Coram Street if Thackeray would otherwise be alone. During one of these visits the novelist drew FitzGerald's bookplate. The design is an elongated plaque, framing the figure of an angel holding a shield. Below is printed, "E. FitzGerald." In one of his books FitzGerald wrote beneath the plate, "Done by Thackeray one day in Coram (Jorum) Street in 1842. E. F. G. 'All wrong on her feet,'—so he said—I can see him now. March 17/78." [5]

2. Thackeray Biographical Edition, IV, xxiv.
3. Thackeray Centenary Edition, VII, xxiv.
4. Letter to Thompson [Feb. 18, 1841].
5. This book is owned by Mrs. Richard Fuller. FitzGerald's, a collector has stated, is one of the rarest and most highly prized of British bookplates. Hutton, Lawrence, *Talks in a Library* (Putnam, N.Y., 1905), p. 404. Copies of it have been made since his death, and probably only those found in his books are genuine.

Anne Thackeray Ritchie, the novelist's daughter declared,

One of my letters to Mr. FitzGerald . . . was written after I had found out from some old letters of my Father's what a friend he had been to my Father. At the time of my Mother's illness, and even before, he had helped him with money, loved him, encouraged him; and my Father, who was as able to *take* generously as to give when the time came, in all his troubles writes back in a brave and grateful and noble way which almost makes me cry even now after all a lifetime . . . though I long to show you what a generous true friend he was I hardly know how to do it.[6]

When in the summer of 1842 Thackeray decided to go to Ireland to gather material for a book, he urged FitzGerald to accompany him. FitzGerald refused, maintaining that, "no sights recompense the often undoing and doing up of a carpetbag." After his friend started in June, he was filled with remorse. "There is that poor fellow Thackeray gone off to Ireland," he told Pollock, "and what a lazy beast I am for not going with him. But except for a journey of two days, I get as dull as dirt." He wrote in the same vein to Thackeray, who twitted him on his misgivings. "I found your dismal letter waiting on arrival here," he replied from Dublin. "What the deuce are you in the dumps for? Don't flatter yourself but that I'll get on very well without you. Such a place as this hotel is itself enough to make a chapter about, such filth and liberality. O my dear friend, pray heaven on bended knee that to-night when I go to bed I find no—Turn-over. Have you ever remarked that the little ones of all sting worst?"

FitzGerald had given Thackeray letters of introduction to his brother Peter and to his uncle at Halverstown, with the exhortation, however, that nothing of his visits was to appear in the book. In that Thackeray failed, for an account of his visit to Halverstown is found in the description of "Mr. P's" estate in Chapter II of the *Irish Sketch Book*. The passage is prefaced with the remark, "And I must begin this tour with a monstrous breach of confidence by first describing what I saw." Thackeray so enjoyed his stay with the Purcells that he returned for a second before leaving Ireland. "Such people," he told his mother, "are not to be met with more than a few times in a man's life." The following June the two friends read proof on the volume in Coram Street; and when it appeared, FitzGerald recommended it to Laurence. "It is all true," he said of the description of Halverstown.

6. Anne Thackeray Ritchie MS. letter.

Thackeray was slowly establishing a reputation. In 1843 he became a member of the *Punch* staff,[7] despite FitzGerald's contrary advice. "The admirers of Mr. Titmarsh" [his pseudonym], he told his mother two years later, "are a small clique, but a good and increasing one." He was an active contributor to various other periodicals and each spring wrote a criticism, usually vitriolic, of the exhibition of the Royal Academy for *Fraser's Magazine*. In these he repeatedly objected to the vacuity and lack of vitality in the work of contemporary English artists. "Why did the poor fellows paint such fiddle-faddle pictures?" he asked in the 1844 article. The following year he continued his bombardment. "These pictures," he asserted, "are like boy's hexameters at school . . . but these verses are not the least like poetry, any more than the great academical paintings of the artists are like great painting. You want something more than a composition, and a set of costumes and figures decently posed and studied." He commented on Charles Landseer's "Charles I before the Battle of Edge Hill."

Charles stands at a tree before the inn-door, officers are round about, the little princes are playing with a little dog, as becomes their youth and innocence, rows of soldiers appear in red coats, nobody seems to have anything particular to do, except the Royal martyr, who is looking at a bone of ham that a girl out of the inn has hold of. Now this is all very well, but you want something more than this in an historic picture. . . . You don't want the *Deus intersit* for no other purpose than to look at the knuckle of a ham.[8]

The critic's remarks on the work of Frank Stone had been generally commendatory, but of one of his paintings he wrote, "By far the prettiest of the maudlin pictures is Mr. Stone's *Premier Pas*. It is that old, pretty, rococo, fantastic Jenny and Jessamy couple, whose loves the painter has been chronicling any time these five years, and whom he has spied out at various wells, porches, etc." Thackeray praised the execution of the piece, however, and spoke of another as "by far the best of Mr. Stone's works, and in the best line." [9]

Shortly after the review appeared, Stone met FitzGerald on the street and, grasping him by the coat, told him "in perfect sincerity, and with increasing warmth, how, though he loved old Thackeray, yet these yearly out-speakings of his sorely tried him; not on account of himself (Stone), but on account of his friends Charles Landseer, Maclise, etc." Stone worked himself up to such a pitch

7. *Punch* began publication in 1841.
8. "Picture Gossip," *Ballads and Miscellanies,* Biographical Edition, XIII, p. 460.
9. *Ibid.,* p. 453.

of excitement that he finally warned that "Thackeray would get himself horse-whipped one day by one of these infuriated Apelleses." FitzGerald, who had half agreed with the artist, laughed heartily at this and replied that "two could play at that game." Thackeray was six feet three inches tall. "These painters," FitzGerald told Frederick Tennyson,

cling together . . . to such a degree that they really have persuaded themselves that any one who ventures to laugh at one of their drawings, exhibited publickly for the express purpose of criticism, insults the whole corps. In the meanwhile old Thackeray laughs at all this; and goes on in his own way; writing hard for half a dozen Reviews and Newspapers all the morning; dining, drinking, and talking of a night; managing to preserve a fresh colour and perpetual flow of spirits under a wear-and-tear of thinking and feeding that would have knocked up any other man I know two years ago, at least.[10]

Thackeray loved good fellowship; and as his reputation grew, he became more and more a clubman. FitzGerald, on the other hand, was becoming more and more attracted to the quietism of Suffolk. The novelist abandoned his house in Coram Street, and after 1845 the meetings of the two men became less frequent.

The publication of *Vanity Fair* serially in 1847–48 ended Thackeray's struggle for recognition. "His book . . . is read by the Great," FitzGerald stated, "and will, I hope, do them good." The story "began dull," he thought, "but gets better every number, and has some very fine things indeed in it. He [Thackeray] is become a great man I am told: goes to Holland House, and Devonshire House: and for some reason or other, will not write a word to me. But I am sure this is not because he is asked to Holland House." [11]

FitzGerald was not so sure as he professed. More than one friend wrote that Thackeray's head was being turned by idolators. He inquired of the novelist himself to determine the truth of the reports. "It is not true," the writer answered,

what Gurlyle [12] has written to you about my having become a tremenjous lion, etc., too grand to, etc., but what is true is that a fellow who is writing all day for money gets sick of pens and paper when his work is over, and I go on dawdling and thinking of writing, and months pass away. All that about being a Lion is nonsense. . . . "Vanity Fair" does everything but pay. I am glad if you like it. I don't care a dem if some

10. Letter to Frederick Tennyson, June 12, 1845.
11. *Ibid.*, May 4, 1848.
12. Thackeray's nickname for Carlyle.

other people do or don't: and always try to keep that damper against flattery.[13]

During 1848 and 1849 FitzGerald was often in London and the old intimacy was resumed. "I have seen Thackeray three or four times," he wrote early in 1849. "He is just the same. All the world admires *Vanity Fair:* and the author is courted by Dukes and Duchesses, and wits of both sexes." Writing from Brighton, Thackeray urged, "Come, Eros! come, boy-god of the twanging bow! Is not Venus thy mother here? Thou shalt ride in her chariot, and by thy side shall be, if not Mars, at least Titmars. How these men of letters dash off these things." [14]

After their visit with Spedding at Mirehouse in 1835 FitzGerald and Tennyson did not often meet until the poet moved to High Beech.[15] The Tennysons occupied that home for only three years; but they remained in southern England thereafter, and Alfred was able more frequently to enjoy the companionship of his friends in London and to indulge his love for the bustle of city streets. Sometimes he rented rooms for his visits to town, sometimes he stayed with one or another of his comrades, thereby relieving the strain on his limited means. "When I got to my lodgings, I found A. T. installed in them," FitzGerald once informed Barton.

He has been here ever since in a very uneasy state: being really ill, in a nervous way: what with an hereditary tenderness of nerve, and having spoiled what strength he had by incessant smoking &c.—I have also made him very out of sorts by desiring a truce from complaints and complainings. Poor fellow: he is quite magnanimous, and noble natured, with no meanness or vanity or affectation of any kind whatever—but very perverse, according to the nature of his illness. So much for Poets, who, one must allow, are many of them a somewhat tetchy race.[16]

At another time when Tennyson announced his intention of staying with him in London, FitzGerald stipulated that the visit "shall be a very short one." Usually, however, the poet was a welcome guest. "We have had Alfred Tennyson here, very droll and wayward," FitzGerald related in 1838, "and much sitting up of nights till two and three in the morning with pipes in our mouths: at which good hour we would get Alfred to give us some of his magic

13. Thackeray Biographical Edition, I, xxxiv.
14. Wright, *FitzGerald,* I, 224.
15. Dr. Warren, in *Tennyson and His Friends,* pp. 104–105, states that FitzGerald once visited Tennyson at Somersby.
16. *Letters to Bernard Barton,* p. 19.

music, which he does between growling and smoking; and so to bed. All this has not cured my Influenza as you may imagine: but these hours shall be remembered long after the Influenza is forgotten." [17] Again, the following year, FitzGerald reported from London, "I have got Alfred Tennyson up with me here, and today I give a dinner to him and two or three others. It is just ordered; soles, two boiled fowls, and an Apple Tart—cheese etc. After this plenty of smoking. I am quite smoke dried as it is."

Convivial evenings were frequent. A group from among Spedding, Thackeray, Pollock, Spring Rice and his cousin, Aubrey De Vere, Savile Morton when he was back from the Continent, and others could usually be collected to dine at the Cock Tavern in the Strand or, more often, at Bertolini's near Leicester Square. They sometimes called it Dirtolini's, said FitzGerald, but not seriously, for the place was clean as well as very cheap and the cookery good for the price. Tennyson's partiality for cold salt beef and new potatoes was the subject of considerable chaffing by his friends; and Spedding described a dinner at the Cock when the poet had "two chops, one pickle, two cheeses, one pint of stout, one pot of port, and three cigars. When we had finished I had to take his regrets to the Kembles; he could not go because he had the influenza." [18]

After dinner the group occasionally attended a theater but more often returned to lodgings, where they drank wine or brandy and water while they discussed the latest books, argued questions of philosophy, debated national and international affairs, or indulged in good-natured banter. They agreed in 1842 that France should be partitioned among other powers as Poland had been. When it was suggested that the democratic influence of France counteracted the absolutism of Russia, FitzGerald maintained that the latter country was "too unwieldy and rotten-ripe ever to make a huge progress in conquest." England, he argued again and again, had fallen into decline. "It seems impossible the manufacturers can go on as they are, and impossible that the demand for our goods can continue as of old in Europe: and impossible but that we must get a rub and licking in some of our colonies: and if these things come at once, why then the devil's in it." However, he faced these possibilities with philosophic detachment, asserting that "in the meantime, all goes on toward better and better . . . and humanity grows clearer by flowing . . . and man shall have wings to fly and something much better than that in the end." Tennyson's

17. Letter to Barton, April, 1838.
18. *Cambridge Apostles*, p. 275.

contributions to these discussions were much respected. Fitz-
Gerald, especially, admired the poet's ability to "let fall—not lay
down—the word that settled the question, aesthetic or other, which
others hammer'd after in vain." "I hope that others have remembered," he said many years later, "and made note of A. T.'s sayings
—which hit the nail on the head. Had I continued to be with him,
I would have risked being called another Bozzy by the thankless
World; and have often looked in vain for a Note Book I had made
of such things." The book has been found; but Tennyson's comments, when read, lack the piquancy which they doubtless possessed when uttered.

No such value was placed on FitzGerald's statements, for he
seems to have been something of an iconoclast in all discussions,
particularly in those relating to literature and art. Spedding, it
will be remembered, had spoken of his judgments as "strange and
wayward . . . though so original and often so profound and luminous." His friends came to expect contradictory opinions from
him and labeled them "Old Fitz's crotchets." Many of his "crotchets" on the literature of his contemporaries, however, have been
endorsed by posterity.

Tennyson was often called upon to entertain his companions with
his "magic music." "There was no declamatory showing off in A. T.'s
recitation of his verse," FitzGerald stated, "sometimes broken
with a laugh, or a burlesque twist of the voice, when something
struck him as quaint or grim. Sometimes Spedding would read the
poems to us; A. T. once told him he seemed to read too much as if
bees were about his mouth. . . ." [19] Nonsense, too, formed a large
share of their entertainment; and the poet, who had considerable
ability as a mimic, would be called upon for imitations. Protesting
that "the oddities and angularities of *great* men should never be
hawked about," he would nevertheless ape the voices and expressions of well-known public characters. He enacted "with grim
humour Milton's 'So started up in his foul shape the fiend,' from
the crouching of the toad to the explosion. He used also, Fitz-
Gerald said, "to do the sun coming out from a cloud and retiring
into one again, with a gradual fluffing up of his hair into full wig
and elevation of cravat and collar; George IV in as comical and
wonderful a way." [20]

FitzGerald contributed liberally to the fun by his drollery. He
and Thackeray found Spedding's forehead an irresistible subject

19. Tennyson, *Memoir,* I, 194.
20. *Ibid.,* p. 184.

for their banter. "Not swords, nor cannon, nor all the Bulls of Bashan butting at it," said FitzGerald, "could, I feel sure, discompose that venerable forehead. No wonder that no hair can grow at such an altitude." He and Thackeray found the impressive brow peering at them from all sorts of objects, from every milestone, for example; and sailors, FitzGerald maintained, hailed it in the Channel, mistaking it for Beachy Head. Thackeray drew a picture of it rising like a sun from behind Mt. Blanc and reflected in Lake Geneva. "The forehead," FitzGerald once told Frederick Tennyson, "is at present in Pembrokeshire, I believe: or Glamorganshire: or Monmouthshire: it is hard to say which. It has gone to spend its Christmas there." In 1844 Thackeray wrote in his diary, "Dined with Quin at a party where FitzGerald was in wonderful cue"; and in his memoirs Aubrey De Vere recorded:

Another most amusing friend of mine was Edward FitzGerald . . . the specialty of whose humour it was that the more comical were his words, the more solemn his face always became. I remember an illustration of this. After a large evening party, when nearly all the guests had departed, the rest remained to smoke. In that party was a man celebrated for his passion for titles. On this occasion he exceeded himself. All his talk was of the rich and great. "Yesterday when I was riding with my friend, the Duke of ——." "On Tuesday the Marquis of —— remarked to me." It went on for a long time; the party listening, some amused, some bored. Edward FitzGerald was the first to rise. He lighted a candle, passed out of the room, stood still with the lock of the door in his hand, and looked back. He could change his countenance into anything he pleased. It had then exchanged in a moment its usual merry look for one of profound, nay hopeless, dejection. Slowly and sadly he spoke: "I once knew a lord, too, but he is dead!" [21]

Most of FitzGerald's friends had vocations which required their attention by day. Thackeray's editors kept him at his desk; Spedding, too, had work to which he conscientiously applied himself. In 1838 he had taken a post in the Colonial Office and four years later went to America as secretary to Lord Ashburton when the latter settled the dispute over the Maine boundary. After his return Spedding was offered a lucrative post in the Foreign Office, but this he declined, choosing to spend the remainder of his life editing the works of Bacon. Spring Rice became a deputy chairman with the Board of Customs. Once during the 'forties he and Fitz-Gerald called on the banker-poet, Samuel Rogers, to view his pictures. As they entered the hallway, Thomas Moore "came tripping

21. De Vere, Aubrey, *Recollections* (London, Edward Arnold, 1897), p. 332.

down the stairs. 'There goes Moore like a gay butterfly,' observed Rogers, 'just alighting on me for a moment, then flying away to somebody else.' " [22]

Compared with their friends, FitzGerald and Tennyson were as unfettered as vagabonds; and together they idled away many days in London. Frequent and long were their discussions of poetry as they sat with lighted pipes in Charlotte Street or Mornington Crescent lodgings. Bookstalls, auction rooms, and art galleries, or merely the activity of the streets, provided entertainment for them when they ventured abroad. Once they took the river-boat to Gravesend, one of FitzGerald's favorite diversions when in town. On the way Tennyson posed for a silhouette-cutter. The result, FitzGerald observed, "though not inaccurate of outline, gave one the idea of a respectable Apprentice." [23]

Often they planned journeys farther afield—to Stratford, to Wales, to Tintagil—but they could never manage to slip their moorings at the same time. Tennyson always found it difficult to launch on a trip, though he meditated many. "Alfred Tennyson has reappeared," Spedding informed John Allen about this time, "and is going today or tomorrow to Florence, or to Killarney, or to Madeira or to some place where some ship is going—he does not know where." Sometimes the poet even bade his friends good-by on the eve of departure, only to turn up the following day with the casual explanation that he had decided not to go. FitzGerald once wrote, also to Allen, "Alfred Tennyson was to have gone with me to the coast, but I have not the least idea where he is now abiding; and if he wrote to fix, he would not do it. One can only rely on Chance for meeting with him." [24] FitzGerald was unaware of the humor of his complaint. In planning trips he was as irresolute as the poet, and he was just as difficult to pin to an engagement. Spedding said that his being *bound* to an engagement served merely to make FitzGerald wish to break it.

It was actually by accident that the two friends made their most noteworthy excursion together. In June, 1840, Tennyson went to Warwick. By luck he had his glass in his eye as the coach approached the town, and he caught sight of FitzGerald walking toward Leamington. He hailed his friend, who returned to town on the coach and persuaded the poet to stay with him at the "George." The inn

22. Spalding diary, March 8, 1868.

23. FitzGerald pasted the silhouette in his copy of Tennyson's *Poems, Chiefly Lyrical*, which is now in Trinity College Library.

24. MS. letter to Allen, July 4, 1845.

was expensive and Tennyson learned with misgivings that the family was in residence at the castle, which meant that it could not be viewed until Saturday. Nevertheless, he remained. The day after his arrival the two went to Kenilworth and "tumbled" about the ruins for three hours. One evening after dinner they strolled down the street skirting the grim walls of Warwick Castle, passed the massive gates, and finally wandered onto the bridge over the Avon. The old fortress loomed above them "grand and black" in the fading light. Rooks cawed, a nightingale sang, and from somewhere came the musical splashing of a waterfall. On Saturday they wandered about the castle gardens, climbed Guy's Tower, and finally went through the castle itself, dividing their admiration as best they could between the portraits and the view from the gallery overlooking the valley toward Eton.

From Warwick they went to Stratford and visited the Shakespeare shrines. In the room where the dramatist was born, Tennyson "was seized with a sort of enthusiasm" and added his name to the hundreds already scribbled on the walls. Afterward, he admitted, he was "a little ashamed of it." They crossed the fields to Shottery by the footpath, climbing stiles, passing behind the ancient manor house, before the row of thatch-roofed dwellings at the Quineys, and finally reached Anne Hathaway's cottage. It was the route which Shakespeare often had followed; and of all that FitzGerald saw at Stratford, the footpath impressed him most.

During these years Tennyson was writing constantly but publishing rarely. His 1832 volume had been universally condemned; and a virulent criticism by John Lockhart in the *Quarterly Review* of April, 1833, had drowned the music of his poetry in a roar of derisive laughter. "Alfred Tennyson is still more laughed at than wept over," the *Oxford Magazine* stated the following year. For ten years he contributed only an occasional poem to some annual or periodical. Edward Moxon, his publisher, proposed a new book; friends begged him to publish; but Tennyson shrank from drawing again the fire of his critics.

FitzGerald was one of the most persistent pleaders and was directly responsible for the poet's finally breaking his silence in 1842. He had heard some of the new poems read from manuscript at Mirehouse in 1835 and had since watched the number increase. In 1839 he told Barton, "I want A. T. to publish another volume: as all his friends do . . . but he is too lazy and wayward to put his hand to the business. He has got fine things in the large Butcher's

Account Book that now lies in my room." [25] He persisted in his entreaties until, in 1841, Tennyson protested, "You bore me about my book; so does a letter just received from America, threatening, tho' in the civilest terms, that, if I will not publish in England, they will do it for me in that land of freemen. Damn! I *may* curse, knowing what they will bring forth. But I don't care." [26] FitzGerald was jubilant in October when Edgeworth wrote to him that Tennyson was busy preparing for the press. The poet was not as busy as reported, however, for six months later he had still not approached his publisher. FitzGerald then took matters into his own hands. "Alfred Tennyson suddenly appeared in town today," he told Barton on March 2. "I carried him off to the auction: and then with violence to Moxon: who is to call on him tomorrow, and settle the publishing of a new volume."

FitzGerald's new method proved effective. Fifteen days later the two were busy preparing the manuscript for the press. The work was done in Spedding's rooms, which Tennyson was occupying, for "Jem" was in the United States with the Ashburton Commission at the time. "The poems were written," FitzGerald told Barton, "in A. T.'s very fine hand . . . toward one side of the large page; the unoccupied edges and corners being often stript down for pipelights, taking care to save the MS., as A. T. once seriously observed." One by one the pages were torn from the "Butcher's Book," corrected, and sent to the printer. They were later thrown into the fire, with the exception of a few which FitzGerald saved and presented to Trinity College in 1861.

"Poor Tennyson has got home some of his proof sheets," he said on March 17, "and, now that his verses are in hard print, thinks them detestable. There is much I had always told him of—his great fault of being too full and complicated—which he now sees, or fancies he sees, and wishes he had never been persuaded to print. But with all his faults, he will publish such a volume as has not been published since the time of Keats: and which, once published, will never be suffered to die. This is my prophecy: for I live before Posterity."

When the poems appeared in May, FitzGerald wrote to Pollock,

I agree with you quite about the skipping-rope,[27] etc. . . . Alfred,

25. Letter to Barton, Nov. 25, 1839.
26. Tennyson MS. letter, 1841.
27. A puerile rhyme included in the volume. Tennyson omitted it from later editions.

whatever he may think, cannot trifle—many are the disputes we have had about his powers of badinage, compliment, waltzing, etc. His smile is rather a grim one. I am glad the book is come out, though I grieve for the insertion of these little things, on which reviewers and dull readers will fix; so that the right appreciation of the book will be retarded a dozen years.[28]

FitzGerald was only partly correct in his predictions. The immediate sale of the poems, although not phenomenal, was satisfactory; and the reviews were favorable. The edition firmly established Tennyson's reputation as the foremost poet in England and laid the foundations of a popularity which eventually developed into idolatry. His success, however, was clouded by misfortunes which befell him in another venture.

While living at High Beech, he had made the acquaintance of Dr. Matthew Allen, a physician who had established a lunatic asylum near by.[29] The doctor was a pioneer in the treatment of insanity by vocational training, and the poet became so interested in these theories that he spent a few days at the asylum to observe the methods practiced. Had the physician confined himself to psychiatry, he would have spared Tennyson considerable anguish and unhappiness. However, he was also an inventor of sorts and had devised a wood-carving machine which he hoped to put into operation on a large scale. Naturally, he needed money to finance his "Patent Decorative Carving and Sculpture Company." Tennyson became enthusiastic about the project, believing that carved paneling and furniture would be produced so cheaply that it could be bought by the masses. The demand would become so great, he thought, that work would be given to the unemployed and fortunes would be made by the investors. The latter could take their profits and at the same time consider themselves philanthropists. Tennyson plunged a legacy of £500 and the proceeds of the sale of a small farm into the company and persuaded other members of his family to invest also. Dr. Allen reported to him in November, 1841, "Yesterday it was the decided opinion of my Bankers and Solicitors that in twelve months your share would be worth Ten thousand Pounds, and that in five years it ought to give you that yearly." [30] In a little more than a year, however, the project collapsed and the

28. Letter to Frederick Pollock, May 22, 1842.

29. It was in Dr. Allen's asylum that John Clare, the rustic poet of Helpstone, was first confined.

30. Schonfield, H. J., *Letters to Frederick Tennyson* (London, Hogarth Press, 1930), p. 55.

Tennysons lost every penny that they had staked. The poet was plunged into despair, "I have drunk one of those most bitter draughts out of the cup of life," he said, "which go near to make men hate the world they move in." [31]

Tennyson became a hypochondriac and resorted to hydropathy to cure his ills, real or imaginary. In December, 1843, FitzGerald declared that he had "never seen him so hopeless." The poet wrote to him from Cheltenham shortly afterward:

It is very kind of you to think of such a poor forlorn body as myself. The perpetual panic and horror of the last two years had steeped my nerves in poison: now I am left a beggar but I am or shall be shortly somewhat better off in nerves. I am in an Hydropathy Establishment near Cheltenham. . . . I have had four criseses (one larger than had been seen for two or three years in Grafenberg—indeed I believe the largest but one that has been seen. Much poison has come out of me, which no physic ever would have brought to light . . . I have been here already upward of two months. Of all the uncomfortable ways of living sure an hydropathical is the worst: no reading by candlelight, no going near a fire, no tea, no coffee, perpetual wet sheet and cold bath and alternation from hot to cold: however I have much faith in it.

My dear Fitz . . . I went thro' Hell. Thank you for inquiring after me. I am such a poor devil now I am afraid I shall very rarely see you, no more trips to London and living in lodgings, hard penury and battle with my lot [sic]. . . . You are the only one of my friends who has asked after me and I really feel obliged to you.[32]

Tennyson's fears of poverty and banishment from London and his friends happily proved groundless. Edmund Lushington, his brother-in-law, insured Dr. Allen's life for the poet, who thereby recovered part of his capital when the physician died in 1845. The following year Tennyson was granted an annual pension of £200 by the government in recognition of his talents. Until the death of the doctor, however, his prospects were decidedly dark. A comment of Carlyle's in a letter to FitzGerald in 1844, therefore, is significant. The historian said that Tennyson had spent a day with him, and continued, "He said of you that you were a man from whom one could accept money; which was a proud saying; which you ought to bless heaven for." [33] Thirty years later the historian told Charles Eliot Norton, one of FitzGerald's American friends, that for many years "in Tennyson's poor days" FitzGerald gave the poet

31. Tennyson, *Memoir*, I, 221.
32. Tennyson MS. letter, Feb. 2, 1844.
33. Wilson, D. A., *Carlyle on Cromwell and Others* (New York, E. P. Dutton & Co., 1925), p. 271.

£300 a year.[34] Carlyle was nearly eighty when he talked with Norton, and his "many years" is probably an exaggeration. Nevertheless, the evidence is sufficiently strong for one to conclude that the poet availed himself of the offer which FitzGerald had made after their Mirehouse visit and accepted money to tide him over his lean years.

Tennyson found it easier to recover from his financial difficulties than from the neurotic state into which he had fallen. He became a valetudinarian and from 1844 to 1848, with the possible exception of 1845, spent many weeks each year taking water cures at Cheltenham, Birmingham, and Malvern. FitzGerald attributed the poet's afflictions to "hereditary tenderness of nerve" and excessive smoking, and once spoke of Tennyson's "ruining himself by mismanagement and neglect of all kinds. He must smoke twelve hours out of the twenty-four." In 1848 FitzGerald said prophetically, albeit inelegantly, "Tennyson is emerged half-cured, or half-destroyed, from a water establishment: has gone to a new Doctor who gives him iron pills; and altogether this really great man thinks more about his bowels and nerves than about the Laureate wreath he was born to inherit." [35] Two years later Tennyson was appointed Poet Laureate.

FitzGerald was convinced that his friend's preoccupation with nerves, water cures, and pills had a deleterious effect on his poetry. The 1842 volumes, he frequently declared, contained "the last of old Alfred's best," a remark dismissed as "another of Fitz's crotchets." Critics have often interpreted the statement as signifying that FitzGerald approved of all that Tennyson wrote before 1842 and condemned everything which he wrote thereafter. That is not true. When the 1842 poems appeared, he said, for example, "It is a pity he did not publish the new volume separately. The other will drag it down. And why reprint the Merman, the Mermaid, and those everlasting Eleanores, Isabels,—which were, and are, and must be, a nuisance. . . . Every woman thinks herself the original of one of that stupid Gallery of Beauties." [36] It is true that FitzGerald's criticism after 1842 was preponderantly adverse, and Tennyson's partisans have resented the frankness and severity of his strictures. These qualities were by no means confined to his judgments of Tennyson's works. He was always uncompromising in criticism, sparing neither himself, friend, nor stranger. "Then Trench is

34. *Letters of Charles Eliot Norton* (London, Constable & Co., 1913), I, 465. 2 vols. Sara Norton and M. A. D. Howe, eds.
35. Letter to Cowell, November, 1848.
36. Letter to Pollock [1842].

coming out!" he told Barton while Tennyson was preparing to publish in 1842, "such wonders is this Spring to call forth. Milnes talks of a popular edition of his poems!—poor devil, as if he could make one by any act of typography." [37]

He watched the progress of Tennyson's work during the remainder of the 'forties without enthusiasm. In June, 1845, he mentioned that the poet had written two hundred lines of a new poem in a butcher's book. This, beyond doubt, was *The Princess,* for which FitzGerald never cared. The work was finished in May, 1848. While Tennyson was reading three books of it to him one evening, FitzGerald, tired with "hacking" about London all day, fell asleep. He thought it monotonous and said that Tennyson's "old fault of talking big on a common matter" was too apparent.[38] His weariness, FitzGerald granted, may have been responsible for the reaction; and, he added, "I may be fast growing out of my poetical age." Nevertheless, when the poem was published later in the year his opinion was unchanged; and he was considered, "a great heretic" for abusing the work. It appeared to him, he said, "a wretched waste of power at a time of life when a man ought to be doing his best; and I feel almost hopeless about Alfred now." Nor did he like the lyrics which Tennyson wrote later "to be stuck between the cantos," because none possessed "the old champagne flavor." As soon as *The Princess* was published, Tennyson began the *Idylls of the King,* for he had long considered basing a poem on the legends of Arthur. FitzGerald, again, was unenthusiastic. "How are we to expect heroic poems from a valetudinary?" he asked; and he urged Tennyson to "fly from England and go among savages."

The same note of regret echoes through FitzGerald's comments on *In Memoriam.* Tennyson had been writing poems commemorating his friendship with Hallam ever since the latter's death in 1833. "A. T. has near a volume of poems—elegiac—in memory of Arthur Hallam," FitzGerald told Donne in January, 1845. "Don't you think the world wants other notes than elegiac now? . . . But Spedding praises: and I suppose the elegiacs will see daylight, public daylight, one day." When the poem appeared in 1850, he said that it was "full of the finest things, but it is monotonous, and has the air of being evolved by a Poetical Machine of the highest order." [39] It would, he feared, "raise a host of Elegiac scribblers."

37. Letter to Barton, March 2, 1842.
38. MS. letter to Cowell [May 8, 1847].
39. Letter to F. Tennyson, Dec. 31, 1850.

FitzGerald's estimate of Tennyson at this time is summed up in his remark to the poet's brother Frederick, "He is the same magnanimous, kindly, delightful fellow as ever; uttering by far the finest prose sayings of any one."

Although FitzGerald was severe in his adverse criticism, he never failed to acknowledge merits which met his standards of poetic values. After reading *Gareth and Lynette* upon its publication in 1873, he re-read the earlier *Idylls* to discover if he had misjudged them. The review, however, confirmed his opinions. "I don't think it is mere perversity that makes me like it better than all its predecessors, save and except (of course) the old 'Morte,' " he told the poet. ". . . I do not know if I admire more *separate* passages in this 'Idyll' than in the others; for I have admired *many* in all."

FitzGerald's later criticism was based on definite convictions. After 1842, he maintained, Tennyson became "more artist than poet," became lost in "coterie worship" and "London adulation," for which Mrs. Tennyson was partly to blame. "She is a graceful lady," he admitted, "but I think that she and other aesthetic and hysterical Ladies have hurt A. T." He believed, moreover, that the poet lived too much within a narrow subjective world and failed to throw himself open to the influences of the world of action about him. "This was the way to write well," he asserted, after reading the passage in which Thucydides describes the fall of Amphipolis, "and this was the way to make literature respectable. Oh, Alfred Tennyson, could you but have the luck to be put to such employment! No man would do it better; a more heroic figure to head the defenders of his country could not be." [40] And later he wrote, "When Tennyson was telling me of how the Quarterly abused him (humorously too) . . . I thought that if he had lived an active Life, as Scott and Shakespeare; or even ridden, shot, drunk, and played the Devil, as Byron, he would have done much more, and talked about it much less." [41] Finally, FitzGerald believed that Tennyson had missed his objective as England's poet. In 1851, when lamenting, as he frequently did, the general decay into which he believed the country had fallen, he exclaimed,

If one could save the Race, what a Cause it would be: not for one's own glory as a member of it, nor even for its glory as a Nation: but because it is the only spot in Europe where Freedom keeps her place. Had I Alfred's voice, I would not have mumbled for years over *In Memoriam*

40. Letter to Cowell, Jan. 25, 1848.
41. Letter to Fanny Kemble, Oct. 24, 1876.

and the *Princess,* but sung such strains as would have revived the Μαραθωνομάχονς ἄνδρας to guard the territory they had won.[42]

Nevertheless, FitzGerald was convinced that Tennyson was the greatest poet of his time, and he jealously defended his friend against anyone who challenged the title. He was particularly scornful of Browning's claims. "To compare Browning with my 'paltry Poet,' " he said in 1870, "is, I say, to compare an old Jew's Curiosity Shop with the Phidian Marbles." [43] He had no more use for the Pre-Raphaelites than for Browning. "When I look at the *Athenaeum,*" he said, "I see there are at least four poets scarce inferior to Dante, Shakespeare, etc., Browning, Morris, D. G. Rossetti, Miss Do." [44]

FitzGerald never doubted that Tennyson had climbed high on Parnassus. His regret was that his friend failed to reach the height won by the triad: Chaucer, Shakespeare, and Milton.

While observing the struggles of Tennyson and Thackeray for a place in the sun during the late 'thirties, FitzGerald was watching more objectively, but with marked interest, the efforts of another and older man to obtain literary recognition in London. In 1833, at the age of thirty-eight, Thomas Carlyle had left his native Scotland to settle in Cheyne Row, Chelsea, and had since been causing a sensation with a succession of strange books. Each new publication furnished FitzGerald and his London companions with topics for animated discussions. "We are all reading Carlyle's *Miscellanies,*" he once told Barton, "some abusing; some praising: I among the latter." On the whole, however, FitzGerald was not at first favorably impressed either by the man or his works. In 1838 he suffered from an attack of influenza which "put a wet blanket" over his brains. "This state of head," he declared, "has not been improved by trying to get through a new book much in fashion— Carlyle's *French Revolution*—written in a German style. An Englishman writes of French Revolutions in a German style. People say the book is deep: but it appears to me that the meaning *seems* deep from lying under mystical language." [45]

FitzGerald attended Carlyle's lectures on "Heroes and Hero Worship" in 1840 and recorded later that the Scotsman "looked very handsome then, with his black hair, fine Eyes, and a sort of

42. Letter to F. Tennyson, December, 1851.
43. MS. letter to A. Tennyson, January, 1870.
44. "Miss Do." is Miss *Ditto.*
45. Letter to Barton, April, 1838.

crucified Expression." However, when the lectures were published
the following year, he branded the volume as "perfectly insane"
and asked Thompson, "Have you read poor Carlyle's raving book
about Heroes? Of course you have, or I would ask you to buy my
copy. I don't like to live with it in the house. It smoulders." To
Pollock he wrote that Carlyle was becoming obnoxious as he became popular. Despite such strictures, FitzGerald at heart was
attracted to the author. "I stumbled upon a Review by Carlyle on
some German Memoirs of a certain Rahel von Ense, in the Westminster, which touched me as all his writings do," he had remarked
to Donne in 1839. "I suppose one day I shall be converted to be a
furious admirer of his French Revolution. All this time I think
Carlyle is a one-sided man; but I like him because he pulls one the
opposite side to which all the world are pulling one." [46]

On September 15, 1842, Samuel Laurence, who had painted the
Scotsman's portrait, took FitzGerald to Cheyne Row. It was a
happy meeting. Carlyle was writing on Cromwell at the time and in
May had gone to Naseby with Thomas Arnold to identify the battlefield from contemporary accounts. This he had done to his own
satisfaction. FitzGerald, who knew the field well, discovered that
Carlyle had walked over "what was not the field of Battle," but
had been misled by an obelisk which FitzGerald's parents had set
up on their estate to commemorate the struggle. Assuming that
the monument indicated where the principal fighting had taken
place, the historian charted all the military positions from that
point. When FitzGerald told him that the obelisk simply marked
the highest elevation on the field, Carlyle was reluctant to believe
that he and Dr. Arnold had erred. His notes, he protested, were
"actual *facts,* gathered with industry from some seven or eight eye-
witnesses, looking at the business with their own eyes from seven or
eight different sides . . . and that no 'theory' by what Professor
soever, can be of any use to me in comparison." [47] FitzGerald, who
had just come from Naseby and expected to return in a day or two,
offered to inquire into the matter. He invited Carlyle to go with
him, but the historian thought "it would be too expensive." He
gave FitzGerald a list of positions which he wished to locate, including "a windmill . . . probably some 300 yards to the west of
where the ass of a column now stands."

On his return to Naseby FitzGerald set laborers to work digging
at various spots where tradition held that the main action had

46. *Donne and His Friends,* p. 49.
47. Letter from Carlyle, Sept. 18, 1842.

taken place. Meanwhile, he "trotted about," drawing sketches of the field, questioning natives, and answering as many of Carlyle's questions as he could. On the evening of the fourth day, one of the laborers reported that he had discovered bones.

"Tomorrow I will select a neat specimen or two," FitzGerald told Barton,

In the mean time let the full harvest moon wonder at them as they lie turned up after lying hid 2400 revolutions of hers. Think of that warm 14th of June when the Battle was fought, and they fell pell-mell: and then the country people came and buried them so shallow that the stench was terrible, and the putrid matter oozed over the ground for several yards: so that the cattle was observed to eat those places very close for some years after.[48]

The following day he continued his letter:

We have dug at a place, as I said, and made such a trench as would hold a dozen fellows: whose remains positively make up the mould. The bones nearly all rotted away, except the teeth which are quite good. At the bottom lay the *form* of a perfect skeleton: most of the bones gone, but the pressure distinct in the clay: the thigh and leg bones yet extant: the skull a little pushed forward, as if there were scanty room . . . Two farmers insisted on going out exploring with me all day: one a very solid fellow, who talks like the justices in Shakespeare: but who certainly was inspired in finding out this grave: the other a Scotchman full of intelligence, who proposed the flesh-soil for manure for turnips.[49]

Carlyle was delighted with the discoveries:
"You will do me and the Genius of History a real favour, if you persist in these examinations and excavations," he replied to Fitz-Gerald's first report,

. . . Clearly enough you are upon the very battle-ground;—and I, it is also clear, have only looked up towards it from the slope of Mill Hill . . . The opening of that burial-heap blazes strangely in my thoughts: these are the very jaw-bones that were clenched together in deadly rage, on this very ground, 197 years ago! It brings the matter home to one, with a strange veracity . . . I will beg for a tooth and a bullet; authenticated by your own eyes and word of honour! Our Scotch friend, too, making turnip manure of it, he is part of the Picture . . . Honour to thrift. If of 5000 wasted men, you can make a few usable turnips, why, do it! . . . But why does the Obelisk stand there? It might as well stand at Charing Cross: the blockhead that it is![50]

48. Letter to Barton, Sept. 22, 1842.
49. *Ibid.*, Sept. 23, 1842.
50. Letter from Carlyle, Sept. [24], 1842.

FitzGerald sent a second report with additional sketches and enclosed in the packet some teeth and a shinbone.

"There is a horrible impressiveness in these jaw-teeth," Carlyle replied,

To think that this grinder chewed its breakfast on the 14th of June, 1645, and had no more eating to do in the world, or services further there—till now, to lie in my drawer, and be a horror! For one thing, I wish you would not open any more mounds till I can be there too: it would have been worth a longer journey to see those poor packed skeletons: that "last of the batch" (or *first*-buried, I suppose he must have been) lying flat on his back; and that one lying across the rest, jammed in, as you describe! Pray explain *him* a little better: was he atop, near the middle, or where? . . . I want no more bones, shin or other . . . I trust in Heaven it was not you or any of your Ancestors that put it [the obelisk] up! . . . Let some charitable mortal clap an index hand upon it, at least, and write "Yonder"! [51]

Then, and many times thereafter, Carlyle was inclined to join FitzGerald at Naseby; but he never did. Once rain deterred him. For the rest—"had I the wings of an eagle, most likely I should still fly to you . . . but with railways and tub-gigs, and my talent for insomnolence, and fretting myself to fiddlestrings with all terrestrial locomotion whatsoever—alas, alas!" [52]

FitzGerald's efforts on behalf of Carlyle and his *Cromwell* did not end with his "bone-rummaging," as he called the Naseby exploits. Before the book appeared, he helped the historian a number of times, drawing sketches, gathering data, and enlisting the help of his friends, the Charlesworths of Bramford, in obtaining information about Cromwell's Lincolnshire campaigns. In 1845 Carlyle told FitzGerald that he expected the book to be published in October. "You should actually raise a stone over that Grave that you opened," he urged. "(I will give you the *shinbone* back and keep the *teeth*): you really should,—with a simple Inscription saying merely in business English: 'Here, as proved by strict and not too impious examination, lie the slain of the Battle of Naseby. Dig no farther. E. FitzGerald,—1843.' By the bye, was it 1843 or 2, when we did those Naseby feats?" [53] There is something humorously typical in Carlyle's use of *we*. The stone was not then set up, and twenty-five years later the two were still fussing over the project.

51. Carlyle MS. letter, Sept. 29, 1842.
52. Letter from Carlyle, Sept. 18, 1842.
53. *Ibid.*, April 8, 1846.

It is not easy to make friends with men of the Carlyle type. Strong-willed and overbearing, they have few points between approval and scorn on the scale by which they judge their fellows. The help which FitzGerald gave the historian, however, led to a lifelong friendship. He became a frequent and welcome visitor in Cheyne Row, sometimes going by himself, at other times in the company of Thackeray, Tennyson, Spedding, or Laurence. Mrs. Carlyle did not at first like him. A day that he spent at Chelsea in March, 1843, did little to endear him to her. He and Thackeray were guests at dinner. Although Mrs. Carlyle was not feeling well, she baked a mutton pie and a raspberry tart. She got through dinner without mishap, she told her sister, and hoped to get through tea; after which, she promised herself, she would go to bed. Just before tea was served, however, her "affairs reached a consummation." She fainted and was carried to bed where she lay for three hours alternating between fainting and retching, while her maid "blubbered" over her. In the meantime Carlyle's guests had been joined by Spedding and John Robertson, a "burly" Scotch journalist with a boisterous laugh. Carlyle took them into a room adjoining his wife's. He was in fine fettle; it was a jolly evening—for the men. They laughed and "raged" in one room, while Mrs. Carlyle suffered in the next. "Oh, I assure you I have not passed such an evening for a good while," she complained to her sister.[54] Not for several years could she wholeheartedly welcome FitzGerald to her home. He called one evening in 1849 with Thackeray. "FitzGerald has lost a good deal of his high colour and was very good and rational," she wrote. "I got to like him." [55]

When season and weather permitted, Carlyle entertained his guests in the garden where clay pipes, stuck into crevices of the wall, awaited those who smoked. Sometimes he took intimate friends to a small den at the top of the house.[56] To this retreat Fitz-Gerald and his host mounted one spring evening in 1844. "The window was open," FitzGerald recorded, "and looked out on nursery gardens, their almond trees in blossom, and beyond, bare walls and houses, and over these, roofs and chimneys, and roofs and chimneys and here and there a steeple, and whole London crowned with darkness gathering behind like the illimitable resources of a

54. Huxley, Leonard, *Jane Welsh Carlyle* (Garden City, Doubleday Page & Co., 1924), p. 102.

55. *Ibid.*, p. 333.

56. Not the famous soundproof room, which Carlyle never liked. That was not yet constructed.

dream." [57] He tried to persuade Carlyle to leave "filthy Chelsea," but the Scot replied that his wife liked London.

At times Carlyle smoked and chatted companionably. Often, however, he was sunk in gloom over the state of England and would then subject his guests to long tirades on the Corn Laws, prison reform, the woeful condition of the poor, or "governments of Jackasserie." He was a victim of dyspepsia and insomnia; and when his nerves were not wracked by one, they were frayed by the other. It was FitzGerald's opinion that Carlyle's attacks of sleeplessness came from "having a great idea which, germinating once in the mind, grows like a tapeworm and consumes the vitals. What a nasty idea!" He spent one evening with Carlyle when his host, he said, "lectured on without intermission for three hours: was very eloquent, looked very handsome: and I was very glad to get away." On another evening, "very dull somehow," FitzGerald again left without regret. "An organ was playing a polka even so late in the street," he related, "and Carlyle was rather amazed to see me polka down the pavement. He shut his street door—to which he always accompanies you—with a kind of groan." [58] Once in 1846 he met the historian at Tennyson's rooms "and they two," he complained,

discussed the merits of this world and the next, till I wished myself out of *this,* at any rate. Carlyle gets more wild, savage, and unreasonable every day; and, I do believe, will turn mad. "What is the use of ever so many rows of stupid, fetid, animals in cauliflower wigs and clean lawn sleeves—calling themselves Bishops—Bishops, I say, of the Devil— not of God—obscene creatures, parading between men's eyes and the eternal light of Heaven," etc. etc. This, with much abstruser nonconformity for two whole hours! And even as it was yesterday, so shall it be tomorrow, and the day after that.[59]

FitzGerald was awed neither by Carlyle's reputation nor by his Juggernaut style of argument. When the "sage" blasted him with his volubility, he remained silent or countered with honest opinions. "I told Carlyle," he said in 1845, "that the more I read of Cromwell the more I was forced to agree with the verdict of the world about him. Carlyle only grunted and sent forth a prodigious blast of tobacco smoke. He smokes indignantly." [60] Though he

57. Letter to Barton, April 11, 1844.
58. *Ibid.,* Jan. 11, 1845.
59. *Ibid.,* May 4, 1846.
60. *Ibid.,* Aug. 15, 1845.

tired sometimes of the Scot's gloomy outlook on men and affairs, FitzGerald rarely went to London without calling at Cheyne Row.

He summed up his opinion of Carlyle and his works after the appearance of the *Latter-Day Pamphlets* in 1850. "They make the world laugh," he said, "and his friends rather sorry for him. But that is because people will still look for practical measures from him: one must be content with him as a great satirist who can make us feel when we are wrong though he cannot set us right. There is a bottom of truth in Carlyle's wildest rhapsodies." [61]

FitzGerald often asserted during the 'forties that if it were not for his friends there, he would rarely go to London. "One finds few in London *serious* men: I mean *serious* even in fun: with a true purpose and character whatsoever it may be," he explained to Frederick Tennyson. "London melts away all individuality into a common lump of cleverness. I am amazed at the humour and worth and noble feeling in the country, however much railroads have mixed us up with metropolitan civilization. I can still find the heart of England beating healthily down here, though no one will believe it." [62] At a party of "modern wits" one night, he felt like crawling inside himself. Although no paragon, he said, the wickedness of London appalled him.

As the decade advanced, he became more and more conscious of the ugliness of the city with its "damn'd smutty atmosphere," and increasingly aware of the charms of Suffolk. When in town he longed to dip into the country if only to rub his hands in the cool dew of the pastures or to sit upon the banks of the "dear old Deben with the worthy collier sloop going forth into the wide world as the sun sinks." And once, while writing to Barton, a cloud came over Charlotte Street and seemed "as if it were sailing softly on the April wind to fall in a blessed shower upon the lilac buds and thirsty anemones somewhere in Essex; or, who knows?, perhaps at Boulge. Out will run Mrs. Faiers, and with red arms and face of woe haul in the struggling windows of the cottage, and make all tight. Beauty Bob will cast a bird's eye out at the shower, and bless the useful wet. Mr. Loder will observe to the farmer for whom he is doing up a dozen of Queen's Heads,[63] that it will be of great use: and the farmer will agree that his young barleys wanted it much. The German Ocean will dimple with innumerable pin points.

61. Letter to F. Tennyson, April 17, 1850.
62. *Ibid.*, May 24, 1844.
63. A common writing paper.

and porpoises rolling near the surface sneeze with unusual pellets of fresh water." [64]

London lost much of its attraction for FitzGerald as most of his older friends gradually abandoned the city. In the meantime his roots were striking deeper at Boulge, and he formed new friends and developed new interests in Suffolk.

64. Letter to Barton, April 11, 1844.

X

The Cowells

'Ah, happy Days! When shall we Three meet again!"
Preface to *Salámán and Absál*

In 1835, when FitzGerald was twenty-six years old, he wrote a significant letter to Thackeray from Wherstead:

. . . and now, my dear Boy, do you be very sensible, and tell me one thing—think of it in your bed, and over your cigar, and for a whole week, and then send me word directly—shall I marry?—I vow to the Lord that I am upon the brink of saying "Miss—do you think you could marry me?" to a plain, sensible, girl, without a farthing! There now you have it. The pro's and con's are innumerable, and not to be consulted. . . . A'nt I in a bad way? Do you not see that I am far gone? I should be as poor as a rat, and live in a windy tenement in these parts, giving tea to acquaintances. I shall lose all my bachelor trips to London and Cambridge, I should no more, oh never more!—have the merry chance of rattling over to see thee, old Will, in Paris, or at Constantinople, at my will. I should be tied down. These are to be thought of: but then I get a settled home, a good companion, and the other usual pro's that desperate people talk of. Now write me word quickly: lest the deed be done! To be sure, there is one thing: I think it is extremely probable that the girl wouldn't have me: for her parents are very strict in religion, and look upon me as something of a Pagan. When I think of it, I know what your decision will be—No! How you would hate to stay with me and my spouse, dining off a mutton chop, and a draught of sour, thin, beer, in a clay-cold country. You would despair. You would forsake me. If I know anything of myself, no imp would ever turn me against you: besides, I think no person that I should like would be apt to dislike you: for I must have a woman of some humour lurking about her somewhere: humour half hidden under modesty. But enough of these things—[1]

Thackeray was already a man of considerable experience in affairs of the heart. In Weimar, he told his mother, he had fallen in love several times—with Mina, with Amelia, with Dorothea. He tumbled from Dorothea's graces when he fell from her arms while

1. MS. letter to Thackeray, July, 1835.

dancing at a ball. A fourth, unnamed charmer deserted him for a young guardsman with magnificent waistcoats and ten thousand pounds a year. It would not have been surprising, after these experiences, if Thackeray had advised FitzGerald that love was naught. His reply may have dampened, but did not quench, FitzGerald's ardor. A few months afterward the latter wrote ecstatically to John Allen:

I have just returned from a dance round my room to the tune of Sir Roger de Coverley, which I dare say you never heard. . . . Here we are all wading through mire, owing to the heavy rains: but I dance and sing merrily. Now you must know that there has been staying here for a fortnight the young damsel I have often told you about: & I like her more than ever. She has shown sense and clear sightedness in some matters that have made me wonder: judging by the rest of the world. Yet have I not committed myself—no, my Johnny, I am still a true Bachelor. What do you think of me? You would like this woman very much, I am sure. She is very pious, but very rational ("poor FitzGerald!" say you internally . . .) she is healthy, and stout, and a good walker, and a gardener, and fond of the country, and thinks everything beautiful, and can jump over stiles with the nimblest modesty that ever was seen. Item, eats very little meat—humph!—drinks no wine—understands good housekeeping—understands children (ill-omened consolation!)—ay, there's the rub. Should I dance round my room to the tune of Sir Roger de Coverley if I were married, and had seven children? Answer me that.[2]

Whether FitzGerald's rapture actually reached the pitch of genuine love is a question. Even in his rhapsodic letter to Allen, he had not been able to ignore possible consequences of marriage, disturbing to a man with celibate leanings. Practical considerations asserted themselves even more forcefully when he wrote to Donne ten months later, "I am ashamed of living in such Epicurean ease: and really think I ought to marry, or open a book at a Banker's, that I may not be more happy than my fellows. Seriously, I do not mean to speak disrespectfully of marriage etc., but I only mean that it must bring some cares, and anxieties. However, don't divulge what I say: for it sounds pert and awkward."[3] Perhaps FitzGerald refused to sacrifice his bachelor freedom. Whatever his reasons, he never declared his love to the young lady who could "jump over stiles with the nimblest modesty that was ever seen." As yet, he had not revealed her name. By 1837 he had apparently abandoned all thoughts of marriage, for he wrote to Allen that he

2. MS. letter to Allen [Feb. 4, 1836].

3. *A FitzGerald Friendship, Letters to W. B. Donne* (New York, William Rudge, 1932), p. 6. N. C. Hannay and Mrs. C. B. Johnson, eds.

intended to settle in Suffolk and wrap himself round with the affection of relatives and friends.

Among FitzGerald's Suffolk friends was the family of the Reverend John Charlesworth, rector of Flowton, near Ipswich. It was possibly at the Charlesworth home at Bramford that he first met Edward Byles Cowell, who later induced him to study Spanish and Persian. Cowell, a scholar by inclination, was a "merchant and maltster" of Ipswich by force of circumstance. He possessed a keen mind and a remarkable memory. At school he had revealed an insatiable hunger for languages, which the prescribed study of Latin, Greek, and French failed to satisfy. With the help of Major W. B. Hockley,[4] a retired officer of the Indian army who lived in Ipswich, he studied Persian. At the time of his father's death in 1842, Cowell, then only sixteen years of age, had been compelled to leave the Ipswich Grammar School and take over the family business. Abandoning his formal education, he applied himself to his uncongenial vocation, but found time to extend his knowledge of languages to Spanish, Italian, old Norse, and various dialects, and to resume Sanskrit, which he had found too difficult as a schoolboy. Although barely nineteen when he first met FitzGerald, probably early in 1845, he had already established a modest reputation as an Oriental scholar through translations from Persian poetry contributed to magazines. Admiration for Cowell's intellectual powers and indefatigable industry, no doubt, first attracted FitzGerald to him.

Cowell met Elizabeth Charlesworth, the younger daughter of the Flowton rector, in 1843. Cowell was then seventeen years old; Elizabeth thirty-one. Two years later their engagement was announced. Their courtship was original, to say the least, for the young suitor undertook to teach Sanskrit to his *fiancée* by correspondence. Elizabeth was a woman of strong will and keen intellect. She wrote verse and in 1839 had published some of her work under the title, *Historical Reveries by a Suffolk Villager*.[5] There is a tradition in the Cowell family that, when the young man told FitzGerald of his intention to marry, the latter exclaimed, "The deuce you are! Why, you have taken my Lady!"[6] There is no reason

4. FitzGerald was also acquainted with Major Hockley, and he may have first met Cowell at the Major's house.

5. Published by G. W. Fuller of Sudbury, Suffolk.

6. Cowell biography, p. 41.

Thomas Wright states in his biography that FitzGerald fell in love with Caroline Crabbe, daughter of the Bredfield vicar (I, 139) and that she refused his offer of mar-to doubt that FitzGerald made the remark at some time, for he subsequently revealed that Elizabeth, who was much nearer his age than Cowell's, was indeed the young lady who had stirred his heart almost ten years before. She had long been intimate with his sisters and visited them frequently, both at Wherstead and at Boulge. The truth is, however, that FitzGerald first learned of the engagement in a letter from Cowell, to which he replied, "I have received both your letters; for which I ought to thank you, written on such an occasion. You are a happy man and — — —" [7] Three words have been torn from the letter, but enough of the script remains to read "I envy you." The words themselves are innocent enough; their deletion is significant. Another remark which FitzGerald added as a postscript has also been torn from the letter.

The Cowells were married in October, 1847, and moved into a cottage at Bramford which the Charlesworths had formerly occupied.[8] FitzGerald was a frequent visitor. For many years he nursed his secret "passion," permitting it at times to sink into adolescent sentimentality. Mrs. Cowell may have suspected the regard in which she was held by her friend, but the easy companionship which he maintained with the couple is sufficient evidence that he never openly revealed his old attachment. That he felt a tenderness for Mrs. Cowell—a tenderness revived and intensified, no doubt, by her removal beyond his reach—is revealed by many passages in his letters, superficially ingenuous, but significant in the light of other evidence.

"It will be a great pleasure to me to do all I can for your poems," he wrote to her in 1851 from London when she proposed to publish a new volume of her verse.[9]

. . . You talk of having all Suffolk about you. I think you should spare me a bit of Bramford. What shall it be? Enclosed with your poems you shall send either one of Cowell's *slippers*—which I used to wear for him —or a little piece of green ribbon cut into a leaf pattern which I remember you used to wear this time last year. Yes, send me that, a memorial

riage (I, 163). I have found no evidence whatever of any such attachment, and John Loder of Woodbridge wrote to Aldis Wright in 1905, ". . . about the engagement of Miss Crabbe. There is an old lady living *here now*—who was ladies' maid to the girls —if anyone knew of a love affair between any of them and E. F. G.—who more likely than this person? She declares there was nothing of the kind, although E. F. G. was often 'in and out and about.' " MS. letter Trinity College Library.

7. MS. letter to Cowell [1845].

8. Mr. Charlesworth had been appointed to the living of St. Mildred's, Bread Street, London, in 1843.

9. Mrs. Cowell did not publish at this time. In 1892 Seeley & Co. of London published her *Leaves of Memory*.

of the past, and that (elderly knight as I am) I may be encouraged to venture on my critical labours with something like the scarf of fair Lady as a guerdon. This suggestion, begun but half earnestly, really is the one I will abide by in good earnest. Send me this.[10]

It was perhaps purely by chance that Mrs. Cowell tied her poems with a ribbon that she had worn, FitzGerald recalled, "when the snow-drops were coming out under your windows in Bramford this time last year." [11] At another time when FitzGerald was forced to decline an invitation to the home of the Cowells, he wrote, "But, in order that I may contribute something to the entertainment I commend you to wear that famous (and Papistical-looking) purple silk gown—seeing how I love all purples and lilacs."

FitzGerald was not so reticent in letters to some of his older friends. In 1852 he wrote to Thackeray, "I used to send you lots of my own wretched verses, I think:—now I will send you some scraps of no great power—of no pretension at all—but yet with a spangle of pure stuff in them, I think: made years ago by the little Suffolk woman you visited at Oxford—who would have been my Poetry if I had had wit enough." [12] Two selections from poems written by Elizabeth Cowell are included in the letter.[13] Fitz-Gerald's restrained criticism is indicative of his partiality for Elizabeth. Her poems are decidedly inferior, and ordinarily he was not lenient with mediocre verse. To Frederick Spalding, a friend of his later years, FitzGerald frankly referred to Mrs. Cowell as his "old Flame." [14]

After FitzGerald's death in 1883, a number of poems in manuscript were found among his effects. One of these, the translation of a sonnet from Petrarch, Cowell identified as having been written by FitzGerald about 1851 or 1852.

> If it be destined that my Life, from thine
> Divided, yet with thine shall linger on
> Till, in the later twilight of Decline,
> I may behold those Eyes, their lustre gone;
> When the gold tresses that enrich thy brow
> Shall all be faded into silver-gray,

10. Letter to Mrs. Cowell [February, 1851].
11. MS. letter to Mrs. Cowell [Feb. 17, 1851].
12. MS. letter to Thackeray, Nov. 15, 1852.
13. One of these selections, beginning "The Winter Skies are tinged with Crimson Still," is quoted on p. 144. These lines are identified as his wife's by Cowell on p. 308 of his biography. The second consists of five stanzas of "The Old Parsonage," which appears in Mrs. Cowell's volume, Leaves of Memory.
14. Spalding diary, Sept. 23, 1867.

From which the wreaths that well bedeck them now
    For many a Summer shall have fall'n away:
Then should I dare to whisper in your ears
    The pent-up Passion of so long ago,
That Love which hath survived the wreck of years
    Hath little else to pray for, or bestow,
Thou wilt not to the broken heart deny
The boon of one too-late relenting Sigh.

In the meantime Cowell was exerting an ever-increasing influence on FitzGerald. Immediately after their first meeting, they began a prolific correspondence in which they exchanged scholarly criticisms of books they were reading. At one time they carried on what Mrs. Cowell described as "the hottest correspondence" in Latin. As early as 1846 Cowell sent FitzGerald passages translated from Persian poetry. It is interesting to note that FitzGerald's interest in that literature at the time was entirely passive. "Your Hafiz is fine," he observed, "and his tavern world is a sad and just idea. . . . It would be a good work to give us some of the good things of Hafiz and the Persians; of bulbuls and ghuls we have had enough."

In his first letters, FitzGerald adopted the tone of an older man writing to a younger, an attitude which he soon dropped. Of Cowell he said, "He ought to do something in the world; for, as far as I can see, his delicacy of discrimination is as great as his capacity for amassing—a rare combination." [15] The young scholar was no less impressed by FitzGerald's capacities. "He is a man of *real* power," he told his mother, "one such as we seldom meet with in the world. There is something so very *solid* and *stately* about him, a kind of slumbering giant, or silent Vesuvius. It is only at times that the eruption comes, but when it does come, it overwhelms you." [16]

During FitzGerald's visits to Bramford, the two men read the classics, particularly Greek drama and history. FitzGerald derived added pleasure from these studies because of the light which the younger man threw on them through his exact scholarship and more varied reading. Cowell's eager enthusiasm vitalized FitzGerald's passive interest. Spurred on by the younger man's example and encouragement, and aided by him, FitzGerald extended his interests to new fields. In August, 1850, he told Frederick Tennyson that he had "begun to nibble at Spanish: at their old Ballads;

15. *A FitzGerald Friendship*, p. 17.
16. Cowell biography, pp. 59–60.

which are fine things . . . I have also bounced through a play of Calderon." [17]

The beauty and quiet of Bramford valley, the happy family life of his friends, the intellectual stimulus which he derived from the Cowells, and his fondness for them all contributed to make Bramford, for FitzGerald, an Arden in Suffolk. He would have been content to have his friends stay there forever. Elizabeth, however, had other plans. She was justly proud of the reputation her young husband was establishing as a scholar. Moreover, she was ambitious and realized that he was capable of greater things than managing an Ipswich business. Originally she had wished him to prepare for the church, but he had progressed too far in his Eastern studies to abandon them; and she resigned herself to his becoming an Oriental scholar. When, in 1849, his younger brother, Charles, was old enough to take charge of the office, Elizabeth proposed that her husband should resume his formal education by matriculating at Oxford. Cowell at first shrank from the prospect. It was no light thing to forsake business for the uncertain livelihood of a scholar. Nor did he relish becoming a married student of twenty-six among youths in their teens. Lastly, he doubted his preparation and abilities. But his wife possessed determination and had set her heart on the Oxford plan. She enlisted the help of George Kitchin, a schoolboy friend of her husband's, who, in 1850, capped a brilliant career at Oxford by taking a double first in mathematics and classics. Together they beat down Cowell's objections and painstakingly established his confidence. He finally decided to matriculate in November, 1850, and go into residence the following term.

FitzGerald was grieved at the prospect of his friends' deserting Bramford, but he appears not to have opposed the plan at first. Less than a fortnight before Cowell was to matriculate, however, FitzGerald visited Donne, who was then living at Bury St. Edmunds. Donne thought the project unwise and easily won Fitz-Gerald to his view. The latter bombarded Cowell with a barrage of letters packed with arguments advanced by Donne, to which, no doubt, he added some of his own. The young man's hard-won resolution began to crumble. His wife was in despair. She wrote frantically to Kitchin.

And now for my story of trouble, all through my own wretched fault! Edward has always told me not to talk of his going to Oxford, but the time drew so near, and it seemed so certain, that I asked him if I might send word by E. F. G. to Mr. Donne, who, being a great scholar, I

17. The play was *El Mágico Prodigioso*.

thought would rejoice in it, feeling a kind interest for Edward. *Par malheur* he has taken up very strongly and impressed E. F. G. with it, the idea that all is done and given at Oxford by favour, etc., all Edward could hope for, and that he had far better try for something (of all *nonsense* to talk!) in the wretched Scotch or London Universities. This is never to be thought of. . . . But the mischief of it is that to prove their point they so *distort* College life, in the dreadfully long letters E. F. G. is rousing up his languid energies to send us, that Edward, who was just beginning, to my heartfelt thankfulness to *rise* to the occasion, and really feel the fitness of his tastes and energies for the career before him, is now almost wholly turned back again.[18]

She also begged FitzGerald to stop writing, "but *quite* in vain; it only brought on fresh arguments."

FitzGerald's greatest fears were that Cowell would be compelled to forego Persian and Sanskrit for the prescribed curriculum at Oxford. Rather than make that sacrifice, he protested, it would be preferable to continue independent study. He urged Cowell to join him and Donne at Bury to reason the matter out. "If he does that," Mrs. Cowell told Kitchin, "I fear, but for God's help, the mischief will be *done!* And that *I* should have done it! whose hope and dream has been his Oxford career! . . . But we must act, not weep." [19] She used all of her wiles to keep her husband at home. She even persuaded him not to reply to FitzGerald's proposal. She outlined for Kitchin arguments which she considered most potent in counteracting those advanced by FitzGerald, and suggested that he write "a long affectionate letter appealing more to his heart than his head."

The battle raged for several days. Fast relays of letters passed between the antagonists. Cowell asked his wife if she had "fairly represented FitzGerald and Mr. Donne" to Kitchin. "Perhaps not," she confided to her ally, "but . . . they . . . were acting according to their *own* view like true friends, and are both really men of the highest principle, as far as *man* can be, who doubts if Scripture be altogether the highest guide . . . but they are men *totally* incapable of appreciating Edward's higher qualities." [20] FitzGerald himself appears to have suspected Mrs. Cowell's methods. "I had begun to suppose," he wrote, "your wife had forbid you to write to me, for fear of my bad communications corrupting your good designs. You both so far misunderstood me that I had no desire to

18. Cowell biography, p. 90.
19. *Ibid.*, p. 90.
20. *Ibid.*, p. 92.

stop your Oxford plans for good and all, but only to advise you to consult so capable a man as Donne before you decided." [21] Finally, Mrs. Cowell, in her more strategic position, supported by timely dispatches from Kitchin, routed her enemies. Cowell's resolution was restored, and he matriculated as he had planned.

The Cowells went to Oxford in January, 1851. There, Fitz-Gerald continued to visit them, though not so often as he had at Bramford. Oxford could never replace the little Suffolk village, which, in his memory, always retained an aura of pastoral beauty. "Ah, happy Days!" he wrote in his preface to *Salámán and Absál*, his first Persian translation.

When shall we three meet again—when dip in that unreturning Tide of Time and Circumstance!—In those Meadows far from the World, it seemed, as Salámán's Island—before an Iron Railway broke the Heart of that Happy Valley whose Gossip was the Millwheel, and Visitors the Summer Airs that momentarily ruffled the sleepy Stream that turned it as they chased one another over to lose themselves in Whispers in the Copse beyond. Or returning—I suppose you remember whose lines they are—[22]

> When Winter Skies were tinged with Crimson still
> Where Thornbush nestles on the quiet hill,
> And the live Amber round the setting Sun,
> Lighting the Labourer home whose Work is done,
> Burn'd like a Golden Angel-ground above
> The solitary Home of Peace and Love—

at such an hour drawing home together for a fireside Night of it with Aeschylus or Calderon in the Cottage, whose walls, modest almost as those of the Poor who clustered—and with good reason—round, make to my Eyes the Towered Crown of Oxford hanging in the Horizon, and with all Honour won, but a dingy Vapour in Comparison.

21. MS. letter to Cowell, Nov. 22, 1850.
22. Mrs. Cowell's, with minor changes by FitzGerald.

XI

"*A Very Lazy Fellow*"

"You know how little I think of my verses. I never wrote
more than twenty good ones in my life."

Letter to Cowell

FITZGERALD is usually described as an intellectual vagabond who spent his liberal allowance of time with reck-
less prodigality. He has himself to blame for the reputation. "I am a very lazy fellow, who do [*sic*] nothing," he
once told Donne, "and this I have been doing in different places
ever since I saw you last." His letters are filled with passages in
which he disparages his interests, activities, and capacities. His
descriptions of himself are caricatures which have been accepted
as portraits. He was far from being the idler he led his friends and
posterity to believe.

Standing at a high desk, for FitzGerald always stood to work, he
spent his mornings at Boulge reading, writing, translating. Although he regretted his imperfect knowledge of foreign tongues,
he insisted upon reading as much as possible in the original. "I can
get at the broad sense," he said while reading Herodotus, "but all
the delicacies (in which so much of the beauty and character of
an author lie) escape me sadly. The more I read, the more I feel
this." He had acquired his knowledge of Latin, Greek, and French
at school. He later mastered Spanish and Persian with Cowell's
help. In Italian, which he began in 1833, and German, begun in
1854, he was self-taught.

It is illuminating to observe the extent of his reading in the
classics alone as revealed by references in his letters during a few
years selected at random. In January, 1837, Aristophanes made him
laugh heartily, but by April the dramatist was "nearly drained:
that is, for the present first reading," and he turned to Plutarch
and Theocritus. In August, 1838, he read Pindar, for whom he did
not much care. The following spring he enjoyed Tacitus; in October was sorry to have finished the *Iliad*. During the summer of 1840
he found Herodotus "the most interesting of all Historians," and

at the close of 1841 he began Livy. This list contains only those authors whom FitzGerald mentioned specifically between 1837 and 1841, but by no means exhausts his reading, even in ancient literatures, during that period. After meeting Cowell, his study of the classics became more extensive. A complete record of the books which he read would form a fairly comprehensive catalogue of ancient and modern literature.

Two or three particular enthusiasms should be noted. His love for Shakespeare was perennial, and in 1834 he bought the Second and Third Folios because "one had need of a big book to remember him by." Scott was another of his favorites. But he did not, by any means, confine his reading in English literature to popular authors. He early exhausted the works of the great English divines who, he thought, "will hereafter be considered our Classics—in Prose, I mean." In 1833 he bought a pamphlet, "very difficult to get," he told Donne, "called The Songs of Innocence, written and adorned with drawings by W. Blake (if you know his name) who was quite mad, but of a madness that was really the elements of great genius ill-assorted: in fact, a genius with a screw loose, as we used to say." In 1837 he stumbled across the poems of "a Poet named Vaughan. Do you know him?" he asked Allen. ". . . He seems to have great fancy and fervour and some deep thought. Yet many of the things are in the tricksy spirit of that time."

FitzGerald kept abreast of contemporary literature in periodicals as well as books. "Then there's an account of Hallam's Literature," [1] he wrote in 1841 after reading a number of the *British and Foreign Review,* "with a deal about *Aesthetics* in it. Oh, Pollock! let you and I [*sic*] and Spedding stand out against these damnable German humbugs." [2] A few months later he wrote "graphically" to Donne, "As to old Niebuhr, it is mean to attack old legends that can't defend themselves." [3]

Like Tennyson, Fitzgerald was profoundly impressed by the revelations of geology in the works of Sir Charles Lyell. In an early letter to Cowell, he said, "The present day teems with new discoveries *in Fact,* which are greater, even as regards the Soul and prospect of Men, than all the disquisitions and quiddities of the Schoolmen. A few fossil bones in clay and limestone have opened a

1. Henry Hallam, *Introduction to the Literature of Europe in the Fifteenth, Sixteenth, and Seventeenth Centuries* (1837–39).
2. MS. letter to Pollock [1841].
3. MS. letter to Donne [1842].

greater vista back into Time than the Indian imagination ventured upon for its Gods: and every day turns up something new." [4]
Two years later he commented, again to Cowell:

I often think, it is not the poetical imagination, but bare Science that
every day more and more unrolls a greater Epic than the Iliad; the
history of the World, the infinitudes of Space and Time! I never take up
a book of Geology or Astronomy but this strikes me. And when we
think that Man must go on to discover in the same plodding way, one
fancies that the Poet of to-day may as well fold his hands, or turn them
to dig and delve, considering how soon the march of discovery will distance all his imaginations, [and] dissolve the language in which they
are uttered. . . . Lyell in his book about America, says that the falls of
Niagara, if (as seems certain) they have worked their way back south-
wards for seven miles, must have taken over 35,000 years to do so, at the
rate of something over a foot a year! . . . And those very soft strata
which the Cataract now erodes contain evidences of a race of animals,
and of the action of seas washing over them, long before Niagara came
to have a distinct current; and the rocks were compounded ages and
ages before those strata! . . . It is not only that this vision of Time must
wither the Poet's hope of immortality; but it is in itself more wonderful
than all the conceptions of Dante and Milton. [5]

Although he constantly dismissed his reading as being of little
worth, it was not superficial. In 1838 he bought the *Biographie
Universelle,* in fifty-three volumes, because "nothing is more pleasant than, when some name crosses one, to go and get acquainted
with the owner." His leisure enabled him to weigh and assimilate,
as few readers have the opportunity of doing. "If you must needs,
however," he said in his first letter to Cowell, "exhaust your eyes
over books which are now pushed back in the shelves that others
may stand more conveniently for use before them, mind you make
extracts of what there *is* good, either in thought or expression. And
then we will keep that, and push the books further back, out of
sight if possible. . . . Keep a good Commonplace book." [6]

This was FitzGerald's own method. He developed what might be
called an "editorial mind" and probably edited mentally, if not
actually, every book he read. He frequently maintained that he had
no skill at original composition, but that he did have a knack for
discovering what was best in the works of others and for presenting
it in an entertaining form. He filled innumerable scrapbooks with
extracts from his reading, with translations, with clippings, with

4. MS. letter to Cowell, Jan. 28 [1845].
5. Letter to Cowell [1847].
6. MS. letter to Cowell, Jan. 28 [1845].

articles from magazines, with prints.[7] Scissors and paste, he said, were his "Harp and Lute." At the time of his death his library contained many volumes which he had revised to suit his taste. He cut down books to one half or one third of their original length and bound them with others which he had treated similarly. Works of two and three volumes he reduced to one. Sometimes he wrote in a paragraph to supply the context of a deletion. Here and there he added marginal notes.

Dickens was one of the first victims of FitzGerald's editorial zeal. While visiting at Geldestone in 1844, he extracted from the *Old Curiosity Shop* the narrative of Little Nell's travels, which he called a "Nelly-ad, or Homeric narration of the child's wanderings." The abstract was made for one of his nieces. "Children," he declared, "do not understand how merriment should intrude in a serious matter. This might make a nice child's book, cutting out Boz's sham pathos, as well as the real fun." [8]

Another book which FitzGerald edited was a volume of *Selden's Table Talk*.[9] He crossed out selections, replaced some with quotations from other sources, and added numerous footnotes explaining allusions. *The Table Talk of John Selden, Esq.*, edited by S. W. Singer, was published in 1847.[10] At the head of his annotations Mr. Singer stated, "Part of the following Illustrations were kindly communicated to the Editor by a gentleman to whom his best thanks are due, and whom it would have afforded him great pleasure to be allowed to name." Aldis Wright, FitzGerald's editor, after comparing Mr. Singer's edition with FitzGerald's copy of the *Table Talk,* stated, "It might have been said with truth that the 'greater part' of the illustrations were contributed by the same anonymous benefactor, who was, I have very little doubt, Fitz-Gerald himself." FitzGerald's annotations, he maintained, "are almost literally reproduced in the Notes to Singer's edition." [11]

FitzGerald, however, did not devote all his working hours to editorial labors. While reading Lucretius in 1848, he sent a free translation "of a fine bit" to Cowell, who urged him to continue the work; but FitzGerald replied that the poet "never could become naturalized in England. . . . so dry is two-thirds of him

7. Nine of these are now in the Christchurch Mansion Museum at Ipswich. There are several in the library at Trinity College, Cambridge, and others have passed into the hands of private owners.

8. This abstract has been published in *A FitzGerald Medley* (Methuen & Co., London, 1933). Charles Ganz, ed.

9. Selden, John, 1584–1654.

10. Published by William Pickering, London.

11. *Letters*, I, 264.

. . . I suppose I could translate a good part of it very fairly:—but the *great bits,* which alone keep alive Lucretius to most men would require a great poet to render." [12] At the same time FitzGerald sent Cowell a translation in blank verse of Lucius Aemilius Paulus' speech to the Roman people after the defeat of Perseus, King of Macedonia.[13] The victorious general, who returned to Rome in triumph only to lose his two sons by death, compares himself with the victim of his conquests, "Two notorious monuments . . . of human instability." The passage closes with the mournful plaint:

> And Paulus is the last of all his Name.

At a later date FitzGerald also converted into blank verse a letter by Sir Charles Napier recording his reflections after his victory at the battle of Meeanee. The poem ends:

> I was running on
> With all that was to be, when suddenly,
> My name was call'd; the glass was fill'd; all rose;
> And, as they pledged me cheer on cheer, the Cannon
> Roar'd it abroad, with each successive burst
> Of Thunder lighting up the banks now dark
> If Indus, which at Inundation-height,
> Beside the Tent we revell'd in roll'd down
> Audibly growling—"But a hand-breadth higher,
> And whose the Land you boast as all your own!"

In 1868 FitzGerald submitted the two selections to *Macmillan's Magazine* under the title, "The Two Generals"; but they were rejected. He subsequently printed them privately, and they were eventually included in his collected works.

He dismissed his occasional verse lightly. "I never do write poetry now," he had told Thackeray in 1831 and immediately contradicted himself by composing two poems [14] which he included in his letter. Many of his lyrics were circulated in manuscript among his Suffolk friends. He avoided, it appears, sending them to his more sophisticated intimates in London. One poem, "Bredfield Hall," was written during the late 'thirties. The lines "are not original," he explained to Mrs. Cowell in 1851, "which is saying, they are not worth anything. They may possess sense, fancy, etc., but . . . you see, all *moulded* rather by Tennyson than *growing* spontaneously from my own mind. No doubt there is original feeling

12. MS. letter to Cowell, June 5 [1848].
13. Livy XIV, 41.
14. See pp. 69–73.

too; but . . . it takes an alien form. . . . The lines which still affect me as the good ones are . . .

> O'er the solemn woods that bound thee
> Ancient sunsets seem to die.[15]

Another of his poems of this period, little more than a rhyme, to be sure, was "Chronomoros," written for Lucy Barton, to be presented with a clock which she once gave to her father as a Christmas gift.

> Wearied with hearing folks cry,
> That Time would incessantly fly,
> Said I to myself, "I don't see
> Why Time should not wait upon me;
> I will not be carried away
> Whether I like it or nay":
>   But ere I go on with my strain,
>   Pray turn me that hour-glass again!

The poet tries to arrest time, first by loading it heavily, then by leaving it "with nothing to carry away."

> Then I cried, in a rage, "Time *shall* stand!"
> The hour-glass I smash'd with my hand,
> My watch into atoms I broke
> And the sun-dial hid with a cloak!
> "Now," I shouted aloud, "Time is done!"
> When suddenly, down went the Sun;
>   And I found to my cost and my pain,
>   I might buy a new hour-glass again!

The poem, which consists of ten stanzas, is unpolished; but the thought is ingeniously developed. Although the verses appeared anonymously in *Fulcher's Poetical Miscellany* [16] in 1841, it is unlikely that FitzGerald submitted them, for they hardly meet his standards of publishable verse. Barton was a regular contributor to Fulcher's publication, the *Sudbury Pocket Book;* and it is most likely that the Quaker was responsible for their appearance.

How much random verse FitzGerald wrote will never be known. When, in 1842, Barton urged him to write more and to publish, FitzGerald replied,

As to my doing anything else in that way, I know that I could write volume after volume as well as others of the mob of gentlemen who

15. MS. letter to Mrs. Cowell [Feb. 17, 1851].
16. Published by G. W. Fulcher, Sudbury, and Suttaby & Co., London, 1841.

write with ease; but I think unless a man can do better, he had best not do at all; I have not the strong inward call, nor cruel-sweet pangs of parturition, that prove the birth of anything bigger than a mouse.

In 1849 he told Cowell, "You know how little I think of my verses. I never wrote more than twenty good ones in my life."

The occasional verse which has come down to us reveals that FitzGerald had a genuine lyric gift which he used sparingly. It is possible that an unsympathetic attitude adopted by his family toward his literary efforts was partly responsible. He was once disturbed to learn that Barton had read one of his poems to his mother. "When I rate you (as you call it)," he told Barton in 1842, "about showing my verses, letters, etc., you know in what spirit I rate you: thanking you all the time for your generous intention of praising me. It would be very hard, and not desirable, to make you understand why my Mama need not have heard the verses: but it is a very little matter: so no more of it."

In the preface to FitzGerald's *Letters and Literary Remains* appears a statement by one of his friends: "He [FitzGerald] was not a great, but he was a good composer." Among his papers in Trinity College Library are eighteen musical compositions in various stages of completion. He set to music poems by Tennyson, Byron, Samuel Rogers, James Hogg, and others. Some, on the other hand, are his own verses. One, with the superscription "Knowest Thou an Isle? (A Northern Mignon) E. F. G.," reads:

> Knowest thou an Isle whose snow-white Walls ascending,
>   Strike as a Star across the purple Wave:
> Whose Sons her ancient Liberty defending,
>   Wise are to counsel as in Battle brave?
> That is the Land where living I would be,
> And, dying, my Beloved, rest with Thee!
>
> Knowest thou a Vale that in that Island nestles,
>   Where Poplars sigh beside a winding Stream:
> Husht into Silence while the Ploughman whistles,
>   Over the golden Upland with his Team?
> That is the Vale where living I would be,
> And, dying, my Beloved, rest with Thee!
>
> Knowest thou some Home a lowly Roof concealing
>   Far from the World within that Vale of Rest:
> Whose slender smoke above the tree-top stealing,

Softly recalls the Wand'rer to his nest?
That is the Home where living I would be,
And, dying, my Beloved, rest with Thee! [17]

The description in the poem closely parallels passages in Fitz-
Gerald's letters which describe Bramford.[18]

A modern student of music described FitzGerald's compositions
as "dated" and said they contained structural weaknesses which
might easily have been corrected. A composer, contemporary with
FitzGerald, was apparently of the same opinion. "You may tell
Mr. Hullah,[19] if you like," FitzGerald wrote to Laurence from
Boulge in 1849, "that in spite of his contempt for my music, I was
very much pleased with a duett of his I chanced to see—'O that we
two were maying'—and which I bought and have forced two ladies
here to take pains to learn. They would sing nicely if they had
voices and were taught." Composing music was merely one of
FitzGerald's many diversions. Although he printed and distributed
some of his songs, none appear to have been published.

17. Trinity College MS. In a letter written to George Crabbe, Jr., in 1851, Fitz-
Gerald said, "I wish you could send me those two alterations which Causton proposed
for the last bar but one of "Knowest Thou an Isle?"

18. Cowell wrote to Aldis Wright in 1887 that his wife thought "the verse beginning
'Know'st thou a village?' refers to our old village Bramford, and its little spire which
rises in the middle of the valley as E. F. G. knew that valley and spire so well."
Cowell biography, p. 304.

19. Hullah, John P. (1812–84), well-known composer and teacher of vocal music.
Prominent in London for his work in choral singing.

XII

Early Works

With them the seed of Wisdom did I sow,
And with mine own hand wrought to make it grow . . .
                                        The Rubáiyát

ON February 19, 1849, after a brief illness, Bernard Barton died at the age of sixty-five. His physician had warned him that his heart was weak, but Barton concerned himself little with possible consequences. Only five days before his death, in a letter to a friend, he complained of shortness of breath and added, "But if the hairs of one's head are numbered, so, by a parity of reasoning, are the puffs of our bellows." FitzGerald attended the funeral and afterward wrote to Cowell, "What solemnity there was at the grave was lost when we got into the Meeting: when three or four very dull but good people spoke in a way that would have been ludicrous but that one saw they were in earnest. At the grave, Mr. Shewell [1] said some few appropriate words; but he began to *sing* when once he was in the Chapel." FitzGerald contributed an obituary and a brief funeral notice to the *Ipswich Journal*.

Barton's daughter, Lucy, decided to issue a volume of his poems and letters; and FitzGerald, at her request, undertook to prepare the manuscript. His "editorial mind" immediately went into action. "I have . . . selected," he wrote to Donne,

what will fill about 200 pages of print—as I suppose—really all the best part out of *nine volumes!* Some of the poems I take entire—some half—some only a few stanzas, and these dovetailed together—with a change of a word, or even of a line here and there, to give them logic and fluency. . . . I am sure I have distilled many pretty little poems out of long dull ones which the world has discarded. I do not pretend to be a poet: but I have faculty enough to mend some of B. B.'s dropped stitches, though I really could not make any whole poem so good as many of his. As a matter of *Art,* I have no doubt whatsoever I am right:

1. A wealthy Quaker who lived at Ipswich.

whether I am right in *morals* to use a dead man so I am not so certain. Tell me candidly what you think of this. I only desire to do a good little job for his memory, and make a presentable book for Miss B.'s profit. . . . I do nothing without Miss B.'s approbation.[2]

FitzGerald persuaded Miss Barton to be named on the title page as editor.

A year before his death Barton had considered writing his memoirs. "Write your biography if you will," FitzGerald replied, when the poet asked his advice, "but think twice before you publish it." The Quaker abandoned the plan, and FitzGerald thereby became his first biographer. Miss Barton shrank from writing the sketch of her father's life which she proposed as a preface to the volume, and FitzGerald agreed to do it. His "Memoir of Bernard Barton," written in his characteristically lucid, rhythmic prose, was the result. The sketch, brightened by delicate humor, is remarkable for its candor. The author glossed no faults; yet gave praise where praise could honestly be given.

The book was published by subscription in the autumn of 1849.[3] While working on it, FitzGerald was also active in obtaining subscribers. He and his family took about fifty copies. George Crabbe took twelve, Spedding, ten; and Thackeray, Carlyle, and others of FitzGerald's friends were among the purchasers.

Working constantly among his books at Boulge, editing the poems of Barton, associating with men who were establishing literary reputations, FitzGerald slowly gravitated toward publication. *Euphranor, A Dialogue on Youth,* published in 1851, was his first book. Written in the form of a Platonic dialogue, *Euphranor* is a criticism of the English system of education of that day. The author charged the schools, first, with neglecting to develop the youth of England physically, and, second, with failing to provide practical training.

FitzGerald, when passing through Cambridge on his journeys between Boulge and the home of W. K. Browne at Bedford, was not favorably impressed by the generations which had succeeded his own at the University. In 1839 he wrote that "the hard-reading,

2. *A FitzGerald Friendship,* pp. 28–29.
3. The book was printed by Charles Childs of Bungay, Suffolk, near Beccles, who had been recommended by Carlyle. This was FitzGerald's first association with Childs, who was to print most of his works. Hall, Virtue & Co., London, the publishers of the book, issued a trade edition in 1853.

pale, dwindled students walking along the Observatory road [4] looked as if they were only fit to have their necks wrung." The undergraduates suffered, in his opinion, by contrast with Browne, who had not attended a university, but had grown to manhood, athletic, alert, and interested in both books and men. For Fitz-Gerald, Browne typified the ideal Briton, a gentleman in the broader sense of the word, one whose interest in books was balanced by participation in business, the affairs of his community, and outdoor life. FitzGerald seems gradually to have attributed the one-sided intellectual development of himself and his university friends to the system of education, and to have concluded that the panacea lay in less formal and more practical education of the type Browne had received. [5]

Each journey to Cambridge brought the contrast more sharply to his attention. Each visit made the evils of the system weigh more heavily on his mind. In October, 1846, he spent several days "in the same rooms in which I sat as a smooth-chinned Freshman twenty years ago." The same prints still hung on the walls; and, in that familiar environment, the ideas which he had been turning over in his mind for years crystallized. Returning to Boulge, he set about "to do something as far as I could against a training system of which I had seen many bad effects."

The dialogue in *Euphranor* is carried on by FitzGerald, in the character of a physician practicing in Cambridge, and four students: Euphranor, an alert, though bookish, graduate student; Lexilogus, a typical, hard-reading honors man; Lycion, an idle, though intelligent, undergraduate; and Phidippus, who represents Browne, good-natured, kindly, intelligent, equally at ease among the sporting element or the scholars.

"I was roused one fine forenoon in May," said the doctor,

by the sound of someone coming up my staircase. . . . then, directly after, a smart rapping at my door; and before I could say, "Come in," Euphranor had opened it, and, striding up to me, seized my arm with his usual eagerness, and told me I must go out with him—It was such a day—sun shining—breeze blowing—hedges and trees in full leaf.

4. This passage (*Letters*, I, 71) reads, ". . . students working along the Observatory road," which I assume FitzGerald wrote in error or that *working* was inadvertently substituted for *walking* by editor or printer.

5. FitzGerald gave a copy of *Euphranor* to Browne, in which he wrote at the time of the latter's death in 1859, "This little book would never have been written, had I not known my dear friend William Browne, who, unconsciously, supplied the moral." Wright, *FitzGerald*, I, 327.

. . . In three minutes we had run downstairs. . . . We struck out briskly for the old Wooden Bridge, where Euphranor said his boat was lying.

On the way to the river they persuaded Lexilogus to join them. They found their boat in the Backs. At Magdalene they threaded their way through the closely packed barges, which were the principal means of transporting heavy freight to Cambridge in the days before the railroad, passed through the locks, pulled three or four miles down the river and back again to the ferry, where they left their boat and crossed the fields to Chesterton. At the Three Tuns Inn, all the billiard tables were in use, "but one, as usual, would be at our service before long." Ale was ordered and quaffed "in one of those little arbours cut into the Lilac bushes round the Bowling-green." Conversation about books, particularly Kenelm Digby's *Godefridus,* and the problem of education engaged them until it was too late to return to Cambridge in time for hall. They ordered dinner at the inn; and, being joined by Phidippus and Lycion, went into

the little Parlour, very airy and pleasant, with its windows opening on the bowling-green, the table laid with a clean white cloth, and upon that a dish of smoking beef-steak, . . . For some time the clatter of knife and fork, and the pouring of ale, went on, mix'd with some conversation . . . about College matters: till Lycion began to tell us of a gay Ball he had lately been at, and of the Families there.

Dinner finished, a song or two was sung; then the friends returned to the bowling green where they engaged in a few bouts until "the shadows lengthen'd along the grass" and they "agreed it was time to be gone." A race was being rowed that afternoon.

We walk'd along the fields by the Church . . . cross'd the Ferry, and mingled with the crowd upon the opposite shore; Townsmen and Gownsmen, with the tassell'd Fellow-commoner sprinkled here and there—Reading men and Sporting men—Fellows, and even Masters of College, not indifferent to the prowess of their respective Crews—all these, conversing on all sorts of topics, from the slang in Bell's *Life* to the last new German Revelation, and moving in everchanging groups down the shore of the river, at whose farther bend was a little knot of Ladies gathered upon a green knoll faced and illuminated by the beams of the setting sun. Beyond which point was at length heard some indistinct shouting, which gradually increased, until "They are off—they are coming!" suspended other conversation among ourselves; and suddenly the head of the first boat turn'd the corner; and then another close upon it; and then a third; the crews pulling with all their might compacted into perfect rhythm; and the crowd on shore turning round to follow along with them waving hats and caps, and cheering, "Bravo, St. John's!" "Go it, Trinity!"—the high crest and blowing forelock of Phidippus's mare, and he himself shouting encouragement to his crew, conspicuous over all, until the boats reaching us, we also were caught up in the returning tide of spectators, and hurried back toward the goal; where we arrived just in time to see the Ensign of Trinity lowered from its pride of place, and the Eagle of St. John's soaring there instead. Then, waiting a little while to hear how the winner had won, and the loser lost, and watching Phidippus engaged in eager conversation with his defeated brethren, I took Euphranor and Lexilogus under either arm, (Lycion having got into better company elsewhere) and walk'd home with them across the meadow leading to the town, whither the dusky troops of Gownsmen with all their confused voices seem'd as it were evaporating in the twilight, while a Nightingale began to be heard among the flowering Chestnuts of Jesus.

The burden of the dialogue, maintained for the most part by Euphranor and the doctor, is a eulogy of youth, with its spontaneous enthusiasms and high ideals. Youth and Chivalry, the doctor maintains, are synonymous; he defines them, in the words of Kenelm Digby, as "that General Spirit or state of mind, which disposes men to Heroic and Generous actions; and keeps them conversant with all that is Beautiful and Sublime in the Intellectual and Moral world." The doctor criticizes English schools, maintaining that, "if they do not 'sacrifice the Living Man to the Dead Languages,' dissipate him among the Fine Arts, Music, Poetry, Painting, and the like." The physical development of a country's youth, he protests, is as great a responsibility of the educational system as the intellectual; and he recommends that physical exercise, military drill, and manual training be included in the school program. "And only think," he adds, "if . . . there were, besides the Playground, a piece of Arable to *work in*—perhaps at a daily wage of provender according to the work done—what illumination might some young Lycion receive, as to the condition of the Poor, 'unquenchable by logic and statistics,' says Carlyle, 'when he comes, as Duke of Logwood, to legislate in Parliament.' " Preparation of this kind, combined with intellectual training, the doctor maintains, would produce a man "sufficiently accoutered for the campaign of ordinary Life. . . . At any rate, he will be sufficiently qualified, not only to shoot the Pheasant and hunt the Fox, but even to sit on the Bench of Magistrates—or even of Parliament—not unprovided with a quotation or two from Horace or Virgil." To clinch his argument, the doctor observes that "neither Yeomanry Drill—nor daily Plough—drove the Muse out of Burns," and he points to Chaucer and Shakespeare as other examples of well-rounded men.

Although FitzGerald began the dialogue in 1846, intending to publish it, the manuscript lay in his study more than four years because, he wrote, "Puseyism and Catholicism were ascendant, and I would not help even by a f——t to fill their sails." In November, 1850, a visit to Cambridge revived his interest in the subject, and on his return to Boulge he "licked" his dialogue "into a sort of shape." After printing it at his own expense, he turned the edition over to William Pickering of London, who appears on the title page as publisher. Until going to press, FitzGerald called the dialogue *Phidippus*. The title was changed, apparently, because Euphranor, who resembles the author, had almost crowded Phidippus out of the discussion.

FitzGerald was very much in earnest about the message in *Euphranor*. "I have it [at] heart the Book should be read," he told Cowell, "drop though it be to sprinkle on the wide world! It is all I can say: I will do what I can to make others hear it. But I know well—were it really a fine thing, done by Plato himself, it would *do* nothing—people would read and admire,—and not practise. The current of a declining nation's history is too strong." [6] The dialogue was reviewed favorably in most of the leading periodicals. [7] At the end of February FitzGerald said that "its sale does not stand still."

While working on *Euphranor*, he had written to Cowell that it was "not easy to keep in good dialectic, and yet keep up the disjected sway of natural conversation." The style of *Euphranor* could hardly be described as natural. It is conversation idealized both in content and manner. FitzGerald drew chiefly on his wide reading for the substance. Philosophers, moralists, poets, and critics are resorted to for precept or example as the debaters thrust and parry. The convolutions of the argument are difficult to follow at first; nevertheless, the reader who will accustom himself to the style will find the discussion interesting, its presentation entertaining. Above all, he will discover in *Euphranor* the beautiful prose of which FitzGerald is master. Tennyson greatly admired the closing paragraph, describing the boat race.

With the appearance of the book, FitzGerald was launched on

6. MS. letter to Cowell, Feb. 10, 1851.
7. Reviews appeared in *The Examiner*, the *Westminster Review*, *The Gentleman's Magazine*, *The Spectator*, and *The Literary Gazette*.
The review in *The Examiner*, Feb. 8, 1851, was written by James Spedding, and in the *Westminster Review*, LV, 260–262, by E. B. Cowell.

his literary career. Within the next five years he published a longer version of the dialogue and three new works. The term "published" must be applied to FitzGerald in a peculiar sense. He usually printed at his own expense, and the publisher named on the title page simply marketed the books.

FitzGerald's second work, *Polonius: A Collection of Wise Saws and Modern Instances,* was published in 1852.[8] "I doubt," he predicted, "it will be a losing affair." He was right, for the sale was limited.

The volume might be called "Polonius, or FitzGerald as a Moralist." "Few books," he said in his preface, "are duller than books of Aphorisms and Apophthegms. A Jest-book is, proverbially, no joke: a Wit-book, perhaps, worse; but dullest of all, probably, is the Moral-book, which this little volume pretends to be. . . . 'Too much of one thing,' says Fuller, 'is good for nothing!' " FitzGerald had long felt a desire to compile a book of aphorisms possessing variety. Another consideration spurred him to publish. "Most of the collections of this nature I have seen," he stated, "are made up mainly from Johnson and the Essayists of the last century . . . when English thought and language had lost so much of their vigour, freshness, freedom, and picturesqueness—so much, in short, of their native character."

Polonius contains quotations, usually brief, on one hundred and thirty-nine topics such as Honesty, Riches, The Poor, Forms and Ceremonies, Envy, War, Liberty, Vanity, and Charity. Carlyle and Bacon are most frequently quoted; but more than a hundred Classical, English, and Continental authors are cited. The majority of passages are from English theologians and philosophers of the sixteenth, seventeenth, and eighteenth centuries. With the exception of Carlyle, FitzGerald rarely quotes his contemporaries, although there are several passages from Newman, three from Tennyson, and one from Thackeray.

His plan was to "put together a few sentences of the wise, and also of the less wise . . . a little Truth, new or old . . . nay, of Truism too, (into which all truth must ultimately be dog-eared) and which . . . widen into new relations with the widening world." He sometimes headed or closed a group of quotations with a proverb to show how the *literati* have expressed ideas which the

8. William Pickering appears on the title page as publisher. The work has twice been reprinted: in the *Variorum and Definitive Edition of the Poetical and Prose Writings of Edward FitzGerald,* edited by George Bentham (New York, Doubleday, Page & Co., 1903, 7 vols.), Vol. V; and in the King's Classics series (London, Alexander Moring, Ltd., 1905).

homely adage states so tersely. More often his method is that illustrated by:

WAR

War begets Poverty—Poverty, Peace—
Peace begets Riches—Fate will not cease—
Riches beget Pride—Pride is War's ground,
War begets Poverty—and so the world goes round.
Old Saw

How all Europe is but like a set of parishes of the same country; participant of the self-same influences ever since the Crusades, and earlier: and these glorious wars of ours are but like parish brawls, which begin in mutual ignorance, intoxication, and boasting speech; which end in broken windows, damage, waste, and bloody noses; and which one hopes the general good sense is now in the way towards putting down in some measure.

Carlyle

"Yet here, as elsewhere, not absurdly does 'Metaphysic call for aid on Sense.' The physical science of war may do more to abolish war than all our good and growing sense of its folly, wickedness, and extreme discomfort. For what state would be at the expense of drilling and feeding dum-drudges to be annihilated by the first discharge of the COMING GUN?"

The sources of many passages are not given, for FitzGerald had copied them into his notebooks without recording the origins. The fragments were not gleaned entirely from his reading, however. Here and there is a statement picked up in his conversations. Such, for example, are the words, "The quick decision of one who sees half the truth," which, FitzGerald says elsewhere, is a casual observation of Tennyson's. Included also is "Taste is the feminine of genius," an aphorism composed by FitzGerald himself.[9] Other unsigned passages are undoubtedly his own. For the most part these are brief comments which elucidate quotations. Occasionally, however, there is a longer passage. The section on "Aesthetics" carries FitzGerald's stamp, both in thought and expression.

AESTHETICS

Memorable—because of the high office of the speaker, and the place he spoke in—was the praise addressed by Lord Palmerston to an Eng-

9. FitzGerald wrote to Frederick Tennyson in March, 1850, "I pretend to no Genius, but to Taste: which according to my aphorism, is the feminine of Genius."

lish gentleman, who had been visiting Naples, not to explore volcanoes and excavated cities, but to go down into the prisons and declare to all Europe the horrors of tyranny and misgovernment.

> Oh would "Young England" half the study thrown
> Into Greek annals turn upon our own,
> Would spell the actual present's open book,
> Where men may read strange matters—learn that Cook
> Tailor, and Dancer, are ill heraldry,
> Compared with LIVING PLAIN AND THINKING HIGH:
> That Fools enough have travelled up the Rhine;
> Discussed Italian Operas, French Wine,
> Gap'd at the Pope, called Raffaelle *"divine"*—
> Yea, could the Nation with one single will
> Renounce the Arts she only bungles still,
> And stick to that which of all nations best
> She knows, and which is well worth all the rest,
> Just government—by the ancient Three-fold Cord,
> Faster secured than by the point of sword—
> Would we but teach THE PEOPLE, from whom Power
> Grows slowly up into the Sovereign Flower,
> By all just dealing with them, head and heart
> Wisely and religiously to do their part;
> And heart and hand, whene'er the hour may come,
> Answer brute force, that will not yet be dumb—
> Lest, like some mighty ship that rides the sea,
> Old England, one last refuge of the free,
> Should, while all Europe thunders with the waves
> Of war, which shall by Tyrants, Czars, or Slaves,
> Suddenly, with sails set and timbers true,
> Go down, betray'd by a degenerate crew! [10]

Polonius is most interesting for the light which it throws on Fitz-Gerald. Many of the opinions which are expressed in the words of other writers appear in essence over and over again in his letters. The book yields, too, examples of his shrewd and sometimes caustic humor. "And are these Fables so fabulous after all?" he asks in his preface. "If beasts do not really rise to the level on which we amuse ourselves by putting them, we have an easy way of really sinking to theirs." More subtle is his indictment of reactionary forces.

10. This criticism of "Young England," the praise of "plain living and high thinking," the "vanity" (to use FitzGerald's word) of foreign travel, the praise of England's capacity for government, and the figure of England's falling into decay like a neglected ship, are topics frequently met with in FitzGerald's letters. The spelling "Raffaelle" is usually used by FitzGerald.

TORY

Tacitus wrote (says Luther) that by the ancient Germans it was held no shame at all to drink and swill four and twenty hours together. A gentleman of the court asked, "How long it was since Tacitus wrote this?" He was answered, "Almost 1500 years." Whereupon the gentleman said, "Forasmuch as drunkenness is so ancient a custom, let us not abolish it."

An old ruinous church which had harboured innumerable jackdaws, sparrows, and bats, was at length repaired. When the masons left it, the jackdaws, sparrows, and bats came back in search of their old dwellings. But these were all filled up. "Of what use now is this great building?" said they. "Come, let us forsake this useless heap."

German.

FitzGerald gave Churchyard a copy of *Polonius* in which he had inserted slips of paper containing two additions. One of these read, "Only early Bird gets Worm—but the Worm?" [11]

11. Prideaux, W. F., *Notes for a Bibliography of Edward FitzGerald* (London, Frank Hollings, 1901), p. 5.

XIII

Spanish and Persian

"Half-a-dozen will buy, and the Critics in the Papers will sneer. For I observe they always take up any Confession of unliteralness, etc., against oneself."

FITZGERALD to COWELL

DURING one of FitzGerald's visits to Bramford in the spring of 1849, Cowell translated a play of Calderon for him.[1] FitzGerald wrote from Boulge in June, "My head sometimes runs on that grand grotesque Spanish Play: fit to be acted in the Alhambra. I shall read Calderon one day." [2] He was at work on the collection of Barton's poems at the time, and it was not until August of the following year that he applied himself to Spanish. By October, 1852, he had made considerable progress and sent Cowell a list of five plays which he had read in his "inaccurate way . . . When I talk of my 'inaccurate' way of reading," he explained,

you understand it to be that I am not distrest when I find a bit of conventional wit in the Clown or some conceit in the Lover, which I do not understand: I do not give so much patience (nor, what is more valuable to me, so much *eye-sight*) as you would to puzzle it out. I have not yet found in Calderon much that, being obscure, was worth much pains to clear up: not, I mean, such things as one finds in Shakespeare, which are worth clearing up. But I believe I get a pretty correct understanding of the *whole*: plot and dialogue too.[3]

He felt sufficiently confident to begin a translation of *El Pintor de su Deshonra*, consulting Cowell on passages which he found difficult. He finished the play by November 9 and asked Donne to submit it to Charles Kean, who, FitzGerald thought, "*might* act it with effect." [4] Kean, however, thought *El Pintor* would not suit an

---

1. Pedro Calderon de la Barca (1600–81), whose life overlapped Shakespeare's, raised the drama of Spain to its greatest heights on the eve of Spanish decadence.
2. MS. letter to Cowell, June 23, 1849.
3. *Ibid.*, Oct. 3, 1852.
4. Donne at this time was acting as Examiner of Plays in the absence of Kemble who was in Germany pursuing his Anglo-Saxon studies. He succeeded Kemble in the office on the latter's death in 1857.

English audience, and declined to stage it. "I dare say he is right," admitted FitzGerald, "though I do not *see* it. Though I should like to have got a few pounds for the translation, and *perhaps* been amused to see the play put in action, yet, on the whole *one has no more trouble.*" [5]

As soon as he began to translate, FitzGerald was tempted to publish some of the plays. "Do you not think," he had asked Cowell in October in almost the same words that he had queried Allen about the *Spectator Papers* nearly twenty years before, "they would make a good Volume: of Spanish Life and Manners? and also of Calderon's Genius? I wonder who would buy and print such a Volume?" [6] When Kean rejected *El Pintor*, FitzGerald's plans for publication took more definite form. By May, 1853, he had sent four plays to the printer and was preparing two more.

Those who consider FitzGerald indolent might well study this timetable of his Spanish translations. In a little more than six months he turned at least six plays into English verse and polished four sufficiently to send to Childs at Bungay. He showed the same dispatch in preparing other works for publication. Although he often debated long whether to do or not to do, when he had once determined on a course of action, he whipped up his "languid energies," as Mrs. Cowell had called them, and worked with astonishing speed.

Six Dramas of Calderon. Freely Translated by Edward Fitz-Gerald was published in July, 1853. The book was the only one of FitzGerald's publications to bear his name as author. Another collection of Calderon's plays, translated by Denis Florence M'Carthy, appeared almost simultaneously; and FitzGerald "was obliged to print with some name . . . and so thought it as well at once to put my own." Pickering was given as the publisher. The firm was about to go out of existence, but FitzGerald "was too tired of the Business" to hunt for another.

The volume contained *The Painter of His Own Dishonour, Keep Your Own Secret, Gil Perez, the Gallician, Three Judgments at a Blow, The Mayor of Zalamea,* and *Beware of Smooth Water.*[7] The object of his selection, FitzGerald explained, was to "give a fair idea . . . of Calderon's Spanish Life." Each play is typical of a group of his dramas: *The Painter,* the efforts of a husband to

5. MS. letter to Cowell, Nov. 20, 1852.
6. *Ibid.,* Oct. 14, 1852.
7. These are translations of *El Pintor de su Deshonra, Nadie fie su Secreto, Luis Perez el Gallego, La tres Justicias en Una, El Alcalde de Zalamea,* and *Guardate de la Agua Mansa.*

restore his damaged honor; *Keep Your Own Secret,* the complications into which a lover falls by failing to guard his tongue; *Gil Perez,* a chronicle play based on the adventures of a historical Spanish Robin Hood; *Three Judgments,* a tragedy of blood; *The Mayor,* the dramatist's only play of humble life; and *Beware of Smooth Water,* a comedy of tangled love affairs. Calderon is noted for his complicated plots and lavish yet beautiful poetry. The poetry is obvious in all of FitzGerald's plays, and all but one reveal the Spaniard's mastery of the involved plot and ingenious complication. The exception is *The Mayor of Zalamea,* the action of which is simple and direct. This play usually appeals most to casual readers.

In reading Calderon, Cowell warned, "We must . . . be prepared to see every principle of art recklessly violated." [8] Another critic stated, "As a dramatist in the highest sense of the word, he must not be estimated; as a play-wright, he ranks with the foremost." [9] His characters lack individuality; they are merely stock figures whose actions are motivated by a ceremonious and unbending code of honor which had survived as tradition in Spanish drama and poetry. The dialogue, frequently bombastic, is garnished with elaborate conceits.

FitzGerald fully appreciated the qualities of his dramatist. He chose, therefore, six of the less famous plays,[10] which seemed to him suited to English taste, and, "while faithfully trying to retain what was fine and efficient; sunk, reduced, altered, and replaced, much that seemed not; simplified some perplexities, and curtailed or omitted scenes that seemed to mar the breadth of general effect, supplying such omissions by some lines of after-narrative." [11] In his preface he defended the freedom of his translation by stating that he did not believe that an exact translation of Calderon could be successful,

retaining so much that, whether real or dramatic Spanish passion, is still bombast to English ears. . . . conceits that were a fashion of the day; or idioms that, true and intelligible to one nation, check the current of sympathy in others to which they are unfamiliar; violations of the probable, nay *possible,* that shock even healthy romantic licence; repetitions of thoughts and images . . . so much, in short, that is not

8. *Westminster Review,* LIV (January, 1851), 292.
9. *Ibid.,* p. 297, G. H. Lewes, quoted by Cowell.
10. "Four of these," FitzGerald wrote in his preface, ". . . as many others in Calderon, may be lookt on as a better kind of what we call melodrama."
11. This, it will be observed, had been FitzGerald's method in editing Barton's poems; and it continued to be his method in all his subsequent works.

Calderon's own better self, but concession to private haste and public taste.

FitzGerald's *purpose* in taking such liberties was his final defense. "If these plays," he wrote, "prove interesting to the English reader, I and he may be very sure that, whatever of Spain and Calderon be lost, there must be a good deal retained; and I think he should excuse the licence of my version till some other interests him as well at less expense of fidelity."

FitzGerald's friends granted him the freedom of translation which he had assumed, and commended his book. A less partial critic, George Borrow, author of *The Bible in Spain,* to whom Fitz-Gerald had sent a copy, added a note of praise.[12] In reply to Borrow's acknowledgment, he wrote, "Though I of course thought the Translations well done (or I should not have printed them), I naturally desired the approval of a competent Judge; since the best of us may make sad mistakes in the estimation of our own handiwork; and it is not pleasant to dub oneself an Ass in print." But FitzGerald was curious, though apprehensive, of the reception which the critics would give his plays. "I fully expect," he wrote to young Crabbe, "that (as I told you, I think) the London press, etc., will either sink them, or condemn them as on too free a principle: and all the more if they have not read the originals. For these are safe courses to adopt." [13]

The *Athenaeum* fulfilled FitzGerald's predictions:

"Freely translated," says Mr. FitzGerald. There is no doubt of it. By way of apology for so much license—for a freedom in dealing with his text so unusual—the translator gives an original reason:—"I have not meddled," he says, "with any of Calderon's more famous plays" . . . We have not taken the trouble to compare these translations with the originals; holding it quite unnecessary to treat as a serious work a book whose author confesses that he has "sunk, reduced, altered, and replaced much that seemed not fine or efficient" . . . supplying such omissions by some lines.[14]

12. This appears to be the beginning of FitzGerald's friendship with Borrow, with whom Donne was already acquainted.

13. Letter to Crabbe, July 22, 1853.

14. *The Athenaeum,* Sept. 10, 1853, p. 1063.

On August 27, the *Literary Gazette and Journal* had stated that it could not "conscientiously recommend Mr. FitzGerald's 'free translations' " on the grounds that they did not give a "just estimate of the spirit and point of Calderon." Nevertheless, the reviewer thought that the plays "will prove interesting to English readers. Mr. Fitz-Gerald has performed his part as a translator with zeal and carefulness, and displays some ingenuity in the difficult task." The passage borrows the deviousness of the "adequate school" of music criticism, a name suggested by critics who observe with astonishing acumen that accompanists' contributions at concerts are "adequate."

In November the same magazine published a eulogistic review of the literal translation of Calderon's plays by FitzGerald's "rival," Denis M'Carthy. Both reviews were written, W. F. Prideaux states, by John Chorley, a contemporary Spanish scholar.[15]

FitzGerald was compelled to wait three years for a champion. In 1856, R. C. Trench, soon to be made Dean of Westminster, published translations of two Calderon plays. In the preface to his book, Trench stated that FitzGerald's versions "are far the most important and worthiest contribution to the knowledge of the Spanish poet which we have yet received. But, written as they are in English of an exquisite purity and vigour, and dealing with poetry in a poet's spirit, they yet suffer, as it seems to me, under serious drawbacks." [16] FitzGerald's selection of plays from among Calderon's less successful works and his use of blank verse instead of the trochee of the original were the two things to which Trench objected. Of M'Carthy's edition, he said, "The translations themselves are sometimes meritorious, yet I cannot consider them generally successful."

Granting the alien qualities inherent in Spanish drama, FitzGerald's plays possess merits which the critics should have recognized even though they resented his method of translation. The story of the *Mayor of Zalamea,* for example, unfolds naturally and dramatically. The characters are well drawn; and the blunt honesty and sturdy independence of Crespo, the mayor, which remind one of Kent in *Lear,* are good *theater. Beware of Smooth Water,* one writer has stated, "goes with unflagging spirit on the stage, if I may testify from an amateur performance." [17] All the plays possess vitality, a quality lacking in the versions of Trench and M'Carthy.

FitzGerald's translations, moreover, are written in a Shakespearean blank verse that is both musical and vigorous. Here and there the lyric quality is crystallized in brief songs which have a decided Elizabethan flavor. In a balcony scene in *The Painter of His Own Dishonour,* one finds:

> Of all the shafts to Cupid's bow,
>   The first is tipt with fire;
> All bare their bosoms to the blow,
>   And call the wound Desire.

15. *Notes for a Bibliography,* p. 8.
16. Trench, R. C., *Calderon's Life's a Dream* (London, John W. Parker & Son, 1856), pp. 120–121.
17. Campbell, A. Y., "Edward FitzGerald," *The Great Victorians* edited by H. J. and Hugh Massingham (Doubleday, Doran, Garden City, N.Y., 1932), p. 179.

Love's second is a poison'd dart,
    And Jealousy is nam'd:
Which carries poison to the heart
    Desire had first inflam'd.

The last of Cupid's arrows all
    With heavy lead is set;
That vainly weeping lovers call
    Repentance or Regret.
                    Act II, Scene 2

In *Keep Your Own Secret,* the lover sings:

O Phoebus, swift across the skies
    Thy blazing carriage post away;
    O, drag with thee benighted day,
And let the dawning night arise!
Another sun shall mount the throne
    When thou art sunk beneath the sea;
From whose effulgence, as thine own,
    The affrighted host of stars shall flee.
                    Act I, Scene 3

One feature which FitzGerald retained is the character of the irrepressible *gracioso,* or buffoon, without which no Calderon play is complete. The comic passages in FitzGerald's versions are particularly well done. Lazaro, the *gracioso* in *Keep Your Own Secret,* who claims that by wearing a ragged coat he had originated the slashed doublet, is at times reminiscent of Falstaff. He tells of a quarrel which arose over a game of cards:

Well, being, as I said, at cards,
And playing pretty high too—mark me that—
I get into discussion or dispute,
(Whichever you will call it) with a man,
If man he may be call'd who man was none—
. . . Well, as I said,
This wretch and I got to high words, and then
(Whither high words so often lead) to blows;
Out came our swords. The rascal having seen
What a desperate fellow at my tool I was,
Takes him eleven others of his kidney,
Worse than himself, and all twelve set on me.
I seeing them come on, ejaculate,
"From all such rascals, single or in league,
Good Lord, deliver us," set upon all twelve,
                    . . .

Beat the whole twelve of them back to a porch,
Where, after bandying a blow with each,

   . . .

Back in a phalanx all came down on me,
And then dividing, sir, into two parties,
Twelve upon this side—do you see?—and nine
On this—and three in front—

Felix   But Lazaro
Why, twelve and nine are twenty-one—and three—
Why, your twelve men are grown to twenty-four!
How's this?

Laz. How's this? why, counting in the shadows—twenty-four,
Shadows and all—you see! [18]

It has been said that FitzGerald was so disconcerted by the review of his *Calderon* in the *Athenaeum,* that he withdrew the unsold copies.[19] The statement has been widely circulated; but there is nothing in his letters to confirm, while there is much to contradict, the report. FitzGerald was disappointed, but he does not appear to have been otherwise affected by the reception of the volume. "If Cowell," he wrote to Mrs. Cowell in September,

looks at the Athenaeum of this week, he will see what treatment his poor friend receives. These Reviewers may have read the Book, and be right: but it seems to me as if they did *not* read, but, laying hold of the confession in the Preface, condemn the principle at once as the safest course to pursue. . . . I always anticipated this might be the case: and perhaps it is scarce to be expected that Critics, who are supposed to know everything, would consent to read the Translations without reference to the Original. On the other hand, they may be *right,* in spite of what Self and company (i.e. Self's *Friends*) say.[20]

FitzGerald had not withdrawn the edition on October 19, for on that date he wrote Spring Rice, "I am certainly glad you and any educated man of intuition should like them: for the Newspaper

18. *Keep Your Own Secret,* Act II, Scene 4. FitzGerald observes in a footnote that this is not the only odd coincidence between Calderon and Shakespeare.

19. Aldis Wright published the statement in his obituary of Edward FitzGerald which appeared in the *Athenaeum* for June 23, 1883. It is significant, however, that it does not appear in the biographical sketch which Mr. Wright later contributed to the *Dictionary of National Biography.*

20. MS. letter to Mrs. Cowell [September, 1853]. FitzGerald wrote to young Crabbe about the same time, "I suppose your sister will send you the Athenaeum in which you will see a more determined spit at me. I foresaw . . . how likely this was to be the case: and so am not surprised. One must take these chances if one will play at so doubtful a game. I believe those who read the Book, without troubling themselves about whether it is a free Translation or not, like it: but Critics must be supposed to know all, and it is safe to condemn."

Critics condemn or sneer and I had almost begun to think I had made an Ass of myself . . . Beside all this, my little bark's *sale* (a pun worthy of A. T.) [21] will fail before the Reviewers' counter blasts." [22] There is evidence, too, that the book was still on sale in 1857.

For a time after the publication of his collection FitzGerald continued to work on Calderon's plays. The criticism led him to attempt more literal translations; but he found that "doing it slavishly so vulgarizes the original" that he abandoned the work. In the meantime he had begun to read *Don Quixote,* which delighted him; thereafter, he confined most of his Spanish reading to that work. Moreover, he had now begun his study of Persian, on which he concentrated for many years.

FitzGerald frequently visited Oxford while Cowell was in residence at the University. He took lodgings near those of his friends and spent a portion of each day in their company. A contemporary undergraduate spoke of seeing him at the Cowells' "wrapped in a plaid and a mysterious atmosphere of cynicism . . . all who knew him believed him capable of great things." [23]

On one of these visits Cowell persuaded FitzGerald to learn Persian. "The first step was taken one wet Sunday," Cowell later told Dr. H. F. Stewart, Dean of Trinity College, Cambridge. "I suggested Persian to him and guaranteed to teach the grammar in a day. The book was Jones's Grammar,[24] the illustrations in which are nearly all from Hafiz. FitzGerald was interested in these and went on to read Hafiz closely." [25]

He probably began his study in December, 1852, for he was at Oxford in that month and went from there to Brighton to spend Christmas with his mother. On December 29 he wrote to the Cowells that he had just visited Alfred Tennyson and his wife at Seaford. "I admired *the Baby* [26] greatly and sincerely: and Alfred nurses him with humour and majesty. He told me I had not seen him in his full glory however—'sitting high and smiling' as he called it

21. Alfred Tennyson.

22. MS. letter to Spring Rice, Oct. 19, 1853.

23. Cowell biography, p. 101. The undergraduate was W. R. Morfil, later professor of Russian at Oxford.

24. Jones, Sir William (1746–94), Orientalist and jurist; founder of the Bengal Asiatic Society.

25. From a marginal note in a volume of FitzGerald's letters belonging to Dr. Stewart. "I knew someone would want this information one day," Dr. Stewart said in 1935, "so I asked Cowell about it and jotted down his account in my book."

26. Hallam Tennyson, the poet's older son, born Aug. 11, 1852.

. . . I told A. T. he was to learn Persian at Oxford: and follow the example of yours truly." [27] FitzGerald signed the letter in Persian, the first time the characters appear in his correspondence.

More than ten years before, his interest had been caught by a bit of Persian literature. In September, 1843, he had sent Barton fourteen lines of poetry which he remembered "versifying . . . out of a passage in one of old D'Israeli's books—when, I forget. . . . The last line is a good one. But my poetical farthing candle is almost burnt out."

> A diver springing darkly to the brim
> Of the full sapphire river as it rolled
> Under palm shadows over sands of gold
> Along the balmy vale of Almahim:
> Brought up what seem'd a piece of common mould,
> But of so rare a fragrance that he cried—
> "Mine eyes are dim with diving—thou'rt no piece
> Of common earth, but musk or ambergrease."
> "I am but common earth," the clod replied,
> "But once within my dusky bosom grew
> The Rose, and so insinuated through
> Her aromatic fibres day by day,
> That time her virtue never will subdue,
> Nor all the rambling water wash away." [28]

FitzGerald carried his Persian grammar about with him for almost a year, studying, now and then translating an apologue, now

27. MS. letter to Cowell, Dec. 29, 1852.
28. *Letters to Bernard Barton*, pp. 70–71. Mr. Barton remarks, "The book he refers to is evidently Isaac D'Israeli's *Mejnoun and Leila*, and the passage therein which caught his fancy . . . runs as follows: 'I was once in the bath, and they gave me a piece of scented clay. It was more than fragrant. And I asked of it, "Art thou pure musk, or ambergris? for thy scent delights my soul." It answered, "I was but Common Earth till I lived in the company of my Rose; then every day I became sweeter, till all her aromatic spirit was infused into mine. Oh! had I not lived with my Rose, I should still have been but a lump of Earth!" ' " Mr. Barton also states that Fitz-Gerald may have seen the story in an album belonging to Lucy Barton. Major Moor had copied the apologue into the book in Persian characters and added a translation.

In the volume on FitzGerald which A. C. Benson contributed to the English Men of Letters Series appears the statement, "Major Moor . . . was always ready to walk with the boy, and would talk for the hour together about the racy provincialisms of the countryside, and about his Eastern experiences. To this influence we can confidently trace FitzGerald's early taste for expressive local words, and his interest in Oriental literature. Indeed Major Moor can, perhaps, be dignified with the title of the true begetter of the Omar Khayyám." (P. 5.)

Mr. Benson does not give the source of his information. I have examined some 2,000 of FitzGerald's letters, but nowhere does he credit Major Moor with having stimulated his interest in Persian. He twice refers to Major Moor's book, *Oriental Fragments*, as "an almost worthless Book . . . to those who did not know him." *Letters*, II, 43–44.

and then sending Cowell an exercise for correction. However, when he finished the grammar in October, 1853, he said, "I am not *greatly* impressed with the desire to poke out even a smatter of Persian." [29] But he did not long remain indifferent. A passage in Jones aroused his interest in Firdusí's *Gulistan;* and, with the aid of Eastwick's translation, he began to read the apologues. In January the idioms and "forms of Eastern Thought" were becoming familiar to him. "This Persian is really a great Amusement to me," he told Cowell. ". . . As to Jones' Grammar, I have a sort of Love for it!"

Before the end of the month he began to translate Sádi and to find fault with the translations which he used as aids. "Certainly Eastwick is *wretched* in the Verse," he said,

and both he and Ross . . . seem to me on a wrong tack wholly in their *Style* of rendering the Prose. Because it is elegant Persian they try to render it into *Elegant* English; but I think it should be translated *something* as the Bible is translated, preserving the Oriental Idiom. It should be *kept* as Oriental as possible, only using the most idiomatic Saxon *words* to convey the Eastern Metaphor. . . . You will think I am Persian mad. . . . I am glad however to make acquaintance with one Oriental Tongue with all its Idioms.[30]

For the next eighteen months he studied poems by Firdusí, Hafiz, Jámí, and Attár and read many books about Persia and its people. For some of the poems there were no English versions; so he had to resort to French and German translations to clarify the difficulties of the Persian. The fact that he knew no German was merely a temporary obstacle, for he had long contemplated learning the language. "The Dscharii I am to have will have a *German* Translation," he informed Cowell in August, 1854, "so as I shall, oddly enough, not so much kill two birds with one stone, as make the two Birds kill each other for my benefit." [31] By this means he also translated Jámí's *Yúsuf and Zuleikhá.*

During the summer of 1854, FitzGerald and Cowell read Jámí's allegorical poem, *Salámán and Absál,* together. FitzGerald continued to translate the work at intervals for the remainder of the year. In January, he wrote to Cowell, "In looking over my Salámán I think I see how *that* could be compressed into a very readable form: and should like to manage it with you." [32] Cowell, however,

29. MS. letter to Cowell, Oct. 7, 1853.
30. *Ibid.,* Jan. 24, 1854.
31. *Ibid.,* Aug. 31 [1854].
32. *Ibid.,* Jan. 10, 1855.

was busy with other translations; so nothing came of FitzGerald's timid proposal. Two weeks later he had completed a "metrical abstract" of the poem, in which he "compacted *the Story* into a producible Drama and reduced the rhetoric into perhaps too narrow a compass." [33] This he sent to Cowell for correction and comment. He still smarted under the lash of the Calderon criticism, apparently, for he assured his friend that he had *"altered* nothing; except the word 'shame.' " In April he submitted his poem to J. W. Parker, publisher of *Fraser's Magazine*. The work was rejected. "I feel a desire," FitzGerald said in telling Cowell of the refusal, "to put it in Type both because I like it so much, and as a record of our pleasant study together."

FitzGerald did not immediately carry out his plan. He became interested in other works, particularly the odes of Hafiz and the dramas of Schiller. He read the latter with the help of a translation. "It is something," he told Cowell, "to get out of the Sweetmeat, Childish, Oriental World back to the Vigorous North! But I shall still go on with a page of Persian daily." Moreover, during the spring of 1855, he revised *Euphranor* "mainly for the purpose of reducing the didactic pretence of the former and casting all in a yet lighter mould." The dialogue was considerably altered in the new edition [34] and an appendix was added, in which Goethe, Richter, and other writers were quoted to support the thesis of *Euphranor*.

In December, FitzGerald again took up *Salámán and Absál*, the "ingenious prattle" of which, he said, "I am stilting into too Miltonic verse." In January, he asked Cowell,

What do you think! I have sent off the Text of Salámán to Childs to print—a few Copies only—for, if for no other reason than the subject, it cannot be expected to *sell*. I have cut away even more than when you saw it: lightened the Stories, as you desired; cut out *all* the descriptions of Beauty etc. which are tedious, and are often *implied;* and I think advantageously condensed and retrenched the Love-making.[35]

The pains which FitzGerald took even with minutiae are revealed in one of his letters.

This illegitimate Comma . . . was restored by me. . . . The reason of my Version—and why it was not quite literal is—that it is the culminating point of the Sentence, and I wanted to secure a palpable image of the Deity *scrutinizing* the World he made and moves in

33. *Ibid.,* May 2 [1855].
34. Published by J. W. Parker & Son, 1855.
35. MS. letter to Cowell, Jan. 3, 1856.

through the Eyes of his Master-work, Man, and to edge and clench it with the sharp cornerstone of rhyme in that very word *"scrutinize."* [36]

The allegory of the poem also provided difficulties, which Fitz-Gerald deftly evaded. "I shall bundle up the Celestial and Earthly Sháh so neatly," he said, "that neither can be displeased, and no reader know which is which. Trust an Irishman where any confusion is wanted." [37]

He had decided to print *Salámán* as a "little monument" to his Persian studies with Cowell. While writing the preface, he heard that his friend had been appointed professor of English history at the Presidency College, Calcutta. Cowell had taken his degree in December, 1854, with first-class honors in humane letters and an honorary fourth in mathematics.[38] He had remained at Oxford, supporting himself by tutoring and working in the Bodleian Library. FitzGerald was deeply stirred at the prospect of losing his friends. "Then one night," he wrote to Mrs. Cowell, "as I sat looking into the Fire by myself and seeing you and him and Bramford in the embers,—then all came into my Head and Heart to write what was written." *What was written* referred to the passage in the dedicatory letter, recalling their companionship at Bramford. The foreword is devoted chiefly, however, to acknowledging his debt to Cowell:

Here is my reduced Version of a small Original. What Scholarship it has is yours, my Master in Persian, and so much beside; who are no further answerable for *all* than by well liking and wishing publisht what you may scarce have Leisure to find due fault with.

FitzGerald mentions the necessity of choosing between the fulsome Persian manner of narration and a simplified style, more acceptable to English taste, in which some of the Oriental flavor is lost.

Of the two Evils?—At least what I have chosen is least in point of bulk; scarcely in proportion with the length of its Apology which, as usual, probably discharges one's own Conscience at too great a Price; people at once turning against you the Arms they might have wanted had you not laid them down. However it may be with this, I am sure a complete Translation—even in Prose—would not have been a readable one—which, after all, is a useful property of most Books, even of Poetry.

36. *Ibid.* [1856].
37. *Ibid.* [1856].
38. Cowell had considered competing for honors in mathematics but, "At the Final Examinations he decided. . . to go in only for a Pass. His papers, however, were so exceedingly good that he was recommended by the Examiners for an Honorary Fourth." Cowell biography, p. 108.

The Bramford description follows,[39] after which he resumes:

But to turn from you Two to a Public—nearly as numerous—(with whom by the way, this Letter may die without a name that *you* know very well how to supply),—here is the best I could make of Jámí's poem . . . here collapsed into a nut-shell Epic indeed; whose Story, however, if nothing else, may interest some Scholars as one of Persian Mysticism— perhaps the grand Mystery of all Religions—an Allegory fairly devised and carried out—dramatically culminating as it goes on; and told as to this day the East loves to tell her Story, illustrated by Fables and Tales . . .

Salámán and Absál, FitzGerald explained, "is one of many Allegories under which the Persian Mystic symbolized an esoteric doctrine which he dared not—and probably could not—more intelligibly reveal." [40] Jámí was a member of the pantheistic sect of Súfís, to which belonged most of the great poets of Persia. According to Súfí belief, the soul had once been absorbed in God; and salvation lay in re-absorption. This could be accomplished only by renunciation of all earthly influences and desires. When the worshiper achieved complete abnegation, "I," the individual, merged with "Thou," or God. The Súfís were considered heretics by the orthodox Mohammedans and were forced to express their beliefs by an elaborate symbolism in which the object of a lover's adoration represented God; the separation of lovers, the separation of the worshiper from the Deity; wine represented the love for God; and drunkenness, religious ardor. The struggle of the soul and its final unity with the Infinite is the subject of *Salámán and Absál.* FitzGerald's version, which stripped much of the confusing allegory from the original, may be summarized as follows:

The Sháh of Yúnan extended his dominion until he ruled the world. He owed his success to the wisdom of a Sage, whose advice he sought in all matters. Finally he had only one desire unfulfilled, his wish for a son. His counsellor advised against marriage, for, he warned, the Sháh would become the slave of his own appetite. On the advice of his counsellor the Sháh resigned the issue to the Supreme Intelligence, and

> . . . Lo! From Darkness came to Light a Child
> Of carnal composition unattaint;

The child was given the name of Salámán which combined the two words, *Salámat,* or security from Evil, and *Asmán,* or Heaven. Absál, a beautiful maiden, was chosen to be his nurse.

39. See p. 144.
40. Preface to *Salámán and Absál.*

Salámán became the fairest of men and "shook down splendour round him like a Sun." He excelled all his fellows on the polo field and in the hunt; "the fine edge of his Wit would split a hair"; his bounty was fathomless. He and Absál, the fairest of women, fell in love. When the Sháh learned of his son's infatuation, he commanded, "Withdraw thee from the minion who from thee Dominion draws." Salámán could find no way out of his dilemma but through flight, and at night escaped with Absál across the desert to the sea, on which they sailed until they reached an island as fair as Paradise. There they remained.

The Sháh was distraught; but the Sage, by hypnotic power, forced Salámán to return to his father. Absál, however, refused to be separated from her lover, who, between Remorse and Love, came to loathe his life and long for death. Again the lovers fled, not, this time, to a Paradise, but to the Wilderness of Death. There Salámán built and lighted a funeral pyre, and the two sprang into the flames. The Sage, however, had watched these preparations, and, by his will, directed the flames so that Absál alone was burned.

The Prince again returned to his Father, but the memory of Absál still haunted him. To alleviate his sorrow, the Sage raised a phantom image of her. When the young man was comforted, the Sage spoke to him of Zuhrah, or Celestial Venus, until she eventually revealed herself to Salámán's soul and

> Celestial Beauty seen,
> He left the Earthly; and, once come to know
> Eternal Love, the Mortal he let go.
>
> . . .
>
> Then he arose, and shaking off the dust
> Of that lost travel, girded up his heart,
> And look'd with undefilèd robe to Heaven.
>
> . . .
>
> Then THE SHÁH crown'd him with the Golden Crown,
> And set the Golden Throne beneath his feet.

Jámí concluded his poem, which is, in fact, an interpretation of the Súfí doctrine, with an explanation of the allegory. It must be understood that, according to Súfí belief, the Universe is governed by Ten "Intelligences," or gradations of the Spirit, of which the tenth and lowest is regent over the earth. The Sháh represents the Tenth Intelligence. The Sage is the Supreme or First Intelligence, from which all others derive their power. Salámán represents the Soul of Man, and Absál, "the Sense-adoring Body." The Paradise to which the lovers flee is the sensual attraction of the physical world, and Salámán's return to the Sháh is the return of the repentant Soul to its "true Parentage." The flight into the desert and the fire into which the lovers spring represents ascetic discipline to which all Súfí novitiates subject themselves to purge the Soul of worldly influences. Zuhrah is Divine Perfection, which alone is worthy of the Soul's meditations.

FitzGerald's book was printed by April 4, and the edition was sent to Parker to be placed on sale. "Half-a-dozen will buy," the author predicted, "and the Critics in the Papers will sneer. For I observe they always take up any Confession of unliteralness, etc., against oneself: and yet one can't honestly put forth a Translation without saying how far one has left the Original." [41] Among those who received presentation copies was Landor, whose acquaintance FitzGerald had made at Bath two years before. The translator received an enthusiastic acknowledgment from "that Generous old Fellow, who deals out furious praise on what is of less worth than Salámán." [42]

Salámán and Absál was reviewed in the *Athenaeum* of August 2 1856. "It shows," the critic said, "some poetic feeling, a diligent use of the dictionary, but a very moderate acquaintance with Persian . . . mistakes are numerous." The criticism is concerned chiefly with minutiae. The review concludes, "As a first attempt, however, to make Jámí accessible to the English reader, this little volume is deserving of commendation." [43]

41. Letter to Cowell [1856].
42. MS. letter to Cowell, April 24, 1856.
43. *Athenaeum*, No. 1501, Aug. 2, 1856.

XIV

Financial Troubles

"I keep on the windy side of care, and don't care half so
much for all these matters as I should for my finger aching."
                                                    Letter to Donne

DURING the late 'twenties, FitzGerald's father had begun
to mine coal on the family estate at Pendleton, near Manchester. His superintendent was Robert Stephenson,[1]
who had been an active pioneer, with his more famous
brother, George, in railroad engineering. By 1832 the mining enterprise was well under way. In that year it was decided to sink the
shaft seven hundred yards deeper, which would make the colliery,
Stephenson claimed, one of the largest in the south of England.

From the very beginning of the venture, John, Edward's eldest
brother, concerned himself with the welfare of the miners and persuaded his father to establish a school for their children.[2] Mr. Fitz-
Gerald provided a building and donated part of the teacher's salary,
the remainder being paid by his philanthropic son. Solicitude for
the education of the laboring classes was not common in that day,
as the report of the Children's Employment Commission to Parliament in 1843 graphically revealed. An area of thirty-two square
miles with a population of 105,000 in the vicinity of Oldham and

1. In the early 'twenties Robert Stephenson constructed an improved steam engine
which, he claimed, eliminated the difficulties and crudenesses of the Watt boiler.
Stephenson Letters, British Museum, Add. 38,781 ff. 6–15. He once conclusively proved
his ingenuity as a structural engineer, to Mr. FitzGerald's great advantage. On June
12, 1831, Peter FitzGerald marched a company of soldiers, "not exceeding seventy in
number," across a chain suspension bridge over the River Irwell at Broughton, adjoining Manchester. He failed to order his men to break step, and the vibration
wrecked the bridge. Fortunately, none of the soldiers were injured. Bids for repairing
the structure ranged from £2,000 to £6,000. Stephenson told Mr. FitzGerald that he
could repair it for £400. "He has been so successful," a correspondent wrote to the
Manchester Guardian, "as to restore the bridge and render it much stronger by a
simple method of preventing the bolts from bending." The cost, the correspondent
stated, was not over £240. The strength of the repaired bridge was fully tested when it
supported a herd of "sixty fat bullocks" which was accidentally permitted to cross
"in a crowded manner." Ordinarily no more than ten bullocks were permitted to cross
a chain bridge at one time. Stephenson Letters, British Museum, Add. 38,781 ff. 49.
    2. *Ibid.,* f. 116.

Ashton, Lancashire, it stated, contained not one public day school for poor children.

The action of Mr. FitzGerald and John was typical of an altruism characteristic of the whole family. At Naseby Mr. and Mrs. FitzGerald built and endowed a school for the natives on property donated by the FitzGerald children.[3] However, their benevolence was not confined to educational philanthropies. Edward's bounty has already been mentioned; John was also sympathetic and generous; and once when the price of coal was raised, Mr. FitzGerald voluntarily set aside one third of the advance to increase the wages of his miners.[4]

Mr. FitzGerald unfortunately proved to be more proficient in giving and losing money than in making it.[5] He has been called a "blundering Irishman" and other hard names as a result of his financial misadventures. It should be noted in his defense, however, that he embarked on his mining enterprises when industrial expansion and overspeculation were rampant in England. In 1836 some 300 or 400 companies, representing an aggregate capital of £200,000,000, were endeavoring to place their shares on the market.[6] Britons blundered with Irish facility, and the bubble burst before William IV died in June, 1837.

Mr. FitzGerald at least had the cold comfort of being associated with the nation's most illustrious engineer in misapplying his energies and fortune at Manchester. In 1835 he had extended his operations by forming the Pendleton Colliery Company with a capitalization of £60,000. The right was obtained to mine coal on land leased from the Duchy of Lancaster, adjoining the FitzGerald properties; and on June 13, 1836, a prospectus was issued. Among the directors was none other than George Stephenson.[7] The company proposed to open the deeper seams on the Duchy lands and to produce 120,000 tons of coal yearly. Statements of George Stephenson and the engineers for the Duchy testified that the proposals formed "a sound and lucrative undertaking," and it was estimated that the

3. Kerrich, Miss Eleanor FitzGerald, "Edward FitzGerald: A Personal Reminiscence," *Nineteenth Century Magazine*, LXV (March, 1909), 469.

4. Stephenson Letters, British Museum, Add. 38,781 f. 74.

5. In 1830, it will be remembered, Mr. FitzGerald's manager at Naseby had absconded with £5,000. In 1833 an agent through whom he retailed coal at Manchester also fled after swindling him out of further sums. Stephenson Letters, British Museum Add. 38,781 f. 59.

6. Walpole, Spencer, *History of England*, IV, 35.

7. Besides Mr. FitzGerald, the other directors were John Kerrich, his son-in-law; Edward Faux, Esq., of Thornby, Northamptonshire; and Horace Twiss, Esq., K. C., M. P. of Park Place, St. James.

investment would yield an annual profit of £14,000. George Stephenson was so optimistic about the project that he recommended that power should be reserved to enlarge the company beyond the scale of the prospectus.[8]

The venture, however, proved disastrous. Water had interfered with production in the old mine and presented formidable engineering problems in the new. It was necessary to "tub," or line, shafts and tunnels to keep out the water, an operation which cost thousands of pounds. As early as December, 1836, Mr. FitzGerald was advising his superintendent to "reserve all the Bills you can, until the end of January, but should any *require* acceptance previously, you must inclose them to me. . . . It is no doubt a very anxious time at present until you can ascertain whether you can so far master the Water as to reach the good foundation for your tubbing." [9] Eventually those subterranean waters swept away the fortunes of Mr. FitzGerald, his son-in-law, John Kerrich, and his old friend, Squire Jenney of Hasketon, who had also invested in the company. In September, 1843, Mr. FitzGerald lost one of his collieries.[10] Matters went from bad to worse until, on August 5, 1848, he filed a petition in bankruptcy.[11]

The London *Times,* in reporting one of the hearings, said that Mr. FitzGerald's debts and liabilities totaled "about £198,000. The assets are considerable. . . . It was stated that the bankrupt had from time to time invested £150,000 in the collieries of which he was the owner." [12] His eight sons and daughters were creditors for £10,000 each. Although he was declared bankrupt on December 20, 1848, litigation arising from the case dragged on for three years. He emerged from the ordeal with health shattered. In the spring of 1849, he and Mrs. FitzGerald separated. Three years later he died in London, murmuring as he lay in the stupor of death, "That engine works well." [13]

The losses which FitzGerald himself suffered through his father's

8. Stephenson Letters, British Museum, Add. 38,781 f. 101.

9. *Ibid.,* f. 109–110.

10. Spring Rice letter, Sept. 28, 1843. This appears to be the new mine operated by the Pendleton Colliery Company. Five years later, when Mr. FitzGerald was declared bankrupt, no mention of the company is made.

11. *Petitions for Arrangement, 1844–1866;* Bankruptcy Courts, London.

12. London *Times,* Jan. 18, 1849. "My father," FitzGerald had written to Barton, "has protection at least as far as all the debts contained in the Schedule are." *Letters to Bernard Barton,* p. 160. The furnishings of Boulge Hall were sold in 1848 to meet the demands of creditors. For a time FitzGerald's possessions in the cottage were threatened with the same fate but that danger was averted. *A FitzGerald Friendship,* p. 25.

13. He was buried at Boulge.

bankruptcy gave him little concern. "I keep on the windy side of care," he told Donne, "and don't care half so much for all these matters as I should for my finger aching." A few weeks later he again wrote to Donne. "In all this matter however I do not desire, nor need, sympathy—many are my defects—but solicitude for money and luxury is not among them: and as I and all my family shall have *enough,* independent of this smash, when my Mother dies, we should be *base* to fret ourselves now." [14] He assured Cowell that he should "delight in Philoctetes as much as ever when I meet you; and I make my apology to books in general, who, in spite of what I have often said of them, have certainly supplied me with better idols than love of wealth and splendour and gentility." [15] His friends commended him on the philosophic calm with which he accepted his reverses, but he parried all compliments. "It really gives me a pain," he told Frederick Tennyson, "to hear you or any one else call me a philosopher, or any good thing of the sort. I am none, never was; and, if I pretended to be so, was a hypocrite. Such things as wealth, rank, respectability, I don't care a straw about; but no one can resent the toothache more, nor fifty other little ills beside that flesh is heir to."

For the plight of others, however, FitzGerald was more solicitous. "I have disposed of my own Bond," he told Barton early in the bankruptcy proceedings, "to the best advantage I can for the *three* creditors, who, I thought, most needed it; and I am determined to draw the line there. I shall do all I can to push my Father's petition through, *not* for his sake, poor man: but for that of his Creditors; who are the only party I feel very much pity for." Although business negotiations were a vexation to him, FitzGerald labored diligently throughout the litigation to protect his sisters' interests. "I seriously believe," he confessed to Cowell as late as 1851, "that if only myself were at stake, I should prefer to take my ease, and let all this take its chance in the Lawyers' hands: but I cannot leave my sisters in their hands. No one helps me. I make a great rout,—get the outline of the whole—and, after all, do no good, I believe." [16]

FitzGerald had been living on the interest from the £10,000 which his father had borrowed, and the bankruptcy made it necessary for him to raise money for the future. He could have done this with a minimum of trouble by selling his reversion; but, he said,

14. *A FitzGerald Friendship,* p. 24.
15. MS. letter to Cowell, Sept. 22, 1848.
16. *Ibid.,* Dec. 1, 1851.

"I wish to leave it to others who will, I hope, make better use of it than I myself shall, or any Annuity Office would, put it to." He negotiated with lawyers at Bedford, who worked at the business during the whole of 1849, only to tender "a large bill for service unperformed." He did not get his affairs settled until November, 1851, when Spedding became his mortgagee. "I cannot tell you," he said to Cowell, "what it has been to me, after mixing with the Rascals and Fools and Blackguards of the three last years, once more to have to deal with a Gentleman! I mean, of course, a Gentleman in Soul." [17] It was, perhaps, not entirely fortuitously that in one of his translations from Calderon FitzGerald has a character assert, "I make no friends with lawyers, and never trust their promises." [18]

Business trips to London gave FitzGerald many opportunities to meet old friends. After Tennyson married in 1850 and settled at Twickenham, FitzGerald assumed the casual liberties of a bachelor friend and occasionally visited the poet and his wife, sometimes at their invitation, sometimes at his own. He took Donne and the Cowells to call, and Mrs. Tennyson and Mrs. Cowell became firm friends. He also spent evenings with Carlyle. Once when Mrs. Carlyle was not at home, the two men "lay down each at a side of the fire, and talked of Life slipping away." Other evenings were passed with "Spedding the Wise" and "Thackeray the Witty." FitzGerald spent a week with the latter at his home in March, 1852; and from there went to visit John Allen in Shropshire, a journey long projected. Allen had been appointed to the living of Prees, near Shrewsbury, in 1846 and the following year was made Archdeacon of Salop, a post which he held until his death. FitzGerald captured the hearts of his old friend's children, one of whom he dubbed "Little Ticket," and he adapted a French play which they performed. One Sunday Allen presided at services in a near-by village; and FitzGerald played the harmonium for him, requesting one of the Archdeacon's sons to announce that the congregation would have the privilege of listening to the performance of the distinguished foreigner, Signor Geraldino.

In October Thackeray left for his first lecture tour in the United States. Shortly before his departure he wrote to FitzGerald:

My dearest old Friend,

I mustn't go away without shaking your hand, and saying Farewell and God Bless you. If anything happens to me, you by these presents

17. *Ibid.*, Nov. 7, 1851.
18. *Gil Perez, the Gallician,* Act II, Scene 3.

must get ready the Book of Ballads which you like, and which I had not time to prepare before embarking on this voyage. And I should like my daughters to remember that you are the best and oldest friend their Father ever had, and that you would act as such: as my literary executor and so forth. . . .

I shall send you a copy of Esmond to-morrow or so which you shall yawn over when you are inclined. But the great comfort I have in thinking about my dear old boy is that recollection of our youth when we loved each other as I do now while I write Farewell. . . . I care for you as you know, and always like to think that I am fondly and affectionately yours.[19]

FitzGerald was deeply stirred by this affectionate letter. Only a fragment of his answer remains:

You see you can owe me no thanks for giving what I can no longer use "when I go down to the pit," and it would be some satisfaction to me, and some diminution of the shame I felt on reading your letter, if "after many days" your generous and constant friendship bore some sort of fruit, if not to yourself to those you are naturally anxious about.[20]

"What I can no longer use" referred to bequests which FitzGerald made to Thackeray's daughters. Harriet (Mrs. Leslie Stephen) died before FitzGerald; Anne (Mrs. Ritchie) survived him and received £500 by his will. The novelist's reply to this was destroyed, but the first letter which FitzGerald sent to him in the United States has been preserved.

My dearest old Thackeray

I had your note—I dare scarce read it as it lies in my desk. It affects me partly as those old foolscap letters did, of which I told you I burned so many this spring: and why:—I was really ashamed of their kindness! If ever we get to another world, you will perhaps know why all this is so. I must not talk any more of what I have so often tried to explain to you. Meanwhile, I truly believe there is no man alive loves you (in his own way of love) more than I do. Now you are gone out [of] England, I can feel something of what I should feel if you were dead: I sit in this seedy place and read over Bouillabaisse till I cry again. This really is so: and is poor work: were you back again, I should see no more of you than before. But this is not from want of love on my part: it is because we live in such different worlds: and it is almost painful to me to tease anybody with my seedy dullness, which is just bearable by myself. Life every day seems a more total failure and mess to me: but it is yet bearable: and I am become a sad Epicurean—just desirous to keep on the windy side of bother and pain. . . .

19. *Letters,* II, 9–10.
20. *Loc. cit.*

This is all very gloomy and stupid. I could tell you of the very few things I have seen and done since I saw you: they would take but little room to write. But this first letter must be as it is. I was relieved to have a note from you: for I had begun to think you were disgusted with me. Donne told me you *couldn't* write. I dreamt so of you the other night. I wish you would tell me your girls' address in Paris: I should like to write to them, and hear from them. . . .

I never dare God Bless people scarcely—for the words have little meaning in my mouth. He is now blessing L. Buonaparte.

But Good bye, Good bye, my dear old Thackeray: and believe (for I can assert) that I am while I live yours ever E. F. G.[21]

21. MS. letter to Thackeray, Nov. 15, 1852.

XV

The Wanderer

"He travels from Dan to Beersheba and says, 'All is naught.'
Paris not improved and the Rhine a cockney affair."
DONNE ON FITZGERALD

FITZGERALD always regarded Boulge Cottage as a temporary home and, throughout his residence there, conducted
a listless search for a more substantial house. He was attracted in turn to Bedford and to Woodbridge, Beccles, Ipswich, and other Suffolk towns but could never force himself to
leave the snug quarters which seemed to fit like an old shoe. However, in 1853 his eccentric brother John took possession of Boulge
Hall. John's idiosyncracies and religious zeal were a constant irritation to Edward, and the two best maintained amicable relations by infrequent meetings. In November, therefore, FitzGerald
abandoned the cottage and stored his belongings with Job Smith
at Farlingay Hall, a farmhouse on the outskirts of Woodbridge.
He intended to "float about for a year and visit some friends." The
year stretched into seven before he again took permanent lodgings.

On trips to London he usually returned to the familiar haunts
of Charlotte Street until 1855; thereafter he took rooms at 31 Great
Portland Street.[1] In 1852 Donne had been appointed librarian of
the London Library and made his home in the building, 12 St.
James's Place, where FitzGerald sometimes stayed. "I have never
been so happy in London before," he wrote from there. Visits to
town, to his brother Peter at Twickenham, to his sister Andalusia
at Bath, to the Kerriches at Geldestone, and to the homes of his
many friends kept his calendar full. When his visits were pro-
tracted, he rented lodgings near the home of his "hosts," with whom
he would spend a few hours each day.

He spent ten days with the Tennysons at Farringford, Isle of
Wight, in June, 1854. While the poet worked, FitzGerald wandered about the hills with his sketchbook, usually returning with
wild flowers—horned poppies, yellow irises, or perhaps an orchid

1. In 1858 the number was changed to 88.

—in addition to his drawings. When Tennyson was free, his guest translated odes of Hafiz for him, for the Persian characters so taxed the poet's eyes that he had been forbidden to read the language. Evenings, FitzGerald would sit at the piano and play "one glorious air after another." He and Mrs. Tennyson stood as proxies at the christening of Lionel, the youngest member of the family, then two months old. The Tennysons enjoyed their guest, who "was in the most delightful spirits and as amusing as man could be." In later years they often urged him to repeat the visit, but he could never be persuaded to do so. "Ah," he said, "if he [Tennyson] did not live on a somewhat large scale, with perpetual Visitors, I might go once more to see him."

FitzGerald had been relieved of attendance on his mother, but he often visited her in Richmond, where she made her home. On the night of January 30, 1855, she died "very suddenly and quite easily" in her sleep at Brighton, and was buried beside her husband at Boulge. FitzGerald again became "plagued by Lawyers, Trustees, and Chancery." It was not until July of the following year that the business was settled. "But what a dry remainder Biscuit is one left after the forty-eight year Voyage!" he exclaimed. His legacy, however, was sufficient to satisfy his simple wants and extravagant whims for the remainder of his life.

He made his home in Suffolk at this period, either with Crabbe at Bredfield vicarage [2] or with the Smiths at Farlingay. His room at the farm, he told Carlyle in 1854, was such "as even you, I think, would sleep composedly in." That was a bold prophecy. Because they disturbed the Scotsman's slumbers, the cocks of Chelsea have won immortality. He had traveled the length and breadth of the British Isles but had found few places in which he could sleep peacefully. FitzGerald must have given him graphic descriptions of the tomb-like silence of the Suffolk countryside, for, in August, 1855, he consented to endure the "shrieking, mad, (and to me quite horrible) rail operations" and visit his friend. Accommodations either at Crabbe's vicarage or at Farlingay were offered him, and Carlyle chose the farm. The conscientious FitzGerald begged Mrs. Carlyle to tell him what her husband should "eat—drink—and avoid," and took every precaution to ensure the comfort of his tetchy guest. "You will be at most entire Liberty," he promised, "with room, garden, and hours, to yourself . . . pipes are the order of the house. . . . Bring some books." Carlyle, who was preparing his work on Frederick the Great at the time, re-

2. FitzGerald usually gave his address at Crabbe's as "Bredfield Rectory."

plied that he would bring reading material. "I am used," he wrote, "to several hours of solitude every day: and cannot be said ever to *weary* of being left well alone."

FitzGerald, "the best of landlords," met his guest at Ipswich and drove him to Farlingay. The Scot was well pleased with his visit. Skies were bright. He took brisk walks along the pleasant lanes and quiet country roads and felt "twice as strong for walking." He found that he could indeed slumber composedly at the farm. "I made an excellent sleep out last night," he informed his wife the second day after his arrival. Alas for Carlyle! Job Smith's cows seemed, in some mysterious way, to discover that the celebrated insomniac from Chelsea was in the vicinity and set up a lusty lowing at two o'clock the following morning. Out rushed the farmer and his son to drive them into the fields. The herd persevered in the chorus while the distracted Carlyle tossed on his bed. At six he abandoned his efforts to sleep and rose to take a walk. On his return he found "poor Fitz" engulfed in sorrow. The rest of the household offered endless apologies. Thereafter, the cows were kept further afield; and Carlyle enjoyed the slumber of the conscienceless for the remainder of his visit.

He spent his mornings beneath an elm in the garden reading Voltaire. In the afternoon he walked or drove with his host; during the evening the two smoked and chatted with the Smiths, whom Carlyle astonished with his knowledge of soils and crops. Fitz-Gerald drove him to Framlingham Castle, Orford, Dunwich, and other points of interest. "Perhaps their pleasantest [drive]," D. A. Wilson records,

was on Sunday . . . to Aldeburgh. They started in the morning, and the pony and trap with the strange uncouth pair—FitzGerald in his scare-crow clothes, and Carlyle with the usual long clay pipe in his mouth—passed the Church just as the worshippers were leaving it after morning service. The shocked look on the face of conventionality and "gigmanity" was entirely to their taste and made them laugh.[3]

Carlyle was attracted to Aldeburgh and coaxed his wife to join him for a holiday. It was, he wrote, "a beautiful little sea town, one of the best bathing places I have seen . . . beach solitary . . . If you have yet gone nowhere, you should think of Aldeburgh. I could like very well a fortnight or so of it. Never saw a place more promising. Adieu, dearest! Drown Nero, and be rea-

3. Wilson, D. A., *Carlyle to Threescore-and-ten*, pp. 170–171.

sonable." [4] But Mrs. Carlyle, who did not care for rustications, did not drown her dog, and did not go to Aldeburgh.

The last three days of the visit were spent at Bredfield vicarage. Crabbe, so Carlyle told his wife, was "a very excellent old Parson . . . who took much to me." At the end of his holiday the historian, refusing to be suffocated again in a railway carriage, "like a great codfish in a hamper," returned to London by steamer. "I feel privately confident," he wrote to his host from Chelsea, "I *have* got good by my Suffolk visit." He had one complaint, which he confided to his sister. "I . . . found the country and the farm house much to my taste—could I have been but 'well let alone' (according to the bargain!) but in that we did rather fail." [5] Nevertheless, Carlyle was sufficiently pleased with his entertainment to propose to FitzGerald, "When you get your little Suffolk cottage, you must have in it a 'chamber in the wall' for me, *plus* a pony that can trot, and a cow that gives good milk: with these outfits we shall make a pretty rustication now and then."

In the course of Carlyle's visit, the subject of the Naseby excavations was revived, and the historian again proposed that they set up a monument to mark the battlefield.[6] However, as FitzGerald and his brother were then negotiating the sale of the Naseby property, it was thought unwise to complicate the matter by requesting permission to erect the stone. A year passed before the estate was sold, and by that time Carlyle's and FitzGerald's interest in the matter had lapsed.

Shortly after the historian's visit FitzGerald went to London to see Frederick Tennyson, who had come from Italy. They talked, one may be sure, of that "wild Irishman," Savile Morton, who had finally been called to account for considering every woman "fair game." While serving as Paris correspondent for the *Daily News*, he had been killed on October 1, 1852, by a fellow correspondent, who stabbed him in the neck. His assailant fled to England but re-

4. *Ibid.,* p. 171.

5. *New Letters of Thomas Carlyle* (London and New York, John Lane, 1904), II, 174–175. 2 vols. Alexander Carlyle, ed.

6. On his return to London, he composed an inscription which he sent to Fitz-Gerald:

SISTE VIATOR

Here, and for — yards rearward, lies the Dust of men slain in the Battle of Naseby, 14 June 1645. Hereabouts appears to have been the crisis of the struggle, hereabouts the final charge of Oliver Cromwell and his Ironsides, that day.

This Ground was opened, not irreverently or with^t reluctance. Sat^y 13 Septr 1842, to ascertain that fact, and render the contemporary records legible. Peace henceforth to these old Dead.

Edwd Fitzg^d (with date)

Letters, II, 34.

turned to stand trial in December and was acquitted upon testifying that his wife, during an attack of fever, had confessed that Morton was the father of her youngest child.[7]

Before returning to Suffolk, FitzGerald took a short cruise in a government cutter with Spring Rice. They touched at Boulogne and Brighton, and FitzGerald was "delighted to sail the salt seas once more before a Breeze unpolluted with Smoke and Grease." Writing from Geldestone in October, he sent Spring Rice a few bars of a song which had floated into their cabin at Brighton. " 'Oh, I am a Bachelor bold humph, humph,' " he wrote below the music. "I am not sure if 'bold' was the word; and the 'humph' was a sort of grunt between Pig and Donkey—very fit for a Bachelor, I dare say." [8] In June of the following year he went to the Continent with Browne and young Crabbe. They visited Paris and Antwerp, and took the Rhine steamer to Heidelberg. "I saw little to care for except the Good-humoured out-of-door Life of the people," FitzGerald told Tennyson. "It was pleasant to sit outside a cafe till 12 p.m. The Prussians looked pleasant too after the French: and I think one could live very happily without 'The Times' under Frederick William." [9] Donne wrote to Fanny Kemble after Fitz-Gerald's return, "He travels from Dan to Beersheba and says 'all is naught.' Paris not improved and the Rhine a cockney affair."

In the meantime, August 1, the date on which the Cowells were to sail for India, was fast approaching. FitzGerald was despondent at the prospect. He urged Cowell to remain at Oxford, and sent him an account of the wretched climate of Calcutta, which Carlyle's brother, a physician, had given him. He conjured up visions of "Bodies floating down the Hooghly, etc." Micawber-like, he insisted that Cowell would eventually be appointed to a professorship in an English university. He continued:

I can't tell how it is in the Interior of your Family Economy, but *I* can't see why you should not prosper well in England instead of this Exile. . . . You rise constantly in Reputation; I, and all who know you, feel sure you will get on. . . . The Calcutta place would be capital were it *not* at Calcutta, which is of course a Truism. Only, if you remain in England you must limit your Number of Pupils . . . not only for your Health, but because *you are wanted* to do other Things— Hafiz, Ramayana, etc. . . . Let me say that should you want Money to make it up, I *have* it, and shall (without regard to you) take care to have some to spare every Year, so long as Public Securities hold. I always

7. Data sent to Aldis Wright by Sidney Lee, then editor of the *Dictionary of National Biography*.
8. MS. letter to Spring Rice, Oct. 15, 1855.
9. MS. letter to Tennyson, July 26, 1856.

must live well within my Income whatever that be, . . . this being my only sense of Riches and great Earthly Luxury . . . On this account, I always lay by something: how glad I should be if you would both now and hereafter ease me of some of it, and keep here in England to do so! Would I not—*will* I not—pay a good sum to keep you both here? What is to become of my Stupendous Learning when you go? I scarce see my old Friends, and make no new ones—I shall die starved of human regard; and besides that shall become a filthy *miser* if I keep laying by . . . I wish you would think of this, and show me you can trust in me by acting upon it. I want you to do work in England, as well as help to keep me alive in it.

Think of this.[10]

Cowell, however, was not to be swerved from his purpose. Many Oriental scholars had gone to India and there established reputations by studying under pundits and tapping the stores of rare manuscripts in the libraries. He was determined to follow their example. FitzGerald spent a fortnight with him at Ipswich after returning from the Continent, and they read Persian together. Just before his friends sailed, FitzGerald wrote:

My dear Edward and Elizabeth Cowell,

I think it is best for many reasons that I should *not* go to see you again—to say a Good-Bye that costs me so much.

I shall very soon write to you; and hope to keep up something of Communion by such meagre Intercourse. Do you do the same to me. Farewell, Both! [11]

10. MS. letter to Cowell, undated.
11. Cowell biography, p. 121.

XVI

Marriage

"Seriously, I do not mean to speak disrespectfully of marriage etc., but I only mean that it must bring some cares, and anxieties."

Letter to Donne

ALTHOUGH the departure of the Cowells was a calamity to FitzGerald, it was merely the prelude to a greater. Four months later, on November 7, 1856, Donne wrote to Fanny Kemble in America:

I am going as Harley says in the Vampire, "not to astonish you, Madam, but to paralyze you." I am going to affirm what, when rumoured of yore, I have often denied: to contradict my own prophetic soul: to approve in a measure what I have repeatedly averred to be improbable, impossible, absurd, out of the way, out of the question, gossip, humbug, twaddle—in short I am now going to announce not—that I am come into a fortune . . . nor anything indeed that you can fancy or dream, or have ever expected or longed for—but simply that Edward FitzGerald is at this moment, or in a very few days or hours will be— "Benedick the married man!" He is married or going to be married to Lucy Barton.[1]

FitzGerald was already married when Donne wrote, for the wedding had taken place at Chichester, Sussex, three days previously.

Lucy Barton was forty-eight years old, a few months her husband's senior. A member of the Barton family has written, "In point of intellect, culture, benevolence, and address, Lucy Barton was doubtless attractive; but she lacked physical charms. Her features were heavy, she was tall and big of bone, and her voice was loud and deep." [2] Though born of Quaker parents, she had adopted the Anglican faith and became a zealous church worker and Sunday-school teacher in Woodbridge. In 1831 she had published *Bible Letters for Children,* addressed to her church-school pupils who "might chance to find therein," stated her preface, ". . . something that would lead you early to think upon that great and good Being who made you and me, and all this beautiful earth, and not these

1. *Donne and His Friends,* pp. 210–211.
2. *Letters to Bernard Barton,* pp. 169–170.

things only, but also a glorious and happy heaven." Such was the woman whom the careless, Bohemian, skeptical, and ascetic Fitz-Gerald had married.

The marriage was no love match. FitzGerald had been bound to Lucy by a quasi-engagement since the death of her father, Bernard Barton, seven years before. In later years he told Frederick Spalding that he became engaged shortly after the poet's death.[3] FitzGerald's references to Miss Barton in his correspondence are, without fail, decidedly impersonal. How the engagement originated is a mystery which has gone with them to their graves. Members of the two families have their theories about the betrothal. They agree that FitzGerald unintentionally became involved in the contract; aferward, his sense of honor would not permit him to withdraw.

The explanation advanced by his family includes a scene at Barton's deathbed in which FitzGerald was a helpless and innocent actor. Mary Eleanor FitzGerald Kerrich, his grandniece, has written:

In his agony, as he was passing, Bernard Barton joined his daughter's and FitzGerald's hands and gave the . . . pair his blessing. Had Fitz-Gerald, at that supreme and last moment of his old friend's life, withdrawn his hand, had he immediately and positively disclaimed all share in the implied promise, the marriage, it is safe to say, would never have taken place. A man of the world (but such FitzGerald was not) would have acted at once, and would have refused to understand anything more than a subconscious expression by an affectionate father of a wish unformulated until then. . . . It is safe, therefore, to suppose . . . that FitzGerald was not immediately conscious of any obligation such as he felt later. . . . When or how they came to an understanding, I do not know.[4]

Barton left his daughter little more than his house, his books, and a few paintings of considerable sentimental but little intrinsic value. During the last year of his life he had lost part of his small capital, and he worried about his daughter's welfare when his death would cut off virtually all of her income. The Barton theory is that, in order to relieve his old friend of anxiety, FitzGerald had assured the poet that he would look after Miss Barton's interests and protect her. F. R. Barton has written:

When Barton's small estate had been realized, FitzGerald saw clearly that it did not provide enough to support her; and, faithful to the

3. Spalding diary, March 4, 1868.
4. Kerrich, [Mary] Eleanor FitzGerald, "Memories of Edward FitzGerald," *East Anglian Magazine* (August, 1935), p. 84.

assurance he had given some months previously to his ailing friend, he impetuously offered to make up the deficiency from his own income. Such an offer her sense of propriety forbade her to accept. One can imagine the effect of her refusal upon a temperament so sensitive as FitzGerald's. He accused himself of having committed an indelicacy— a breach of good taste. His disordered fancy prompted him to believe that he had grossly outraged the feelings of his old companion's daughter by offering her money. The thought was intolerable to him. He must make amends at any cost. And so, heedless of the consequences, he proposed, and she—blind to the distraction of mind that had impelled him —accepted his offer.[5]

Whatever the means, FitzGerald was convinced that the only honorable course left to him was marriage. Thus the engagement. He was involved in the financial troubles resulting from his father's bankruptcy at the time, and his means did not permit him to establish a home. Matrimony was deferred, therefore, until after the death of his mother.

His customary philosophic calm was disturbed at the prospect of marrying a woman whom he did not love. He shrank, too, from abandoning forever his bachelor freedom. Nevertheless, he tried to convince himself that marriage might be a desirable step and that Lucy Barton, reared in the simplicity of a Quaker household and accustomed to the somnolent life of Woodbridge, would make as near an ideal companion as he could hope to find. The long engagement robbed him even of that scant consolation. Miss Barton spent her last seven years of spinsterhood as companion to the two grandnieces of a wealthy Quaker, Hudson Gurney, of Keswick Hall, Norwich. She was accepted as one of the family by the Gurneys, who were active in Norfolk society. "She forgot," FitzGerald told Spalding, "the plainness and simplicity of the Quakeress and, attending Parties, Operas, etc., branched out into a fine . . . Lady." [6] The Lucy Barton of Keswick Hall was not the Lucy Barton whom FitzGerald had engaged to marry. Eventually he came to the conclusion that "they were unsuited to each other, and, *love* between two of their age and feelings being out of the question, he *suggested* through a letter to Mrs. Jones a breaking off of the engagement—but Miss Barton, on receiving this letter

5. *Letters to Bernard Barton,* pp. 170–171.
   No doubt a promise of some kind was involved. "In 1849," young Crabbe told Aldis Wright, "Bernard Barton died, and it was then that E. F. G. seemed more unhappy. I suppose on account of his promise." MS. letter to Aldis Wright.
   6. Spalding diary, May 4, 1868.

from Mrs. Jones, returned it to him saying *she* had no fears for the future, but that he was always looking on the worst side, etc." [7]

Thus ended FitzGerald's feeble effort to avert the catastrophe. Before he broached the matter again, if he ever did propose to press his suggestion further, his mother died, and he inherited a fortune.

"What could I do?" he asked Spalding rhetorically.

He struggled with himself to make the best of the situation. As November, 1856, approached, he notified his closest friends of his intention. "I am going to be married to Miss Barton," he told Spring Rice, "a very doubtful experiment—long thought of—not fixt beyond all Cause and Impediment till lately—and now 'Vogue la Galère!' I shut my Eyes to the Consequences, and read trash in Hafiz. . . . Oh, I am very tired of writing this News to Relatives etc." [8] He was calm but not hopeful when he wrote to Allen, "Thank Mrs. Allen for all her sanguine wishes—sanguiner than my expectations." [9] He was doleful when he told young Crabbe, in words that would be comic were it not for their pathos, "George, I am going to be married—don't congratulate me." Crabbe said later, "I shall never forget his miserable tones." [10]

The reactions of his friends differed greatly.

I am delighted at the news! [wrote Carlyle] There was a faint semi-invisible hint at such a thing in your former letter, but nobody, except myself, would take it; even my Wife was blind; and Donne . . . pleaded ignorant,—tho', he said, there had been for years back some rumour . . . of the kind, in reference to—the very Lady who now turns out to be the veritable Fact! For the rest, his character of her was at once credible and superlatively favourable. Indeed, it is difficult to fancy . . . that Miss Barton can be other than an eligible Wife. You may fairly look forward to a Home in this world henceforth such as you have not had before, and might very easily have missed ever to have. In all which I am the more interested as I hope to see said Home, with my own eyes, some day or other, and to have a kind of vested interest in the same for the rest of my time. I will say only, long may you live, and see and do good in the land, you and the amiable Life-Partner you are now to have. And may the gods "send never worse among us!" as our Scotch people pray.[11]

7. *Loc. cit.*
8. MS. letter to Spring Rice, Oct. 21, 1856.
9. MS. letter to Allen [1856].
10. MS. letter from Crabbe to Aldis Wright.
11. *Letters to Bernard Barton,* pp. 172-173.

W. K. Browne was baldly frank. "My dear Fitz," he remonstrated, "I would have kicked you to the Land's End, rather than this should have happened." [12]

FitzGerald's announcements to his friends indicate that whatever resolution he had summoned was slowly evaporating as the wedding approached. The preparations for the event, and finally the ceremony itself, swept away the last of his meagre consolation. When one considers his attitude toward polite society and its trumperies, it is easy to imagine the sort of wedding that he favored. Since some ceremony must be, he would not care what it was so long as there was no fuss and, above all, no smart, coxcombical wedding party. "All Cockney!" he branded such functions. But Miss Barton's relatives at Chichester expected the customary formalities. Miss Barton insisted upon them. It was her first mistake in managing a very difficult husband.

The wedding was held on November 4, with all the trappings of a formal ceremony. The bridegroom was hardly coöperative. One concession he flatly refused to make and that was in the matter of dress. His apparel, at best, never approached sartorial perfection and he appeared for the function wearing an old slouch hat and everyday clothes. Nor did he attempt to play the role of happy bridegroom. One of the Bartons records that "on the fateful day he looked like a victim being led to his doom. He walked by her side as one walking in his sleep, mute, and with head bowed." [13] A guest said that he spoke only once during the wedding breakfast. When offered some blanc mange, he waved it away with a gesture of disgust, muttering as he did so, "Ugh! Congealed bridesmaid!" [14]

The couple were as ill-suited to each other as any two mortals could be. Moreover, FitzGerald assumed that he would merely occupy the place in the life of Lucy Barton vacated by her father and that their home would be as unpretentious as that to which she had been accustomed in Woodbridge. FitzGerald had, in fact, attempted to ensure this by stipulating, before they were married, that they were "to see no company, to keep no establishment, and to live very quietly." [15] To this Miss Barton had agreed. Perhaps she made her promise early in the engagement; at any rate, she forgot, or chose to ignore, the pact. Life at Keswick Hall had given her an intimate knowledge of the way in which the well-ordered home of

12. Spalding diary, May 4, 1868.
13. *Letters to Bernard Barton*, pp. 173–174.
14. *Ibid.*, p. 174.
15. Spalding diary, May 4, 1868.

an English gentleman of means was run. She presumed that such a home was to be hers. The rub was that FitzGerald did not care how the homes of other English gentlemen were managed. He did not want his to be "managed" at all.

After the wedding the couple went to Brighton, which indicated another choice and another mistake of Mrs. FitzGerald's. To her husband, Brighton was "the hatefullest of all places." Nevertheless, it was one of the most fashionable—a feature which made it as attractive to Mrs. FitzGerald as abhorrent to her husband. The honeymoon was a dismal failure; and, after about six weeks on the coast, husband and wife temporarily separated. Mrs. FitzGerald returned to Norfolk to visit the Gurneys and, later, FitzGerald's sister, Mrs. Kerrich. At the same time she was to search for a house which would satisfy her own and her husband's antagonistic tastes. FitzGerald went to London to attend to business matters.

He returned to the Great Portland Street lodgings in which he had lived as a carefree bachelor. Resuming life in those surroundings was like donning dressing gown and slippers and settling at one's fireside after an unquiet day. Familiar surroundings assuaged, but could not remove, the anguish of his mind. Life, which had always been relatively simple, had suddenly become complex. He had already come to look upon his marriage as a rash act which, he told Cowell,

had good Sense and Experience prevailed instead of Blind Regard on one side . . . never *would* have been completed! You know my opinion of a "Man of Taste"—never so dangerous as when tied down to daily Life Companionhood—and with one very differently complexioned and Educated, and who might have been far far happier and usefuller untied to me. She wants a large Field to work on, and to bestow her Labour on a Field that will answer to Tillage. . . . I believe before long I shall offer a Field for some sort of Labour, if not the best; for I am not well, and shall, I really believe, very soon be laid by (if not dead) and *then* I shall put all my Taste into the Fire, I suppose; and my Wife will be rejoiced at last to be a Slave with a Master who can at last thank her for her Pains.[16]

He had planned to join his wife in Norfolk when he finished his business. However, the transaction completed, he tarried in his old rooms. He was reluctant to abandon them, unwilling to forego the subtle comfort derived from familiar surroundings. His wife could not find a satisfactory house in Norfolk. Finally, after a

16. MS. letter to Cowell, Jan. 22, 1857.

separation of five weeks, she joined him in London and they rented temporary lodgings at 24 Portland Terrace, Regent's Park. The evening of the day following her arrival, FitzGerald had not yet moved to his new quarters. "I positively stay behind here," he wrote to Cowell, "in the old Place on purpose to write to you in the same condition you knew me in and I you. I believe there are new Channels fretted in my cheeks with many unmanly tears since then, 'remembering the days that are no more' . . . I have seen scarce any Friends even while in London here. Carlyle but once; Thackeray not once—"

The next moment Thackeray was announced and entered the room "looking gray, grand, and good-humoured." Doubtless "Old Thack" tried to cheer his bewildered and depressed friend. But to no avail. After the novelist left,[17] FitzGerald closed his letter because "Thackeray's coming in overset me, with one thing and another. Farewell. Write to me; direct—whither? For till I see better how we get on I dare fix on no place to live or die in."

The FitzGeralds expected to stay in London two months; they remained four. The selection of a home was a thorny problem which kept them for weeks in a "total Quandary." FitzGerald was the difficult one to please. "I wish my Wife would go and choose and suit herself," he said, "and leave me to find out if it suits me." He disliked making decisions, and persuading him to make one which involved burning the last bridge between him and his old freedom was probably an impossibility.

Spring came early to London that year. From a little balcony outside their windows FitzGerald watched a fresh green spread over the lawns and hedges of Regent's Park. Peddlers, bearing huge baskets of crocuses, hepaticas, and primroses passed below. But color and blossom, for once, failed to stir his sense of beauty. Rather, the cry of the flower hawkers rose ominously from the street— "Growing. Growing. Growing! All the Glory going!"

One morning in April as he sat on the balcony, letters from the Cowells were brought to him. "My wife cried a good deal over your wife's Letter, I think—I think so," he told Cowell. "Ah me! I would not as yet read it, for I was already sad." [18] FitzGerald sought forgetfulness in Persian studies, but passages which he had read with his tutor constantly distracted him. "How it brought all back to me!" he said of an ode of Hafiz, first translated at Oxford. "Oriel opposite, and the Militia in Broad Street, and the old Canary-

17. This was probably the last meeting of the two men.
18. Cowell MS. letter, April 21, 1857.

coloured Sofa and the Cocoa or Tea on the Table! . . . I should think Bramford begins to look pretty about this time, hey Mr. Cowell? And Mrs. Cowell? . . . 'The Days are gone when Beauty bright, etc.' " [19]

Confinement within the rooms of a London lodging strained the relations of the uncongenial pair to the breaking point. The acrimony and asperity of FitzGerald's nature had rarely been aroused when he lived undisturbed, ordering every feature of his life by making a minimum of contacts with persons and conditions incompatible with his peace of mind. Like Sir Anthony Absolute, he was compliance itself—when not thwarted. Being compelled to live with one who made constant demands upon his time, attention, and consideration was an alien experience, and one that he could not—perhaps would not—brook. Nor was Mrs. FitzGerald's nature such as to make the cataclysm in his life an easy one. She was strong willed, and her mannish stride (the children of Woodbridge had nicknamed her Step-a-Yard) strengthened an impression of indomitable determination.

Each had resolved on the essentials to future happiness. FitzGerald wanted to live with as little change in his life and habits as possible. His wife's existence was the only concession he considered necessary. Mrs. FitzGerald's resolution was to mold the bachelor into the husband she wanted: one who observed all social punctilios, attired himself as a gentleman, dressed for dinner, helped to entertain his wife's guests, and did not smoke whenever and wherever he pleased. All this meant a great change in the life of the man who had once been unable to attend his mother, when she visited him at college, because his only pair of shoes was at the cobbler's. It meant that he could not spend his evenings reading, wrapped in the old plaid shawl in which he felt so comfortable. It meant that he would be unable to indulge in any of the Bohemian habits which gave rise to the story, whether true or not, that he had once been seen walking barefooted along a Woodbridge road, his shoes slung over his shoulder. He was not in the slightest respect like his wife's imaginary husband. She had ever been a crusader, and now she set out to reform her refractory spouse.

Apparently FitzGerald had retracted some of the conditions laid down before his marriage. He had consented, for instance, to keep an "establishment." But Mrs. FitzGerald was not satisfied. She "wanted to stay out, receive friends, and go into society, etc.," he said, "in fact wishing for everything the very opposite to, as she

19. *Ibid.*, March 29, 1857.

always knew, his taste and feelings." [20] To his wife's importunities on these matters FitzGerald made further concessions, though with bad grace. He permitted Donne, Pollock, and others of his London friends to entertain them, and entertained his friends in return. These occasions were hardly festive, to judge from the words of Pollock, with whom the FitzGeralds took dinner and whom they later had to tea in Portland Place. "Both occasions were altogether uncomfortable ones," wrote Pollock, "and it was a relief when the evening at our house—and the afternoon at his place—came to an end. The wretchedness of the terrible mistake he had made was apparent all the time—and in leaving his own place, he came away with us—very much the worse for some wine he had been taking— a condition in which I never saw him at any other time." [21] Nothing could demonstrate more clearly than the testimony of Pollock, who had known him for many years, the dejection and hopelessness into which FitzGerald had fallen. He had never been a teetotaler; but no one despised more any man who drank to excess.

Although FitzGerald made these two halfhearted concessions to his wife's desires regarding their home and entertainments, he was more perverse in accepting other marital responsibilities. To a degree he endured his wife's whims and her objections to his antisocial habits. For the most part, however, he maintained a moody silence and continued to do as he pleased. When Mrs. FitzGerald crusaded, he withdrew into himself and thought of happier times. He turned continually in memory to the carefree days he had spent with the Cowells at Bramford and Oxford. He sang in a doleful voice, until his wife was sick of hearing him, an old song, "When shall we three meet again?," particularly a stanza which ran, "Though in foreign lands we sigh, Parcht beneath a hostile sky." He repeated to himself over and over again the words of "Evan Banks," a Scotch poem, substituting for Evan, *Orwell*, the name of the stream on which Bramford and Ipswich are situated.

> Slow spreads the Gloom my Soul desires,
> The Sun from India's Shore retires:
> To *Orwell's* Bank, with temperate ray—
> Home of my Youth!—he leads the Day:
> Oh Banks to me for ever dear,
> Oh Stream whose murmur meets my Ear:
> Oh all my Hopes of Bliss abide
> Where *Orwell* mingles with the Tide.

20. Spalding diary, May 4, 1868.
21. Pollock MS. letter.

Music came to him for the words, and he sang the song to himself, thinking of the Cowells until, "It seems to me it would be easy to get into the first great Ship and never see Land again till I saw the Mouth of the Ganges! and there live what remains of my shabby Life." [22]

But FitzGerald did not go to India. Instead, he stayed in Portland Terrace, hoping, though hardly striving, for some solution to the enigma of his married existence. It must not be thought that their life was one of uninterrupted dissension. They tried, in so far as their discordant natures would permit, to tolerate each other and to bring order out of chaos. There is no doubt that Mrs. FitzGerald felt a genuine affection for her husband; but, says F. R. Barton, "the more she tried in her fond, tactless way to win his regard, the more she repelled him."

In addition to the major problems confronting them, small irritating clashes arose. FitzGerald's clothes were a persistent trouble. He obstinately refused to humor his wife's whims, as he called them, by "dressing for this and dressing for the other." He remained a Bohemian; Mrs. FitzGerald remained a model of Victorian propriety. He found her irksome and made no attempt to conceal the fact. "Your account of Edward FitzGerald," wrote Mrs. Sartoris, Fanny Kemble's sister, to Donne, "is very droll, but not comfortable I think. At least if I were his wife, I should not like him even to play at being bored by me." [23] To Donne he referred to his wife as "the Contemporary" and "the Elder." He did not like their apartment. It looked in front upon the wild beasts in Regent's Park, and behind upon a cemetery. He liked the living room least of all. The windows were narrow and lighted the room only dimly; the paper was a dark green, and, he told Donne, "My Contemporary looks in this chamber of horrors like Lucretia Borgia." Donne wrote to Fanny Kemble, "Most extraordinary of Benedicks is our friend. He talks like Bluebeard. Speaks 'O' leaping o'er the line': really distresses even Spedding's well-regulated mind. I have however so much confidence in him that I believe all this [to be] irony with a rooted regard for Lucy, and so much confidence in Lucy as to believe she'll tame Petruchio, swagger as he list."

On May 18, after four months of strife, the FitzGeralds again sought respite in separation. They gave up the London rooms. FitzGerald went to Bedford to stay with Browne for two weeks;

22. Letter to Cowell [1857].
23. *Donne and His Friends,* p. 217.

Mrs. FitzGerald visited friends at Gorleston, near Yarmouth, on the Norfolk coast. She rented lodgings, and her husband joined her early in June. The change was made to conform as nearly as possible to his desires. "Instead of the Regent's Park, and Regent Street, here before my windows are the Vessels going in and out of this River: and Sailors walking about with fur caps and their brown hands in their Breeches Pockets. Within hail almost, lives George Borrow who has lately published, and given me, two new Volumes of Lavengro called 'Romany Rye.' " [24] They now declined all formal invitations. FitzGerald refused one from Borrow, but added, "If one happens to drop in at tea, or Grog, time—all very well. I shall hope to give you a look before you go." Relieved of social obligations, and living among people who dined at one and did not object to early teas or old clothes, FitzGerald was happier for a time. "Moreover," Donne told Fanny Kemble, "his nieces have been staying with him who, as he improperly says, are, since his marriage, his chief comfort." Mrs. FitzGerald probably derived little pleasure from their new life, for her husband's happiness was but transitory. Fresh discords or the same old ones broke out, and FitzGerald again became steeped in misery. One evening Borrow accepted his suggestion to "drop in." Spalding records, "Borrow drank strong port, and had a contempt for anyone who could drink Sherry. It was just at the time when Mr. FitzGerald was very unhappy and this night drank a good deal of it, walked home with Borrow, and coming back, being very sleepy and tired, lay down in the grass by the roadside and fell asleep, not waking till three or four in the morning." [25]

Unwise as their marriage had been, shortsighted as they had been in attempting it, the FitzGeralds could not remain blind to the inevitable. In August they decided that the attempt was an irremediable failure, and separated permanently. FitzGerald left for Geldestone Hall. His wife remained at Gorleston. He made a generous settlement; thereafter, although they were never divorced, they lived apart.

That a full share of the blame for the failure of his marriage should be heaped upon FitzGerald's head cannot be denied. At the time, no doubt, he felt justified in his course of action. He had married on definite conditions. These had not been met and un-

24. Letter to Cowell, June 5, 1857.

Spalding records in his diary, "Mr. FitzGerald . . . told him [Borrow] that part of it [Romany Rye] he didn't believe, and *never could have happened,* quite expecting to be knocked down while telling him so." Spalding diary, Oct. 13, 1867.

25. *Ibid.,* Oct. 13, 1867.

happiness had resulted. Doubtless there would have been no other outcome, had the conditions never been made. The desires and habits of the two, both approaching fifty, had become firmly fixed. Husband and wife alike were strong willed, and neither could sacrifice enough to ensure the happiness of the other.

FitzGerald rarely mentioned his marriage to friends; but when he did, he took all the blame upon himself. "My married Life has come to an end," he told Mrs. Tennyson, "and I am back again in old Quarters, living as for the last thirty years—only much older, sadder, uglier, and worse! If People want to go further for the cause of all this Blunder than the fact of two People of very determined habits and Temper, first trying to change them at close on fifty—they may lay nine-tenths of the Blame on me." [26] Spalding recorded in his diary, "He does not in the least excuse himself —but says that he acted very wrongly, and for the worst—in not bearing and forbearing—after carrying out his engagement and contract, speaks most highly of her—excuses her of any *design* in the matter—of her willingness to undergo anything, in the way of *self*—or great things for him—but great People, great sights, great praise, great anticipations, and great confidence in her own power and management spoiled her." [27]

The separation by no means brought about an absolute break in the relations of the hapless couple. FitzGerald sympathized with his wife's lot and did what he could to relieve it. When Crabbe of Bredfield died in September, 1857, FitzGerald wrote to the vicar's son,

I want your Sisters so much to go to my Wife at Gorleston, when they can, and for as long as they can; and I have had a Letter from her to-day, hoping so they *will* but let her in that way return them some of the Sympathy they showed her when *her* Trial was. I am convinced that their going to her would be the very thing for herself, poor Soul: taking her out of herself, and giving her the very thing she is pining for; namely, some one to devote herself to. I write to your Sister to say this.

By *"her* Trial" FitzGerald did not refer, as one might almost assume, to the months that she lived with him; but to the time of Barton's death.

In the years immediately following their separation, FitzGerald occasionally visited his wife. In March, 1859, he spent a few days with her in Kent, where she had gone to live. To Donne, he de-

26. MS. letter to Mrs. Tennyson, March 19, 1858.
27. Spalding diary, May 4, 1868.

scribed the district as "a kind of park where elders are turned out to graze," for two other women who were separated from their husbands were in the same locality. In later years, "that poor lady" replaced "the Elder" and "the Contemporary" as the term by which he referred to his wife.[28]

28. Mrs. FitzGerald lived until Nov. 28, 1898. She died at Croydon at the age of ninety.

XVII

The Romance of The Rubáiyát

"I was . . . thinking to myself how it was fame enough to
have written but one song—air, or words—which should in
after days solace the sailor at the wheel, or the soldier in foreign
places!—be taken up into the life of England!"

Letter to Mrs. Cowell, 1851

I HAVE been the last Fortnight with the Cowells," FitzGerald
told Tennyson in July, 1856, after visiting his friends at Ipswich before they left for India. "We read some curious In-
fidel and Epicurean Tetrastichs by a Persian of the Eleventh
Century—as Savage against Destiny etc. as Manfred—but mostly
of Epicurean Pathos of this kind—'Drink—for the Moon will often
come round to look for us in this Garden and find us not.' " ¹

FitzGerald referred to the *rubáiyát*,² or quatrains, of Omar
Khayyám which Cowell had discovered in a Persian manuscript at
the Bodleian Library shortly before leaving Oxford. Omar was
then barely known to Western scholars, and Cowell had not previously heard or read of him. He copied the verses and made a
second transcript for FitzGerald while the latter was visiting at
Ipswich. After a cursory examination, FitzGerald put the quatrains
aside for almost a year. In the spring of 1857, however, he wrote to
Garcin de Tassy, a scholar of Persian literature living in Paris, to
inquire if there were any Omar manuscripts in the libraries there;
later he sent a copy of his quatrains to the Frenchman.³ When Fitz-
Gerald left London and his wife to visit Browne in June, he "put
away almost all Books, except Omar Khayyám!, which I could not

1. MS. letter to Tennyson, July 26, 1856.
2. *Rubáiyát* is the plural form of *rubái*. The translation of *rubái* as "quatrain" is
convenient but not literal. See p. 220.
3. Garcin de Tassy used FitzGerald's transcript to write a paper, "Note sur les
Rubâ'iyât de 'Omar Khaïyâm" for the *Journal asiatique* (Paris), No. 9, 1857. He intended to acknowledge his indebtedness to FitzGerald and Cowell, but at the former's
urgent request refrained from doing so. M. de Tassy wrote to FitzGerald that he had
also read his paper before the Oriental Society, of which he was vice-president, when
the Persian ambassador was present. "So," FitzGerald told Cowell, "you see I have
done the part of an ill Subject in helping France to ingratiate herself with Persia
when England might have had the start."

help looking over in a Paddock covered with Buttercups and brushed by a delicious Breeze." Some of the quatrains he turned into "monkish Latin." [4] He was in the midst of the confusion over his marriage problem at the time, and Omar, he told Cowell, "breathes a sort of Consolation to me!"

About the middle of June, he received the transcript of a second manuscript of Omar's verses, which Cowell had found in the Library of the Bengal Asiatic Society at Calcutta. In his letter of acknowledgment, FitzGerald mentioned the "human interest" which manuscripts possess, as compared with printed books, having been

written by a living hand at the end of which was a living Soul like my own—under a darker skin—some "dark Indian face with white Turban wreathed" and under an Indian Sun. And you spoke to him those thousands of miles away, and he spoke to you and this manuscript was put into your hands when done; and then deposited in that little box, made also by some dark hand, along with its aromatic Companion: you and your dear Wife saw them after they were nailed down . . . and so they have crossed the Atlantic, and . . . have reached my hands at last.[5]

The new manuscript quickened FitzGerald's interest, and he studied the quatrains closely. On July 14, 1857, exactly a year after he had parted from Cowell at Ipswich, he completed his first survey of the new collection. Walking in the garden of his Gorleston lodgings, where roses were blowing as, he presumed, they were in Persia, a translation of one of the stanzas formed in his mind; and with the lines he closed a letter to Cowell:

> I long for wine! oh Sáki of my Soul,
> Prepare thy Song and fill the morning Bowl;
> For this first Summer month that brings the Rose
> Takes many a Sultan with it as it goes.[6]

Within six months FitzGerald had translated many of Omar's quatrains. When Parker, who had published *Salámán and Absál,* asked him to contribute to *Fraser's Magazine,* FitzGerald selected thirty-five of his "less wicked" stanzas and sent them to the pub-

4. FitzGerald's Latin translation is in the Trinity College Library. A collation of the Latin with the English translation by Sir E. Denison Ross and Charles Ganz was published in 1938 by the Golden Cockerel Press.

5. MS. letter to Cowell, June [1857].

6. FitzGerald composed the first drafts of much of his poetry on lonely walks. It will be noted that his first quatrain consists of two couplets. He had not yet adopted the customary rhyme scheme of the Persian, a-a-b-a.

lisher in January, warning him, however, that he might find them "rather dangerous among his divines." The editors, apparently, were of the same opinion, for they kept them almost a year, neither publishing nor rejecting. Omar's freedom of thought on religion and morality, it is true, were somewhat daring for the conservative theology of Victorian England. FitzGerald finally decided that the magazine had no intention of printing his verses. "So, S'Death," he told Pollock, "I must shame the fools." He retrieved his manuscript, added forty quatrains, and had two hundred and fifty copies of the poem printed and bound in ordinary brown paper. Forty of them he kept; the remainder he turned over to Bernard Quaritch, a bookseller who specialized in Oriental works, to be placed on sale in his shop in Castle Street.[7] On April 9, 1859, the following advertisement appeared in the *Athenaeum* and the *Saturday Review:*

Just published, price 1s.
Rubaiyat of Omar Khayyam, the
Astronomer-Poet of Persia, translated into English Verse.
B. Quaritch, London, Castle Street,
Leicester-square.[8]

Review copies were sent at FitzGerald's request to various magazines.

Few books have so dramatic a history as has FitzGerald's *Rubáiyát*. Although its fame has declined since the time when its lines were on every tongue, it is still one of the most popular poems in the language. The collections of most booklovers contain copies, and no other poem is seen so frequently in the meager libraries of those who make no claim to being lovers either of books or of literature. But before the merit and beauty of the poem became known, it was almost lost to posterity. Few modern books have so narrowly escaped oblivion and yet survived; none have so nearly perished, finally to achieve so great a triumph. The recognition of the masterpiece and the identification of the translator, for the poem was published anonymously, hinged upon so strange a concatenation of events that the story reads like romance.

7. This street has since become part of Charing Cross Road, and the Quaritch firm still occupies the former Castle Street premises, now 30 Charing Cross Road.

8. *Athenaeum*, No. 1641; *Saturday Review*, Vol. VII, No. 180. The first line of the advertisement in the latter periodical reads, "Just published, 8vo., price 1s." Both were inserted at FitzGerald's suggestion.

Writers on FitzGerald have given the original price of the edition at anywhere from one to five shillings.

Many notable Victorians appear as characters in the "Romance of the *Rubáiyát*." Among those who rescued the book from oblivion were Swinburne, Dante Gabriel Rossetti, William Morris, and Whitley Stokes, a lawyer and Celtic scholar. They discovered the poem after Bernard Quaritch had consigned the edition to the pit of forgotten books, the penny box. Another group, which included Ruskin, Carlyle, Browning, Charles Eliot Norton, professor of fine arts at Harvard and editor of the *North American Review,* and Edward Burne-Jones, the Victorian painter, also appear in the story. They identified the author of the poem.

Of the forty copies which FitzGerald reserved, he gave away only three, one each to Cowell, Donne, and that omniverous student of languages, George Borrow. "I hardly know," he wrote in a letter which accompanied the copy to India, "why I print any of these things, which nobody buys; and I scarce see the few I give them to. But when one has done one's best, and is sure that that best is better than so many will take pains to do, though far from the best that *might be done,* one likes to make an end of the matter by Print." The distribution of the book seems to have ended with FitzGerald's gifts. Cowell, a pious man, was "naturally alarmed at it"; reviewers ignored the poem; and the sales, if any, were so few as to be negligible.

For almost two years the *Rubáiyát* lay on Quaritch's shelves. Finally the pamphlets were dumped into the bargain box outside the door of 15 Piccadilly, to which the dealer had moved from Castle Street;[9] and the poem seemed doomed to vanish ignominiously. One day early in 1861, however, some unknown person passing the shop caught sight of the homely booklets. One pictures him casually picking up a copy and indolently turning the pages. What was it that captured his attention? One can only conjecture. Sufficient it was that either his admiration or curiosity was piqued so that he bought copies at a penny each and gave them to friends. The *Rubáiyát* had won its first public.

Among those first attracted to the poem was a member of the *Saturday Review* editorial staff, who bought a number of copies. Strangely, it did not occur to him to review, or even to mention, the book in his magazine.[10] The poem fared better in the hands of

9. Quaritch told FitzGerald that the edition had been "as much *lost* as sold" when his business was moved from Castle Street.

10. FitzGerald wrote to Cowell in 1870, "Bye the bye, he [Quaritch] sent me of his own accord a funny account of what he calls the 'Disappearance' of the first Edition—which was bought up, he says, by the editor of the *Saturday Review* (Wilks?), who (at a penny a piece) gave them to friends. Why he did not say so much in his Paper I don't know." Cowell biography, p. 158.

others, however. Someone, perhaps the editor, perhaps another purchaser, told Rossetti of the discovery; Rossetti told Swinburne, and the two bought copies for themselves. The unprecedented demand caused the price to soar. "Next day," Swinburne told Lady Burne-Jones several years later, "when we were returned for more, the price was raised, to the iniquitous and exorbitant sum of two-pence. You should have heard, but you can imagine, the eloquent and impressive severity of Gabriel's humorous expostulations with the stall-keeper, on behalf of a defrauded if limited public. But we were extravagant enough to invest in a few more copies, even at that scandalous price." [11] One wonders what Rossetti would have said, could he have known that seventy-five years later a copy of the *Rubáiyát* in original wrappers and containing a note by Swinburne would be offered for sale by the Quaritch firm for $9,000. At the same time another copy, bound in green morocco, was valued at a paltry $4,500.

Not even the severest critics of the Pre-Raphaelites have ever charged them with lack of enthusiasm. The *Rubáiyát* caught their fancy, and their praises advertised the poem. Rossetti, Swinburne, and Morris were eager to discover the translator; but there was no clue to his identity. Swinburne gave one of the books to Burne-Jones, who praised the work highly and copied it for many of his friends. When he showed the poem to Ruskin in 1863, the critic was so impressed that he immediately wrote a note addressed "To the Translator of Omar Khayyam" and left it with the artist to deliver when the author was discovered. None of the group saw the following item which appeared in a catalogue issued by Quaritch in the autumn of 1868:

Omar Khayyam, the astronomer-poet of Persia, Rubaiyat, translated into English verse by E. FitzGerald, Esq. 8 vo., sd. RARE, 3s. 6d.

Upon seeing the advertisement, FitzGerald wrote to Quaritch that the price made him blush. In the same year (1868) FitzGerald published a second and longer edition of the poem. Still another, that of 1872, appeared before he was identified as the author.

11. Rossetti is usually credited with buying the first copy at the penny box, but Swinburne states in his letters that he believed Whitley Stokes called Rossetti's attention to the poem. It is impossible to identify, beyond doubt, the first purchaser.

Swinburne closed his account with the statement, "I think it was within a month that Quaritch was selling copies at a guinea,—so at least we heard, and read." *Memorials of Edward Burne-Jones* (London, Macmillan & Co., Ltd., 1902), I, 234. This may have been true but appears to have been rumor, as the advertisement quoted in the following paragraph indicates.

Charles Eliot Norton, who visited England frequently, had met Burne-Jones at the home of Robert Browning in 1857. In 1868, while Norton was visiting Ruskin, his acquaintance with the artist ripened into friendship. Burne-Jones at that time showed the American his *Rubáiyát* and spoke of the note which Ruskin had left with him five years before. When he returned to the United States, Norton carried with him a copy of the second edition as well as a translation of Omar's quatrains published the year before by J. B. Nicolas, a Frenchman. The two works were the basis of an article which Norton contributed to the *North American Review* in October, 1869. His comments on FitzGerald's poem, the first public recognition of the work, reveal the enthusiasm of those early patrons. Norton stated:

He [the translator] is to be called "translator" only in default of a better word, one which should express the poetic transfusion of a poetic spirit from one language to another, and the re-presentation of the ideas and images of the original in a form not altogether diverse from their own, but perfectly adapted to the new conditions of time, place, custom, and habit of mind in which they reappear. In the whole range of our litera-ture there is hardly to be found a more admirable example of the most skilful poetic rendering of remote foreign poetry than this work of an anonymous author affords. It has all the merit of a remarkable original production, and its excellence is the highest testimony that could be given, to the essential impressiveness and worth of the Persian poet. It is the work of a poet inspired by the work of a poet; not a copy, but a reproduction, not a translation, but the redelivery of a poetic inspira-tion . . . There is probably nothing in the mass of English transla-tions or reproductions of the poetry of the East to be compared with this little volume in point of value as *English* poetry. In the strength of rhythmical structure, in force of expression, in musical modulation, and in mastery of language, the external character of the verse cor-responds with the still rarer interior qualities of imagination and of spiritual discernment which it displays.[12]

The *Rubáiyát* won immediate recognition and popularity in the United States as a result of Norton's article, and Quaritch carried on a brisk trans-Atlantic trade, which was largely responsible for the third and fourth editions. FitzGerald dismissed this demand as inconsequential, for he understood that Americans "took up a little *Craze* of this sort now and then." Fanny Kemble's daughter, Mrs. Sarah Wister, who was acquainted with FitzGerald's other translations, almost intuitively, it appears, fixed upon him as the

12. *North American Review,* CIX (October, 1869), 575-576.

author. She questioned her mother and Donne when she visited England in the spring of 1870, but they maintained that they knew nothing of the matter. Mrs. Wister then wrote to FitzGerald and learned that she was correct in her assumption. Through her the author's identity became known to a limited circle in the vicinity of Philadelphia. One of her friends, Horace H. Furness, the Shakespeare scholar, wrote to Quaritch in December, 1870:

> Many thanks for the promptitude with which I received the two copies of Omar Khayyam's Rubaiyat. Please send me (by Post) eight (8) more copies of it.
>
> If you ever communicate with Mr. Edward FitzGerald, I wish you would express to him, if he care to learn it, the keen delight with which his translation has been read by quite a circle of my friends here in this city; and I must confess so exquisite is the English and rhythmical is the verse that we all, ignorant as we are of the original, mistrust that the beauties of Omar are largely due to the genius of the translator.[13]

Quaritch immediately forwarded this tribute to FitzGerald, who was gratified by the "good words."

In England, however, the author was still unidentified; and it was not until 1870 that an English publication reviewed the poem. In June a writer in *Fraser's Magazine* likewise compared Fitz-Gerald's version with that of Nicolas, and paid tribute to the unknown Englishman

> who can hardly be too much congratulated on the excellence and elegance of his performance. . . . He has certainly achieved a remarkable success, and it would be difficult to find a more complete example of terse and vigorous English, free from all words of weakness or superfluity. The rhythm of his stanzas is admirable. . . .[14]

FitzGerald read the article and told Cowell that he "was well pleased to be so belauded."

As fame of the poem spread, it became rumored in London that the translator was "a certain Reverend Edward FitzGerald, who lived somewhere in Norfolk and was fond of boating." Setting FitzGerald's reverence aside, the identification came as close as one should require of a rumor. FitzGerald *was* fond of boating, and Norfolk adjoins Suffolk. Burne-Jones told Norton of the report

13. MS. letter, Trinity College Library.
14. Hinchcliff, Thomas W., "Omar Khayyám, the Astronomer-Poet of Persia," *Fraser's Magazine*, New Series, I (June, 1870), 777–784. The review was unsigned, but Mr. Hinchcliff identified himself as the author in a letter written to Quaritch in 1876. *Edward FitzGerald's Letters to Bernard Quaritch* (London, Bernard Quaritch, Ltd., 1926), pp. 42–43. C. Quaritch Wrentmore, ed.

when the latter returned to England in the autumn of 1872. The following spring, the American, while walking with Carlyle, whom he had known since 1869, mentioned his admiration for the *Rubáiyát.*

"He had never heard of it," Norton related.

He asked me whose work it was, and I told him what I had heard, that the translation was made by a Rev. Edward FitzGerald, who lived somewhere in Norfolk and spent much time in his boat. "The Reverend Edward FitzGerald?" he said in reply. "Why, he's no more Reverend than I am! He's a very old friend of mine—I'm surprised, if the book be as good as you tell me it is, that my old friend has never mentioned it to me" . . . I told him I would send him the book, and did so the next day. Two or three days later, when we were walking together again, he said: "I've read that little book which you sent to me, and I think my old friend FitzGerald might have spent his time to much better purpose than in busying himself with the verses of that old Mohammedan blackguard." I could not prevail on Carlyle even to do credit to the noble English in which FitzGerald had rendered the audacious quatrains of the Persian poet; he held the whole thing as worse than a mere waste of labour.

Upon hearing of Norton's discovery, Burne-Jones sent him Ruskin's note, which the American posted to Carlyle with the following:

I enclose a note which Ruskin wrote some year or two, or even more, since, addressed to the Translator of Omar Khayyam, that "old Mohammedan blackguard" as you call him. He took a fancy to the productions of the reprobate poet, and left this note with an acquaintance of mine to be forwarded to the translator if ever his name should be discovered.

The note has been lying all this while in a desk, and I am asked now to ask you to forward it,—that is to give to it the right address and let it be sent to the post office.

Will you have the kindness to do this? unless you think that such a part of the Persian poet blackguard's sins rests upon the shoulders of his translator, as to make him unworthy to be cheered by the knowledge that his work has given pleasure to others no better, if indeed not worse than himself.[15]

Carlyle wrote immediately to FitzGerald:

Mr. Norton, the writer of that note, is a distinguished American . . . an extremely amiable, intelligent, and worthy man; with whom I have had some pleasant walks, dialogues and other communications, of late months;—in the course of which he brought to my knowledge, for the

15. MS. letter, Trinity College Library.

first time, your notable *Omar Khayyam,* and insisted on giving me a copy from the third edition, which I now possess, and duly prize. From him, too, by careful cross-questioning, I identified, beyond dispute, the hidden "FitzGerald," the Translator;—and indeed found that his complete silence, and unique modesty in regard to said meritorious and successful performance, was simply a feature of my own *Edward F.!* The translation is excellent; the Book itself a kind of jewel in its way. I do Norton's mission without the least delay, as you perceive. Ruskin's message to you passes through my hands sealed.

Ruskin's note read:

> 2nd. September
> 1863
>
> My dear and very dear Sir,
>　　I do not know in the least who you are, but I do with all my soul pray you to find and translate some more of Omar Khayyam for us: I never did—till this day—read anything so glorious, to my mind as this poem— (10th. 11th. 12th pages if one were to choose)—and that, and this, is all I can say about it—More—more—please more—and that I am ever gratefully and respectfully yours.
>
> J. Ruskin.[16]

In his acknowledgment of Carlyle's letter, FitzGerald said, "It is lucky for both R. and me that you did not read his Note: a sudden fit of Fancy, I suppose, which he is subject to."
FitzGerald also wrote to Norton:

> Two days ago Mr. Carlyle sent me your Note, enclosing one from Mr. Ruskin. . . . You will be a little surprised to hear that Ruskin's Note is dated September 1863: all but ten years ago! I dare say he has forgotten all about it long before this: however, I write him a Note of Thanks for the good, too good, messages he sent me; better late than never; supposing that he will not be startled and bored by my acknowledgements of a forgotten Favour rather than gratified. It is really a funny little Episode in the Ten years' Dream.

16. MS. letter, Trinity College Library.
　FitzGerald wrote to Ruskin immediately to acknowledge the letter. In the Trinity College collection is Ruskin's reply.

> Brantwood,
> Coniston, Lancashire
> 18th. April [1873]
>
> My dear Sir,
>　　I hope the address you gave is enough—for I want to say how glad I am of your letter—though I have time to say no more than that
>
>　　　　　　I am
>
>　　　　　　　　Most truly yours,
>　　　　　　　　J. Ruskin.

FitzGerald was first credited in a literary journal with being the author of the *Rubáiyát* in 1875. In February of that year Fitz-Edward Hall, who described himself enigmatically as "a social leper," with whom the translator carried on a sporadic correspondence, contributed a paragraph on FitzGerald's works to "Our Monthly Gossip" column of *Lippincott's Magazine*. After mentioning the current admiration for the translation, Mr. Hall praised the poem which "has gone far to prove that the acceptableness among us of Oriental poetry may depend very largely on the skill with which it is transplanted into our language. The translator of the *Rubáiyát* is Mr. Edward FitzGerald, of Woodbridge in Suffolk." A complete list of FitzGerald's works was given. It included not only those published and printed privately, but also his *Bird Parliament*, a translation of Attár's *Mantik-ut-tair*, which then existed only in manuscript. Mr. Hall concluded, "Mr. Allibone knows nothing of Mr. FitzGerald and he is similarly passed over in silence by the compiler of *Men of the Time*. Everything that he has produced is uniformly distinguished by marked ability; and, such being the case, his indifference to fame, in this age of ambition for literary celebrity, is a phenomenon which deserves to be emphasized."[17] FitzGerald was formally acknowledged as the author of the poem in 1876. The *Contemporary Review* for March carried a criticism of the *Rubáiyát* by H. Schütz-Wilson, who had applied through Quaritch for permission to use FitzGerald's name.[18]

Although FitzGerald lived to see the *Rubáiyát* recognized as a masterpiece, he died before "the little Craze" for the poem, which he had noted among American readers, became a mania which swept the world. Its popularity has declined from its zenith, reached at the turn of the century, but editions still pour from the presses and still find buyers. Some publishers consider their lists incomplete if they fail to contain at least two editions of the poem, one for ordinary trade and one "fine" edition. Private presses have found the poem ideally suited to their purposes. It is doubtful if the total number of editions which have been published can ever be determined. The first to appear without benefit of consent by either author or publisher was printed in Calcutta in 1862. The poem seems to hold the same fascination for illustrators that the role of Hamlet holds for actors. Not all who have illustrated it have

17. The article was unsigned, but Mr. Hall identified himself as the author after FitzGerald's death. The paragraph appeared in *Lippincott's Magazine,* XV (February, 1875), 261.

18. Schütz-Wilson, H. "The Rubá'iyát of Omar Khayyám," *Contemporary Review,* XXVII (March, 1876), 559–570.

understood the ideas which they were attempting to interpret. The work has been translated into many languages, including Latin and Erse. One edition, the creation of the late Eben Thompson of Worcester, Massachusetts, for some years has held the world's record for miniature books. It is so small as to require a magnifying glass to be read.

The influence of the poem has been tremendous. It created an inquisitive public which stimulated the work of Persian scholars. Mr. Thompson, who was tempted to study Persian and to make his own translation of Omar, was neither the first nor the last to be so influenced by FitzGerald. Some have mastered the language to elucidate his work. Others have wished to read Omar's poetry in the original.

The *Rubáiyát* has probably revealed the full beauty of lyric poetry to more readers than any other poem in the language. The appeal of its philosophy cannot be denied. FitzGerald has inspired poets. Swinburne adapted the stanzaic pattern of the poem in writing "Laus Veneris." One of the most successful achievements by those who have dared comparison with FitzGerald is that of Richard Le Gallienne, who converted portions of Justin McCarthy's prose translation into poetry.

Aspiring, as well as proved, poets have tried their hands at the measure. I have seen a manuscript copy of a *Rubáiyát* written by the late Clarence Darrow, the criminal lawyer. A "Rubáiyát of a Persian Cat" had a considerable vogue for a time. Doubtless, *rubáiyát* have been written to celebrate quadrupeds and perhaps even bipeds of greater length of ear. If FitzGerald's poem could be killed, the efforts of versifiers who have been inspired by him would have killed it.

XVIII

The Persian Poet and the English Poem

"But in truth I take old Omar rather more as my property than yours: he and I are more akin, are we not? You see all his Beauty, but you don't feel *with* him in some respects as I do."

Letter to Cowell

THE Persian poet, Omar Khayyám or, to give his full name, Ghiyas Uddin Abul Fath Omar Ibn Ibrahim al-Khayyámi, was a native of Naishápúr in the province of Khorassán, "the Land of the Sun." The exact date of his birth is unknown, but he had reached middle age in 1066 when Harold, England's last Saxon king, was defeated by William the Conqueror. The date of his death is usually given as A.H. 517, or A.D. 1123–24; but E. G. Browne, formerly lecturer in Persian at the University of Cambridge, author of the standard history of Persian literature, states that he can find no strong authority for the date. He adds, "It is, however, certain . . . that he died between A.D. 1115 and 1135, and 'some years' before the latter date." [1] In one of his quatrains Omar mentions that he had lived for more than a century.

> That which I am I am, O lord, by Thy decree;
> An hundred years in ease Thy grace hath fostered me. [2]

This statement, according to J. K. M. Shirazi, a Persian of the present century, is supported by evidence found in other Persian sources. [3] FitzGerald followed the evidence available to European scholars of his time when, in writing the preface to his *Rubáiyát*, he placed Omar's birth "in the latter half of our Eleventh century."

Shirazi says that the poet was probably of Arabian stock. "Up to the present," he writes,

1. Browne, Edward G., *A Literary History of Persia* (London, T. Fisher Unwin, 1906), II, 255. 4 vols.

2. Payne, John, *The Quatrains of Omar Kheyyam* (London, Villon Society, 1898), Quatrain 681, p. 166.

3. Shirazi, J. K. M., *Life of Omar al-Khayyámi* (Edinburgh and London, T. N. Foulis, 1905), p. 29.

it has been pretty generally accepted that Omar was of purely Persian descent, European authors either taking his origin for granted or refusing to enter into complicated questions of family history. My contention is that Omar, though a native of Persia, was not of Persian origin but belonged to an Arab tribe, al-Khayyámi, a name which is commonly used as his surname and has given rise to the legend that his father and even the poet himself followed the trade of tent-making. Now, except in conjunction with that of Omar the poet, the name occurs nowhere in Persian MSS, and the best authorities are agreed that neither in ancient nor in modern Persia does the name al-Khayyámi exist as a patronymic. Among Arabs, on the other hand, the name is fairly common, as also among the nomadic tribes of Khuzistan and Luristan.

Mr. Shirazi explains that, to escape political and religious strife, which were common among nomadic tribes, individuals and groups frequently left their own people and settled in more peaceful provinces in Persia. Khorassán was a favorite refuge. "Early in the ninth or tenth century," the writer continues,

there is supposed to have existed an Arab tribe called al-Khayyámis (tent-makers). . . . To this tribe the ancestors of Omar probably belonged, and doubtless had good reasons of their own for migrating to Khorassán, where the power of the Caliphs was merely nominal, and ample opportunities existed for gaining a peaceful livelihood. . . . There are many families in Persia today, Persian of the Persians, who yet pride themselves on their Arab descent.[4]

This assumption is supported by W. F. Prideaux, who, writing independently, points out that Omar's quatrains breathe more of the spirit of Arabian than of Persian verse. In a work printed privately Prideaux quotes a few lines of Arab poetry to illustrate its similarity to Omar's:

> Alas, my Soul, for Youth that's gone—
> no light thing lost I when he fled!
> What time I trailed my skirts in pride
> and shook my locks at the tavern's door.
>
> Nay, envy not a man that men say,
> "Age has made him ripe and wise";
> Though thou love life and live long safe,
> long living leaves its print on thee! [5]

4. *Op. cit.*, pp. 30–33.
5. Prideaux, Col. W. F., *Omar and His Translator* (Ely, Cambs., private press of E. H. Blakeney, 1909), quoted here from a review of the book in *T. P.'s Weekly*, Oct. 8, 1909.

Much more has been written about Omar than is actually
known about him, the sources of information for the most part
being works of questionable authority. Persian and Arabic writers
who lived before 1300, that is, within one hundred and seventy-five
years of Omar's death, provide us with the meager information
that Omar was famous as a philosopher, astronomer, and mathematician, and that he was denounced by devout contemporaries as
a free thinker. To these few facts have been added many legends,
the most persistent of which might be called "The Story of the
Three Friends." According to the tale, Omar, as a young man,
studied under the Imám Mowaffak, one of Persia's most renowned
teachers, whose pupils, it was commonly believed, rose to fortune.
Omar and two fellow students, Nizám al Mulk and Hassan al Sab-
báh, became close friends. At Hassan's suggestion the three agreed
that whichever of them achieved greatest success should share his
fortune with the other two. Nizám al Mulk became vizier, or prime
minister, under Malik Shah, one of the early Seljuk rulers of Persia.
Applying to his friend, Omar was granted a yearly pension of
twelve hundred *mithkáls* of gold, estimated as being the equivalent
of between $3,000 and $4,000. Hassan was given a place at court
and plunged into a career of intrigue which ended when he attempted to supplant his benefactor in the Sultan's favor. He then
fled and became founder of the band of outlaws known as the
Hassaniyeh, or Assassins. Nizám al Mulk eventually became a victim of the band.

Browne is supported by other modern scholars in his dismissal
of the story as pure fiction. He states that the *Wasaya* or *Testa-
mentary Instructions* attributed to Nizám al Mulk, in which the
legend first appears, has been proved spurious and of fifteenth-
century composition. Furthermore, the story involves chronolog-
ical assumptions which cannot be accepted without question.
Finally, although there is evidence that Nizám al Mulk was acquainted with Hassan, a later and less famous minister stated that
he had been a student with Hassan. It is possible, Mr. Browne
suggests, that the identities of these two men may have become
confused.[6]

Persian sources leave little room to doubt, however, that during
a long life spent in study Omar became renowned and respected
for knowledge and wisdom. He was an *imám* or priest, and one of
the earlier sources states that his knowledge of Arabic philology
and the seven readings of the Koran was remarkable. The same

6. Browne, *Literary History*, II, 190–192.

source says that, after having read a certain book seven times, Omar later wrote it out almost word for word from memory. He was one of the eight astronomers appointed by Malik Shah to reform the calendar. The result was the Jaláli Era, which was inaugurated on March 15 (the Persian New Year's Day), 1079. Their computations, Gibbon states, surpassed the Julian and approached the accuracy of the Gregorian calendar. Omar is known to have written a book on algebra and one on geometry. Various other mathematical, meteorological, and metaphysical works are attributed to him; and there is evidence that he had studied the works of Avicenna, the Arabian physician and philosopher, and had written on medicine.

Among his countrymen Omar's reputation rested almost entirely on his philosophical, mathematical, and scientific studies, for orthodox Mohammedans ignored his poems as containing a freedom of thought to which they could not subscribe. In *The Book of Learned Men,* an Arabic biographical work of the thirteenth century,[7] appears the following:

Omar al-Khayyámi, Imám of Khorassán, was the most learned man of his day. Not only was he versed in all the wisdom of the Greeks, but he encouraged the search after the One. . . . He also taught the necessity of studying science according to the principle of the Greeks. The later Sufis have professed to find in his verses confirmation of their own doctrines. . . . But their [i.e., Omar's verses] inner meanings are as stinging serpents to the Musselman law, hence the men of his day hated him and exposed the secrets he would fain have concealed, so that, fearing for his life, he controlled his tongue and pen. . . . There was no one equal to him in astronomy and philosophy; in these his name was a proverb.[8]

Research by modern scholars has confirmed the implication in the foregoing quotation that Omar was not a Súfí, the sect of Mohammedan mystics with whom the poet is frequently linked.[9] In FitzGerald's day, however, opinion was divided on the question, despite the fact that the poet, in his verse, freely ridiculed the sect.

From the beginning of his studies FitzGerald discarded the Súfí interpretation of Omar's *rubáiyát.* "His Worldly Pleasures," he stated, "are what they profess to be without any pretence at divine Allegory: his Wine is the veritable Juice of the Grape: his Tavern,

7. Browne gives the title as *History of the Philosophers.* The author was al-Quiftí.
8. Shirazi, *Omar,* pp. 58–60.

9. Browne translates the passage referring to the Súfís as follows: "The latter Súfís have found themselves in agreement with some part of the apparent sense of his verse, and have transferred it to their system." *Literary History,* II, 250.

where it was to be had: his Sáki, the Flesh and Blood that poured it out for him." [10] In the preface to his second edition FitzGerald observed that "very few of the more mystical Quatrains are in the Bodleian MS., which must be one of the oldest, as dated at Shiraz, A.H. 865, A.D. 1460." Originally, Cowell likewise had denied Omar's affiliation with the Súfís. "We have said," he wrote in the *Calcutta Review* in 1857, "that Omar was no mystic—we find no trace of Sufeyism in his book." [11] Cowell was a conservative, ortho- dox Victorian, however, and viewed with great concern the later popularity of FitzGerald's translation. When Edward Heron-Allen, a Persian scholar, proposed to dedicate a book on the poem to him in 1898, Cowell replied,

I yield to no one in my admiration of Omar's poetry as literature, but I cannot join in the *Omar Cult,* and it would be wrong in me to pretend to profess it. So, I am deeply interested in Lucretius . . . but here again I only admire Lucretius as "literature." I feel this especially about Omar Khayyám, as I unwittingly incurred a grave responsibility when I intro- duced his poems to my old friend in 1856. I admire Omar as I admire Lucretius, but I cannot take him as a *guide*. In these grave matters I prefer to go to Nazareth, not to Naishapúr.[12]

So disturbed did Cowell become over the growth of an "Omar Cult" that he eventually professed to believe that the poem was an allegory. Fear that FitzGerald's reputation would suffer unless the poem were so explained was probably responsible for Cowell's revised interpretation.

Omar's philosophy has been frequently discussed and often mis- represented. Anyone who studies his poetry closely discovers that the poet was neither an atheist nor an agnostic. "His addresses to the Deity," writes one Persian scholar, "even when most audacious, are those of a convinced believer; sometimes offering the advice of an intrepid subject to his sovereign, sometimes throwing out the shrewd comments of a court jester; always recognizing supremacy, often implying goodness." Nor does he expound any formal phi- losophy in his *rubáiyát*. "We . . . have seen," the writer states, "that he had no plan or 'principle,' no set intention of writing a continuous *Apologia pro vita sua*." [13] Another authority concludes,

10. Preface to the *Rubáiyát*.

11. *Calcutta Review,* Vol. XXX, January, 1858. Quoted by N. H. Dole, *Rubáiyát of Omar Khayyám* (Boston, L. C. Page & Co., 1898), 1, xxiii. 2 vols.

12. Heron-Allen, Edward, *Rubá'iyát of 'Umar Khayyám* (London, Duckworth & Co., 1908), p. xv.

13. Keene, H. G., "Loose Stanzas," *Calcutta Review,* 1895. Quoted in Dole, *Rubái- yát,* II, 433 and 437.

after quoting a number of passages from Omar, "Of course, in such a collection, much stress cannot be laid upon one or two quatrains, but there is much else to justify us in holding that our poet was not without some faith in God and duty." [14]

Omar's quatrains are epigrams, the random thoughts of a learned, wise, and frank scholar who revolted against the bigotry, dogma, and fetters of Mohammedanism. He satirized the pietists and fanatics who substituted hollow ritual for true worship. He challenged the beneficence of a God who, having ordained both good and evil, yet punished man for transgression.[15] That which bewildered him most was the riddle of existence to which he "found no key." His consolations were women and wine. The *rubáiyát* were struck off as he speculated on all these matters during the course of his long life.[16] There is no consistency of belief in the collection, for none was attempted. There is no continuity of thought, for the quatrains are arranged, as is customary with Persian epigrammatic verse, in diwan, or alphabetical, order, the sequence being determined by the final letter of the rhyming word.

It is simply for convenience that the Persian term *rubái* is translated into English as "quatrain." Actually, the *rubái* is a two-lined stanza which breaks very naturally into the four lines of the English quatrain. In every variety of Persian poetry, the unit is the *bayt*, a line which consists of six or eight feet. Each *bayt* in a *rubái* is divided into two symmetrical halves called *misrá*. Usually the first, second, and fourth *misrá*, rhyme, resulting in the *a a b a* pattern used in English translations. In other words, a *rubái* consists of two lines divided into hemistichs with the first, second, and fourth hemistichs rhyming.

In his translation FitzGerald adopted the rhyme pattern (*a a b a*) which predominates in the original, but he simplified the rhyme itself. Persian poets sometimes use the single rhyme to which English readers are accustomed; usually, however, their rhyme is more complicated than our own. One form which Omar frequently used is illustrated by the following quatrain quoted from Payne's literal translation of the *Rubáiyát*:

14. Cadell, J. E., "The True Omar Khayyám," *Fraser's Magazine*, XCIX (May, 1879), 659.
15. See FitzGerald's letter to Thackeray, written in 1831, p. 57.
16. It is impossible for scholars to say how many of the quatrains attributed to Omar were actually written by him. In the process of transcribing, many stanzas were added to the various manuscripts. "While it is certain," E. G. Browne states, "that 'Umar Khayyám wrote many quatrains, it is hardly possible, save in a few exceptional cases, to assert positively that he wrote any particular one of those ascribed to him." *Literary History*, II, 257.

> Bethink thee that soulless and bare thou shalt go;
> The veil of God's mysteries to tear thou shalt go;
> Drink wine, for thou knowest not whence thou hast come;
> Live blithe, for thou knowest not where thou shalt go.[17]

The selection illustrates the Persian practice of throwing the rhyme (bare, tear, where) back into the line by repeating a clause. Sometimes the rhyme is followed by a word or two, at others by a phrase. This introduces a repetition which is alien and usually awkward to English ears. The repetition frequently takes more complicated and sometimes more effective forms. For example:

> An hundred thousand Moses Time's Sinaï hath seen;
> An hundred thousand Jesus its azure sky hath seen;
> An hundred thousand Caesars its hall go by hath seen;
> An hundred thousand Kisras its vaults on high hath seen.[18]

Occasionally, as in this quotation, four rhymes appear in a *rubái,* a pattern which FitzGerald followed in three of his quatrains.[19] The thought expressed or the whim of the poet suggests the form of the lines, and no uniformity of meter is observed by the Persian in a group of *rubáiyát.* Within single *rubái* the meter of the third hemistich, particularly when unrhymed, may differ from that of the other three. These liberties FitzGerald also abandoned in deference to English practice.

The belief that FitzGerald's poem contains many passages interpolated by him has been current ever since the work gained recognition. One scholar has asserted that FitzGerald, in calling his poem a translation, committed "a sin against literary morality." Another stated, "It is a poem on Omar, rather than a translation of his work." [20] FitzGerald's editor said in a note, "It must be admitted that FitzGerald took great liberties with the original in his version of Omar Khayyám. The first stanza is entirely his own." [21] The statement about the first stanza is an error,[22] and careful research has disclosed that he interpolated little.

17. Payne, *Quatrains*, No. 188.
18. *Ibid.,* No. 143.
19. Fourth edition, quatrains 32, 46, 69.
20. First statement: Payne, *Quatrains*, p. lxvii; second: Cadell, *Fraser's Magazine,* XCIX, 650.
21. FitzGerald, *Literary Remains*, VII, 186.
22. Mr. Heron-Allen comments on this point, "It is not surprising that Mr. Aldis Wright . . . states that 'the first stanza is entirely his own,' for, in this precise form the rubá'i is only to be found in the Calcutta MS and in a recently discovered MS copied largely from it . . ." Heron-Allen, *Edward FitzGerald's Rubá'iyát of Omar Khayyám* (London, Bernard Quaritch, 1899), p. 5.

Edward Heron-Allen, a Persian scholar, spent twelve years surveying the entire range of FitzGerald's Persian studies and tracing his quatrains to their sources. His object was "to set at rest, once and for ever, the vexed question of how far Edward FitzGerald's incomparable poem may be regarded as a translation of the Persian originals, how far as an adaptation, and how far as an original work. . . . The results of my observations," he stated,

may be summarized as follows:

Of Edward FitzGerald's quatrains, forty-nine are faithful and beautiful paraphrases of single quatrains to be found in the Ouseley or Calcutta MSS or both.

Forty-four are traceable to more than one quatrain and may therefore be termed the "Composite" quatrains.

Two are inspired by quatrains found by FitzGerald only in Nicolas' [23] text.

Two are quatrains reflecting the whole spirit of the original poem.

Two are traceable exclusively to the influence of the Mantik ut-tair of Ferid ud dín Attár.

Two quatrains primarily inspired by Omar were influenced by the Odes of Hafiz.[24]

The list accounts for the one hundred and one stanzas which make up the poem in its final form. The last eight quatrains to which Heron-Allen refers are: those "inspired" by Nicolas, 46 and 98; those traced to Attár's *Mantik,* 33 and 34; those influenced by Hafiz, 2 and 3; those which cannot be attributed to any particular quatrains in the original but which reflect the philosophy of many of Omar's stanzas, 5 and 86.

Heron-Allen also traced the source of nine additional quatrains which appeared in FitzGerald's second edition. "Three," he states, "which appeared only in the first and second editions and were afterwards suppressed by Edward FitzGerald himself, are not—so far as a careful search enables me to judge—attributable to any lines of the original texts." He pointed out, in conclusion, that "FitzGerald's tendency, after the second edition, was to eliminate quatrains which were merely suggested by the general tone and sentiment of the original poem, and not the reflection or translation of particular and identifiable *rubá'iyát.*" [25]

FitzGerald's censors have favored a literal rendering of the Per-

23. Nicolas, J. B., A French scholar who published *Les Quatrains de Khèyam,* a Persian text and translation of 464 quatrains (Paris, The Imperial Press, 1867). FitzGerald used this text in the preparation of his second edition, London, 1868.

24. Heron-Allen, *FitzGerald's Rubá'iyát,* pp. xi–xii.

25. *Ibid.,* p. xiii.

sian. From their viewpoint they were justified in their criticism, for his method was that which he had already applied to Calderon's plays and Jámí's allegory. "My translation will interest you," he wrote to Cowell in 1858, "from its *Form*, and also in many respects in its Detail: very unliteral as it is. Many Quatrains are mashed together: and something lost, I doubt, of Omar's Simplicity, which is so much a Virtue in him."

There is much to be said for the freedom which FitzGerald invariably exercised in recasting a work, and he often defended his method in letters to friends. He protested that a translation cannot be literal and at the same time retain the spirit of the original; and, above all, the spirit must be retained. "The live Dog better than the dead Lion" or "better a live Sparrow than a stuffed Eagle," he declared. To appreciate the validity of his contention, one has merely to compare his *Rubáiyát* with a literal translation. Mr. Payne's version, for example, although interesting for its attempt to reproduce the very idiom and rhythms of the Persian, is so painfully literal as to be worthless from the standpoint of art. And FitzGerald has had his champions—many of them. One, Hugh Walker, observes that the number of translations which are likely to maintain a permanent position in English literature thus far might be limited to five: the Authorized Version of the Bible, Chapman's Homer, Pope's Homer, FitzGerald's *Rubáiyát*, and Jowett's Plato. Not one of these, he points out, attempts a literal translation.[26]

The approval of FitzGerald's poem by *all* types of readers, from tyro to pundit, is its best defense, if any defense is required. With the exception of the Bible, FitzGerald's *Rubáiyát* is probably quoted more frequently than any other work in English literature. Despite the strictures of pedants, a term which excludes most scholars, the *Rubáiyát* has become one of the immortal poems of the language.

FitzGerald studied three different collections of Omar's quatrains before his paraphrase reached its final form: the Ouseley manuscript at the Bodleian, Nicolas' translation, and the Calcutta manuscript of the Bengal Society.[27] The Bodleian, the shortest,

26. Walker, Hugh, *The Literature of the Victorian Era* (London, Cambridge University Press, 1921), pp. 482–483.

27. The Ouseley manuscript is dated A. H. 865 (A.D. 1460); the Calcutta manuscript has disappeared from the library of the Bengal Asiatic Society and its date is unknown. It is, however, of later date than the Ouseley. The French translation by J. B. Nicolas was published in Paris in 1867 and contains four hundred and sixty-four quatrains.

contains one hundred and fifty-eight stanzas; the Calcutta, the longest, five hundred and sixteen. The first and shortest of FitzGerald's versions contains seventy-five quatrains; the second and longest, one hundred and ten. By his method he achieved, in his poem, a distillation of Omar's thought. Sometimes, though not often, he drew out an idea contained in one Persian stanza through two or three of his own. This occurs occasionally in Persian epigrammatic verse, but only by accident. Finally, FitzGerald grouped quatrains containing allied thoughts. Disjointed as his poem appears, it possesses a unity not found in the original.

The principal difference between FitzGerald's version and the Persian, however, is one of mood. "The general spirit," writes H. G. Keene of Omar's work, "is one of freedom and cheerfulness; and everything is tolerated but intolerance." [28] Mrs. Cadell says of FitzGerald's poem, ". . . the existing translation harmonizes with a special phase of modern thought. . . . Its inexactness has allowed for the infusion of a modern element, which we believe to exist in the Persian only in the sense in which the deepest questions of human life are of all time." [29] Reynold A. Nicholson, who, like Browne, was a lecturer in Persian at the University of Cambridge, also recognizes the intrusion of a modern note and the liberties which FitzGerald took with his material but observes that the translator's very deficiencies as a Persian scholar were an advantage to him as an artist. He states:

Persian is not a difficult language, but to read Persian religious and philosophical poetry with full understanding of the sense intended by the writer, is an achievement of which few professed scholars are capable, since it requires not only mastery of the language but also intimate acquaintance with the general history of Moslem thought, and in particular with theology and mysticism. FitzGerald, luckily, did not trouble himself about such matters; the poetry was what he cared for, and he read it by the light of his own speculations and those of the age in which he lived . . . the point of view has shifted from the twelfth century to the nineteenth. The unique popularity of FitzGerald's poem was and is in large measure due to the fact that it spoke to a past generation, as it speaks to the present, of modern problems, conflicts, doubts and perplexities, in language coloured by the remote and mysterious charm of medieval Persia.[30]

28. Keene, quoted by Dole, II, 437.
29. Cadell, *Fraser's Magazine*, XCIX, 650.
30. Nicholson, Reynold A., *Rubáiyát of Omar Khayyám Translated by Edward FitzGerald* (London, Adam and Charles Black, 1909), pp. 28-30.

FitzGerald was fully aware that the *motif* of his poem differed from that of the original. "Those [quatrains] here selected," he wrote in his preface, "are strung together into something of an Eclogue, with perhaps a less than equal proportion of the 'Drink and make-merry' which . . . recurs over-frequently in the Original." He could truthfully have stated that he had included "a less than equal proportion" of amatory stanzas. On the other hand, his poem has proportionally more to do with death and life after death than the Persian.

A comparison of one or two quatrains in the English poem with the literal rendering of those they represent will reveal FitzGerald's skill in reproducing the sense of the orginal, while parting from a strict translation.[31]

30.

> What, without asking, hither hurried *Whence?*
> And, without asking, *Whither* hurried hence!
> Oh, many a Cup of this forbidden Wine
> Must drown the memory of that insolence.

Mr. Heron-Allen traces this to two of Omar's stanzas:

> Seeing that my coming was not in my power at the Day of Creation,
> And that my undesired departure hence is a purpose fixed (for me),
> Get up and gird well thy loins, O nimble cup-bearer,
> For I will wash down the misery of the world in wine.

> Had I charge of the matter I would not have come,
> And, likewise, could I control my going, how should I have gone?
> There could have been nothing better than that, in this world,
> I had neither come, nor gone, nor lived.[32]

46.

> And fear not lest Existence closing your
> Account, and mine, should know the like no more;
> The Eternal Sáki from that Bowl has pour'd
> Millions of Bubbles like us, and will pour.

This originates in:

> Khayyám! although the pavilion of heaven
> Has spread its tent and closed the door upon all discussion,

---

31. FitzGerald's quatrains quoted here are from the fourth edition of his poem. The fifth edition is virtually the same.
32. Heron-Allen, *FitzGerald's Rubá'iyát*, pp. 49–51.

> In the goblet of existence, like bubbles of wine,
> The Eternal Sáki brings to light a thousand Khayyáms.[33]

FitzGerald published four editions of his *Rubáiyát* during his life; a fifth, which appeared after his death, contained only a few minor changes.[34] Except for the quatrains which he created and later omitted, the first two translations most nearly correspond to the original. In later versions, refinements of the first and second, he departed further and further from literalness. A comparison of any two editions reveals the purpose of his emendations. Here he deleted an expletive; there he replaced one word with another, more exact, more musical, or of richer connotation; here he improved the rhythm; there he inserted a bolder or clearer figure. It is illuminating to trace the changes in one or two stanzas through successive editions. In the first edition, quatrain twelve reads:

> "How sweet is mortal Sovranty!"—think some:
> Others—"How blest the Paradise to come!"
>   Ah, take the Cash in hand and waive the Rest;
>   Oh, the brave Music of a *distant* Drum!

This appears as thirteen in the second and subsequent editions:

> Some for the Glories of This World; and some
> Sigh for the Prophet's Paradise to come;
>   Ah, take the Cash, and let the Promise go,
>   Nor heed the music of a Distant Drum!

The quatrain reached its final form in the third edition:

> Some for the Glories of This World; and some
> Sigh for the Prophet's Paradise to come;
>   Ah, take the Cash, and let the Credit go,
>   Nor heed the rumble of a distant Drum!

Quatrain forty-eight in the first edition reads:

> While the Rose blows along the River Brink,
> With old Khayyám the Ruby Vintage drink:
>   And when the Angel with his darker Draught
> Draws up to Thee—take that, and do not shrink.

In the second edition it appears as quatrain forty-six:

> So when at last the Angel of the drink
> Of Darkness finds you by the river-brink,

33. *Ibid.,* p. 73.
34. These changes were found in one of his own copies of the fourth edition after FitzGerald's death.

> And, proffering his Cup, invites your Soul
> Forth to your Lips to quaff it—do not shrink.

In the third edition, the only variation is the substitution of "offering" for "proffering." The final form, fourth edition, quatrain forty-three, reads:

> So when that Angel of the darker Drink
> At last shall find you by the river-brink,
> And, offering his Cup, invite your Soul
> Forth to your Lips to quaff—you shall not shrink.

The alterations have not won the approval of all readers, who generally prefer the version with which they first became acquainted. As successive editions appeared, the translator's publisher received many complaints about the changes.

FitzGerald's *Rubáiyát* possesses a structure which has escaped the attention of many. It was pointed out by the translator in a letter which he wrote after the publication of the second edition. The longer version, he said, "gave Omar's thoughts room to turn in, as also the Day which the Poem occupies. He begins with Dawn pretty sober and contemplative: then as he thinks and drinks, grows savage, blasphemous etc., and then again sobers down into melancholy at nightfall." [35] This development may easily be traced. The poem begins:

> Wake! For the Sun, who scatter'd into flight
> The Stars before him from the Field of Night,
> Drives Night along with them from Heav'n and strikes
> The Sultán's Turret with a Shaft of Light.

In the early stanzas Omar reflects tranquilly on the transitoriness of life and the futility of worldly endeavor:

> 7.
>
> Come, fill the Cup, and in the fire of Spring
> Your Winter-garment of repentance fling:
> The Bird of Time has but a little way
> To flutter—and the Bird is on the Wing.
>
> 16.
>
> The Worldly Hope men set their Hearts upon
> Turns Ashes—or it prospers; and anon,

35. *Letters to Bernard Quaritch*, p. 18.

> Like Snow upon the Desert's dusty Face,
> Lighting a little hour or two—is gone.

Turning his attention to the riddle of the universe, Omar proceeds, step by step, to a blasphemous passion of rebellion:

27.

> Myself when young did eagerly frequent
> Doctor and Saint, and heard great Argument
>   About it and about: but evermore
> Came out by the same door where in I went.

28.

> With them the seed of Wisdom did I sow,
> And with mine own hand wrought to make it grow;
>   And this was all the Harvest that I reap'd—
> "I came like Water, and like Wind I go."

61.

> Why, be this Juice the growth of God, who dare
> Blaspheme the twisted tendril as a Snare?
>   A Blessing, we should use it, should we not?
> And if a Curse why, then, who set it there?

63.

> Oh threats of Hell and Hopes of Paradise!
> One thing at least is certain—*This* Life flies;
>   One thing is certain and the rest is Lies;
> The Flower that once has blown for ever dies.

68.

> We are no other than a moving row
> Of Magic Shadow-shapes that come and go
>   Round with the Sun-illumined Lantern held
> In midnight by the Master of the Show;

69.

> But helpless Pieces of the Game He plays
> Upon this Chequer-board of Nights and Days;
>   Hither and thither moves, and checks, and slays,
> And one by one back in the closet lays.

Omar reaches the height of his rebellion in a series of exclamatory protests against man's lot:

79.

What! from his helpless Creature be repaid,
Pure Gold for what he lent him dross-allay'd—
    Sue for a Debt he never did contract,
And cannot answer—oh the sorry trade!

81.

Oh Thou, who Man of baser Earth didst make,
And ev'n with Paradise devise the Snake:
    For all the Sin wherewith the Face of Man
Is blacken'd—Man's forgiveness give—and take!

Quatrain 81 has been much discussed. In his 1903 edition of Fitz-Gerald's works, Aldis Wright quotes the following from a letter written to him by Cowell,

There is no original for the line about the snake: I have looked for it in vain in Nicolas; but I have always supposed that the last line is FitzGerald's mistaken version of Quatrain 236 in Nicolas's Edition. . . . FitzGerald mistook the meaning of *giving* and *accepting* . . . and so invented his last line out of his own mistake. I wrote to him about it when I was in Calcutta; but he never cared to alter it.[36]

FitzGerald's answer to Cowell's criticism has survived. "As to my making Omar worse than he is in that stanza about Forgiveness," he wrote,

you know I have translated none literally, and have generally mashed up two—or more—into one. Now, when you look at such Stanzas as 356, 436, and many besides, where "La Divinité" is accused of the Sins we commit, I do not think it is going far beyond by way of Corollary to say—"Let us forgive one another." I have certainly an idea that this *is* said somewhere in the Calcutta MS. But it is very likely I may have construed, or remembered, erroneously. But I do not *add* dirt to Omar's face.[37]

FitzGerald had indeed read a reference to the snake somewhere, but not in any of Omar's quatrains. Heron-Allen traced the lines to an apologue in Attár's *Mantik-ut-tair*.[38]

After his outburst the poet, as if exhausted by passion, falls back on the reflective strain with which he began. He laments the loss of youth and reveals a wistful longing for a single sign to justify faith:

36. *Literary Remains,* VII, 186.
37. Cowell MS. letter, Dec. 17, 1867.
38. Heron-Allen, *FitzGerald's Rubá'iyát,* p. 119.

96.

Yet Ah, that Spring should vanish with the Rose!
That Youth's sweet-scented manuscript should close!
  The Nightingale that in the branches sang,
Ah whence, and whither flown again, who knows?

97.

Would but the Desert of the Fountain yield
One glimpse—if dimly, yet indeed, reveal'd
  To which the fainting Traveller might spring,
As springs the trampled herbage of the field!

He concludes his reflections in melancholy resignation as the day
ends:

100.

Yon rising Moon that looks for us again—
How oft hereafter will she wax and wane;
  How oft hereafter rising look for us
Through this same Garden—and for *one* in vain!

101.

And when like her, Oh Sáki, you shall pass
Among the Guests Star-scatter'd on the Grass,
  And in your joyous errand reach the spot
Where I made One—turn down an empty Glass!

FitzGerald's religious views, expressed in *Euphranor* and his
letters, have already been mentioned.[39] In appraising his religion
and philosophy, the *Rubáiyát* alone is usually examined and all else
is ignored. Although he paraphrased Omar's panegyric of Today,
he likewise translated in Attár's *Mantik:*

And if so vain the glittering Fish we get,
How doubly vain to doat upon the Net,
Call'd Life, that draws them, patching up this thin
Tissue of Breathing out and Breathing in,
And so by husbanding each wretched Thread
Spin out Death's very Terror that we dread—

It is true that FitzGerald included in the *Rubáiyát:*

For all the Sin wherewith the Face of Man
Is blacken'd—Man's forgiveness give—and take!

39. Pp. 62–64.

On the other hand, when he translated Calderon's play *El Mágico Prodigioso,* he purposely increased "the religious Element." The action in that drama is set in Antioch early in the Christian era. The protagonist, Ciprian, a lesser Faust who had sold his soul to Lucifer, is converted to Christianity. The climax is reached when, before the Senate, Ciprian proclaims his conversion, an admission punishable by death. His speech in FitzGerald's version runs:

> I come to you, to witness and make known:
> One God, eternal, absolute, alone;
> Of whom Christ Jesus—Jesus Christ, I say—
> And, Antioch, open all your ears to-day—
> Of that one Godhead one authentic ray,
> Vizor'd awhile his Godhead in man's make,
> Man's sin and death upon Himself to take;
> For man, made man; by man unmade and slain
> Upon the cross that for mankind He bore—
> Dead—buried—and in three days ris'n again
> To His hereditary glory, bearing
> All who with Him on earth His sorrow sharing
> With Him shall dwell in glory evermore.
> And all the gods I worship'd heretofore,
> And all that you now worship and adore,
> From thundering Zeus to cloven-footed Pan,
> But lies and idols, by the hand of man
> Of brass and stone—fit emblems as they be,
> With ears that hear not; eyes that cannot see;
> And multitude where only One can be—
>   .   .   .
> Lo, here I stand for judgment; by the blow
> Of sudden execution, or such slow
> Death as the devil shall, to maintain his lies,
> By keeping life alive in death, devise.
> Hack, rack, dismember, burn—or crucify,
> Like Him who died to find me; Him that I
> Will die to find: for whom, with whom, to die
> Is life; and life without, and all his lust,
> But dust and ashes, dust and ashes, dust—
>   (He falls senseless to the ground.) [40]

The truth is, of course, that any writer who speaks through characters may be made, by a judicious selection of quotations, to contradict himself endlessly. Nevertheless, one has no difficulty determining the direction a stream flows despite innumerable eddies;

40. *The Mighty Magician,* Act III, Scene 3.

and one may discover the trend of a writer's thoughts despite contradictions.

FitzGerald has been the victim of his *Rubáiyát*. The power of its philosophy has been multiplied by multiple reading. Although resembling Omar in his hearty contempt for sanctimony, hypocrisy, and bigotry, he had no desire to indoctrinate the world with the Persian's heresies. When Quaritch proposed an edition of the poem in 1879, he insisted that *Salámán and Absál* be included in the volume, although he realized that it would not be "half so welcome." He was more partial to Jámí's allegory than to Omar's quatrains and always considered the former his best work.

In any judgment on FitzGerald's heterodoxy, the man himself and his *milieu* must be considered. He was an intelligent, widely read Victorian, watching the revelations of science slowly unfold and observing the opening skirmishes of the long struggle between modern science and religion. He was no more unorthodox, although he was more outspoken, than many contemporaries who acknowledged doubts while searching for faith. In the *Rubáiyát* he discovered "a desperate sort of Thing, unfortunately found at the bottom of all thinking Men's minds; but made Music of." The eleventh-century poem echoed nineteenth-century thoughts. FitzGerald set about to reveal Omar to his generation. He wished, furthermore, to unveil the beauties which he had himself discovered in the poetry of the Persians. These, and the desire to give form to a formless creation, were his reasons for translating the poem.

As for FitzGerald himself, the limits of his heterodoxy were skepticism toward the theology of the Old Testament, and uncertainty of a life after death. He never expressed any doubt of the existence of a Supreme Being; he revered and admired Christ; and throughout his life he respected, supported, and defended the Established Church.

XIX

Market Hill

"Then you shall see all the faded tapestry of country town life: London jokes worn threadbare; third rate accomplishments infinitely prized; scandal removed from Dukes and Duchesses to the Parson, the Banker, the Commissioner of Excise, and the Attorney."

FITZGERALD to LAURENCE

GEORGE CRABBE, the elder, died at Bredfield on September 16, 1857.[1] FitzGerald usually avoided funerals; but, after some hesitation from fear of "becoming too sad with remembering our old Days," he attended the service. He paid a last visit to "the Cobblery," as he called the vicar's tobacco-fumed study, and took away as souvenirs a china ash tray and a silver nutmeg grater which had once belonged to the poet Crabbe and had given the finishing touch "to many a Glass of good hot Stuff." At the family's request he wrote an obituary which was published the following month in *The Gentleman's Magazine*.[2] Later he completed a biographical sketch similar to his memoir of Barton, intending to offer it to some periodical, but he never submitted it.

Fifteen months after Crabbe's death, in January, 1859, W. K. Browne, returning from a day's hunting, stopped to remonstrate with a rider who was punishing his mount. Browne's mare was kicked by the other horse, reared, slipped on the wet shelving turf, and fell, crushing her rider beneath her. Browne was injured beyond any hope of recovery, but for two months lay in bed fighting the inevitable. On March 24 FitzGerald was summoned from Donne's home in London. He was not permitted to see Browne until the day after his arrival when the patient sent him a fragment of a note written "in the hand of a Child's first Attempt . . . 'I love *you* very—whene-v-e-r—W. K. B.'" Steeling himself for the ordeal, FitzGerald went to the sickroom. In place of the usual

---

1. He was seventy-two years old.
2. "The Rev. George Crabbe," signed "E. F. G.," *The Gentleman's Magazine*, CCIII (November, 1857), 562–563.

cheery greeting came the familiar words uttered slowly and painfully, "My dear Fitz—old Fel—low," and tears filled Browne's
eyes. Despite his resolution, FitzGerald also broke down. For two
days more he wandered about the house, to be on hand in case his
friend should again ask for him. On the walls were pictures which
the two men had bought on their trips to London during their
twenty-year friendship. In the bookcases were many volumes bearing the inscription, "E. F. G. to W. K. B." "I came away," Fitz-
Gerald wrote to young Crabbe, "wishing to be alone, or in other
Company, when the Last came. So I am now going to Geldestone." [3]

Browne died on March 30. FitzGerald attended the funeral,
conducted by Airy, but never again returned to Bedford.

The loss of these two friends had a profound effect on Fitz-
Gerald's life, for their deaths snapped the last ties which bound
him to inland Suffolk. Almost within a decade had died Major
Moor and Squire Jenney, both closely associated with his childhood, Barton and Crabbe, companions of his young manhood, and
finally Browne, in whom he had always found an exhaustless source
of contagious vigor. "Somehow," he wrote to Mrs. Cowell in 1860
from Farlingay, "all the Country round is become a Cemetery to
me: so many I loved there dead."

His old haunts were further spoiled for him by "the petty race
of Squires" who succeeded his friends and, he complained, "only
use the Earth for an *Investment:* cut down every old Tree: level
every Violet Bank: and make the old Country of my Youth hideous
to me in my Decline." London, too, had finally become genuinely
obnoxious to him. He had long felt a distaste for the metropolis,
but the attraction of friends, theaters, and art galleries had always
overcome his aversion. He and Browne had visited the city together
annually, and the memory of his friend was so closely connected
with the streets and taverns as to "fling a sad shadow over all."
Nevertheless, hardly a year of his life passed without at least one
trip to London. Although his later visits were short and were usually made necessary by business or to see some old friend who had
fallen on evil days through failing health or fortune, he generally
crowded in a few calls on friends, an hour or two at the National
Gallery or one of the exhibitions, and a hasty tour of art shops to
snap up pictures which caught his fancy. Several times during the
early 'sixties he visited the Crystal Palace, "the sight of the Century," as he called it.

3. Crabbe MS. letter of March 29, 1859, which also contains the details in this
passage.

For three years after separating from his wife, FitzGerald, when in Suffolk, made his home at Farlingay. In December, 1860, he moved to Woodbridge, taking lodgings with Sharman Berry, a gunsmith and sporting-goods merchant who lived on Market Hill. Some years earlier he had declared that in Woodbridge could be seen "all the faded tapestry of country town life: London jokes worn threadbare; third rate accomplishments infinitely prized; scandal removed from Dukes and Duchesses to the Parson, the Banker, the Commissioner of Excise, and the Attorney." [4] The sluggish life of the town was boldly advertised by the monotonous routine of the chimes in the tower of the parish church. "Oh, if you were to hear," FitzGerald moaned in a letter to Pollock,

"Where and oh where is my Soldier Laddie gone" played every three hours in a languid way by the Chimes of Woodbridge Church, wouldn't you wish to hang yourself? On Sundays we have the "Sicilian Mariners' Hymn"—very slow indeed. I see, however, by a handbill in the Grocer's Shop that a Man is going to lecture on the Gorilla in a few weeks. So there is something to look forward to.

Despite these strictures he loved Woodbridge and the activity in its square on market days. He had, of course, again taken lodgings only "temporarily," until he could find a house of his own; but when Farlingay was offered for sale, he was "afraid to leave the poor Town with its little bustle! As one grows older, lonelier, and sadder, is not the little Town best . . . ?" He did not expect that he would be able to stay long at Berry's, for Mrs. Berry, who paid her maid a shilling a week, found it difficult to keep help. "She has one now," FitzGerald once said, "who has this strong recommendation: that she can neither read nor write." Another inconvenience was having his lodgings thoroughly cleaned once a year. This his landlady insisted upon, despite his objections. Nevertheless, he remained at Berry's for thirteen years.[5] Mrs. Berry bought his food and prepared his simple meals. From time to time he gave his landlord a five-pound note with a casual, "Let me know when that is gone."

"I do very well here," he told Crabbe of Merton soon after he took possession, "the Lodging cheerful, warm, and convenient (only the Privy quite public), the People quiet, honest, careful, and

4. Letter to Laurence [June 20, 1847].
5. The building, situated on the north side of Market Hill, still stands and is marked by a tablet bearing FitzGerald's initials and the dates of his residence, 1860–73.

old-fashioned . . . Peter Parley is my chief Company . . . He is a worthless Man enough: but he does for me at a Pass." [6]

His quarters consisted of two rooms which he filled with "pictures, gewgaws, and knickknacks," till they looked like "a back shop in Wardour Street." [7] For a time the furnishings included a "party-coloured Mop, so agreeable to my colour-loving Eyes that I have kept it in my Sitting-room instead of giving it over to be trundled in the Kitchen." His pictures were spoiled by a "vile" wallpaper, but they still gave him much pleasure. He puttered over them during winter evenings, sometimes painting the dark corners with gold so as to form an oval, a shape which he liked within a square. By this means he eliminated much black background which he abhorred. He cut one of his canvases down the middle, "making two very good Pictures, I assure you." His books and his writing also occupied hours when he was not entertaining callers, who dropped in frequently for a chat and a glass of Scotch ale or grog. However, no friend ever presumed to enter his rooms unannounced, and any acquaintance who thoughtlessly committed that blunder was received with frosty formality and was not asked to repeat the call.

When he moved to Woodbridge, FitzGerald's reputation was under a cloud. His wife was popular among the townspeople, and the virtuous burghers severely criticized his treatment of her. "If I must tell the unwelcome truth," one of her friends stated, "she has now enough to bear from the atrocious proceedings of her husband, who is highly unprincipled or insane." [8] There is no doubt that the indignant citizens were outspoken in their censure, and one suspects that a resolution to face his detractors was partly responsible for FitzGerald's decision to live in Woodbridge.

Although he participated little in the town's activities, he took a genuine interest in them. He was always ready to give help to a worthy cause, although most of his benefactions were privately and quietly distributed. He paid a medical man a fixed sum each year to visit the poor. [9] He lent wholehearted support to the Third Suffolk Volunteers, organized at Woodbridge in 1859, [10] and encouraged the militiamen by attending what they called their "manuring and skrimmaging." The indifference of the gentry ir-

6. Peter Parley was an Ipswich journalist and miscellaneous writer.
7. Wardour Street, London, in FitzGerald's time a street of pawnshops.
8. Glyde, *FitzGerald*, p. 249.
9. Wright, *FitzGerald*, II, 146.

10. In 1859–60 a war mania seized the country and a conflict with France under Louis Napoleon seemed inevitable. Organization of a volunteer militia was promoted by the government.

ritated him. "It is a shame the Squires do nothing in the matter," he protested, "take no Interest: offer no Encouragement, beyond a Pound or two in Money. And who are those who have most interest at stake in case of Rifles being really wanted? But I am quite assured that this country is dying, as other Countries die, as Trees die, atop first. The lower Limbs are making all haste to follow." [11] He donated prizes for shooting competitions and persuaded his brother John to invite the company to Boulge for maneuvers and entertainment. FitzGerald himself was sometimes host to the company. "If you will kindly take charge of this little Entertainment of mine," he once wrote to the secretary of the regiment,

say, if possible, nothing about me at all: but, if my name should be mentioned, please to say I only wish to show a little Interest in so good a cause, and in those who are active in it; and that I hope the little I offer may be pleasant. If I ever went to such Meetings, I would go to this to say so much for myself—if *necessary:* and you will perhaps [do] so for me—*if necessary:* and only if necessary. And don't let my name creep into the Newspaper . . . So leaving you to manage this for me: and also to settle the amount of *Beer and Grog* for the younger, and less seasoned, Apprentices, I will say Farewell for the Present. No doubt the thing to secure, if possible, is *Cheerfulness* and even *Merriment,* so long as without any Noise or Disorder that would discredit a Good Cause.[12]

The indifference of the gentry to what he considered their civic responsibilities was a constant source of irritation to FitzGerald; and he became, in very fact, a "village Hampden," opposing the "petty Tyrants" of the surrounding fields. He was particularly incensed by their blocking public footpaths, and on one occasion, at least, angrily tore down an obstacle of brush which had been set up at a stile. After an acquaintance of long standing built a cottage over a lane which FitzGerald had used for fifty years, he wrote a sharp letter to the malefactor, who replied that he "was always intending" to replace the path with one more convenient to the public. "It's a Sanctimonious *Lie,*" FitzGerald maintained, "he wanted quietly to do away with the Footpath and make his nasty Property 'snug.'" Two years later he asked Spring Rice:

Does your Trinity Board control the *River Banks?* And, if so, do you know what the Law is about *Right of Way* by River sides: and if you do, what is it?—

11. Letter to George Crabbe, June 4, 1861.
12. MS. letter to Spalding, undated.

Hereabout—along this Deben—we have for the most part raised Banks, called *Walls,* all along the River to the Sea; on the *Top of which* has been, during the oldest Memory, a *Right of Way* for Men. But now we have a Set of Squires who—(all Screws!)—whether to entrench in their Land for *Crops,* or for their d——d *Game*—are sticking up Placards of Prosecution against all who travel along these *walls*— which many want to do, in going from Woodbridge to the Ferry at the River's Mouth. We have one Great Squire—Tomline—inheritor of the Scoundrel Bishop's wealth—who keeps buying up Acre after Acre between the Rivers Deben and Orwell—(so as purposes, they say, to own all the Peninsula between—d——n him!) and to make a Game-preserve of it! So now any poor Man, who used to walk these *walls,* is now collared by Gamekeeper after Gamekeeper—even if the Poor Man has no *Gun* in his hand. . . .

I have been told there is by Law a certain *Right of Way just above High-water Mark:* and if so then is Right of Way along these Walls which *embank* the High Water, and are raised for that purpose? Can your Trinity *insist* on this? The Board already *has,* I am told, prevented Tomline enclosing a Creek of the River, which he destined for a Fish and Fowl Preserve.

And now this new *Bad Act* for *Police-poaching* will arm the Police with Power to arrest Men who go *trespassing on their own Ground.*[13]

FitzGerald's bitterness once stung him to unaccustomed action, for in 1867 he actively opposed Lord Rendlesham's election to Parliament. His role during an election the following year was more characteristic. He gave instructions to Berry that if any canvassers called, he was to say, "Mr. FitzGerald would *not* vote, advised everyone to do the same and let the rotten old ship go to pieces of itself."

The failure of his marriage made FitzGerald sensitive about visiting friends; but, although he warned them not to come to Woodbridge for the sole purpose of seeing him, he urged them to visit him if they could conveniently include the town on their journeys to other destinations. He usually lodged his out-of-town guests at the Bull Inn at the foot of the market place; and Donne, Airy, and Robert Hindes Groome, rector of Monk Soham, often accepted his hospitality. When Groome was made Archdeacon of Suffolk in 1869, FitzGerald surmised that he would never dare come again to sing old Cambridge songs with him; but in that he erred. W. H. Thompson, who became Master of Trinity College in 1866, occasionally joined him in Suffolk, and Frederick Tennyson twice visited him, and Laurence and other old friends were also

13. MS. letter to Spring Rice, Sept. 23, 1862.

his guests. FitzGerald's brother Peter sometimes came to Woodbridge; and John and his sons, when at Boulge, called at Market Hill several times a week. FitzGerald, however, never went to the Hall.

Although he shunned Woodbridge society, he nevertheless made friends among the townspeople. The Reverend Mr. Bernard, a former editor of the *Christian Advocate,* who lived at Woodbridge during the 'sixties, sometimes called at his lodgings and joined him on his walks. One evening the mate of a three-masted schooner visited with him before weighing anchor for Genoa with a cargo of red herring. Herman Biddell, William Airy's cousin, of Playford, near Ipswich, a successful farmer and a man of culture, often called on Woodbridge market days. Biddell valued FitzGerald's friendship highly. Across the Deben at Sutton Hoo lived Alfred Smith, son of FitzGerald's former landlord at Farlingay. Punctually at two o'clock on Sunday, when not otherwise engaged, FitzGerald appeared at the little ferry by which he crossed the river to spend the afternoon at Smith's farm.

Among the tradespeople, too, FitzGerald found friends. One of these, George Manby, a corn merchant and churchwarden, he described as "a good fellow; a John Bull with Sense, Veracity, Experience, and Decision; better to me than all the colourless Squires, who know nothing that I don't know better: and that's not much." [14] Another was John Loder, the stationer and bookseller. There was also Frederick Spalding, secretary for the Woodbridge riflemen and merchant's clerk with tastes far beyond his means. Relics, objects of art, books, and pictures were far more interesting to him than merchandise and ledgers. FitzGerald once lent him £500 to establish a business and soon afterward burned the bond which Spalding's father and a friend had signed; then, after the merchant had punctually paid the interest on his note several times, told him, Spalding recorded, that "£7.10 half yearly made no difference to him, but might to me in my little Business and with my children." [15] Eventually, FitzGerald burned the note itself.

One of the local squires who mortgaged a farm with FitzGerald fared differently. He was not always prompt in paying the interest; and when the mortgage expired at the end of two years, the loan was promptly collected.

14. *Ibid.,* July 27, 1863.
15. Spalding diary, April 18, 1868.

XX

Sailing

"We rayched down and copped hold on him and h'isted
him aboord . . . He come up a-laughin', playsed as Punch,
an' give orders to cast off . . . an' he jest lay down in the lee
scuppers, and 'I can't get no wetter, Posh,' he say, and let the
lipper slosh oover him. Ah! He was a master rum un, was my
ole guv'nor!"

POSH FLETCHER

WHEN the Suffolk countryside lost its attraction for
FitzGerald, he turned to the River Deben and
the sea, "where Friends are not buried, nor Path-
ways stopt up." For a number of years his chief
seaside haunt was Lowestoft on the easternmost point of the English coast, thirty-three miles northeast of Woodbridge and eleven
miles east of Geldeston. Ten miles northward were Great Yarmouth and Gorleston, where he had spent the last weeks of his
"married life." Since young manhood, FitzGerald had occasionally
visited Lowestoft, a popular resort. However, he avoided the "new
town" which catered to holiday visitors. He was drawn, rather, by
the teeming life of the basin where, in season, the herring luggers
were warped in to unload their catches.

He usually took lodgings at 12 Marine Terrace on what is now
called London Road, North, in the "old town." He spent the winter of 1859–60 there, longing for companionship to replace that
which he had lost with Browne's death. He spent his mornings
reading or writing in his parlor which faced the sea; during the
afternoons he walked. After coffee, he would wander about the
streets, observing the rugged sailors and looking into shops. Returning to his rooms, he would write letters or lose himself in
Hakluyt's *Voyages,* "a very good book." After "a glass (or two) of
grog" he would go to bed about ten. "Dull enough, to be sure,"
he confessed, "but it is dull enough everywhere in the Country
now, and almost *less* so by the Sea who always keeps alive . . .
here are Ships innumerable: Colliers, to be sure; but they tack
about and keep moving. I have the sailors, too . . . when one is

in London one seems to see a decayed Race; but here the old English Stuff." [1]

He admired particularly the sturdy independence of the seamen. When groundless fears of an invasion by the French under Louis Napoleon temporarily shattered Victorian composure in 1860, the Admiralty tried unsuccessfully to enlist the fishermen in the naval reserve. "They won't compromise their half-starving Independence," FitzGerald explained to Spring Rice.

. . . They are obstinate Fellows with wonderful Shoulders: won't take one out in one of their Yawls for a Sovereign though they will give one a ride when they go out to get nothing at all: and they rather suspect one has a Design in being civil to them. But I give them Tobacco and Rum now and then, and have had a Chat on the Beach this very moonlight Night before coming in to Patience and Grog.[2]

When they were not engaged in fishing, the men followed a questionable vocation which they called "salwagin" (salvaging). When vessels went aground on the shoals outside the roads, the "salwagers" put out in their yawls to offer their services to the captain in freeing his ship. If they could so much as get a line aboard, which they sometimes did despite resistance by the crew, they collected charges for "assistance." The captain usually refused all aid, fully aware of the exorbitant costs, sometimes a high as $6,000, which would result.[3] Oftentimes the "salwagers" returned to shore drenched and as penniless as when they had launched their boats. "Wouldn't it be better," FitzGerald would argue, "to let half-a-dozen of your Men take me off for a Sovereign which will buy them five Bottles of Rum?" But the fishermen could not see it that way. Some hundred and fifty men had a share in each yawl and such small returns could not be satisfactorily divided. "But," FitzGerald said, "we are capital friends."

At Aldeburgh, resort of his childhood, the natives were more coöperative; and he ran over from Woodbridge now and then "to have a Toss on the Sea, and a Smoke with the Sailors. We have Grog and Pipes in a little Tavern Kitchen: and sometimes in a

1. MS. letter to Spring Rice, Dec. 24, 1859.
2. *Ibid.*, March 2, 1860.
3. One writer states: "The methods of the beach men were sometimes rather questionable, and Colonel Leathes, of Herringfleet Hall, tells a tale of a French brig, named the *Confiance en Dieu*, which took the ground on the Newcome Sand off Lowestoft about the year 1850. The weather was perfectly calm, but a company of beach men boarded her and got her off, and so established a claim for salvage. As a result she was kept nine weeks in port, and her skipper, the owner, had to pay £1200 to get clear." Blyth, James, *FitzGerald and "Posh"* (London, John Long, 1908), pp. 37–38.

sort of *Net-House* where (on a Saturday Night) we sing songs too. One of the Songs is *'The Pride of Aldboro,'* and I gain Applause in 'Pretty Peg of Derby O!' The Childishness and Sea Language of these People pleases me." He sailed with a lad "as strong as a Horse, and simple as a Child," who was in love and sang sentimental songs. One day FitzGerald abstractedly repeated aloud some verses from Scott's *Pirate.* "I should like to hear that again, Sir," the boy said. "Somehow you know Songs something like ours, only better." "I gloried," FitzGerald told Spring Rice, "in Sir Walter finding his place at once in a common Sailor's Heart." [4] In 1861 Cowell repaid £100 which he had borrowed from FitzGerald, who immediately spent most of it on boats, sails, and fishing gear for his sailor-boy's family. "They were all united in their Poverty," he later told Cowell, "but when the Boats and Nets came, *the Devil* came too, stirring up a little Jealousy among them." He asserted his authority, adjudicated the various claims, and harmony was restored.

The racy speech of the seamen captured FitzGerald's interest. "One of my pleasures with Sailors," he declared,

is their very fine *old English:* some of it not known elsewhere, and missed by the Compilers of Provincial Glossaries, who busied themselves with the *Land-labourers* rather than *Sea.* There are words for *Nets* etc. at Lowestoft which must have kept to that Neighbourhood alone for these one thousand years. Then the Sailors as you know have a fine Poetry about them—of its sort. I admire their Phrase of a Ship "beginning to *complain"* when she is strained.[5]

FitzGerald owned a small boat in which he sailed on the Deben. Occasionally he took the helm, but staring at the white sail and watching for beacons in the tortuous channel strained his eyes; so, he said, "I generally take my Ease and call out to my Man, 'Now then! Luff, Luff!' and insist on his weathering such and such a point." His sailor was "a poor careless Devil" whom he employed "because no one else would." Having nothing else to do during the winter of 1860–61, this worthy broke into a house and was committed to fifteen months' imprisonment. "So he is off my hands," FitzGerald told Spring Rice. "But he had *Fun* in him: and the more respectable Men are duller."

In the spring of 1861 he had a new boat, the *Waveney,*[6] built at Beccles. It measured sixteen feet long, five-and-a-half feet broad,

4. MS. letter to Spring Rice, April 20, 1861.
5. *Ibid.,* Sept. 23, 1862.
6. Named after the river on which Beccles is situated and which flows past Geldestone.

and twenty-seven inches deep, and carried a crew of two, Ted West, the captain, a one-legged man, and Jack Howe, both of Woodbridge. "She'll do all but speak," West said of the *Waveney* after a trial; and FitzGerald was delighted when a sailor at Aldeburgh remarked, "Ah—she go like a *wiolin,* don't she?" Although designed for the Deben, the crew managed to sail her to Aldeburgh whenever FitzGerald wished.

During his summer visits there as a child, his imagination had been fired by the sight of the Berwick smacks or "clipper Schooners" beating along the Suffolk coast between Berwick-on-Tweed and London. During the summer of 1861 he took passage to Scotland on one of them. The skipper was "a fine handsome fellow— a larger *Carlyle,*" who talked so like the writer that his passenger asked if they were related; but the sailor had not heard of "Great Tom!" FitzGerald found that the vessel was not so fast as he had expected. "Some light Brigs," he said, "came very close upon us, though the Captain turned a deaf Eye that way." Nevertheless, FitzGerald had a delightful voyage from Saturday noon, when they left the London docks, until four o'clock Tuesday morning. "When I got on shore," he told Spring Rice, "I ought to have gone on by rail to Edinburgh which was but two hours off: but the next Train was—homeward!—and home I came—like an Ass—for I had always wanted to see Edinburgh, and *ought* to have seen it—Dickey!" "Dickey" is Suffolk for donkey.

This venture, no doubt, was responsible for the anecdote that FitzGerald, after wishing for a lifetime to go to Edinburgh, once started on the journey. Arriving at Newcastle, he found a train about to leave for London; so he seized the opportunity to return thereby. The story is one of many often repeated to illustrate Fitz-Gerald's eccentricity. Most of them appear to have grown from just such a seed of truth as is found in the Berwick trip. It is entirely possible that FitzGerald himself first circulated the tales in their revised form. He was always berating himself as a "Paddy," "Paddy" for him signifying the most irresponsible member of the *Blunder* family. "Paddy doubting Paddy," he once told Aldis Wright when seeking his advice, "is apt to blunder more than Paddy pure and simple."

FitzGerald was not satisfied with river boats and Berwick smacks. He wanted a yacht with sleeping quarters and enough deck space to accommodate parties of friends and relatives, particularly the Kerriches who spent their summers at Lowestoft. In the spring of 1862 a Woodbridge glazier praised a boat which he had seen lying

in the Thames at Greenwich, and FitzGerald commissioned him
to buy it. The man, however, had neglected to ascertain

what she was made of, what her stores were, nor whether she was good
to go etc. But he was so *sure* of all this, that he was also sure she must
be worth twice as much as I gave for her (£43) and down she comes
with two men from London: and is found so ill provided that she
must have new ropes etc.; then *hatches* added to cover her in: and, after
all, she turns out worth *nothing:* neither safe, *nor* fast: so as I lose the
£60 she cost from first to last: and *he,* poor man, gets badgered by the
Wits of Woodbridge for his Folly. I am really more sorry for him than
for the money: which, now gone, I don't care a bit about: and, after
some bad Bargains, such as these are *Flea-bites.* But I never can escape
my Bally-blunder Destiny: if I confess I can't judge and act for myself
in one way, I forthwith choose one of the biggest owls in Woodbridge—
(and that is no small thing)—to choose and act for me.[7]

His purchase proving worthless, FitzGerald hired the *Criterion,*
a yacht of ten tons, from an Ipswich owner. It, too, was a "shabby
Concern" which he had to patch and repair to make seaworthy;
but summer and autumn were such as he never remembered, "so
sunshiny," he wrote, "yet with a constant *Breeze* to make my little
Boat go." A shifting bar at the mouth of the Orwell, however,
gave him considerable trouble. "I wish you were in office," he told
Spring Rice on September 15, "to order us *a larger Buoy* at one
end of the Shoal. For what we now have is scarce bigger than a
Fisherman's Float, and is scarce discernible when there is any
'Spuffle' of Water, nor when Dusk comes on. . . . Can't you advise some of your Old Board to set this to right?"[8] Spring Rice, who
had been deputy chairman of the board of customs, was interested
and asked for further particulars, which he forwarded to Trinity
House. One day in December, as FitzGerald was walking toward
the river, he saw a new buoy waiting to be taken to the harbor; the
customshouse officer, "rushed out to congratulate me on *our* Success. I have already risen," he said, "in the Eyes of my Townsmen."
The following spring the float was in place and, FitzGerald reported, "is called by my Name, I believe." Later he informed
Spring Rice,

I shall go out in Glory by—my new buoy! which has brought me the
only *kudos* I ever had in these parts: it being supposed (from it) that I
am all-powerful in Official Quarters, only that I am tender of putting

7. MS. letter to Crabbe, May 17, 1862.
8. MS. letter to Spring Rice, Sept. 15, 1862.

forth all my Power. But really my Boy—("at last I *have* got one" is the saying here)—is a good Boy, not only to his Parent, but to other way-farers over the Bar:—they bless the useful Light, as I do.[9]

During the winter of 1862 he searched and advertised for a yacht. He wanted one "between ten and fifteen Tons—fast, but not a Racer, a good Sea-boat." He sent West to London and the Isle of Wight to search for such a vessel but could find none. All of that size were built to draw six or seven feet of water, too great a draught to navigate conveniently in the Deben and across the bar at its mouth. Finally, early in 1863, he ordered a schooner to be built by J. Harvey, a boatbuilder at Wivenhoe, near Colchester in Essex. The yacht, which cost £350, was forty-three feet long, nine-and-a-half feet broad, and drew five feet of water. She was launched as the *Shamrock* in June, but FitzGerald changed the name to the *Scandal,* which he said was "the staple product of Woodbridge." His skiff was called the *Whisper.* He found his new boat awkward in the narrow Deben, but she "did well without a reef" in a "tuning" which they gave her at sea on July 17. He described her to Spring Rice as "not a Racer—but not a Cart-horse—a good Sea Boat; with a Cabin that every one can sleep in, except myself."

The rigging of the *Scandal* consisted of mainsail, boom foresail, stay foresail, jib and gaff topsail, and a small square sail which was only occasionally used.[10] Shortly before FitzGerald took over the ship, his captain, West, "forfeited his confidence"; and FitzGerald had to engage another. "But where shall I find such *English?*" he asked Donne. He found both a good navigator and a master of picturesque speech in Thomas Newson, one of the Trinity pilots at Bawdsey, whose official duties sometimes interfered with Fitz-Gerald's sailings; Ablett Parsifal,[11] another of the pilots, then filled in. Newson, generally called "Bassy," tilted his head to one side as he talked, "like a jack-daw looking into a pint pot." The *Scandal,* he once observed, "looked no bigger on the water than a pocket comb." Jack Howe, second man in the crew, served as deck-hand and cook. His duties in the galley were simple, because Fitz-Gerald subsisted on cold fare while on board. He never sailed on Sunday, and, when cruising over a week end, invariably put into harbor that his men might enjoy a hot Sunday dinner. When be-

9. *Ibid.,* July 27, 1863.
10. *FitzGerald Medley,* pp. 16–17.
11. Parsifal's name had a protean quality, for it is spelled interchangeably, Parsifal, Pasifal, and Percival.

ing landed in the skiff, he would impatiently leap out as soon as shallow water was reached, and wade ashore.

He gave the day's sailing orders each morning. Having once decided upon a course, he never changed it, even though another destination along the coast might subsequently appeal to him. The rougher the sea, the better he liked it. Once in rough weather Newson suggested that he go below. "Mind your own business, Tom," he replied. "Never mind if I am washed overboard."

The number of anecdotes about FitzGerald's being swept from the deck would account for his spending almost as much time in the sea as on it. Many of these, no doubt, are variations of a few authentic duckings. Once the boom knocked him from the deck while he was reading. When he floated to the surface, he still held the book in his hand. He was hauled on deck where, in dripping clothes, he continued to read, unperturbed. At another time he fell overboard in Lowestoft Harbor and Newson fished him out. "Thank you," he said when safely on deck. "I didn't want to be drowned in that dirty water." One of his men told of another time when he went overboard at Lowestoft.

I remember one day when the *Scandal* was a layin' agin' the wharf where the trawl market is now. Mr. Sims Reeves, the lawyer, . . . and some other friends came over for a sail, and they and Tom . . . was below while me and Jack and the guv'nor was on deck, astern. The mains'l was h'isted, but there wasn't no heads'l on her, and we lay theer riddy to get unner way. There was a fresh o' wind blowin' from the eastard, not wery stiddy, and as we lay theer the boom kep' a wamblin' and a jerkin' from side to side, a wrenchin' the mainsheet block a rum un. The guv'nor was a readin' of a letter as had just been brought down by the poost. . . . "Here's a letter with some money I niver expected to git," he say . . . when just then the boom come over wallop and caught him fair on the side of his hid, and knocked him oover into the harbour like one o'clock. He was a wearin' of his topper same as us'al, and all of a sudden up he come agin just as Jack an' me was raychin' oover arter him. His topper come up aisy like, as though 'twas a life-buoy if I may say soo. . . . And as true as I set here he was still a holdin' that letter out in front of him in both hands. Well, I couldn't help it. I bust out a laughin', and soo did Jack an' all, and then we rayched down and copped hold on him and h'isted him aboord all right and tight, but as wet as a soused harrin'. He come up a laughin', playsed as Punch, an' give orders to cast off and git up headsail ta oncet. And would yew believe me, he wouldn't goo below ta shift afore we got right out to the Corton light, though Mr. Reeves axed him tew time and time agin! Not he. That was blowin' a fresh o' wind, an' he jest lay down in the lee scuppers, and "I can't get no wetter, Posh," he say, and let the lipper slosh oover him. Ah! He was a master rum un, was my ole guv'nor! [12]

In April, 1863, while the *Scandal* was being built, Mrs. Kerrich died. She was, FitzGerald claimed, "the only one of my family I cared much for, or who cared much for me. I had built this Boat partly to have it at Lowestoft two months this Summer, when she was to have been there; and now all that way of the Coast is sad to me." To Mrs. Browne he wrote, "For herself it is well: she never, I believe, would have had tolerable health any more. But for her family! . . . The good die, they sacrifice themselves for others; she never thought of herself, only her children. Ay, and would fret about any cold *I* might have, when she was lying overcome with illness herself, and with the whole weight of that large and anxious family depending on her." [13] FitzGerald did not go to "the wretched funeral where there are plenty of mourners," but he said that he would go to Geldestone when wanted.

His pleasure in the *Scandal* was marred for a time by his sister's death; but he soon came to love his "dear little Ship," as he called it. After the boat was turned over to him, he took one or two short cruises along the coast and then crossed to Holland with Manby, the corn merchant, for a trip which he had contemplated for many years. The *Scandal* anchored early one Thursday morning in July in a Rotterdam canal. FitzGerald wanted to go at once to the art gallery at The Hague, but Manby persuaded him to tour the port first. The next day they went to Amsterdam, returning to The Hague just as the museum was being closed for the day, not to be opened again until Sunday noon. "Hearing all this," he related to Crabbe,

in Rage and Despair I tore back to Rotterdam: and on Saturday Morning got the Boat out of the muddy Canal in which she lay and tore back down the Maas, etc., so as to reach dear old Bawdsey shortly after Sunday's Sunrise. Oh, my Delight when I heard them call out "Orford Lights!" as the Boat was plunging over the Swell. All this is very stupid, really wrong: but you are not surprised at it in me . . . Oh dear!— Rembrandt's Dissection—where and how did I miss that? [14]

The *Scandal* was FitzGerald's summer home for eight years. He went to Lowestoft for several weeks each summer and placed his boat at the disposal of the Kerrich family. He also invited friends

12. *FitzGerald and "Posh,"* pp. 113–115.
13. Wright, *FitzGerald,* II, 44.
14. One suspects that this journey was responsible for another anecdote. It is said that he once sailed to Holland to look upon Paul Potter's "Bull"; but, arriving at his destination, he noted a favorable homeward breeze; so he immediately put about and sailed home. Paul Potter, 1625–54, Dutch painter, noted for his paintings of animals.

to sail with him; the Cowells, after their return from India, Donne and his sons, George Crabbe, and others were his frequent guests on board. Cruises were usually confined to the East Anglian coast between Cromer and the River Colne, but FitzGerald sometimes sailed to the south coast. In August, 1865, after spending six weeks at Lowestoft, he went to Ramsgate where his brother Peter and his wife were staying. They sailed about the coast for two weeks and ended the cruise by crossing to Calais, "just to touch French Soil, and drink a Bottle of French Wine in the old Town." He was pleased to find Calais, except for the soldiers' uniforms, just as he remembered it from forty years before.

Peter's wife, a devout Catholic who had persuaded her husband to change his faith, died the following year. "I have now before me on the table," FitzGerald wrote in July, "the little, well-used missal she used for twenty-five years, and this being Sunday, I have read in it, and can very well believe that she who acted up to what she read there may be as safe in another world as any of us Protestants who are most bitter in denouncing it." [15] Peter spent six weeks of the summer sailing with his brother at Lowestoft and about the Isle of Wight.

"We got here very well on Tuesday evening," FitzGerald wrote from Cowes.

Wednesday I sent Newson and Crew over to Portsmouth, where they didn't see the one thing I sent them for, namely, Nelson's Ship, the "Victory," but where they bought two Pair of Trousers, which they call "Dungaree." Yesterday we went to Poole—a place I had long a very slight Desire to see; and which was not worth the seeing. To-day we came back here: I regretting rather we had not run further along the Coast to Weymouth and Teignmouth, where I should have seen my Friend Mansfield the Shipwright. It was a little weakness of mine, in *not* changing orders, but, having talked of going only to Poole, I left it as it was. The weather has been only *too* fine; the sea too calm. Here we are in front of this pretty place, with many Yachts at anchor and sailing about us: nearly all Schooners, little and great, of all which I think we are the "Pitman." [16] I must say I am very tired of seeing only Schooners. Newson was beaten horribly yesterday by a Ryde open Boat of about 7 or 8 tons, which stood right into the wind, but he soon afterwards completely distanced a Billy-boy, which put us in Spirits again. [17]

"Billy-boys" were cumbersome, wind-driven scows used to transport coal,

15. Wright, *FitzGerald*, II, 62–63.
16. Pitman, Suffolk for runt.
17. Letter to Spalding, June 30, 1866.

FitzGerald usually avoided regattas, but Newson was keen to race the *Scandal,* and his employer often let him take her for that purpose. FitzGerald accompanied him once. While in the harbor at Yarmouth, he was informed that his boat was wanted for a race. "As Newson would secure £5 for himself even by losing," he explained to Crabbe, who was at the port, "I let him go; and went with him. The latter, as I afterward found, I need not have done; but at Harwich Regatta they insisted on the Presence of the owner, or some Yacht Club Member. The Trumpet of Fame may already have informed you that we came in second—*out of Two*—perhaps some of your Party saw the Strife, the Victory and the Defeat." [18]

While on board ship FitzGerald spent most of the time sitting or lying near the mainmast, reading and smoking. His book fare at sea was usually Dante, Homer, and the Greek dramatists which he took with him "as Johnson took Cocker's Arithmetic with him on travel, because he shouldn't exhaust it." It was wonderful, he told Donne, how the sea whetted his appetite for Greek. The murmur of the Aegean, he believed, had wrought itself into the language.

When alone on his yacht, he was the absolute vagabond, footloose, carefree. Once at Lowestoft the *Scandal* fell in with another vessel from Woodbridge, and he and his men boarded her to drink "a Bottle of Blackstrap round with the crew." From Harwich he wrote to Pollock:

Now I am lying here again, simply on the principle of leaving Well—a Pretty Well—alone—coming yesterday with the intention of returning to my own River at Evening; but there was a German Band playing Rossini's boatman to Gazz Ladra [19] so pleasantly that I stopped to hear them again in the Evening. . . . Here we lie, abreast of the Town, and almost under shadow of a huge, hideous, Iron-clad called the *Penelope* —who, I hope, won't begin thundering her 98 Pounders over our heads. "Shall we stop here this day also?" "Let us get our Dinners first, and then see." . . .

Dinner

Bread	Sherry	Cheese

"No, we'll stop here today, Newson; and hear the Band; and also the Cheap-Jack on the Battery Green; and then see about Tomorrow." "Very good, Sir." [20]

18. MS. letter to Crabbe, Aug. 1 [no year].
19. *La Gazza Ladra,* comic opera in two acts. Produced at King's Theatre, London, March 10, 1821.
20. MS. letter to Pollock, June 22, 1870.

XXI

Winter Quarters

"Since then I have been still more diligently cultivating (as Spedding said) the stupid part of my Nature; seeing none of the Wise People, and only reading Memoirs, Travels, etc., just one grade above Novels."

FITZGERALD to COWELL

FITZGERALD dreaded the approach of winter, which forced retirement to his Market Hill lodgings. There he spent the time reading, revising his poems from the Persian, translating Greek plays, busying himself with scissors and paste, his "Harp and Lute," making readable books from dull ones. From Mudie's lending library in London he borrowed memoirs and biographies, the type of narrative he most enjoyed. Novels enabled him to slip into society without stirring from his rooms. Trollope's, he thought, were very good; "not perfect, but better than a narrower Compass of Perfection like Miss Austen's." Certain books he read over and over again. One of these was Wilkie Collins' *The Woman in White,* first published in 1860; in 1862 he went through *Clarissa Harlowe* for the fifth time. He also read the new publications of his friends, but generally with disappointment. "I don't think you ever told me," he wrote to Cowell in 1863,

if you had got, or read, Spedding's two first volumes of Bacon. My opinion is not the least altered of the Case: and (as I anticipated) Spedding has brooded over his Egg so long he has rather addled it. . . . I say this Life of his wasted on a vain work is a Tragedy pathetic as Antigone or Iphegenia. Of Tennyson I hear but little: and I have ceased to look forward to any future Work of his. Thackeray seems dumb as a gorged Blackbird too: all growing old!

A few days later, however, he read "a very charming Paper about Holland in Thackeray's Roundabouts."

Many hours were spent on the correspondence which has gained for FitzGerald a high place among English letter writers. In the opinion of James Russell Lowell, with whom he corresponded, FitzGerald's letters are superior to those of Walpole and Lamb;

and many readers would concur in that estimate. His observations
on life, opinions on the arts, reports of activities, his gossip, anecdotes, and bits of humor, all phrased in FitzGerald's rhythmic prose,
have been so freely quoted in these pages that readers may evaluate
the correspondence for themselves. If the *hors d'œuvres* provided
here have proved appetizing, a rich banquet awaits those who may
wish to feast on the published correspondence.[1]

In criticism of the arts FitzGerald was often narrow minded and
dogmatic. For the most part, his judgments were dictated by an
intense loyalty to early attachments. He developed new enthusiasms from time to time, but his attitude toward new artists and
new forms was generally hostile. In spite of, rather, because of,
his many prejudices, FitzGerald's criticism is always entertaining.

He believed that art should idealize. "If we take the mere rep-
resentation of common Nature as the sum total of Art," he maintained, "we must put the modern Every day life Novel above Shakespeare. . . . Nor can I think that Frith's veracious Portraitures
of people eating Luncheons at Epsom [2] are to be put in the Scale
with Raffaelle's impossible Idealization of the Human made Divine." [3]

In art FitzGerald was a competent judge of composition and
color, but, above all, he demanded "feeling" in pictures. "There
is as genuine a feeling of Nature in one of Nursey's [4] sketches," he
once asserted, writing to Barton from London, "as in the Rubenses
and Claudes here: and if that is evident, and serves to cherish
and rekindle one's own sympathy with the world about one, the
great end is accomplished." Claude and the two Poussins, Fitz-
Gerald believed, were the great ideal painters of landscape.

Nature looks more steadfast in them than in other painters: all is
wrought up into a quietude and harmony that seem eternal. This is
also one of the mysterious charms in the Holy Families of Raffaelle
and of the early painters before him: the faces of the Madonnas are
beyond the discomposure of passion, and their very draperies betoken
an Elysian atmosphere where wind never blew. The best painter of the
unideal Christ is, I think, Rembrandt. . . . Rubens and the Venetian
Painters did neither one thing nor the other: their Holy figures are
neither ideal nor real: and it is incongruous to see one of Rubens'

---

1. For further sampling, the author recommends particularly *Some New Letters of
Edward FitzGerald* (F. R. Barton, ed.), a small but very human and entertaining collection of FitzGerald letters. Four volumes of his correspondence are available in his
Letters and Literary Remains.
2. An allusion to Frith's picture, "Derby Day."
3. Letter to Biddell [1863].
4. Perry Nursey, a Suffolk artist.

brawny boors dressed up in the ideal red and blue drapery with which
the early Italians clothed their figures of Christ.[5]

Gainsborough's "Watering Place," FitzGerald maintained, was
superior to all the Claudes in the National Gallery. "But this," he
added, "is perhaps because I am an Englishman and not an Italian."
In a letter to Laurence he said, "I will not argue how far he [Gains-
borough] was superior to Reynolds in Colour; but in the Air of
Dignity and Gentility (in the better sense) he was surely inferior;
it must be so, from the Difference of Character in the two men.
. . . Sir Joshua was by much the finer Gentleman: indeed Gains-
boro' was a scamp." He considered the devotion of a whole room
at the National Gallery to Turner to be "a national Absurdity."

For the Academicians of his time he had little use. "The Exhibition is like most others you have seen; worse perhaps," he wrote to
Frederick Tennyson in 1848. "There is an 'Aaron' and a 'John
the Baptist' by Etty far worse than the Saracen's Head on Ludgate
Hill." The Pre-Raphaelites fared no better. After viewing Holman
Hunt's "The Finding of Christ in the Temple" in 1860, he commented,

No doubt, there is Thought and Care in it: but what an outcome of
several Years and sold for several Thousands! What Man with the Elements of a Great Painter could come out with such a costive Thing after
so long waiting! Think of the Acres of Canvas Titian or Reynolds
would have covered with grand Outlines and deep Colours in the Time
it has taken to niggle this Miniature! The Christ seemed to me only
a wayward Boy: the Jews, Jews no doubt: the Temple I dare say very
correct in its Detail: but think of even Rembrandt's Woman in Adul-
tery at the National Gallery; a much smaller Picture, but how much
vaster in Space and Feeling! Hunt's Picture stifled me with its Little-
ness. I think Ruskin must see what his System has led to.[6]

Discussing music in a letter to Frederick Tennyson in 1842, Fitz-
Gerald said, "I grow every day more and more to love only the
old God Save the King style: the common chords, those truisms of
music, like other truisms so little understood in the full." His para-
mount requirement was melody, and he loved waltzes and polkas.
Handel, Rossini, Mozart, Beethoven, and Bellini, whose works
he had heard and played in youth and young manhood, remained

5. Letter to Barton, June 8, 1838.
6. Letter to Crabbe, Dec. 28, 1860. "The Finding of Christ in the Temple" had been
started in 1854. For four years, however, Hunt had been forced to abandon work on
the canvas while painting "pot-boilers" to enable him to complete it. The picture was
sold in 1860, when it was finished, for £5,500.

his favorites through life. He admitted, however, that Handel "never gets out of his wig: that is, out of his age," but his "coursers, with necks with thunder clothed and long resounding pace, never tire." His love for Handel, fostered at the University when "Camus" programs invariably included one of his compositions, could not, for FitzGerald, redeem oratorios from dullness. "I never heard one that was not tiresome," he told Donne,

and in part ludicrous. . . . Even Magnus Handel—even Messiah. He (Handel) was a good old Pagan at heart, and (till he had to yield to the fashionable Piety of England) stuck to Opera, and Cantatas, such as Acis and Galatea, Milton's Penseroso, Alexander's Feast, etc., where he could revel and plunge and frolic without being tied down to Orthodoxy. And these are (to my mind) his really great works: these, and his Coronation Anthems, where Human Pomp is to be accompanied and illustrated.

He thought "Rossini's vein was Comic, and the Barber his Masterpiece: but he is always melodious and beautiful, and that will make him live when Meyerbeer, Gounod, Mendelssohn, Wagner, and Co. lie howling, by the side of Browning and Co., in some limbo of Dante's first Act of the Comedy." [7]

His first reaction to Mendelssohn had been favorable, for in 1842 FitzGerald had considered him "by far our best writer now," combining qualities of Beethoven and Handel. Mozart, he believed, was

the most universal musical genius: Beethoven had been too analytical and erudite: but his inspiration is nevertheless true. . . . He tried to think in music: almost to reason in music: whereas perhaps we should be contented with *feeling* in it. It can never speak very definitely. . . . Beethoven's Sonata—Op. 14—is meant to express the discord and gradual atonement of two lovers, or a man and his wife: and he was disgusted that every one did not see what was meant: in truth, it expresses any resistance gradually overcome— Dobson shaving with a blunt razor, for instance. [8]

In his literary criticism, FitzGerald was a decided reactionary. "As for modern Poetry," he declared in 1880, "I have cared for none of the last thirty years, not even Tennyson, except in parts: pure, lofty, and noble as he always is. Much less can I endure the *Gargoyle* school (I call it) begun, I suppose by V. Hugo." Browning was "the great Prophet of the Gargoyle School," in whose "un-

7. Letter to Pollock, July 13, 1870.
8. Letter to F. Tennyson, March 31, 1842.

couth" works FitzGerald saw "little but Cockney Sublime, Cockney Energy, etc." For the late Victorian poets generally he had only scorn. "Dear me, how thick great poets grow nowadays!" he exclaimed after reading a criticism of the Pre-Raphaelites.

Some of his friends to whom such broadsides were sent did not permit them to go unanswered. In 1870 Spedding bluntly took him to task for his prejudices:

I *do* admire Morris very much—though I have not found time to read any part of his last volume: and I do not find any difficulty in understanding him: nor can I well see where the difficulty should be; for his fault if any is being too full and explicit about everything. He affects a mode of expression, and perhaps of thought, which belongs to a past time; just as C. Lamb did in his Adventures of Ulysses and Tales of Shakespeare: and I am not sure that it is not a defect in both. But then the stories are old, and the setting is old, and altogether it has not to me the disagreeable effect of affectation: and they are beautifully told. Rossetti's last volume I have not seen, and I have only read a few extracts from it and I think I once read some translation from Dante by him, and thought it sounded good. But I cannot say whether I understand him or not. I do not know what you mean to imply by asking if the chair is empty. I know of no chair in poetry in which only one man can sit, nor do I find any difficulty, more than is due to the increasing dullness and ineptitude of my own faculties, in admiring as many new poets as the land can produce. Jealousy of competition is a poor and unworthy feeling even in a man who suffers by it; but jealousy in another man's behalf is absurd. I have seen such a thing. I have seen dislike expressed for a new man, not because he was overpraised by others or because he was himself unworthy, but because he seemed likely to *excel* an old favourite. It seems to me that the new thing ought to be the more welcome the better it is; and I am glad to hear of a fresh poet. Even when I have not eyes to see him or opportunity to make his acquaintance. At the same time Alfred still lives, and is (as far as I see) as well and as young—in his genius I mean—as ever. I hear some of his old admirers accuse him of senescence and it may be my own senescence that prevents me from perceiving it: or it may be *their* senescence that enables them; but I see nothing in his last book [9] that would suggest to me any decay of power or delicacy or freedom or activity. And if he would take up a greater subject I think he has it in him to make a greater poem than those he has yet made.[10]

Through Spedding's letter one may reconstruct that which provoked it. "I *do* admire Morris," "effect of affectation," the "decay" of Tennyson's power—perhaps every remark was an answer to a

9. *The Holy Grail and Other Poems,* 1869.
10. MS. letter from Spedding, May 11, 1870.

statement by FitzGerald. By the "empty chair" Spedding probably
referred to an implication that if Tennyson no longer occupied
the throne of English poetry, the chair must be empty. The words,
"I have seen such things," in reference to jealousy on another man's
behalf, was a thrust which must have caused FitzGerald to wince.

No doubt the majority of Spedding's strictures were as deserved
as they were pointed. The difference of opinion between the two
men over the merits and weaknesses of Tennyson's poetry, however, was of long standing. "Jem" had been an idolator from the
first and had even approved of "The Skipping Rope," a childish
bit of doggerel which Tennyson had included in his 1842 volume.
In the main, posterity has sustained FitzGerald's judgments and
repudiated Spedding's.

FitzGerald had little use for women writers. He admitted however, that Jane Austen was "capital as far as she goes: but she never
goes out of the Parlour." Moreover, she dealt with a circle which
he had "found quite unendurable to walk in." He referred, of
course, to the gentry. One of his criticisms of Elizabeth Barrett
Browning resulted in a bitter attack on FitzGerald by her husband.
When the poetess died in 1861, FitzGerald wrote to Thompson,
"Mrs. Browning's Death is rather a relief to me, I must say: no
more Aurora Leighs, thank God! A woman of real Genius, I know:
but what is the upshot of it all? She and her Sex had better mind
the Kitchen and their Children; and perhaps the Poor: except in
such things as little Novels, they only devote themselves to what
Men do much better, leaving that which Men do worse or not at
all." [11]

Superficially considered, the remark on Mrs. Browning's death
is painfully callous; but it should be interpreted, as it was intended,
solely as literary criticism. While writing, it is apparent, Fitz-
Gerald was thinking more of the poem than of the poetess. Most
people, in communicating with friends, spice their letters and
conversation with remarks which they would suppress if they had
any reason to suspect the comments would reach a wider public.
Among intimates, they are confident that the spirit in which their
opinions are expressed will be understood.

In preparing FitzGerald's correspondence for publication, Aldis
Wright took exceptional care to delete passages which might cause
pain to any living person. This item, however, escaped his vigilance
and appeared in the first edition of the letters, published in 1889,
six years after FitzGerald's death. As luck would have it, Brown-

11. *Letters* (1889 ed.), I, 280–281. The passage was deleted from subsequent editions.

ing saw the remark while casually leafing through the volume which he found on a friend's table. In white anger the aged poet, then seventy-seven, dashed off twelve lines of verse which, however much they may have relieved his feelings, contributed nothing to his dignity. He sent his rhyme to the *Athenaeum*.

> I chanced upon a new book yesterday:
> I opened it, and where my finger lay
> 'Twixt page and uncut page those words I read,
> Some six or seven at most, and learned thereby
> That you, FitzGerald, whom by ear and eye
> She never knew, "thanked God my wife was dead."
>
> Ay, dead! and were yourself alive, good Fitz,
> How to return you thanks would pass my wits.
> Kicking you seems the common lot of curs—
> While more appropriate greeting lends you grace:
> Surely to spit there glorifies your face—
> Spitting from lips once sanctified by Hers.[12]

It is to be regretted that Browning could not know of another passage, hitherto unpublished, which FitzGerald had written in 1851:

I see extracts in the *Athenaeum* from a new poem of Mrs. Barrett Browning—"Casa Guidi Windows"—[13] a Dantesque survey of Italy—and really I am compelled to think *her* now a greater Poet than Tennyson! That it should come to this! I don't mean that what she writes is equal to what he *wrote,* and was born to write; but better than what he has lately done or (as I fear) ever will do again. Mrs. Browning writes on a noble, stirring, and nineteenth century subject; dashing away at rhyme and rhythm; often failing, often succeeding; at all events preserving the charm of impulse and *go;* not "added and altered many times till all is ripe and rotten." Yet I do not believe her Poems are good enough to *live* . . . [14]

As has been apparent, FitzGerald was just as severe in criticizing his friends as in appraising other writers. The fact that much praise is mixed with his censure has often been ignored. It was from principle, and not from pure captiousness, that his letters contain a preponderance of adverse criticism on the books which friends sent him. No writer, he assumed, would publish a work without believing that it had good qualities. He should be inter-

12. *Athenaeum*, No. 3220 (July 13, 1889), p. 64.
13. *Casa Guidi Windows*, published in 1851; *Aurora Leigh* in 1856.
14. MS. letter to Cowell, June 13, 1851.

ested, therefore, only in hearing how readers thought the work could be improved. "I dare say you will feel bound to acknowledge the Book," he wrote to Archbishop Trench when sending his edition of Crabbe in 1880, ". . . but I always maintain it best to say nothing, unless to find fault, with what is sent to one in this Book line. And so to be done by."

FitzGerald spent Christmas of 1863 at Market Hill. In the evening as he strolled through the gardens of the Seckford Almshouse, his friend Manby sought him out to tell him that news of Thackeray's death on the previous day had just been received. "I have thought little else than of W. M. T. ever since," FitzGerald told Cowell a month later,

what with reading over his Books, and the few Letters I had kept of his; and thinking over our five and thirty years' Acquaintance as I sit alone by my Fire these long Nights. I had seen very little of him for these last ten years; *nothing* for the last five; he did not care to write; and people told me he was become a little spoiled; by London praise, and some consequent Egotism. But he was a very fine Fellow. His Books are wonderful: Pendennis, Vanity Fair, and the Newcomes, to which compared Fielding's seems to me coarse work.

As he read the novels, FitzGerald seemed to hear Thackeray "saying" much of them, he told Laurence, "and it seems to me as if he might be coming up my Stairs, and about to come (singing) into my Room, as in old Charlotte Street, etc., thirty years ago."

A short time before his death, as the novelist was gazing from a window of the home which he had built in Kensington two years before, his daughter Anne asked him, "Which, of all your friends, have you cared for most?"

"There was 'Old Fitz,' " Thackeray replied, "and I was very fond of Brookfield once." After a pause, he added, "We shall be very good friends again in hell together." [15]

In the spring FitzGerald visited "Old Thack's" home the day before its furnishings were auctioned. Later he commissioned Laurence to copy a portrait which the artist had made of Thackeray. "When I had unscrewed the last Screw," he wrote after receiving the picture, "it was as if a Coffin's Lid were raised; there

15. In writing his introduction to the *Letters and Literary Remains,* Aldis Wright deleted from Thackeray's remark everything, as FitzGerald's mother was fond of quoting, "that might offend the chastest eye or ear." Mr. Wright gives Thackeray's reply as, "Why dear old Fitz, to be sure; and Brookfield." My version is taken from a letter sent by Anne Thackeray Ritchie to Mr. Wright while he was preparing the correspondence for publication.

was the Dead Man. I took him up to my Bedroom; and when morning came, he was there—reading; alive and yet dead."

Every winter for several years after the novelist's death, Fitz-Gerald read his books with keen enjoyment. "I must think we have *no Novels* in the Language like them," he declared in 1867, ". . . in spite of what People say, the Good, the Amiable, and the Noble, preponderate." [16] In later years he could not enjoy the realistic novel. "I cannot get on with Books about the Daily Life," he said in 1875,

which I find rather insufferable in practice about me. I never could read Miss Austen, nor (later) the famous George Eliot. Give me People, Places, and Things, which I don't and can't see; Antiquaries, Jeanie Deans, Dalgetty's etc. . . . As to Thackeray's, they are terrible; I really look at them on the shelf, and am half afraid to touch them. He, you know, could go deeper into the Springs of Common Action than these Ladies: wonderful he is, but not delightful, which one thirsts for as one gets old and dry.[17]

Despite his love and admiration for Thackeray, FitzGerald refused to subscribe to the fund collected in 1864 for the purpose of placing a bust of the novelist in Westminster Abbey. "I wouldn't subscribe," he told Pollock,

. . . because, on the one hand, I think no one should be monumented there till a hundred [years] have proved that any one knows of him; and, on the other hand (rather contradictory), there are already such a heap of vulgar Statues to People no one, even now, cares for that I shouldn't care to see W. M. T. lumped among them, next to—Sir W. Follett, for instance. What Foreigner, looking into the Noble Abbey, but must wonder at such an Intrusion; the Name not known, I suppose, out of Britain, and not exciting any very lively recognition here. Does it? I feel sure W. M. T. will be known and admired a hundred years hence: Laurence's likeness will be kept, and repeated; and then the New Zealander may make a Bust or a Statue, as he pleases.[18]

More or less content with his books, his pictures, and his Wood-bridge friends, FitzGerald took relatively little interest in the affairs of the nation and the world. "Don't write Politics—I agree

16. MS. letter to Cowell, March 25, 1867.
17. Letter to Laurence, Dec. 30, 1875.
18. The funds collected at this time provided for the bust by Marochetti in the Poets' Corner.
On the same grounds FitzGerald had approved the action of Trinity College in refusing to place Woolner's bust of Tennyson in the library in 1859, although, he asserted, there was no doubt that Tennyson would be known one hundred years hence. The Woolner bust, however, was eventually placed in the library.

with you beforehand," he had warned Frederick Tennyson in 1852. At times he abandoned reading newspapers entirely because he was convinced that he could no nothing to remedy conditions, and he resented having them imposed upon his attention. His indifference was rather assumed than genuine, however. Sensational news topics captured his interest, and he usually kept abreast of major events of the day. He told Spring Rice in 1860:

No, I am no Napoleonist. I think he is one of whom I have seen more, who, having lived a life of Lying up to Middle Age, get to believe in themselves. The Light is dead within them. I can hardly think Louis Napoleon could else believe the World would be gulled by his con- tradictory Words and Acts. Or does he know that 700,000 armed Men will persuade any Men any Belief? Anyhow, I feel persuaded the Day of Peace—the long, long, Day of lovely Peace—is gone from us, accord- ing to the fatal Destiny of Men and Nations who must fight when they have grown rich and proud by *not* fighting. I think it would have been for the Dignity of England *not* to have allied again with so convicted a Scoundrel: nor do I believe that the Nations ever *can* ally. The Blood is so opposite. With the German tribes, we, or rather the English, would do well. But yet it may be all right to try what unlimited Commerce may do. I am rather glad to be turned of Fifty, being weary, if not Dis- gusted, with the Concern—of the World! [19]

His *laissez faire* attitude was revealed in another discussion of the same topic in a letter written a few weeks later.

I took the *Times* to look at till a Fortnight ago: when I got bothered with this new Squabble about Switzerland: and would see no more. Come what will, I do think England has acted honourably in the Mat- ter: and I am glad our Disagreement with France has arisen from no national Interest of our own. *This* Break may be soldered up for a Time: but I think it is impossible the two Nations can go on long together: and the French, whom we blame for Ambition have some- thing to say against us for the Past: they have got rich and proud: and the old Story goes on about War being the Result of a Peace that brings Wealth and Pride. "Give Peace in our Time, oh Lord!" But I doubt "I wish you may get it" is the Answer from that Destiny under which this wretched Planet rolls. So, as I can't help these things, why should I be plagued with them, till they knock at my Door too unmistakably loud not to be heard? One wonders that any clever Man, like Louis Napoleon, doesn't see what a mere Puppet of old Destiny he is: to be kicked over himself when he has done his Mischief.[20]

19. MS. letter to Spring Rice, March 2, 1860.
20. *Ibid.*, April 13, 1860.

He had little sympathy for the French in the Franco-Prussian War.

I must say that my savageness against France goes no further than wishing that the new and gay part of Paris were battered down; not the poor working part, no, nor any of the People destroyed. But I wish ornamental Paris down, because then I think the French would be kept quiet till they had rebuilt it. For what would France be without a splendid Palace? . . . Only Notre Dame, the Tuileries, and perhaps the beautiful gilt Dome of the Invalides do I care for. They are historical and beautiful too.

But I believe it would be a good thing if the rest of Europe would take possession of France itself, and rule it for better or worse, leaving the French themselves to amuse and enlighten the world by their Books, Plays, Songs, Bon Mots, and all the Arts and Sciences which they are so ingenious in. They can do all things but manage themselves and live at peace with others: and they should themselves be glad to have their volatile Spirits kept in order by the Good Sense and Honesty which other Nations certainly abound in more than themselves.[21]

The *Trent* and *Alabama* affairs during the American Civil War *would* be heard, FitzGerald said, "by the deafest adder." Analyzing the *Trent* affair, when most Englishmen were demanding action, he wrote:

I don't quite understand you, or the Press, about America. Is it so certain they meant to *insult* us etc? They are savage Snobs, and wanted to seize suspected Traitors, and did seize them in an English Vessel: there being at least *a Doubt* at first if they were not justified in so doing—And if they *have* intended to insult us, should we go to war with them *now,* when their hands are otherwise tied, after we have, as you say, submitted to insult heretofore when their hands were free?—I do think that England, which has begun so many good things, should, or might, begin now to discountenance the Duelling of Nations *for mere Honour,* as she has so long discountenanced that of *Individuals;* and that she might now well say (supposing America declines to concede) "Well—we *could* strike you now you're half down: but we won't—wait till you are up again, and see if you are as angry with us then." And who knows if even America would not be so angry after being treated—as only one English Boxer treats another in the Ring?

This may be all wrong, and you and others who are versed in Papers and Politics may *know* that America's outrage is much worse than *I* know it—They are a bad set—really, a Continent of Pirates—and I can't doubt it is England's *Interest* to deal them the Blow *now* which they draw on themselves. But—but—is it not time for the Better Soul

21. Letter to Pollock, Nov. 1 [1870].

to prevail, and strike a *Blow at War itself* rather than to give War new Life by re-making it?—(I was going on, but won't—with all this)—[22]

Spring Rice wrote to defend England's position in the matter, and FitzGerald responded:

I dare say you are right about the fact that a Breach of international Law has been done by America toward us: but, anyhow, it was not so clear at first but that Lawyers were obliged to be called in to decide it; and American Lawyers see it just the different way from the English. It is natural therefore that the *People* should, as well as their lawyers. "*Prima facie,*" I should have supposed America *had* a right to board a ship in which she knew there was *Treason* sailing—Treason, as she considers it—and if she took the treason out, and then let the Ship go her way without further Damage, I should hardly have thought we could complain. If however our Lawyers, and European Opinion, agree that it *was* unlawful, I am quite ready to agree. Only I don't think we should be so fierce against America not seeing it as we *now* do. Do we, in judging, put *her* case as if it were *our own?* Eh?—We might not *justify* the case by so doing, but we should, I think, look at it with less Animosity.[23]

When the trouble over the privateer, the *Alabama,* arose in 1863, FitzGerald commented, again to Spring Rice, "I expect we shall be over head and ears in an American War by Mid-summer. I never cared much about it so long as I thought we had a clear Conscience. So we may have now; but it seems to me even the *Saturday Review* hesitates a little about the Alabama. What do you think?" [24]

He was no imperialist. "A Nation with great Estates is like a Man with them," he asserted at the time of the Indian mutinies in 1857, "more trouble than Profit: I would only have a *Competence* for my Country as for myself." [25] In 1861 he wrote to Cowell,

I am sure there is no longer any great pleasure living in this Country, so tost with perpetual Alarms as it is. One Day we are all in Arms about France. Today we are doubting if To-morrow we may not be at War to the Knife with America! I say still, as I used, we have too much Property, Honour, etc., on our Hands: our outward Limbs go on lengthening while our central Heart beats weaklier: I say, as I used, we should give up something before it is forced from us. The World, I think, may justly resent our being and interfering all over the Globe. Once more I say, would we were a little, peaceful, unambitious, trading Nation, like—the Dutch.[26]

22. MS. letter to Spring Rice, Dec. 12, 1861.
23. *Ibid.,* Dec. 18, 1861.
24. *Ibid.,* April [15, 1863].
25. Letter to Mrs. Allen, Aug. 15, 1857.
26. Letter to Cowell, Dec. 7, 1861.

For twenty years FitzGerald had been looking for a house in which to establish his home. After moving to Market Hill, he "intensified" his search, for he feared being caught "some sudden fine day with death, disease, and disability" in a strange house. "I am quite clear," he declared in 1861, "I must live the remainder of my Life in a Town: but a little one, and with a strip of Garden to saunter in." He considered Lowestoft and Beccles, that he might be near the Kerriches, but eventually concentrated on Woodbridge. Satisfactory dwellings, however, were few. "All the better houses," he complained, "are occupied by Dowagers like Myself: the Miss Tolls: Mrs. Pulham: the Miss Silvers: and Billy Whincopp: and none of them will die, or otherwise migrate, for Love or Money." George Moor, FitzGerald's lawyer, pointed out several houses which his client rejected. "At last," Moor stated, "he said he had made up his mind; and, as he had not been able to find anything that did suit him, he had fully decided to buy one that did not suit." [27] In the spring of 1864 a cottage on Pytches Road in the northern outskirts of the town, not far from the main thoroughfare, was advertised for sale; FitzGerald bought it and four acres of ground for £510. Two acres of meadow before the house were purchased for £200. "I don't know that I want either," he told Crabbe, "but having talked so long of buying *something*, I bought those which I believe I shall be able to sell with scarce a loss in case something else offers." [28]

The cottage, which consisted of a single living room, a large scullery, and a kitchen on the ground floor, and three bedrooms above, was an old building and, according to the new owner, "a rotten affair." He had plans drawn for two immense drawing rooms to be added, one on each story, at the south side, overlooking the garden. Halls and a new stairway were also capacious. [29] William Dove, a Woodbridge builder whom FitzGerald engaged, recommended that four rooms be made of the projected two, but the owner insisted on his original plan. Some delay occurred when it was discovered that the ground on which the house stood was copyhold and not freehold as had been thought. By February, 1865, however, men were at work on the property, "not only for the improvement sake," FitzGerald said, "but because it gives employment. Even now I have six men filling up a ditch, etc., who

27. Moor MS. letter.
28. MS. letter to Crabbe, June 5, 1864.
29. FitzGerald also added a small conservatory to the house, but whether at this time or later cannot be determined.

would else have been out of work. It is better than buying a picture of some old Jew, is it not?"

He was so hard to please that building proceeded at a snail's pace. He suggested changes as construction advanced, and sometimes ordered work to be torn down and rebuilt. The addition was not completed until March, 1866; in June, Dove submitted a bill for £1,150. This sum far exceeded the owner's expectations. To a Woodbridge cabinetmaker who congratulated him on the completion of the house, he replied, "It isn't finished yet—it isn't paid for. Dove is a nice bird, but he has a very long bill." [30] He maintained that the charges were one third more than they should be, and engaged another builder to make an appraisal. The claim was haggled over by lawyers for two years before being settled for £1,030.

"I shall never live in it," FitzGerald said of his new home, "but I shall die there." Both predictions proved false.

He engaged as caretakers John and Mary Howe, an old couple who had been tenants of the cottage, and furnished the house as a summer home for his Kerrich nieces and for friends who came to Woodbridge. For seven years after its completion, however, he persisted in remaining at his Market Hill lodgings.

While FitzGerald was negotiating the purchase of his "chateau," as he often called it, the Cowells returned to England. They had expected to spend eight years at Calcutta, but Cowell's vitality had been sapped by the tropical climate; and, at the end of seven years, he was granted a furlough. Upon arriving home, he notified Fitz-Gerald, who replied with strange diffidence:

It was indeed a surprise to find a Letter of yours dated from Ipswich. Well you have come at a good time of the year so far as English nature is concern'd; I suppose you must be out in it, and away from Sanskrit, as much as you can.

Ah, I am afraid you will find me a torpid and incurious Man compared to what you left me; and *then* I was fast wearing that way, you know. Since then I have been still more diligently cultivating (as Spedding said) the stupid part of my Nature; seeing none of the Wise People, and only reading Memoirs, Travels, etc., just one grade above Novels. . . .

In a week or ten Days, I shall be embarking on my little Ship; you must come one day and see our River in her—you and Elizabeth—though my Boat does not shine in a River way. You know I go nowhere . . .

30. Information given by Richard Hayward, son of the cabinetmaker.

But you will let me hear of you before long, I dare say; and Time will clear up what it has to unfold.[31]

A great change had come over FitzGerald during his friend's absence. His confidence in himself had been sadly shaken by the blunder of his marriage. The deaths of Crabbe, Browne, Thackeray, and Mrs. Kerrich had broken many old ties. He was convinced that he had gone to seed intellectually, although references to his reading hardly bore him out. A passage from a letter to Donne is but one of many such. "Sophocles," he said, "has almost shaken my Allegiance to Æschylus. Oh, these two Œdipuses! but then that Agamemnon! Well: one shall be the Handel and t'other the Haydn: one the Michel Angelo, and t'other the Raffaelle, of Tragedy." He read Newman's *Apologia pro Vita Sua* as soon as it appeared in 1864 and recommended it to Crabbe as "deeply interesting; pathetic, eloquent, and, I think, sincere." During the summer he read Juvenal and Lucretius.

It had been easy to write to Cowell in India; to meet him in England was quite another matter. The younger man tried to arrange a meeting in June but was unsuccessful. "Our next arrangement," he told his wife, "will be more *precise*. One need be a lawyer and weigh one's expressions with an ultra grammatical nicety to be sure of meeting him." They met before the summer was ended, but it was several years before FitzGerald overcame his shyness.

His regard for the Cowells had nevertheless survived. "Oh, never go back to India!" he pleaded as the furlough drew to a close. "You both of you like a retired Life, in the country, with Books at home, and poor People abroad, and Providence over all. Why can't EBC get Orders, and a quiet Living, and see the last of old England, and read the Service of the Dead, in Charitable Hope, over E. FG. Oh yes! All this can be done; perhaps even I might help you: Stay, Stay!" [32] Other friends and Cowell's family also urged him to remain in England, and he finally decided to do so. He was appointed examiner for the Indian Civil Service and, with this work and writing, supported himself until 1867. In that year a chair of Sanskrit was established at Cambridge. Thompson, who had been elected Master of Trinity the previous year, asked FitzGerald if his friend would apply for the post. Cowell eagerly offered himself. Only one candidate, a German at Edinburgh, opposed him.

FitzGerald took an active part in his friend's campaign for the position. He wrote to Pollock:

31. Cowell MS. letter, May 25, 1864.
32. MS. letter to Cowell, March 25 [1865].

Unless you are predestined to vote for a German to fill the chair of Sanskrit to be set up at Cambridge, do vote, and get those you can to vote, for Edward Cowell. What the other Candidates may be, I don't know; I am sure he is fit for the Place; first, because, though I am not a proper Judge of Sanskrit, or any other Scholarship, I believe I am a Judge of the Stuff a Scholar should be made of: and, of all my learned Friends, I have known none of so unmistakable Metal as Cowell. And, secondly, among the Qualities that so clearly distinguish him, none is more to be trusted than his Reverence and Modesty, which I know would not let him set up for any Office he was not competent to fill: for which very reason he may not profess the Omniscience, or the sublime Theories, which the Germans have dazzled us with: but he will be sure of what he does profess. Beside having studied Oriental Literature these twenty years, he has been for eight years at Calcutta . . . where he studied Sanskrit with the native Pundits, etc. He told me, on his return . . . that he had been surprised to find how extremely inaccurate the German Scholars were in that direction: that their grand and plausible Theories would not stand Examination: this he told me long before this Cambridge Professorship was talked of . . . I repeat this, whatever the other Candidates may be, I am certain Cowell is a fit man; and if he be so, I should wish him success over a German, even were he not my Friend, but only an Englishman: whose national Good Sense I have more respect for than all the German Aesthetics, etceterorum.[33]

He also solicited the votes of Tennyson, Groome, and other Cambridge friends. To the poet he wrote:

And do ask others to vote this way. Your Voice will go a very long way, without your having the trouble to exert it much. Do, like a good Fellow, and *"paltry Poet."* O dear! How shocked would be some of your aesthetic Worshippers at my Impudence! I am relying upon it that *you* won't, you see; on the strength of Old Times . . . and believe me your sincere old unaesthetic Worshipper.[34]

Mrs. Cowell wrote to thank FitzGerald for his help. He replied:

You have surely gone astray when you talk of *my* Influence about—a Professorship!—and of Sanskrit!! Don't you think Max Müller, and your Husband's late Professorship—and present Employment—and Editings and Writings—do the work—if it is to be done at all?

However you will persist, I dare say, in giving me too much Credit in the matter. I can only say that I have always spoken of EBC as a real Scholar—a very rare thing—whom men may be *sure* will not pretend to know what he does not know *thoroughly;* and who has the Gift of making others know it also.

I dare say Groome will do all he can; and that will be *something,*

33. Letter to Pollock, May 8, 1867.
34. MS. letter to A. Tennyson, May 7, 1867.

but EBC's real Testimonials lie apart from all such efforts. If I could, or can, do any more in the same line, tell me, of course.[35]

Cowell was elected to the chair in June and held it until his death in 1903. During his long career he established an enviable reputation as a scholar, as an indefatigable teacher, and as a considerate and sympathetic adviser to all who sought his help.

35. MS. letter to Mrs. Cowell, May 18, 1867.

XXII

FitzGerald and Fletcher:
Herring Merchants

"So now I shall be very glad to drop *Esquire,* and be addressed as '*Herring-merchant*' for the future."

Letter to Spalding

DURING the spring of 1864, FitzGerald met Joseph Fletcher, a Lowestoft fisherman, who for several years seemed to him to be the embodiment of all that was worthy in man. They were introduced by Newson one day as the *Scandal* lay at Felixstowe Ferry. "Posh," as Fletcher was generally called, was twenty-six years old, a stalwart, bearded sailor of six feet, with ruddy-brown complexion, blue eyes, and auburn hair, "a grand Fellow," said FitzGerald, "like one of those first British sent over to Rome—a very humane Savage." [1] He combined simplicity of soul and an almost womanly tenderness of nature with the sturdy independence of the beachmen. Moreover, he expressed himself in the racy colloquialisms, larded by unconscious humor, which always attracted FitzGerald to sailors. On cruises to Lowestoft during the next two years he came more and more to admire the rough seaman until Posh became the ideal man and Carlyle's hero rolled into one—such a person, FitzGerald said, "as I think I would rather be than—Tennyson or Thackeray." [2] Fletcher also reminded him of Browne, both in feature and character "so that," he told Mrs. Browne in 1867, "I seem to have jumped back to a regard of near forty years ago; and while I am with him feel young again, and when he goes shall feel old again." [3]

Posh made his living by "inshore" fishing for cod, haddock, sole, and other fish with which the coastal waters teemed. He also belonged, of course, to a boat company which engaged in salvaging. "You sea pirates!" FitzGerald would exclaim, laughing heartily at the latest "salwagin" episode, "You sea pirates!" In 1866 Posh

---

1. MS. letter to Cowell, April 2, 1867.
2. *Loc. cit.*
3. Wright, *FitzGerald,* II, 50.

bought an old lugger, the *William Tell;* and with £50 borrowed from FitzGerald and a like sum from Newson, he equipped it for herring fishing.[4] The ship was barely seaworthy, and after a year Posh sold it. FitzGerald then proposed a partnership with his young friend, wherein he was to finance the building of a new lugger and Posh to contribute his nets and gear and serve as captain. Arrangements were completed on January 5, 1867, and the lugger was begun by Dan Fuller, a Lowestoft shipwright, according to specifications outlined by Posh. "I dare say I had better have left all this alone," FitzGerald confided to Spalding, "but, if moderately lucky, the Vessel will pay *something,* at any rate: and in the meanwhile it really does me some good, I believe, to set up this little Interest here: and even if I lose money, I get some Fun for it. So now I shall be very glad to drop *Esquire,* and be addressed as 'Herring-merchant,' for the future." [5]

The lugger, which cost £360, was forty-five feet long, fifteen broad, and seven deep: two feet less in length than the beam called for by Lowestoft ideas. Because of her stubby appearance, Fitz-Gerald called her a "Cart-horse," but she proved to be a faster vessel than the *Scandal.* He first considered calling her the *Marian Halcombe,* after the heroine of *The Woman in White;* but she was launched as the *Meum and Tuum.* This the sailors read *Mum and Tum,* and so she was known along the coast. The lugger put out on her first voyage in August, but the season proved to be a poor one. When FitzGerald went to Lowestoft at the end of December to settle accounts, he found them "much against us." He commented to Cowell,

My dear Captain, who looks in his Cottage like King Alfred in the Story, was rather saddened by all this, as he had prophesied better things. I tell him that if he is but what I think him—and surely my sixty years of considering men will not so deceive me at last!—I would rather lose money with him than gain it with others. Indeed I never proposed Gain, as you may imagine: but only to have some Interest with this dear Fellow.

He had invested about £500 in the partnership, first considered to be a three-quarters interest. However, the nets and gear contributed by Posh proved to be of greater value than had been estimated; and before the lugger put to sea, it was decided that the two men should be equal partners. FitzGerald's friends urged him to secure his investment by a mortgage on boat and equipment,

4. FitzGerald subsequently took over Newson's loan.
5. *Two Suffolk Friends,* p. 108.

and this he proposed the following spring. The captain acquiesced, although he resented changing the agreement. "I believe that he and I shall now sign the Mortgage Papers," FitzGerald wrote to Spalding in April, 1868, ". . . I only get out of him that he can't say he sees anything much amiss in the Deed." To the end of his life, however, Posh resented the activities of "interfarin' parties" who came between him and his "guv'nor."

During the winter nets for mackerel fishing had been purchased for the lugger; but poor luck dogged the *Meum and Tuum* through 1868, and another loss was recorded when accounts were closed. Fortune changed the following year, however, and the vessel made £450 in the North Sea fishing. FitzGerald rejoiced that "the poor fellows all came home with something to carry to Wife and Children; £18 a Share: never was Money more gladly dispensed with." On the other hand, "only for fun's sake," he had wished

to realise £5 in my Pocket. But my Captain would take it all to pay Bills. But if he makes another £400 this Home Voyage! Oh, then we shall have money in our Pockets. I do wish this. For the anxiety about all these People's lives has been so much more to me than all the amusement I have got from the Business, that I think I will draw out of it if I can see my Captain sufficiently firm on his legs to carry it on alone.[6]

The lugger had average luck for the remainder of the year; and in December the partners divided £35, the first return on their investment.

FitzGerald was too tenderhearted for a business man. Whenever the vessel was at sea in rough weather, he worried about the safety of the crew and was as apprehensive about the health of his captain as a fussy mother with an only child. "He came up," he once informed Spalding after Posh had put into Lowestoft to leave some nets, "with a very bad cold and hoarseness: and so went off, poor fellow: he never will be long well, I do think." [7] Members of Posh's family had suffered from gallstones and FitzGerald feared that his model man would become a victim also. He plied him with advice. "You should take plenty of *Tea*," he had written while the *Meum and Tuum* was on her first voyage, "some Gin and Water every night; and *no* Ale or Beer: but only Porter; and not much of that. If you do not choose to buy Gin for yourself, buy some for *me:* and keep it on board: and drink some every Day, or night, Pray remember this: and *do it.*" [8] Posh was probably not averse to

6. Letter to Mrs. W. H. Thompson [1869].
7. *Two Suffolk Friends*, p. 118.
8. FitzGerald and "Posh," p. 72.

drinking gin and water at the "guv'nor's" expense, but his reaction to such solicitude may easily be guessed.

The partnership did not operate without friction. Posh was as careless about financial obligations as FitzGerald was meticulous; and the latter, though an inactive, was not a silent partner. "Remember your debts. Remember your debts," he admonished the younger man in 1866. But Posh did not always remember them, and his careless bookkeeping and slipshod methods of conducting business were a constant vexation to his benefactor. Posh, on the other hand, resented what he considered interference. A letter written by FitzGerald in the autumn of 1869 reveals the grievances which each held against the other.

I cannot lay blame to myself, Posh, in this matter, though I may not have known you were so busy with the boat as you tell me. Hearing of great disasters by last week's gale, I was, as usual, anxious about you. Hearing nothing from you, I telegram'd on Thursday Afternoon to Mr. Bradbeer: his answer reached me at 5 p.m. that you had come in on Tuesday, and were then safe in harbour. Being then afraid lest you should put off paying away the money, which, as I told you, was a positive *danger* to Wife and Children, I directly telegram'd to *you* to do what I had desired you to do the week before. Busy as you were, five minutes spent in writing me a line would have spared all this trouble and all this vexation on both sides.

As to my telegrams telling all the world what you wish to keep secret; how did they do that? My telegrams to Mr. Bradbeer were simply to ask if you were *safe*. My telegram to you was simply to say, "Do what I bid you"; Who should know *what* that was, or that it had anything to do with paying the Boat's Bills? People might guess it had *something* to do with the Boat: and don't you suppose that everyone knows pretty well how things are between us? And why should they not, I say, when all is honestly done between us? . . .

You say truly that, when we began together, you supposed I should leave all to you, and use *no* Authority (though you have always asked me about anything you wished done). Quite true. I never did wish to meddle; nor did I call on you for any Account, till I saw last year that you forgot a really important sum, and that you did not seem inclined to help your Memory (as everyone else does) by writing it down in a Book. In two cases this year I have shown you the same forgetfulness (about your liabilities I mean) and I do not think I have been unjust, or unkind, in trying to make you bring *yourself* to Account. You know, and ought to believe, that I have perfect confidence in *your honour;* and have told you of the one defect I observed in you as much for your sake as mine.

Quite as much, yes! For the anxiety I have suffered these two years about your eleven lives is but ill compensated by all these squalls between us two: which I declare I excuse myself of raising. If, in this last case, you really had not time to post me a line or two to say you were all safe, and that you had done what I desired you to do; I am very sorry for having written so sharply as I did to you: but I cannot *blame* myself for the mistake. No: this I will say: I am not apt to think too much of my doings, and dealings with others. But, in my whole sixty years, I can with a clear conscience say that I have dealt with *one man* fairly, kindly, and not ungenerously, for three good years. I may have made mistakes; but I can say I have done *my* best as conscientiously as he can say he has done his. And I believe he *has* done his best, though he has also made mistakes; and I remain his sincerely, E. FG.[9]

FitzGerald was aware of another blemish in his hero. While the partnership was being formed, he wrote to Spalding from Lowestoft:

The Man is, I do think, of a Royal Nature. I have told him he is liable to one Danger (the Hare with many Friends)—so many wanting him *to drink*. He says, it's quite true, and that he is often obliged to run away: as I believe he does: for his House shows all Temperance and Order. This little Lecture I give him—to go the way, I suppose, of all such Advice . . .[10]

Posh rarely touched spirits, but more than once he distressed his patron by getting "fuddled" on beer. FitzGerald loathed drunkenness, but he was chiefly concerned about Posh because he believed that the cheap "two-penny" brew, of which the sailor was exceedingly fond, undermined his health. Time and again Posh promised temperance, but his resolution usually weakened in the company of convivial friends.

Posh drove in here . . . to tan his nets: could not help making one with some old friends in a Boat-race on the Monday, and getting very fuddled with them on the Suffolk Green (where I was) at night. After all the pains I have taken, and all the real anxiety I have had. And worst of all, after the repeated promises he had made! I said, there must now be an end of Confidence between us, so far as *that* was concerned, and I would so far trouble myself about him no more. But when I came to reflect that this was but an outbreak among old friends on an old occasion, after (I do believe) months of sobriety; that there was no concealment about it; and that though obstinate at first as to how little drunk, etc., he was very repentant afterwards—I cannot let this one flaw weigh against the general good of the man. I cannot if I would: what then is the use of trying? But my confidence in *that* respect must

9. *FitzGerald and "Posh,"* pp. 133–136.
10. *Two Suffolk Friends*, p. 109.

be so far shaken, and it vexes me to think that I can never be *sure* of his not being overtaken so. I declare that it makes me feel ashamed very much to play the Judge on one who stands immeasurably above me in the scale, whose faults are better than so many virtues. Was not this very outbreak that of a great genial Boy among his old Fellows? True, a Promise was broken. Yes: but if the Whole Man be of the Royal Blood of Humanity, and do Justice in the Main, what are *the people* to say? *He* thought, if he thought at all, that he kept his promise in the main. But there is no use talking: unless I part company wholly, I suppose I must take the evil with the good.[11]

FitzGerald was so diligent in finding excuses for the weaknesses of his hero that he completely spoiled him. The sailor, independent by nature, became headstrong under indulgence.

After the division of their first profits, FitzGerald believed that he had set Posh in the way to independence. "He and I will, I doubt, part Company," he told Laurence in January, 1870,

. . . he likes to be, what he is born to be, his own sole Master, of himself, and of other men. So now I have got him a fair start, I think he will carry on the Lugger alone: I shall miss my Hobby, which is no doubt the last I shall ride in this world: but I shall also get eased of some Anxiety about the lives of a Crew for which I now feel responsible. And this last has been a Year of great Anxiety in this respect.

A further exhibition of independence by Posh no doubt strengthened FitzGerald's half-formed resolution. Apparently assuming that the comparative success during 1869 justified an expansion of business, Posh, without consulting his partner, bought another lugger, the *Henrietta*. FitzGerald at first objected; but, after conferring with Spalding, who, incidentally, was himself a poor business man, wrote to Posh,

He [Spalding] would not go so far as to say I was *wrong;* but he thought that you were not to blame either. Therefore I consider that I *was* wrong; and, as I told you, I am very glad to find myself wrong, though very sorry to have been so. . . . Mr. Spalding thinks you would have done better to stick to *one* Lugger, considering the double trouble of two. But he says he is not a proper judge. *I* think the chief evil is that this new Boat will keep you ashore in the Net-room, which I am persuaded hurts you.

FitzGerald, nevertheless, advanced money for the boat; and amity was restored, though not for long. A few weeks later he asked Posh about the operating costs of a lugger. The captain apparently resented the query, for FitzGerald wrote,

11. *Ibid.,* pp. 115–117.

I never wanted you to puzzle yourself about the Accounts any more, but only to tell me at a rough estimate what the chief expenses were— as, for instance, Shares, etc. . . . And my reason *for* asking, was simply that, on Monday Mr. Moor here was asking me about what a Lugger's expenses were, and I felt it silly not to be able to tell him the least about it: and I have felt so when some one asked me before: and that is why I asked you. I neither have, nor ever had, any doubt of your doing your best: and you ought not to think so.[12]

He had now had enough of his captain as a partner. On April 12, 1870, an appraiser at Lowestoft evaluated the luggers and their gear. FitzGerald reduced the valuation and took a mortgage on equipment and ships, retaining title to the latter. In June he announced, "I am advertised in the Gazette as being no longer a Fishmonger; and my last Hand is played."

There was no breach in the friendship of the two men upon the termination of the partnership. FitzGerald continued to take a keen interest in Posh's venture and went frequently to Lowestoft to see him. Before the year was out, however, the younger man's conviviality resulted in another rupture. "I must speak very plainly to him," FitzGerald told Spalding,

that, with all his noble Qualities, I doubt that I can never again have Confidence in his Promise to break this one bad Habit, seeing that he has broken it so soon, when there was no occasion or excuse: unless it were the thought of leaving his Wife so ill at home. The Man is so beyond others, as I think, that I have come to feel that I must not condemn him by general rule; nevertheless, if he asks me, I can refer him to no other. I must send him back his own written Promise of Sobriety, signed only a month before he broke it so needlessly; and I must even tell him that I know not yet if he can be left with the Mortgage as we settled it in May. . . . I think that Posh ought to be made to feel this severely: and, as his Wife is better, I do not mind making him feel it, if I can. On the other hand, I do not wish to drive him, by Despair, into the very fault which I have so tried to cure him of.[13]

The breach was again patched, and FitzGerald gave Posh his support for two more years, during which dissension broke out repeatedly. Although Fletcher prospered and drove a mare and smart gig, he still neglected to pay his bills promptly; and he never overcame his fondness for drink. In December, 1873, he revolted against his patron's continued intervention. FitzGerald wrote to him with chilly formality:

12. *FitzGerald and "Posh,"* pp. 150–151.
13. *Two Suffolk Friends,* pp. 120–121.

Joseph Fletcher,

As you cannot talk with me without confusion, I write a few words to you on the subject of the two grievances which you began about this morning.

1st. As to your being *under* your Father: I said no such thing: but wrote that he was to be *either* Partner, or, (with your Mother) constantly employed, and consulted with as to the Boats. It is indeed for *their* sakes, and that of your own Family, that I have come to take all this trouble.

2ndly. As to the Bill of Sale to me. If you could be calm enough, you would see that this would be a Protection to *yourself*. You do not pay your different Creditors *all* their Bill at the year's end. Now, if any one of these should happen to want *all* his Money; he might, by filing a Bankruptcy against you, seize upon your Nets and everything else you have to pay his Debt.

As to your supposing that *I* should use the Bill of Sale except in the last necessity (which I do not calculate upon), you prove that you can have but little remembrance of what I have hitherto done for you and am still willing to do for your Family's sake quite as much as for your own. . . .

If you cannot see all this on reflection, there is no use my talking or writing more about it. You may ask Mr. Barnard, if you please, or any such competent person; if *they* object to the Bill of Sale, I shall not insist. But you had better let me know what you decide on before the end of the week when I shall be going home, that I may arrange accordingly.

Edward FitzGerald.[14]

Despite his anger, FitzGerald was still able to condone Posh's waywardness. "Yet there is Greatness about the Man," he insisted, "I believe his want of Conscience in some particulars is to be referred to his *Salwaging* Ethics; and your Cromwells, Caesars, and Napoleons have not been more scrupulous. But I shall part Company with him if I can do so without Injury to his Family." [15] However, he gave Posh yet one more chance. "I certainly shall not let you have the use of my Boats," he told him on January 19, 1874, "unless under *some* conditions, *none* of which you seemed resolved to submit to. It will save all trouble if you take the offer I have made you, and the sooner it is settled the better." But, Posh said during an interview in 1907, he "worn't a goin' ta hev his faa'er put oover him, nor he worn't a goin' ta take no pledge." [16] On February 17, therefore, the *Meum and Tuum* and the *Henrietta* were

14. *FitzGerald and "Posh,"* pp. 181–182.
15. *Two Suffolk Friends*, p. 123.
16. *FitzGerald and "Posh,"* p. 188.

auctioned at Lowestoft. Fletcher tried to buy the "Mum and Tum," but it sold for £300, more than he could bid.

After a temporary estrangement FitzGerald again resumed friendly relations with Posh, although he had no more business dealings with him. In 1870 he had commissioned Laurence to paint the sailor's portrait "to hang up by old Thackeray and Tennyson, all three having a stamp of Grandeur about them in their several ways, and occupying great places in my Soul." [17] In 1877 he could still say,

The Great Man . . . is yet there [at Lowestoft]: commanding a Crew of those who prefer being his Men to having command of their own. And they are right; for the man is Royal, tho' with the faults of ancient Vikings . . . His Glory is somewhat marred; but he looks every inch a King in his Lugger now. At home (when he is there and not at the Tavern) he sits among his Dogs, Cats, Birds, etc., always with a great Dog following him abroad, and aboard. This is altogether the Greatest Man I have known. [18]

Posh did not retain the economic security to which his patron had helped him. Bad luck continued to dog his boats and, Fitz-Gerald said two years later, he seemed to be "sinking into disorder." He spent his last years as a beachman, picking up a precarious livelihood by shrimp fishing. Nor did he return FitzGerald's high opinion of him. "It may interest you to know," a correspondent informed Aldis Wright in 1906,

that "Posh" Fletcher seems still to be hale and hearty. I meet him sometimes in my rambles along the North Beach there [Lowestoft]; [19] but I don't like the man because, notwithstanding all FitzGerald's kindness to him—and he gave him a grand chance to prove himself, at least, something like what FitzGerald imagined—he is ungrateful, and blames FitzGerald for "spoiling him." [20]

17. Letter to Pollock, Jan. 16 [1870].
18. Letter to Laurence, Jan. 15, 1877.
19. Posh died at Lothingland House, a workhouse at Oulton, Suffolk, on Sept. 7, 1915, at the age of seventy-six.
20. MS. letter from A. W. Dutt, author of *Literary Associations of East Anglia*, to Aldis Wright, dated April 26, 1906.

XXIII

More Persian and Spanish

"I hardly know why I print any of these things which nobody buys; . . . But when one has done one's best, and is sure that that best is better than so many will take pains to do . . . one likes to make an end of the matter by Print."

Letter to Cowell

AFTER publishing the *Rubáiyát* in 1859, Fitzgerald did not appear publicly in print until Quaritch issued the second edition in 1868. He was not idle during those years, however. His restless mind drove him constantly into literary activity of one kind or another, and his first undertaking after the *Rubáiyát* was to finish his translation of the *Mantik-ut-tair,* or *Parliament of Birds,* by the Persian, Farid-uddin Attár. Like *Salámán and Absál,* the work is a Súfí allegory. The *Mantik* interprets Súfí pantheistic beliefs.

FitzGerald had translated the poem during the hectic months of his married life, before he began the *Rubáiyát.* About the middle of December, 1856, he borrowed a manuscript from Napoleon Newton of Hertford, and five weeks later had translated about two thirds of it.[1] "He [Attár] has not so much Fancy or Imagination as Jámí," he told Cowell, "nor I dare say, as much depth as Jeláluddín; but his touch is lighter. I mean to make a Poetic Abstract of the Mantik, I think." He worked on the translation until March, when he put it aside "so as to happen on it again one day with fresh eyes." This process he repeated a number of times, using for the later stages of the work a printed text published by Garcin de Tassy.

In 1862 he sent his translation to Cowell in India, evidently proposing that it be submitted to the *Journal of the Bengal Asiatic Society,* of which Cowell was Oriental secretary. In December, however, FitzGerald wrote,

1. FitzGerald was aided in his translation by an analysis of the poem which Garcin de Tassy included in his *Mémoire sur la poésie philosophique et religieuse chez les Persans.* The French scholar published a prose translation in 1863, but FitzGerald had completed his poem by that time.

By the bye, if you have made any Annotations on my *Birds,* I think you might as well have the whole *printed* in an independent Pamphlet for me—say 100 copies or so: and, keeping what you care to keep, send the rest over to me. I do not think, after all, your Asiatic Society will care for it in their Magazine: it is not literal enough to serve their purpose; and I certainly do not wish you to have any trouble in forcing it on them. And, as I have a copy here, I could print it for myself: only, as you said you had made some Elucidations and Notes I should wish above all to have the benefit of them. I do not think it would cost you much trouble to write a short Introduction about Attár's Life and the Nature of his Poem etc.—a very little would do: and it would be *everything* for me: for I am always so afraid of blundering in Names, Facts, etc. (as Irishmen do) that I generally blunder the worse for over-anxiety to be accurate. Of course I shall pay for all the Expense of Printing.[2]

Cowell was too busy to attend to the matter, however, and Fitz-Gerald did not care to "meddle" with it himself. "Indeed," he said in August, 1863, "I dare say I should only be bored with the Copies when they were printed: for I don't know a Soul here who would care for the Thing if it were ten times as well done as I have done it." The poem was not printed until the first edition of FitzGer-ald's *Letters and Literary Remains* was published in 1889, six years after his death.

The *Bird Parliament* (the title which FitzGerald chose for his translation) is the very antithesis of the *Rubáiyát,* for it urges the abandonment of all that Omar held dear. The poem describes a pilgrimage to the sacred mountain Káf, in search of Sýmurgh, a gigantic bird of great wisdom.[3] The birds typify the Súfís, and Sýmurgh represents God, *the Truth.* The pilgrims pass through seven valleys of probation: Search, Love, Knowledge, Independ-ence, Unification, Amazement, and Destitution and Annihilation.

The original poem contains between nine and ten thousand lines written in couplets, which form FitzGerald retained. He simplified the elaborate allegory and reduced "the Mass into something of an Artistic Shape," until, as he said, it presented a "bird's-eye view" of the *Parliament of Birds.* "What I have done for amuse-ment," he explained, "is not only so unliteral, but I doubt *un-oriental,* in its form and expression, as would destroy the value of the Original without replacing it with anything worth reading of my own." Nor was he satisfied with the verse. Despite his criticisms, the result is an entertaining birds' *Pilgrim's Progress* in which types of human beings are cleverly represented by various fowls.

2. MS. letter to Cowell, Dec. 1, 1862.
3. Sýmurgh is coined from *si murgh,* meaning "thirty birds."

"The *Bird Parliament* well deserves to be published," Cowell declared shortly after the translator's death. "Some parts of it are really magnificent." [4]

FitzGerald's version opens with the assembling of the birds for the purpose of selecting a Sultan from among their number. The Tájidár,[5] credited by the Arabs with having the power of speech, first addresses the parliament.

> And now *you* want a Khalif: and I know
> Him, and his whereabout, and How to go:
> And go alone I could, and plead your cause
> Alone for all: but, by the eternal laws,
> Yourselves by Toil and Travel of your own
> Must for your old Delinquency atone.

The Sultan, to whom the Tájidár promises to lead them, is Sýmurgh.

> Who then this Travel to Result would bring
> Needs both a Lion's Heart beneath the Wing,
> And even more, a Spirit purified
> Of Worldly Passion, Malice, Lust and Pride.

The majority are eager to set out at once on the pilgrimage with the Tájidár as their leader.

> But some there were
> Who listen'd with a cold disdainful air,
> Content with what they were, or grudging Cost
> Of Time or Travel that might all be lost.

One by one these come forward and lodge their objections, which are answered by the leader, who illustrates his arguments by apologues. The debate with the nightingale is typical of these discussions:

> Then came *The Nightingale,* from such a Draught
> Of Ecstasy that from the Rose he quaff'd
> Reeling as drunk, and ever did distil
> In exquisite Divisions from his Bill
> To inflame the Hearts of Men—and thus sang He—
> "To me alone, alone, is giv'n the Key
> Of Love; of whose whole Mystery possesst,
> When I reveal a little to the Rest,
> Forthwith Creation listening forsakes

4. Cowell MS. letter, July 19, 1883.
5. The Tájidár, a kind of lapwing, is the hoopoe of Aristophanes' *Birds*. In Persia it is also called the hudhud.

The Reins of Reason, and my Frenzy takes:
Yea, whosoever once has quaff'd this wine
He leaves unlisten'd David's Song for mine.
In vain do Men for my Divisions strive,
And die themselves making dead Lutes alive:
I hang the Stars with Meshes for Men's Souls:
The Garden underneath my Music rolls.
The long, long Morns that mourn the Rose away
I sit in silence, and on Anguish prey:
But the first Air which the New Year shall breathe
Up to my Boughs of Message from beneath
That in her green Harím my Bride unveils,
My Throat bursts silence and *her* Advent hails,
Who in her crimson Volume registers
The Notes of Him whose Life is lost in hers.[6]
The Rose I love and worship now is here;
If dying, yet reviving, Year by Year;
But that you tell of, all my Life why waste
In vainly searching; or, if found, not taste?"

So with Division infinite and Trill
On would the Nightingale have warbled still,
And all the World have listen'd; but a Note
Of sterner Import check'd the love-sick Throat.

"Oh watering with thy melodious Tears
Love's Garden, and who dost indeed the Ears
Of men with thy melodious Fingers mould
As David's Finger Iron did of old:
Why not, like David, dedicate thy Dower
Of Song to something better than a Flower?
Empress indeed of Beauty, so they say,
But one whose Empire hardly lasts a Day,
By Insurrection of the Morning's Breath
That made her hurried to Decay and Death:
And while she lasts contented to be seen,
And worshipt, for the Garden's only Queen,
Leaving thee singing on thy Bough forlorn,
Or if she smile on Thee, perhaps in Scorn."

The Tájidár upbraids the parrot for his love of the present, the
peacock for love of the lost Eden, the owl and the partridge for love
of riches, the falcon for pride, the ringdove for sloth.

6. It was sometimes fancied that the Rose had as many petals as her Lover had
Notes in his voice. [FitzGerald's note.]

Then from a Pond, where all day long he kept,
Waddled the dapper *Duck* demure, adept
At infinite Ablution, and precise
In keeping of his Raiment clean and nice.
And "Sure of all the Race of Birds," said He,
"None for Religious Purity like Me,
Beyond what strictest Rituals prescribe—
Methinks I am the Saint of all our Tribe,
To whom, by Miracle, the Water, that
I wash in, also makes my Praying-Mat."

To whom, more angrily than all, replied
The Leader, lashing that religious Pride,
That under ritual Obedience
To outer Law, with inner might dispense;
For, fair as all the Feather to be seen,
Could one see *through*, the Maw was not so clean:
But He that made both Maw and Feather too
Would take account of, seeing through and through.

The Tájidár cheers the weak, and counsels the timid.

And then, with drooping Crest and Feather, came
Others, bow'd down with Penitence and Shame.
They long'd indeed to go; "but how begin,
Mesh'd and entangled as they were in Sin?"

. . .

Whom the wise Leader bid be of good cheer,
And conscious of the Fault, dismiss the Fear.

Then follows one of the finest figures in the poem:

"For like a Child sent with a fluttering Light
To feel his way along a gusty Night
Man walks the World: again and yet again
The Lamp shall be by Fits of Passion slain:
But shall not He who sent him from the Door
Relight the Lamp once more, and yet once more?"

Still the birds hesitate. How can they gain an audience with an emperor mightier than Mahmúd the Great, having neglected to bring rich gifts from home? To which the Tájidár replies:

"Let him that with this Monarch would engage
Bring the Gold Dust of a long Pilgrimage:
The Ruby of a bleeding Heart, whose Sighs
Breathe more than Amber-incense as it dies;
And while in naked Beggary he stands

Hope for the Robe of Honour from his Hands.
And, as no gift this Sovereign receives
Save the mere Soul and Self of him who gives,
So let that Soul for other none Reward
Look than the Presence of its Sovereign Lord."

The Tájidár's description of the road which the pilgrims must follow causes many birds to desert the council. Finally, however, a mighty band sets out. At the very border of the Vale of Search a freezing wind sweeps down on the host, and the ranks break. When order is restored, fewer than half of those who had started are left. They struggle on, but each mile sees the ranks further depleted. Pilgrims fall from exhaustion; others are either scorched or frozen; some die of hunger, some of thirst, others from drinking poisoned water. Some go mad; others commit suicide. When the foot of Káf is reached, only a small band remains of the host which had begun the journey. Of these, only a handful survive the climb to the summit of the sacred mountain,

> But *Thirty*—thirty desperate draggled Things,
>   . . . fell upon
> The Threshold of the Everlasting *One*,
> With but enough of Life in each to cry,
> On THAT which all absorb'd—

Suddenly there flashes before them "a winged Harbinger of Flame," which demands to know who they are and whence they came. The Tájidár replies:

>   . . . "We are
> Those Fractions of the Sum of being, far
> Dis-spent and foul disfigured . . .
> Let us but see the Fount from which we flow,
> And, seeing, lose Ourselves therein!"

Before the Tájidár has finished speaking and without any door being opened, the thirty find themselves before the Throne. So bright is the glory that the pilgrims have to drop their gaze, and each finds before him a scroll that flashes back the "half-forgotten Story of his Soul." The thirty

> By full Confession and Self-loathing flung
> The Rags of carnal Self that round them clung;
> And, their old selves self-acknowledged and self-loathed,
> And in the Soul's Integrity re-clothed,
> Once more they ventured from the Dust to raise
> Their Eyes—up to the Throne—into the Blaze

And in the Centre of the Glory there
Beheld the Figure of—*Themselves* . . .[7]

. . .

They That, That They: Another, yet the Same;
Dividual, yet One: from whom there came
A Voice of awful Answer . . .
"The Sun of my Perfection is a Glass
Wherein from *Seeing* into *Being* pass
All who, reflecting as reflected see
Themselves in Me, and Me in Them: not *Me*,
But all of Me that a contracted Eye
Is comprehensive of Infinity:
Nor yet *Themselves:* no Selves, but of the All
Fractions, from which they split and whither fall.

. . .

"All you have been, and seen, and done, and thought,
Not *You* but *I*, have seen and been and wrought:
I was the Sin that from Myself rebell'd:
I the Remorse that tow'rd Myself compell'd:
I was the Tájidár who led the Track:
I was the little Briar that pull'd you back:
Sin and Contrition—Retribution owed,
And cancell'd—Pilgrim, Pilgrimage, and Road,
Was but Myself toward Myself: and Your
Arrival but *Myself* at my own Door:

. . .

"Come you lost Atoms to your Centre draw,
And *be* the Eternal Mirror that you saw:
Rays that have wander'd into Darkness wide
Return, and back into your Sun subside."

While corresponding with Cowell about the *Birds* in 1862, Fitz-Gerald had said, "I still think I shall one day finish an impudent Version of the Agamemnon, and of Calderon's *Vida* and *Mágico*.[8] But I have now a sort of Terror at muddling with Pen and Paper in that way, and make no hand of it when I try. The old *Go* is gone—such as it was. One has got older: one has lived alone: and, also, either one's subjects, or one's way of dealing with them, have little Interest to others." [9] He seems to have done nothing with the plays until after Cowell's return to England in 1864. "I don't know if it's your coming home," he said in November,

7. Thus the origin of Sýmurgh, Thirty Birds.
8. The complete titles are *El Mágico Prodigioso* and *La Vida es Sueño*.
9. MS. letter to Cowell, Dec. 1, 1862.

or my being better this Winter, or what: but I have caught up a long ago Version of my dear old *Mágico,* and have so recast it that scarce a Plank remains of the original! Pretty impudence: and yet all done to conciliate English, or modern, Sympathy. This I shan't publish. . . . only I shall print some Copies for you and one or two more. . . . There is really very great Skill in the Adaptation, and Remodelling, of it.

These two Calderon plays had first aroused FitzGerald's interest in the Spanish dramatist. He had not included them in his former volume of translations, because they belonged to Calderon's more famous productions, with which he had not wished to "meddle." After the criticism of his 1853 volume, he had attempted more literal translations of the two plays but had abandoned the work when he found that he could not transfuse the spirit of the original while following it closely. Now, however, he polished up his early drafts and sent *The Mighty Magician,* as he called his translation of *El Mágico,* to Childs, the Bungay printer. He then set to work on *La Vida.* In February, 1865, he sent copies of the first play to a number of friends. To R. C. Trench, who had been made Archbishop of Dublin the previous year, he wrote:

I . . . have licked the two Calderons into some sort of shape of my own, without referring to the Original. One of them goes by the Post to your Grace; and when I tell you the other is no other than your own "Life's a Dream," you won't wonder at my sending the present one on Trial, both done as they are in the same lawless, perhaps impudent, way. I know you would not care who did these things, so long as they were well done; but one doesn't wish to meddle, and in so free-and-easy a way, with a Great Man's Masterpieces, and utterly fail: especially when two much better men have been before one. One excuse is, that Shelley and Dr. Trench only took parts of these plays, not caring surely —who can?—for the underplot and buffoonery which stands most in the way of the tragic Dramas. Yet I think it is as a whole, that is, the whole main Story, that these Plays are capital; and therefore I have tried to present that whole, leaving out the rest, or nearly so; and altogether the Thing has become so altered one way or another that I am afraid of it now it's done, and only send you one Play . . . which will be enough if it is an absurd Attempt.

Such Stuff as Dreams Are Made Of had also been printed by May 3, and the two plays were stitched together in a single volume.[10] "I don't publish," FitzGerald explained to Cowell, "because I found there was no use, in the other Translations: more

10. FitzGerald had ordered 500 copies of each play. Only 50 copies had been printed by May 10, however, and in 1875 he wrote to Fanny Kemble that he had had 100 copies printed "and have not had a hundred friends to give them to."

trouble to others and oneself than Good. If any Magazine or Miscellany chooses to print this Play—[11] (supposing you and others approve it) well and good." [12] Neither of the plays was published until the appearance of his collected works.

FitzGerald replaced the swift and often improbable action of the original plays with introspection, and engaged his protagonists in subjective struggles which have no parallel in Calderon. He ignored the underplot and comedy of *El Mágico* entirely and all but deleted them from *La Vida*. As a result of his omissions *The Mighty Magician* contains little action, and the conflict is almost entirely confined to the intellectual clash between the protagonist and Lucifer. *Such Stuff as Dreams Are Made Of* retains more action because the original play is melodramatic.

The Mighty Magician relates the story of Ciprian, a pagan scholar of Antioch in the early days of Christianity. He sells his soul to Lucifer, whose true identity he does not know, in order to win the love of Justina, a Christian maiden who spurns the advances of all suitors. The sorcery in which the demon instructs him has no effect upon the maiden, and Ciprian demands to know the source of her strength. Lucifer refuses to tell him, and the scholar invokes his diabolical powers to force the truth. Discovering that his antagonist is proof against them, he resorts to other means.

Cipr.   Then if your own hell
          Cannot enforce you; by that Unknown Power
          That saved Justina from your fangs, although
          Yourself you cannot master, if you know,
          I charge you name him to me!—
Luc.   (after a great flash of lightning and thunder) Jesus Christ!
Cipr. (after a pause) Ev'n so!—Christ Jesus
          Jesus Christ—the same
          That poor Lisandro died suspected of,

                    .   .   .

          The prophet-carpenter of Nazareth,
          Poor, persecuted, buffeted, reviled,
          Spit upon, crown'd with thorns, and crucified
          With thieves—the Son of God—the Son of man,
          Whose shape He took to teach them how to live?

                    .   .   .

          Luc.   Yea!
          Cipr. Of the one sun of Deity one ray

11. *The Mighty Magician.*
12. MS. letter to Cowell, Nov. 19, 1864.

> That was before the world was, and that made
> The world and all that is within it?

Luc.   Yea!

. . .

Cipr. All one, all when, all where, all good, all mighty,
> All eye, all ear, all self-integrity—
> Methinks this must be He of whom I read
> In Greek and Roman sages dimly guess'd,

. . .

> Is this the God for whom I sought so long
> In mine own soul and those of other men,
> Who from the world's beginning till to-day
> Groped or were lost in utter darkness?

Luc.   Yea!

Cipr.   . . . Oh,
> Like a flogg'd felon after full confession
> Released at last!

Luc.   To bind you mine for ever.

Cipr. Thine! What art thou?

Luc. The god whom you must worship.

Cipr. There is no God but one, whom you and I
> Alike acknowledge, as in Jesus Christ
> Reveal'd to man. What other god art thou?

Luc. Antichrist! He that all confessing Christ
> Confess; Satan, the Serpent, the first Tempter,
> Who tempted the first Father of mankind
> With the same offer to a like result
> That I have tempted thee with . . .

Cipr.

> I fling myself and all my debt on Him
> Who died to undertake them—

. . .

Luc. (seizing him)   Take my answer—

Cipr. Oh, Saviour of Justina, save Thou me!

Ciprian escapes and confesses his conversion to Christianity before the senate of Antioch. He is sentenced to die on the scaffold with Justina. As they await execution, he tells the maiden of his change of faith and pleads:

> Oh, Justina,
> Who upward ever with the certain step
> Of faith hast follow'd unrepress'd by sin;
> Now that thy foot is almost on the floor
> Of heav'n, pray Him who opens thee the door,
> Let with thee one repenting sinner in!

Of the second drama FitzGerald said, "I call the Play *Such Stuff as Dreams Are Made Of* to hook on Calderon with his Contemporary.[13] Isn't it a good Title? Yes; of course much the best Part of the whole." [14] He printed the following lines as a preface:

> For Calderon's Drama sufficient would seem
> The title he chose for it—"Life is a Dream";
> Two words of the motto now filch'd are enough
> For the impudent mixture they label—"such Stuff!"

The scene of the play is Poland. Segismund, heir to the throne, has been imprisoned in a mountain tower to thwart a prophecy that he will destroy his father, King Basilio, and many of his subjects. The prince has reached maturity, and Basilio decides to restore him to his place at court in order to determine whether or not he is viciously inclined. Segismund is given a sleeping potion and awakens at the palace, surrounded by courtiers and servants. When told that he is a prince, the memory of the indignities which he has suffered drives him to violence. Having failed his father's test, he is given a second potion. He awakens in his tower and is told that the brief interlude amid luxury was merely a dream. Aware now that an heir to the throne lives, the army rebels and releases Segismund, who overthrows his father. After his triumph, however, the prince accords clemency to his enemies, thereby proving that he has gained wisdom.

The action, as in all of FitzGerald's translations, follows that of the original far more closely than one would expect from his comments, for he always warned readers of more radical changes than he effected. He eliminated much which detracted from unity; but, in what he retained, he was faithful to the original. On the other hand, he introduced ideas of his own into the dialogue, expanded thoughts merely hinted in his source, and forged bolder figures to express ideas found in the original. In this way he instilled life into his versions and infused them with poetic beauty. A speech from a literal translation of *La Vida* and its parallel in FitzGerald's play will serve for comparison. In Denis M'Carthy's version, when Segismund awakens after his return to prison, his jailer, a nobleman, addresses him:

> Clotaldo   . . .
> But in dreams, however bright,

13. Shakespeare, although the two men were not exactly contemporaries. Calderon's dates were 1600–81.

14. Fragment of a MS. letter to Cowell, undated.

       Thou shouldst still have kept in sight
       How for years I tended thee,
       For 'twere well, howe'er we be,
       Even in dreams to do what's right. (Exit.)
Segis. That is true: then let's restrain
       This wild rage, this fierce condition
       Of the mind, this proud ambition,
       Should we ever dream again:
       And we'll do so, since 'tis plain,
       In this world's uncertain gleam,
       That to live is but to dream:
       Man dreams what he is, and wakes
       Only when upon him breaks
       Death's mysterious morning beam.
       The king dreams he is a king,
       And in this delusive way
       Lives and rules with sovereign sway;
       All the cheers that round him ring,
       Born of air, on air take wing.
       And in ashes (mournful fate!)
       Death dissolves his pride and state:
       Who would wish a crown to take,
       Seeing that he must awake
       In the dream beyond death's gate?
       And the rich man dreams of gold,
       Gilding cares it scarce conceals,
       And the poor man dreams he feels
       Want and misery and cold.
       Dreams he too who rank would hold,
       Dreams who bears toil's rough-ribbed hands,
       Dreams who wrong for wrong demands,
       And in fine, throughout the earth,
       All men dream, whate'er their birth,
       And yet no one understands.
       'Tis a dream that I in sadness
       Here am bound, the scorn of fate;
       'Twas a dream that once a state
       I enjoyed of light and gladness.
       What is life? 'Tis but a madness.
       What is life? A thing that seems,
       A mirage that falsely gleams,
       Phantom joy, delusive rest,
       Since is life a dream at best,
       And even dreams themselves are dreams.

This soliloquy is given by FitzGerald to Clotaldo:

Clot. So sleep; sleep fast: and sleep away those two
    Night-potions, and the waking dream between
    Which dream thou must believe; and, if to see
    Again, poor Segismund! that dream must be.—
    And yet, and yet, in these our ghostly lives,
    Half night, half day, half sleeping, half awake,
    How if our waking life, like that of sleep,
    Be all a dream in that eternal life
    To which we wake not till we sleep in death?
    How if, I say, the senses we now trust
    For date of sensible comparison,—
    Ay, ev'n the Reason's self that dates with them,
    Should be in essence or intensity
    Hereafter so transcended, and awoke
    To a perceptive subtlety so keen
    As to confess themselves befool'd before,
    In all that now they will avouch for most?
    One man—like this—but only so much longer
    As life is longer than a summer's day,
    Believed himself a king upon his throne,
    And play'd at hazard with his fellows' lives,
    Who cheaply dream'd away their lives to him.
    The sailor dream'd of tossing on the flood:
    The soldier of his laurels grown in blood:
    The lover of the beauty that he knew
    Must yet dissolve to dusty residue:
    The merchant and the miser of his bags
    Of finger'd gold; the beggar of his rags:
    And all this stage of earth on which we seem
    Such busy actors, and the parts we play'd,
    Substantial as the shadow of a shade,
    And Dreaming but a dream within a dream!

For many years FitzGerald had been collecting material, in a leisurely way, for a vocabulary of provincial English. He first referred to this pastime in 1858.

I amuse myself with jotting down materials (out of vocabularies, etc.) for a Vocabulary of *rural* English, or *rustic* English: that is, only the best country words selected from the very many Glossaries, etc., relating chiefly to country matters, but also to things in general: words that carry their own story with them, without needing Derivation or Authority, though both are often to be found. I always say I have heard the Language of Queen Elizabeth's, or King Harry's Court, in the Suffolk Villages: better a great deal than that spoken in London Societies, whether Fashionable or Literary: and the homely [strength] of which has made Shakespeare, Dryden, South, and Swift, what they could not have been without it. But my Vocabulary if ever done will be a very little Affair . . . for here again it is pleasant enough to jot down a word now and then, but not to equip all for the Press.[15]

When he began to visit Lowestoft frequently, FitzGerald discovered a new store of graphic provincialisms in use among the seafolk. In July, 1860, he called attention to this vocabulary in a letter written to *The East Anglian,* a periodical of notes and queries edited by Samuel Tymms of Lowestoft. FitzGerald proposed that the readers "who live on the spot, would do well to gather what of these they can lay hold of, and contribute them to the *East Anglian* . . . before the modern SCHOOLMASTER has drubbed them out of the language." [16]

FitzGerald himself began to collect sea words and phrases, his chief authority being Posh, although the sailor was not aware that his speech was being anatomized. Two Suffolk vocabularies had already been published, one, *Suffolk Words and Phrases,* edited by FitzGerald's old friend, Major Moor; and the other, *The Vocabulary of East Anglia,* edited by the Reverend Robert Forby, rector of Fincham, Norfolk.[17] For a time FitzGerald proposed a fusion of these two works, "taking the more accurate Forby for groundwork, to be illustrated with Major Moor's delightful Suffolk Humour, and adding the Sea Phrases in which both are wanting." [18] He was anticipated by J. G. Nall, who, in 1866, published a guide to Great Yarmouth and Lowestoft, appending a vocabulary of sea words. FitzGerald thereupon sent Nall his own collection to be used in any future edition of the work. Late in 1868 he sent his vocabulary to Tymms. "On the whole," he wrote, "I think if you print them as I send them, it must be in some Christmas number, a season when even antiquarians grow young, scholars unbend, and grave men are content to let others trifle." [19] At the Christmas season for three years, 1868–70, FitzGerald contributed vocabularies to *The East Anglian,* as well as notes of local interest pertaining to John Wesley and Crabbe the poet. Binding his glossaries, which contained about four hundred definitions, in pamphlets entitled *Sea Words and Phrases,* he distributed them among his friends.

He sent letters, on subjects of local interest for the most part,

15. Letter to Cowell, Sept. 3, 1858.
16. *East Anglian Notes and Queries,* I (July, 1860), 141.
17. Moor, Edward, *Suffolk Words and Phrases* (London, R. Hunter, 1823); Forby, the Rev. Robert, *The Vocabulary of East Anglia* (London, J. B. Nichols & Son, 1830).
18. *East Anglian Notes and Queries,* III (December, 1868), 347.
19. *Loc. cit.*

to *The East Anglian,* as well as to *Notes and Queries.* For the latter he used the signature "Parathina." Ten years later Archdeacon Groome's son, Francis, edited "Suffolk Notes and Queries," a weakly feature of the *Ipswich Journal.* Writing under a number of aliases, father and son managed to fill the column, FitzGerald occasionally helping them with contributions signed "Effigy," coined from his initials.

As early as 1865 Quaritch urged him to republish the *Rubáiyát,* but he did not think it worth while, although he "saw where some things might be transposed, and some added." Nevertheless, he toyed with the idea and in September, 1867, wrote to the publisher, "You must tell me . . . whether you care to take charge of such a shrimp of a Book if I am silly enough to reprint it." A few weeks later he received a letter from Mrs. Tennyson, who carried on the bulk of her husband's correspondence, in which she spoke of the poet's admiration for the *Rubáiyát.* "To think of Alfred's approving my old Omar!" FitzGerald replied. "I never should have thought he even knew of it. Certainly I should never have sent it to him, always supposing that he would not approve anything but a literal Prose translation—unless from such hands as can do original work and therefore do not translate other People's!" Tennyson's praise clinched FitzGerald's half-formed resolution. He forwarded the letter to Cowell. "It gives me a *Spurt,*" he said, "to look what I can do further with Omar; adding some Quatrains; which may do more harm than good. But a few more will, at any rate, allow for the Idea of *Time passing* while the Poet talks, and while his Humour changes." [20] He added thirty-five quatrains, making the total in the new edition one hundred and ten.

While FitzGerald was revising his poem, J. B. Nicolas, a French scholar, published a prose translation of Omar's verses, maintaining in his preface that the poet was a Súfí. FitzGerald had abandoned the theory in his first edition, and he examined the text closely in view of the Frenchman's claims. "I cannot see reason to alter my opinion," he stated in his revised preface, "formed as it was a dozen years ago when Omar was first shown me." To support his interpretation, he cited the article in the *Calcutta Review* in which Cowell had denied that Omar was a Súfí. "And if more were needed to disprove Mons. Nicolas' Theory," FitzGerald continued, "there is the Biographical Notice which he himself has drawn up in direct contradiction to the Interpretation of the

20. MS. letter to Cowell, Nov. 24, 1867.

Poems given in his Notes." He concluded with the thrust, "The reader may understand them [the quatrains] either way, literally or mystically, as he chooses. Whenever Wine, Wine-bearers, Cypress, etc., are named, he has only to suppose 'La Divinité'; and when he has done so with Omar, I really think he may proceed to the same Interpretation of Anacreon—and even Anacreon Moore."

Childs printed two hundred copies of the new edition, which was placed on sale by Quaritch in February, 1868. The translator's agreement with his publisher was informal to say the least. "It seems absurd," he told Donne,

to make terms about such a pamphlet likely to be so slow of sale, so I have written to Quaritch . . . that he must fix the most *salable* price he can; take his own proper profit out of it; and when fifty copies are sold give me mine . . . I should be inclined to make the whole Edition over to him except such copies as I want to give away (to W.B.D. and Cowell, etc., and a few more), but one only looks more of a Fool by doing so—so I say after fifty copies, etc., when I believe my Ghost will have to call upon Bernard Quaritch for a reckoning.

His prophecy, happily, was not fulfilled. Norton's praise of the poem in the *North American Review* the following year and the favorable criticism in *Fraser's Magazine* in 1870 created a market for the book, particularly in America. By 1872 Quaritch was urging a third edition. A number of readers who knew the first version had been displeased by the changes in the second, and the publisher proposed that the two be combined in the new issue. "I wonder," FitzGerald replied,

that, with all your great Business, you care to be troubled again with this little one: but if you really wish to set [sic] off old Omar once more to America, I would do what I could for his outfit. . . . But the truth is, that on looking over the two Versions, and ready to adopt your plan of reconciling two in one, I consider that such a scheme, with brackets etc., would be making too much of the thing: and you and I might both be laughed at for treating my Omar as if it were some precious fragment of Antiquity. . . . I doubt therefore that, if Omar be republished, he must go forth in one Shape or another—in his first, or second, suit. And I certainly vote for Version 2, with some whole Stanzas which may be "de trop" cut out, and some of the old readings replaced. . . . My Eyes have been so bad these last two years that I have scarce read anything: and feel a little reluctant to revert even to my little Omar for any purpose of revision. If, however, you still wish it, I will send you the Poem curtailed, and altered back, as I have proposed.[21]

21. *Letters to Bernard Quaritch*, pp. 18–19.

Eventually he sent a manuscript containing one hundred and one quatrains for the third edition, which was published in 1872. Quaritch assumed full responsibility for preparing the volume, and it appeared in a half-Roxburgh binding which, though modest enough, contrasted markedly with the simple paper bindings of the two former editions. FitzGerald wrote to Quaritch in August:

I found Omar on my return home yesterday. I can only say that I doubt you have put him into a finer Dress than he deserves—and that some other Critics will have their Bile raised to say so—if they take any notice now of the old Offender. I only hope you have not over-estimated your Transatlantic friends who I fancy are our chief Patrons—The Americans (as I found from Mrs. Wister—a daughter of Mrs. Kemble's) taking up a little *Craze* of this sort now and then.

Well—you have chosen to run the risk: and you are such a clever man that I suppose you know that your Edition may evaporate in time: and I hope you may live to see it.

Meanwhile, when Edition II is exhausted, you will owe me something for it—of so little consequence to me, or to you, that I shall desire you to give it to some Charity—public or private. If the Persian *Famine Fund* still subsists, the money might properly be added to that —as I dare say old Omar would have done—had he translated the works of yours truly—[22]

But Quaritch had forgotten the terms of their agreement; and FitzGerald wrote a few days later:

In re The Profits of Omar the Second—scarce worth writing about—I write to you from a recollection of our agreeing to share them, as we shared in the publishing: you taking all the trouble etc., I the expense of Printing etc. I did not keep your letter: you forget all about it; 'tis a case of "Equity." You are an equitable Man: "argal" be you Judge, and pay what Costs you judge fair (I should think your £5 more than covers them) to the Persian or any other Charity; and say no more to me about it.

On September 3 Quaritch sent a check for £5 to the Persian Relief Fund, 79, Great Tower Street, in "Omar Khayyám's Memory."

22. *Ibid.*, p. 20.

XXIV

The Laird of Little Grange

"Now I have written enough for you as well as for myself:
and am yours always the same
                    LITTLEGRANGE *

* 'What foppery is this, Sir?'—*Dr. Johnson."*
                    Letter to Fanny Kemble

I CAN'T make up my mind to go into my Chateau," FitzGerald
confessed to Cowell in 1867, a year after his home was ready
for him. He spent one night there in January, 1870, when
Mrs. Berry died; but "the rooms were so large, cold, and solitary," he complained, "that I was obliged to run away to the Bull
Inn, get to the kitchen fire, and there at last thaw, the Landlord
assisting with hot Punch." [1] The following day he went to Lowestoft where he stayed for several weeks, finally returning to his
lodgings. In 1873, however, he was evicted from his old rooms.

"This fall from not very commodious or comfortable quarters,"
Donne reported to Fanny Kemble,

is, like the fall of man, a woman's work. His landlord, a . . . meek man,
though dealing in deadly weapons, guns, pistols, etc., and though a
widower, again rushes into wedlock, and whereas his deceased wife
was a thin thread-paper sort of person, he has now taken to himself a
widowed giantess of at least fifteen stone I hear, strong in arm, mighty
in tongue, and in short stalwart enough to turn E.FG. out of doors! [2]

F. H. Groome, the archdeacon's son, preserved FitzGerald's account of the eviction. The new Mrs. Berry, it developed, was too
genteel to keep lodgers. Groome recorded:

So one day—I have heard FitzGerald tell the story—came a timid rap
at the door of his sitting room, a deep "Now Berry, be firm," and a mild
"Yes, my dear," and Berry appeared on the threshold. Hesitatingly he
explained that "Mrs. Berry, you know, sir—really extremely sorry—
but not used, sir," etc. etc. Then from the rear, a deep, "And you've got
to tell him about Old Gooseberry, Berry," a deprecatory "Certainly, my

1. MS. letter to Pollock, Jan. 30, 1870.
2. *Donne and His Friends,* p. 294.

love"; and poor Berry stammered forth, "And I am told, sir, that you said—you said—I had long been old Berry, but now—now you should call me Old Gooseberry.[3]

Although forced from his rooms, Fitzgerald still shrank from taking possession of his own house. His reason, he said, was that he wished it always to be available for his Kerrich nieces, who spent several months there each summer. "It is not my fault that they do not make it their home," he told Mrs. Kemble. He first rented lodgings next door to Berry's and, while they were being prepared, alternated between his "chateau" and Lowestoft. The new quarters, however, involved housekeeping, which he was loathe to undertake. That consideration alone finally drove him to his home. He moved in on trial in the spring of 1874 and there spent the remainder of his life.

Despite FitzGerald's interference and Dove's shortcomings, if any, the builder had provided him with a comfortable and attractive home. The new wing was larger than the original cottage, but proportions had been well maintained in making additions. Fitz-Gerald kept one room on the ground floor of the old house as an entrance hall; the others were assigned to Mrs. Howe. A billiard table taxed the capacity of the hall, and in one corner stood a small organ, "which might almost be carried about the Streets with a handle to turn, and a Monkey on the top of it." From this instru-ment, Archdeacon Groome said, FitzGerald drew "such full har-monies . . . as did good to the listener." When his nieces visited him, FitzGerald occupied only the large living room on the ground floor. A partition of folding doors shut off one end of the chamber for use as a bedroom. The remainder, his study, was furnished comfortably but simply. The walls were lined with bookshelves. Near a French window was a high desk, at which he stood to work. He rather enjoyed being restricted to this apartment, for it re-minded him of his cabin on the *Scandal*. The rest of the house, particularly the second-floor drawing room, which was reserved for his nieces, was luxuriously furnished. The appointments included much china and many Oriental art objects. "I . . . like Oriental Things," he once declared, "their quaint shapes, fine Colours, and musky sandal-wood Scents; and, though I do not so much look at these things individually, yet their Presence in the Room creates a cheerfulness which is good as one grows old, blind, deaf, and dull."

The garden, into which he could step through the French win-

3. *Two Suffolk Friends,* p. 91.

dows of his study, was small and was bounded by a decorative brick wall. Regular beds alternating with gravel paths contained, not the roses of Omar, but fragrant or colorful old-fashioned flowers: mignonette, honeysuckle, morning glories, geraniums, poppies, nasturtiums, and marigolds, forming, Miss Kerrich said, "an Oriental blaze of colour." The house faced eastward and overlooked a lush meadow of some two acres. The property to the rear, shared by lawn and a grove of lofty trees, sloped upward toward the summit of Mill Hill. Beside a hedge which bordered the road ran a path which he called his "Quarterdeck." Here he sometimes paced for hours. "It is worth your coming to England to see his earthly Paradise," Donne told Mrs. Kemble, "(several Eves in it when his nieces are there, but harmless Eves—timid, and fearers of the devil in all shapes). Eve, proper and wedlocked, never enters his garden; the which garden is as nicely laid out as his house." [4]

John Howe, FitzGerald's man-of-all-work, was an old seaman, a year or two older than his master. FitzGerald called him "The King of Clubs" or, because he carried the letters to the post, "my old Hermes." When Howe made more than the usual noise in raking ashes from the stove in the hall, FitzGerald would sing out—

> Gaily old Puddledog
> Banged his guitar.[5]

Howe wore a sailor's pea-jacket of blue, while his wife, at her master's request, wore a skirt of red with cloak to match. To Mrs. Howe, a bright, cheerful woman, he gave the name "the Fairy Godmother." Considerate always of those who attended him, he rarely asked to have anything done for him which he could do himself. When Mrs. Howe was unwell, he took lodgings at Lowestoft or Aldeburgh until she recovered. "So kind he was," she told F. H. Groome, "not never one to make no obstacles. Such a joky gentleman he was, too."

At first FitzGerald called his home "Grange Farm" to distinguish it from "The Grange," of which his property had formerly been a part. Soon after he moved in, however, he was visited by Anna Biddell, a sister of Herman Biddell's, who suggested "Little Grange." For a time FitzGerald spelled the name interchangeably "Littlegrange" and "Little Grange," but eventually fixed upon the second form. In letters to friends he sometimes jokingly signed him-

4. *Donne and His Friends*, p. 319.
5. A parody of the popular lyric:
> Gaily the troubadour
> Strummed his guitar . . .

self "The Laird of Little Grange." He concluded a letter to Fanny
Kemble in 1881 with the signature, "Littlegrange," and added,
" 'What foppery is this, sir?'—*Dr. Johnson.*"

The name "Grange Farm" had not been entirely a misnomer,
for he stocked the place with diminutive flocks of chickens and
ducks. He was a meticulous poultryman.

"It occurs to me," he once wrote to Biddell,

that, when I last saw you, you gave me hopes of finding a *Chanticleer*
to replace that aged fellow you saw in my Domains. *He* came from
Grundisburgh; and surely you spoke of some such Bird flourishing in
Grundisburgh still. I will not hold out for the identical plumage—
worthy of an Archangel—I only stipulate for one of the sort: such as
are seen in old Story books; and on Churchvanes; with a plume of Tail,
a lofty Crest and Walk, and a shrill trumpet-note of Challenge; any
splendid colours; black and red; black and Gold; white, and red, and
Gold! Only so he be "gay," according to old Suffolk speech.

Well, of course you won't trouble yourself about this: only don't
forget it, next time you ride through Grundisburgh. Or, if, in the course
of any Ride, you should see any such Bird, catch him up at once upon
your Saddle-bow, and bring him to the distressed Widows on my
Estate.[6]

A few weeks later he wrote again to Biddell:

You were very good to have thought of me and my disconsolate Widows. What I shall do with them as Spring advances I don't know. But I
don't like your Cochins and Dorkings, thank you: no, we must wait for
an old-fashioned, Æsop-fable fellow. . . . I believe I shall have to advertise if it can be decently done.

Then again, I want a *Drake* (three Widows in this case also!); and in
this case also I deprive them of their lawful rights till I find an Old-
fashioned Drake (Have you one?) nearest akin to the *Wildfowl*—small,
grey, and game-like: not your overgrown prize-fowls.

I think it will end in Hens and Ducks quitting my premises if I
delay much longer.

The demands of both sets of widows and of the exacting owner
were eventually satisfied. A few years later he spoke of his "two
broods of Ducks, who compete for the possession of a Pond about
four feet in diameter: and but an hour ago I saw my old Seneschal
escorting home a stray lot of Chickens." One hot day, Spalding
watched Howe as he stood motionless, peering intently at the
ducks as they swam about the pond. "What is it, Howe?" he asked,
and the old man answered, "How fond them ducks dew seem of

6. Letter to Biddell, Dec. 22, 1867.

water, *to* be sure." The remark so amused FitzGerald that he added it to his store of anecdotes.

About the time that he moved to Little Grange, FitzGerald was photographed at Ipswich and was well pleased with two of the pictures. "I shouldn't know that either was meant for me," he told Pollock, to whom he sent a copy,

nor, I think, would anyone else, if not told: but the Truth-telling Sun somehow did them; and as he acted so handsomely by me, I take courage to distribute them to those who have a regard for me, and will naturally like to have so favourable a Version of one's Outward Aspect to remember one by. . . . The up-looking one I call "The Statesman," quite ready to be called to the Helm of Affairs: the down-looking one I call "The Philosopher." [7]

In sending his photograph to Quaritch, he said that it was "*a Miracle* of one favourable Sitting. By such means I, a Sinner, turn out [a] much better Man than my Brother, who is a Saint: only he didn't know how to sit for one. Isn't it *Beautiful?* Had the Original Omar a more contemplative look—even when drunk? or Polonius, the Original?"

The success of his photographs so intrigued him that he analyzed the conditions under which he had sat and advised friends on the art of being photographed. Women might wear a collar of yellowish lace, he suggested, and men would do best to sit in a dirty shirt. "Of course," he told Fanny Kemble,

the whole Figure is best, if it can be artistically arranged. But certainly the safe plan is to venture as little as possible when an Artist's hand cannot harmonize the Lines and the Lights as in a Picture. And as the Face is the Chief Object, I say the safest thing is to sit for the Face, neck, and Shoulders only. By this, one not only avoids any conflict about Arms and Hands (which generally disturb the Photo) but also the Lines and Lights of Chair, Table, etc.

His final rule, he said, was "not to sit on a Sunshiny Day: which we must leave to the Young."

His photographs reveal the rather severe aspect which his countenance assumed in repose but lost in the animation of conversation.[8]

7. MS. letter to Pollock, March 30, 1873.
8. FitzGerald's wife wrote on the appearance of the *Letters and Literary Remains* in 1889, "I had seen the photograph which was so unlike the brighter expression of some few years ago, not that it was a face ever perfectly free from sadness, or perhaps I should rather say thoughtfulness—still it had not that painful drooping of the mouth which pained me to look at—but the engraver has in great measure toned down the sadness which gave the face a heaviness, which certainly it *never* had." Mrs. FitzGerald MS. letter, June 30, 1889.

The full lips are tightly closed, and the corners of his mouth droop downward. His head is bald to a line just behind the crown, and one wonders if Spedding ever retaliated for the banter which Fitz-Gerald and Thackeray formerly directed at his "Mt. Blanc forehead." His hair is long and straggly at the neck, and he wears side beards and a thin fringe of whiskers below the chin. His eyes, deeply lined beneath shaggy brows, were, Miss Kerrich said, "wonderfully blue" and "with his incomparable smile, . . . unforgettable." He had lost weight since his years at Boulge Cottage, when he weighed fourteen stone, and was spare of frame. Though still above average height, some of his six-foot stature had been lost, for he had become slightly stooped.

Although FitzGerald's wardrobe was stocked with well-tailored clothes of good quality, he preferred to wear old garments which fitted him "like a sack." His trousers were usually short, and gray socks appeared above his shoe tops. His collar was of the "Gladstone" type; and a silk scarf, carelessly tied in a bow, served for a cravat. He presented a melancholy appearance as he walked through the streets of the town with a distant air which discouraged familiarity.

To the citizens of Woodbridge, according to Pollock, he was "a benevolent oddity." His fellow townsmen were not so charitable in their choice of epithet. "In the intensely Philistine and circumscribed Woodbridge mind," wrote one, "he was regarded as a harmless semi-lunatic." [9]

Descriptions of him at this time of his life are numerous. "I can see him now," F. H. Groome wrote, "walking down into Woodbridge, with an old Inverness cape, double-breasted, flowered satin waistcoat, slippers on feet, and a handkerchief, very likely, tied over his hat. Yet one always recognized in him the Hidalgo." [10] Fitz-Gerald's appearance, however, was not such as to command respect from those who knew him only by sight. Edward Clodd, a Suffolk writer who frequently saw him at Aldeburgh, described him as "a tall sea-bronzed man . . . wearing a slouch hat, often tied on with a handkerchief, and wrapped in a big cloak. . . . Everybody knew old Fitz by sight, and many called him 'Dotty.' " Sidney Colvin, who became curator of the Fitzwilliam Museum at Cambridge, lived near Woodbridge as a boy and has recorded his recollections of FitzGerald.

9. Recollections of Stephen Gravely, a native of Woodbridge, in possession of the Omar Khayyám Club.

10. *Two Suffolk Friends*, p. 72.

By report we youngsters knew also, not without envy, of the sailing yacht he kept upon our neighbouring river the Deben. But of his being a writer and the friend and intimate correspondent of the most famous writers of his time, Carlyle, Tennyson, Thackeray, and the rest, we never heard or dreamed. All we saw in him was an old, tall, sad-faced, middle-aged or elderly gentleman wandering, say rather drifting, abstractedly about the country roads in an ill-fitting suit with a shabby hat pushed back on his head, blue spectacles on nose and an old cape cast anyhow about his shoulders.[11] Few figures were more familiar to me by sight, few less regarded; and many a time must my pony's hoofs have bespattered this forlorn-looking figure as we cantered past him, in the neighbouring lanes.[12]

He walked slowly and, Miss Kerrich has said, "always with the air of one constrained to be a spectator at a show . . . He saw most things, and that with the air of seeing none."

Groome's observation that one always recognized in FitzGerald "the Hidalgo" was corroborated by all who knew him personally. "A perfect gentleman" was the description of one of the Crabbe sisters, recalling his visits to Bredfield vicarage; "a courtly gentleman" stated a man who knew him in his last years. However, FitzGerald maintained such high standards of honesty, courtesy, and propriety, and was so blunt and undeviating in applying them that he did not appear as the "courtly gentleman" to all who came in contact with him. Two things which he could not brook were forwardness and discourtesy. If any townsman to whom he had not been introduced was so bold as to address him, FitzGerald was apt to reply brusquely, "Sir, I do not know you." But he could be polite even in rebuke. In a Woodbridge shop he once overheard a lady telling another of his brother John's eccentricities. Turning, he said quietly, "He is my brother, madam."

A Woodbridge boy once witnessed a severe test of FitzGerald's gravity and courtesy. "It was on a very wintry day in the late 'seventies," he recorded, "that a friend and I were busily engaged making up a pile of snowballs, ready for bombarding, when Fitz passed us walking in his usual stately style with his top hat on. The target was irresistible, and a shot was launched and recorded a bull, his topper rolling some yards away." He recovered his hat, passed a silk handkerchief around it, replaced it on his head, and retraced

11. FitzGerald has frequently been described as wearing a gray shawl on his walks about Woodbridge. This, Mr. Vincent Redstone, the Woodbridge antiquarian stated, is pure fiction. Occasionally, in pacing his "Quarterdeck," FitzGerald would wear such a shawl which he had snatched from a chair or couch as he left the house.

12. Colvin, Sir Sidney, *Memories and Notes of Persons and Places* (London, Edward Arnold & Co., 1921), pp. 34-35.

his steps. The marksman, meanwhile, had retreated. "No doubt," FitzGerald said to the second youth, "your companion thought it fine fun from his point of view. Taking youthful tendencies into consideration, I overlook it and trust, from a gentlemanly point of view, he will desist from repeating. Kindly inform him when next you meet." [13]

He was not always content merely to speak his mind. One day as he walked along the footpath beside the Melton Road, a young man on a "penny-farthing" bicycle approached, riding on the path. Two ladies stepped into the road to allow the cyclist to pass, but FitzGerald drew up against the fence and awaited his approach. As the vehicle came opposite, he thrust his walking stick under the front wheel, heaved, and tumbled cycle and rider into the highway. "That's the best place for an ungentlemanly cad," he said. The young man picked himself up and began to abuse FitzGerald, concluding with a threat to prosecute. "Very well," was the reply, "I will counter-summons you for breaking the law by riding on a public footway. Think it over. Stick to the road in the future and respect public rights. Good afternoon." He then approached the ladies and apologized for the fellow's rudeness. [14]

Mistreatment of animals always aroused his ire. One day he saw a man beating a dog in Pytches Road. He remonstrated, arguing that it was unbecoming to lose one's temper with dumb animals. The man protested that the dog must be disciplined. "Well, don't repeat it in my presence," replied FitzGerald, "or I will take my stick and pay you back with some of the same medicine." On another occasion he encountered a portly couple riding in a trap drawn by a small pony which strained at the traces as it mounted the hill beside Little Grange. "Don't you think you could get out?" FitzGerald asked the pair; then added, "You look as able to draw the trap as he does." One summer day, as he walked past the home of a neighbor, he saw a small girl giving water to a stray dog and praised the child for her thoughtfulness. Shortly afterward, returning from town, he stopped at the house and left a present "for the kind little girl who gave the dog a drink." [15]

He never lost his love for children, and enjoyed having them about him. When his nephew, Walter Kerrich, moved to Woodbridge as adjutant of the Suffolk Volunteers and took a house near Little Grange, FitzGerald gave the family the freedom of his

13. Recollections of Edward Fosdike, in possession of the Omar Khayyám Club.
14. *Ibid.*
15. *Ibid.*

grounds, for their own garden was small. He treated children, Miss Kerrich, one of those who benefited by the arrangement, has written, "with a dignified courtesy which, while it appalled their elders had no other effect on those infallible judges of character . . . than to make them anxious of attracting his attention." [16] He liked to watch them at their games. "No, no, play fair, play fair," was his frequent adjuration. The children, who had no intention of playing unfairly, resented the warning, and, among themselves, called their great-uncle "Old Playfair." [17] Once when he asked a small girl her name and she did not reply, he remarked quietly, "She is very discreet." The Kerrich children were frequently his guests at tea. When Mrs. Howe appeared, he would say "with an air of pleasant surprise, 'Enter Mrs. Howe with the tea tray.' "

"He spoke to us," Miss Kerrich said,

of simple things: our pet doves—he gave them a round wicker cage; "It should always be wicker," he said—the amber he had lately had the rare good fortune to find on Felixstowe Beach . . . the probability that his hens would give us a basketful of brown eggs; Mrs. Howe's gingerbread; or a book left open on the Little Grange library table; into which we might look . . . or there was a delightful and mysterious-looking parcel awaiting us there.[18]

FitzGerald appreciated, too, the children's healthy sense of humor and, during his younger years, sent them into gales of laughter with his many stories. One, which delighted the boys particularly, was of a culprit, sentenced by a pompous magistrate at Woodbridge, who retorted by thumbing his nose, which gesture FitzGerald executed in elaborate pantomime. They were delighted, also, by his corruption of Borret and White, the name of the family solicitors, into "Worret and Bite." [19]

John FitzGerald frequently gave family parties at Boulge; and, since Edward could not be persuaded to join them, his relatives called upon him at Woodbridge. The older children, at first awed by his superficial frostiness, were soon put at their ease by being treated as equals. Leopold de Soyres, one of his nephews, described a "duty call" which he once made on FitzGerald. "I presented myself at the famous lodgings on Market Hill," he wrote,

feeling very nervous and awkward at having to introduce myself and explain who I was. But all my alarms vanished in Uncle Edward's

16. Kerrich, Miss Eleanor FitzGerald, "Edward FitzGerald: A Personal Reminiscence," *Nineteenth Century Magazine* (March, 1909), p. 461.
17. Information given by Miss Olivia Kerrich, a grandniece.
18. Recollections of Miss Kerrich.
19. Recollections of John de Soyres, MS. in possession of Miss Madeleine de Soyres.

presence. His reception was most kind and friendly. He was robed in an ancient smoking cap and dressing gown. He was full of pleasant talk and astonished me by saying how fond he was of novels. We soon found a bond of union in our mutual liking for Anthony Trollope's stories. It was a blazing July day, and Uncle very kindly asked me if I should like some claret. Like an idiot, I said "Thanks," and immediately perceived that I had said something foolish. He gravely declined my answer thus: "Thanks, Thank you, I thank you." It was only long afterwards, when his *Letters* were published, that I learnt how much he disliked the word "Thanks" . . . In 1878, when Julian [20] and I were at Boulge with our Mother, we all paid him a call at Little Grange and he took Julian and myself up to the "quarter-deck" and talked to us in his delightful way. [21]

Descriptions of FitzGerald at this time of his life usually mention the blue spectacles or the green eyeshade which he often wore. The innumerable hours that he spent poring over books and manuscripts, often with inadequate light during the evenings, had weakened his vision so that, at times, he was in danger of losing his sight altogether. During the later years at Boulge Cottage he had so taxed his eyes that he was compelled to rest them. He employed Alfred Smith, then a lad, to read to him for part of each evening. Some of the time was spent in discussing books which they read, and Smith afterward came to the conclusion that his employer was also trying to help with his education. FitzGerald treated him, Smith said, "more like a nephew than an acquaintance."

FitzGerald's eyes again became affected in 1866, but he did not spare them until, three years later, they were almost "blazed away by paraffin." His sight was sufficiently strong to permit him to read in moderation during the day, but his oculist forbade reading by artificial light; and FitzGerald again resorted to readers. The first, son of a cabinetmaker, was paid a shilling a night for reading about two hours. The boy assisted his father in the shop by day and was more accustomed to using his hands than his head. He made so many mistakes that FitzGerald called him "the Blunderer." He transformed "her future husband" into "her furniture husband," and read "ironclad laughter from the left," "face-smiles of letters" and "consolations closed at 91." At these mistakes FitzGerald would cry, "Hold, hold, hold!" The first hour was devoted to the newspaper, and by this means FitzGerald closely followed the developments of the famous Tichborne case, which fascinated

20. Leopold's brother.
21. Recollections of Leopold de Soyres. MS. in possession of FitzGerald's grand-niece, Miss Madeleine de Soyres.

him. As he listened, he imagined himself in the courtroom. After an hour of reading FitzGerald provided refreshments, cake, and fruit essence for the boy, sherry, or a glass of brandy and water for himself. The session closed with a novel or, occasionally, a game of piquet. One night in Market Hill, the reader related, a mouse climbed to the table top as they were playing cards. "Don't interfere with that!" FitzGerald warned. "There's plenty of room in the world for that and you too." The mouse came often, thereafter, to eat crumbs purposely left for it.

"The Blunderer" left Woodbridge in 1872 and was replaced by a butcher's son, who became so agitated at the first appearance of the mouse that FitzGerald had to dismiss him for the evening. The boy returned the next night with poisoned wheat and the rodent was dispatched. The new reader was a good scholar and went through the Tichborne reports "without missing a syllable" but "was not half so agreeable or amusing . . . as his Predecessor." He was followed in 1876 by a son of the local bookbinder, an intelligent lad who enjoyed what he read, laughed heartily, and did not mind being told not to read through his nose. He was so punctual in his arrivals that his employer called him "The Ghost." The boy left Woodbridge in 1879 and was succeeded by his younger brother, FitzGerald's last reader. He was a bright little fellow of fifteen but occasionally made errors which reminded his listener of the old "Blunderer."

When FitzGerald was well, "The Ghost" told an interviewer, it was a pleasure to read to him. "I really give the best proof I can of the Interest I take," FitzGerald wrote when they were reading Trollope's novels, ". . . by constantly breaking out into Argument with the Reader (who never replies) about what is said and done by the People in the several Novels. I say, 'No, no! She must have known she was lying!' 'He couldn't have been such a Fool!' etc." When FitzGerald was indisposed, however, he was difficult to please and "applied hard words sometimes to reader and author." After he had been severe in his remarks, he would either apologize or, as he said, "insult" the boy "in a pecuniary manner." He always sat in a high-backed, low-seated, red-covered armchair, often in dressing gown and slippers. He invariably kept his hat on, and never removed it except when he wanted a red handkerchief from the interior. When not interested in what was being read, he took snuff frequently and shifted uneasily. If annoyed, he ordered his reader to "pass that damn'd rot." When the reading ended, he took a new clay pipe from a drawer and smoked. The pipe was always broken after the tobacco had been consumed, and the pieces were thrown into the fireplace.

One evening "The Ghost" arrived to find FitzGerald greatly perturbed, having mislaid his spectacles. When the boy asked if he could help, FitzGerald replied testily, "Oh, no! It is just about the way I shall get to heaven, searching for what I can't find."

The trouble with his eyes led FitzGerald to part with the *Scandal* in 1871. "My little Yacht is—sold!" he announced to Mrs. Cowell in May,

for a mess of £200. It was not the money I wanted: nay, I told the man [22] who came to buy her that he had better buy another and a bigger which I knew of. But he came from Town on purpose to buy mine; and I let her go. . . . But one main reason for my decision was—these Eyes of mine which will not let me read; and that was nearly all I had to do on board. But I should scarce have thus decided, if Newson had not been offered a much better Berth, which he boggles at accepting; and Jack is engaged to go with the new owner of the Scandal, as he went with me. But his heart was almost up to his eyes when all was settled.[23]

West, the one-legged sailor, was again restored to grace; and Fitz-Gerald reverted to sailing in his smaller boat, the *Waveney*. He confined his boating to the Deben, "looking at the Crops as they grow green, yellow, russet, and are finally carried away in the red and blue Waggons with the sorrel horse." [24]

22. The *Scandal* was sold to Mr. (later Sir Cuthbert) Quilter.
23. Letter to Mrs. Cowell, May 17 [1871].
24. "The sorrel horse," the Suffolk Punch, a famous and popular breed.

XXV

Old Friends and New

Old Fitz, who from your suburb grange,
Where once I tarried for a while,
Glance at the wheeling orb of change,
And greet it with a kindly smile . . .
"To E. FitzGerald," TENNYSON

EVEN during the closing years of his life it is impossible to make FitzGerald conform to his reputation as a recluse. It is true that he lived estranged from the social life of Woodbridge and that until his death he remained hostile to the Suffolk gentry, for whom he frequently reiterated his dislike. While yachting at Felixstowe in 1865, he made the acquaintance of a wealthy London merchant, who, he declared, "has a truly enviable character for his Goodness to the Poor. Therefore it is they call him 'Squire'—which I told him was but a bad Compliment: for Squire is but another name for Screw down here." [1]

Actually, FitzGerald led a fairly social life. He spent many weeks of each summer at Lowestoft, Dunwich, and Aldeburgh. Every year he went to London for brief visits, and sometimes traveled farther afield. At Little Grange he entertained friends old and new, although he felt a certain shyness about having his older companions seek him out. "It may seem odd to you at first," he replied when Pollock proposed a visit in 1871,

. . . that I feel more—nervous, I may say—at the prospect of meeting with an Old Friend, after all these years, than of any indifferent Acquaintance. . . . I always tell Donne not to come out of his way here—he says he takes me in the course of a visit to some East-Anglian kinsmen. Have you ever any such reason?—Well; if you have no better reason than that of really wishing to see me, for better or worse, in my home, come—some Spring or Summer day, when my Home at any rate is pleasant. This all sounds mock-modesty: but it is not; as I can't read Books, Plays, Pictures, etc. and don't see People, I feel, when a Man comes, that I have all to ask and nothing to tell; and one doesn't like to make a Pump of a Friend.

1. MS. letter to A. Tennyson, Oct. 22, 1865.

Apparently Pollock was not deterred by the prospect of being "pumped" for he visited FitzGerald the following May.

Since 1872, the mid-point of FitzGerald's residence in Woodbridge, fairly represents his last years, a sketch of his manner of life during the twelve months is enlightening. He spent the early part of the year at his Market Hill lodgings. His eyes were in a bad state, but he managed by day to read "a little Shakespeare . . . which seemed astonishingly fresh to me: some of De Quincey's Essays: and some of Ste. Beuve." The *Athenaeum,* to which he subscribed, announced the death of H. F. Chorley, a music critic whom he had met at the Kembles' in London forty years before. "I think," he said, "the Angels must take care to keep in tune when he gets among them." His new reader, the butcher's son, read to him evenings—reports of the Tichborne case, to be sure, D'Israeli's *Lothair,* and Thackeray's novels with their "monumental Figures of 'pauvre et triste Humanité,' as old Napoleon called it." One night the boy came to him as curfew was ringing; and FitzGerald quoted for him the first lines of Gray's "Elegy," which the reader had never heard. "This shows how things have altered since my young days," he commented, ". . . then we only heard too much of Gray's Curfew."

In March he went to London to visit an artist friend who was "slowly dying in a Garret with scarce a friend to go and see him." FitzGerald had written to Laurence immediately upon hearing of the man's plight to inquire about his circumstances. "I know not what his means are," he said, "and I should wish to supply what is wanted at such a time. Mr. R— is a delicate and proud man, and has always refused any offer I made him." When he went to London, FitzGerald arranged to have the artist's landlord send him reports on the invalid's health; later, he joined with two friends in providing for the man's needs. While in town he called on Donne.

With the advent of warm spring days he sailed on the Deben and "dabbled" about the grounds at Little Grange. Late in April he went to Playford to visit Biddell and, coming away, left his spectacles and a scarf behind. His host sent them to the train by which FitzGerald had intended to return to Woodbridge, but he could not be found. "I did go home by the Train you sent to," FitzGerald disclosed when he thanked Biddell for sending his belongings, "but in *the Horse-box,* with John Grout, his Man, half-a-dozen Horses, two Dogs, and a Cat—all come from Lincoln that morning."

Pollock spent the Whitsun week end at the Bull as FitzGerald's guest. On Sunday evening Spalding called at Market Hill and found the two men looking over a scrapbook which contained drawings by Thackeray. After a bottle of port the three walked about the grounds at Little Grange, and Spalding recorded in his diary scraps of the conversation. Pollock had recently spent a few days with Tennyson at Farringford and said that real estate agents advertised houses as being within one, two, or three miles of the poet laureate's home. "What does old Alfred say to that?" asked FitzGerald. "He doesn't care," Pollock replied, "so long as they keep out of his way and away from his place." Telling Fanny Kemble of the visit, FitzGerald said, "Sir Frederick Pollock has been to see me here for two days, and put me up to much that was going on in the civilised World. He was very agreeable indeed: and I believe his Visit did him good."

In July FitzGerald spent two days at Sydenham, visiting his brother Peter, whom he had not seen for six years. He visited the Royal Academy, where he saw pictures by Millais, which pleased him. "Just as I was going out," he related,

who should come up to me but Annie Thackeray, who took my hands as really glad to see her Father's old friend. I am sure she was; and I was taken aback somehow; and, out of sheer awkwardness, began to tell her that I didn't care for her new Novel! And then, after she had left her Party to come to me, I ran off! It is true, I had to be back at Sydenham: but it would have been better to forgo all that: and so I reflected when I had got halfway down Piccadilly: and so ran back, and went into the Academy again: but could not find A. T.[2]

He wrote immediately to apologize for his rudeness and received a kind reply in which Annie Thackeray told him that their chance meeting had been like "a message from Papa."

FitzGerald entertained another old friend early in August, when Frederick Tennyson spent three days at Woodbridge.[3] Tennyson had long been a firm believer in table tapping, spirit writing, and all the mysteries of spiritualism. He had come to England from his home in Jersey with a deaf old gentleman who maintained that he had discovered the original mystery of Freemasonry by means of spiritualism. "The Freemasons," FitzGerald observed,

have for Ages been ignorant, it seems, of the very Secret which all their Emblems and Signs refer to: and the question is, if they care enough for their own Mystery to buy it of this ancient Gentleman. If they do not, he will shame them by Publishing it to all the world. Frederic Tennyson, who has long been a Swedenborgian, a Spiritualist, and is now

2. Letter to Pollock [1872].
3. Frederick Tennyson had last visited FitzGerald in Woodbridge just ten years before.

even himself a Medium, is quite grand and sincere in this as in all else: with the Faith of a Gigantic Child—pathetic and yet humourous to consider and consort with.[4]

The English Masons evinced no interest in the old man's information; but, before exposing them, he decided to offer his knowledge to the brotherhood in Ireland; and so he disappeared.

While Frederick was with him, FitzGerald had another guest, Arthur Charlesworth, a nephew of Mrs. Cowell's. Arthur wanted to go to sea as two of his brothers had done, but his mother begged him not to. Much against his inclination, he became a clerk in London. FitzGerald, sympathizing with the boy's love for the sea and dislike for the city, frequently invited him to spend his holidays in Suffolk. Sometimes FitzGerald purposely went to Lowestoft for the period of these visits so that Arthur could spend his vacation amid the boats which he loved. The lad stayed for more than a week after Frederick's departure. "He was very happy," FitzGerald told Mrs. Cowell,

with a Canoe on the River by day, and sitting with me and F. Tennyson at night; polite, quiet, and amused. The last Evening, I found him a *Revolver* to shoot with—at his own straw hat; and I consoled him at going away by lending him the Revolver, and bidding him bring it back to me at Christmas if I be here at that time. I like him much: as he now is, I say, what a Lad should be: and I wish I could get him some place in the *Country*. He says he should not mind what work he had to do if he could but get into the fields or upon the water often. I believe this would keep him from spoiling, more than London is likely to do.[5]

FitzGerald devoted part of the year to preparing the third edition of the *Rubáiyát,* which was published in August. He visited Lowestoft the following month and one evening took Posh to see the *Merchant of Venice.* The "great man" admired the *Gays,* as he called the scenes, "but fell asleep before Shylock had whetted his knife."

Soon after returning home, FitzGerald was visited by Edwin Edwards, a London etcher and painter,[6] whose acquaintance he had made two years before. At that time the artist and his wife were spending a vacation in Woodbridge, and FitzGerald offered them Little Grange for their visit. For several years thereafter the Edwardses spent about a month each autumn at the "chateau." "I have found both Mr. and Mrs. Edwards very agreeable," FitzGerald told Donne.

4. Letter to Fanny Kemble, Aug. 9 [1872].
5. MS. letter to Mrs. Cowell [August, 1872].
6. Edwards was a native of Suffolk, having been born at Framlingham in 1823.

. . . He left a good and lucrative Clerkship in the Admiralty to become a Painter—a little too late in life, I think, to succeed in that; but he would rather live that life on £100 a year, he says, than be restored to his Clerkship at £1,200—and I believe him.[7] He has a strong understanding, much intuitive perception, Humour, and Love for Literature as well as Art: Courage, Determination, Generosity, and the Heart of a Boy. *She* is a very clever, shrewd, and good woman: the very woman for an Artist's wife.

As FitzGerald sat in his lodgings one evening in October, a boy with a tin can passed beneath his windows, crying—

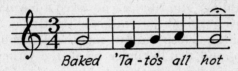

Baked 'Ta-to's all hot

a sure sign that he had got into winter quarters. For the remainder of the year he hugged his fireside. He read Tennyson's idyll, *Gareth and Lynette,* which interested him more than "the Enids, Lily Maids, etc., of former volumes," he told Pollock, "but Time *is*— Time *was* to have done with the whole Concern; pure and noble as all is, and in parts more beautiful than anyone else can do. I was so far interested in this Gareth; that I looked back to the previous Idylls to see if I might not have judged too hastily of them. But I saw nothing to alter my opinion." [8]

His reader again came each evening, and FitzGerald delighted in *Yesterdays with Authors* by the American publisher, James T. Fields. The first volume of Forster's biography made him "love" Dickens. Frederick Tennyson sent him Victor Hugo's *Toilers of the Sea,* but FitzGerald could not "get up an Appetite" for it. In December he read *Henry V,* and the repudiation of honest Jack Falstaff by Prince Hal made him "blubber." At Christmas he sent his annual gifts of pheasants to various friends, among them Barry Cornwall, "my dear little Barry," now over eighty.

And so FitzGerald's year drew to a close. The calendar is not complete, for it barely touches upon his reading, neglects his writing, and does not include his normal intercourse with near-by friends. Nor does he mention in 1872 the visit which he usually paid each spring to George Crabbe at Merton. The year is not one from the busy life of a man of the world, to be sure; but few would recognize it as a year in the life of a recluse.

7. Edwards was not by any means restricted to living on £100 a year. It is apparent that he had a source of income other than his art.
8. MS. letter to Pollock, Nov. 1, 1872.

The Reverend Robert Hindes Groome, rector of Monk Soham, who, in 1869, became Archdeacon of Suffolk, was one of Fitz-Gerald's most frequent visitors at Woodbridge. He was the type of man to capture FitzGerald's heart—simple, genuine, honest, frank, and earnest. Not the least endearing of his qualities was his hearty sense of humor. Like FitzGerald, he appreciated and respected the solid worth of the laboring classes of Suffolk. During his work among them he collected a store of anecdotes which he recounted in the native dialect, to FitzGerald's delight. He told of one of his parishioners who had decided to emigrate to America. "How are you going, Wilding?" the archdeacon asked a few days before the man's departure. "I don't fare to know rightly," was the answer, "but we're going to sleep the fust night at Debenham [a village four miles off] and that'll kinder break the jarney." [9] Another story was a particular favorite with FitzGerald. The archdeacon found one of the churchyards under his jurisdiction partly sowed with wheat. "Really, Mr. Z—," he said to the clergyman, "I must say I don't like to see this." The old church warden chimed in, "That's what I säa tew, Mr. Archdeacon; I säa to our parson, 'Yeou go whatin' it and whatin' it, why don't yeou tater it?' " [10]

Like FitzGerald, Groome was fond of music and had also been a member of "Camus," the musical society at Cambridge. He had a good voice and often appeared on the programs at local concerts. Once at Ipswich a precise young clergyman announced that "the Reverend Robert Groome will sing . . . *Thomas* Bowling." [11] When the archdeacon visited at Little Grange, FitzGerald often entertained him by playing favorite selections on his organ. "Sometimes it would be a bit from one of Mozart's Masses," Groome related,

or from one of the finales of some one of his or Beethoven's Operas. And then at times he would fill up the harmonies with his voice, true and resonant almost to the last. I have heard him say, "Did you never observe how an Italian organ-grinder will sometimes put in a few notes of his own in such perfect keeping with the air which he was grinding?" He was not a great, but he was a good composer. Some of his songs have been printed, and many still remain in manuscript. . . . Pleasant was it also to hear him speak of the public singers of those early days. Braham, so great, spite of his vulgarity; Miss Stephens, so sweet to listen to, though she had no voice of power; and poor Vaughan, who had so

9. *Two Suffolk Friends,* p. 32.
10. *Ibid.,* pp. 35–36.
11. *Ibid.,* p. 34.

feeble a voice, and yet was always called "such a chaste singer." How he
would roar with laughter when I would imitate Vaughan singing

> His hiddeus [sic] love provokes my rage,
>
> Weak as I am, I must engage,

from Acis and Galatea.[12]

During one of Groome's visits in November, 1867, FitzGerald
mentioned some parallel passages which he had noted in the essays
of Montaigne and Bacon, and the archdeacon remarked that Aldis
Wright, librarian of Trinity College, had observed the same and
was collecting examples. FitzGerald had long known Wright, a
native of Beccles, by reputation, and the following month wrote to
him on the subject. "Your 'Master' [13] wrote me word the other
day," he said in closing his letter,

. . . that you as well as he wished for my own noble works in your Library. I quite understand that this is on the ground of my being a Trinity man . . . As I think some of the Translations I have done are all I
can dare to show, and as it would be making too much fuss to wait for
any further asking on the subject, I will send them if you think good
one of these days all done up together.

It was not until two years later, after further solicitation, that
FitzGerald sent the promised book.[14] His first letter to the librarian
was the origin of a close friendship between the two men. Wright
later became bursar of Trinity and often visited at Little Grange
while in Suffolk on college business or during holidays. He edited
the *Letters and Literary Remains*.

FitzGerald maintained some of his friendships entirely by correspondence. One of these was with Charles Eliot Norton, who
had been instrumental in identifying him as the translator of the
Rubáiyát. Norton described the note in which FitzGerald thanked
him for forwarding Ruskin's letter as "the beginning of a delightful
epistolary acquaintance. I might indeed more justly call it an
epistolary friendship, which was drawn close during the ten years
from the beginning till FitzGerald's death." [15] Their correspondence was chiefly concerned with literary topics. FitzGerald had no
reason to fear that Norton would dismiss his opinions as "crotchets," as did many of his older friends, and the letters contain some

12. Introduction to the *Letters*, I, ix–xi.
13. W. H. Thompson, Master of Trinity College.
14. The volume (Trinity College Library, Adversaria d. 11. 24) contains the translations of the eight Calderon plays and the *Agamemnon* of Aeschylus.
15. *Norton Letters*, I, 427.

of his best criticism. Two passages, selected for interest rather than depth, are worth noting. In 1876 he expressed his appreciation of a number of the New England writers with whom Norton was personally acquainted.

I know of course (in Books) several of those you name in your Letter: Longfellow, whom I may say I love, and so (I see) can't call him *Mister:* and Emerson whom I admire, for I don't feel that I know the Philosopher as well as the Poet: and Mr. Lowell's "Among my Books" is among mine. I also have always much liked, I think rather loved, O. W. Holmes. I scarce know why I could never take to that man of true Genius, Hawthorne.

Although he could not read Hawthorne's novels with pleasure, FitzGerald enjoyed his English, French, and Italian journals. "Then Milton," he wrote two weeks later, "I don't think I've read him these forty years: the whole Scheme of the Poem, and certain Parts of it, looming as grand as anything in my Memory; but I never could read ten lines together without stumbling at some Pedantry that tipped me at once out of Paradise, or even Hell, into the Schoolroom, worse than either."

Norton sincerely admired FitzGerald's literary powers. "It pleases me," he wrote after the latter's death, "that four years before I had the happiness of coming into personal relations with FitzGerald, and before I knew his name as that of the translator of Omar Khayyám, I wrote a paper on his version. . . . I don't think I ever mentioned it to him." [16] The American was directly responsible for the printing of the translations of Sophocles' *Oedipus Tyrannus* and *Oedipus Coloneus.*

Through Norton, FitzGerald formed a similar "epistolary friendship" with James Russell Lowell. "I think," FitzGerald said in 1879, "he is altogether the best Critic we have; something of what Ste. Beuve is in French." In 1877 Lowell was appointed United States ambassador to Spain and proposed to visit FitzGerald at Woodbridge in July on his way through England. Although the American intended to spend only a day in Suffolk, FitzGerald prepared to entertain him at Little Grange for a longer period. Plans miscarried, however, and Lowell crossed to the Continent without their meeting.

"Indeed, I chiefly flinched," FitzGerald wrote after the ambassador's arrival at Madrid,

at the thought of your taking the trouble to come down only for a Day: which means, less than half a Day: a sort of meeting that seems a mock-

16. Norton MS. letter, Jan. 2, 1890.

ery in the lives of two men, one of whom I know by Register to be close on Seventy. I do indeed deprecate any one coming down out of his way: but, if he come, I would rather he did so for such time as would allow of some palpable Acquaintance. And I meant to take you to no other sight than the bare grey walls of an old Grey Friars' Priory near the Sea; [17] and I proposed to make myself further agreeable by showing you three or two passages in your Books that I do not like amid all the rest which I like so much . . .

Thereafter the two corresponded. "Tell me something of the Spanish Drama, Lope, or Calderon," FitzGerald once requested. "I think you could get one acted by Virtue of your Office." Three years before FitzGerald's death Lowell was appointed ambassador to the Court of St. James's, but they never met.

"It is one of my greatest regrets that I never saw him," Lowell wrote in 1889, "one of my most poignant that he may have thought me neglectful. I was so overwhelmed with bothers, Irish and other, so bewilderingly busy with duties official and social, that I could never find time to visit him at Woodbridge, and the state of Mrs. Lowell's health [18] was such that I could not, most of the time, ask him to make his home with me, if by some rare chance he came to London." [19]

By correspondence FitzGerald preserved, not only new, but many of his old friendships. In 1867 he began an exchange of letters with Fanny Kemble, who lived in the United States although she paid frequent visits to England and the Continent.[20] Eventually, he made a practice of writing to her once a month when the moon reached the full. "You smile at my 'Lunacies,' as you call my writing periods," he said in one letter. "I take the Moon as a signal not to tax you too often for your inevitable answer." By "inevitable answer" he referred to her practices in correspondence, from which nothing short of a miracle caused her to deviate. She never wrote unless written to, she always replied, and she invariably returned the same amount of paper that she received. This, FitzGerald called her "law of the Medes and Persians." By similar rules she governed the most minute details of her life. She wore her dresses in a definite rotation and might appear at some festivity clad in black, or, on the other hand, at some funereal ceremony clad in flaming colors.

17. At Dunwich.
18. In a letter to Aldis Wright, written in 1880, FitzGerald said, "I have only heard of Lowell that he has nursed his Wife night and day: which Mrs. K[emble] also says is usual with American husbands."
19. Lowell MS. letter, July 4, 1889.
20. In 1848 she had divorced her American husband, Pierce Butler.

Evening after evening she played an appointed number of games of patience, ignoring completely her mood and inclinations.

She was an enthusiastic admirer of FitzGerald's translations and did much to make them known in America by praising them to her friends. FitzGerald, on his part, was an avid reader of her diffuse memoirs, published in the *Atlantic Monthly* from 1875 to 1877 under the title, "Old Woman's Gossip." After reading the first three instalments, he wrote, "Of course somewhat of my Interest results from the Times, Persons, and Places you write of: almost all more or less familiar to me; but I am quite sure that very few could have brought all before me as you have done—with what the Painters call so free, full, and flowing a touch." In one portion of her work, however, Mrs. Kemble's touch became too "free, full, and flowing" for FitzGerald's comfort. In December, 1875, her memoirs contained the following in a passage which described her early acquaintance with the FitzGeralds:

One member of her [Mrs. FitzGerald's] family—her son Edward FitzGerald—has remained my friend till this day . . . He was distinguished from the rest of his family, and indeed from most people, by the possession of very rare intellectual and artistic gifts. A poet, a painter, a musician, an admirable scholar and writer, if he had not shunned notoriety as sedulously as most people seek it, he would have achieved a foremost place among the eminent men of his day, and left a name second to that of very few of his contemporaries. His life was spent in literary leisure, or literary labours of love of singular excellence, which he never cared to publish beyond the circle of his intimate friends.

The article continued with a brief catalogue of his works and a description of his manner of life.

"Now—talking of illustrious names, etc." FitzGerald protested after reading the passage,

oh, my dear Mrs. Kemble, your sincere old Regard for my Family and myself has made you say more—of one of us, at least—than the World will care to be told: even if your old Regard had not magnified our lawful Desserts. But indeed it has done so: in Quality, as well as in Quantity. I know I am not either squeamishly, or hypocritically, saying all this: I am sure I know myself better than you do, and take a juster view of my pretensions. I think you Kembles are almost Donnes in your determined Regard, and (one may say) Devotion to old Friends, etc. A rare—a noble—Failing! Oh, dear!—Well, I shall not say any more: you will know that I do not the less thank you for publickly speaking of [me] as I never was spoken of before—only *too* well. Indeed, this is so;

and when you come to make a Book of your Papers, I shall make you cut out something.

FitzGerald saved the instalments of the "Gossip" and had them bound together for his library, but he carefully pasted a sheet of paper over the objectionable passage. When the memoirs were published as *Records of a Girlhood*, the reference to him was deleted.

FitzGerald had not seen Carlyle since the late 'fifties. In the spring of 1859 he had called at Cheyne Row, but the historian was not at home. From Suffolk, he wrote to him,

I really had wished to go and see Mrs. Carlyle again: I won't say you, because I don't think in your heart you care to be disturbed: and I am glad to believe that, with all your Pains, you are better than any of us, I do think. You don't care what one thinks of your Books: you know I love so many: I don't care so much for Frederick [21] so far as he's gone: I suppose you don't neither.

After settling at Woodbridge, FitzGerald wrote annually to the historian unless some topic prompted a rapid exchange of letters. His infrequent correspondence and his lapses in reading newspapers resulted, in 1866, in his committing an awkward blunder. He wrote his usual Christmas letter, "begging to have my annual remembrances made to *Mrs. C.*" Carlyle replied that his wife had died the previous April. "Here is one mischief of living out of the world," remarked FitzGerald, much distressed.

Almost invariably he included in his letter an apology for imposing himself on the historian's attention. "It seems an impertinence to stir up your recollection of me once a year" is a typical beginning.

Still, that may be enough for you, if not too much: and I don't like wholly to lose an intercourse that has lasted, more or less, these eighteen [twenty-eight] years—yes, since I was staying with Thackeray at his house in what he called Jorum Street. . . . Many pleasant evenings do I remember—cups of Tea made by her that is gone: and many a Pipe smoked with you—in your little garden, when weather was fair—and all kind and pleasant at all times. Though I do not write—for the reason that I have nothing worth telling you—you are often in my thoughts, and often on my Tongue when I happen to visit any of the few friends I now see.

21. Carlyle's *Frederick the Great,* on which he worked from 1851–65.

Carlyle assured his correspondent that the letters were always welcome. "Thanks for enquiring after me again," he wrote in 1868,

. . . Your letter has really entertained me: I could willingly accept twelve of that kind in the year—twelve, I say, or even fifty-two, if they could be content with an answer of *silent* thanks, and friendly thoughts and remembrances. But, within the last three or four years my right hand has become captious, taken to shaking as you see, and all writing is a thing I require *compulsion* and close necessity to drive me into. Why not call when you come to Town? I again assure you it will give me pleasure and be a welcome and wholesome solace to me.

Carlyle often urged FitzGerald to call; but the latter, instead of accepting, countered with timid invitations of his own. In 1855, it will be remembered, the historian had urged FitzGerald to include "a chamber in the wall" for him in the new Suffolk home. FitzGerald intimated from time to time that his house was ready. "Sometimes," he said in 1873, "I have thought you might come to my pleasant home, . . . where you should be treated with better fare than you had at Farlingay." From experience, however, Fitz-Gerald well knew Carlyle's hatred for travel and added, "But I may say this: you would not come; nor could I press you to do so."

After resting quietly for fifteen years, the gray ghost of the Naseby monument again began to haunt the lives of the two men. Replying to his friend's Christmas letter in 1871, Carlyle again suggested that they set up a monument and offered to pay half the expense. FitzGerald was loath to bother with the matter, for he feared that it would require a trip to Naseby to point out the site of the grave. "You will think me very base," he said, "to hesitate about such a little fact as a Journey into Northamptonshire for this purpose. But you know that one does not generally grow more active in Travel as one gets older: and I have been a bad Traveller all my life. So I will promise nothing that I am not sure of doing." Nevertheless, he again attempted to obtain permission to erect the monument. It developed, however, that the property had been inherited by a minor, and permission of three trustees, "all great people," was necessary. Negotiations stretched out for almost two years. FitzGerald even forced himself to go to Naseby for two days in June, 1873, to identify the spot where he had dug. On the way he spent three hours in Cambridge, which he had not seen for twelve years. He called on none of his friends, not even the Cowells.

After all his efforts the attempt to set up the stone, again ended in failure. The trustees, he was told, approved neither the stone nor the inscription because they were not *"florid* enough." He notified

Carlyle of the decision and received a reply which showed, Fitz-Gerald said, that the "Sage of Chelsea" was in "full Vigour."

"There is something," Carlyle wrote,

at once pathetic and ridiculous and altogether miserable and contemptible in the fact you at last announce that by one caprice and another of human folly perversity and general length of ear, our poor little enterprise is definitively forbidden to us. Alas, our poor little "inscription," so far as I remember it, was not more criminal than that of a number on a milestone; in fact the whole adventure was like that of setting up an authentic *milestone* in a tract of country (spiritual and physical) mournfully in want of measurement; that was *our* highly innocent offer had the unfortunate Rulers of the Element in that quarter been able to perceive it at all! Well; since they haven't, one thing at least is clear, that our attempt is finished, and that from this hour we will devoutly give it up.[22]

FitzGerald was inspired to write to Carlyle a number of times in 1874. "This time last year," he said in June,

I was preparing to go to Naseby on that fruitless Errand; and last Night I dreamt of you: which may be the immediate cause of my now writing. I thought you were sitting in some room, and you would insist on how much more white-headed you were than I seemed to see you: and you were very kind, and even affectionate; but I said, "You know you often call me a d—d fool, now, don't you?" and then somehow Spedding laughed from a corner of the room. What an Old Woman's Dream to write to Thomas Carlyle!

The following month FitzGerald went by sea to Edinburgh, a journey that he had been promising himself for thirty years. His purpose was to visit the home of Scott, whose novels he never wearied of reading. He had expected to find Abbotsford "a Cockney Castle" but was pleased to find it a dignified home with "Grounds well and simply laid out: the woods he planted well-grown: and that dear Tweed running and murmuring still—as on the day of his Death." After visiting the writer's grave at Dryburgh, his pilgrimage was complete; but some pleasant tourists whom he met at Abbotsford persuaded him to accompany them the following day to the Trossachs, and to Lochs Katrine and Lomond. He was disappointed in these places; they seemed much better to him "in Pictures and Drop-scenes." He was as pleased with Edinburgh, however, as he had been with the Scott shrines and later found himself wishing to see the city again, "as I scarce ever felt for any strange Place." On the fourth day he returned to London by rail

22. *Letters*, III, 85.

and spent two days visiting Peter and Donne. He "looked in" at the Royal Academy, "as poor a show as ever I had seen."

Carlyle had always bantered FitzGerald about his affection for Scott and, when he heard of the intended journey, sent him a picture of John Knox to worship instead. "In spite of you," Fitz-Gerald wrote after his return,

I worshipped at the Scott Monument. . . . Oh, I know you think Scott a brave, honest, good-natured man, and a good Story-teller, only not a Hero at all. And I can't help honoring and loving him as such. Come; he is at least as good as old Bacon, whom Spedding has consumed near forty years in white-washing.

Carlyle replied,

By all means go again to Edinburgh . . . worship Scott, withal, as vastly superior to the common run of authors, and indeed grown now an affectingly *tragic* man. Don't forget Burns either and Ayrshire and the West next time you go. . . . not to speak of Dumfries with Sweet-heart Abbey and the brooks and hills a certain friend of yours first opened his eyes to in this astonishing world. . . . Adieu, dear F., I wish you a right quiet and healthy winter, and beg to be kept in memory as now probably your oldest friend.

Shortly before Carlyle's eightieth birthday in 1875, Professor David Masson of the University of Edinburgh proposed to eighty of the historian's friends that they present him with a congratulatory address and a gold medal bearing his likeness. FitzGerald was asked to join in the tribute and was at loss how to respond, for he did not approve of the plan. Learning that Spedding and Pollock, after some hesitation, had decided to coöperate, he sent a subscription. "Our Names," he told Mrs. Kemble, "are even to be attached somehow to a—White Silk, or Satin, Scroll! Surely Carlyle cannot be aware of that? I hope devoutly that my Name come too late for its Satin Apotheosis; but, if it do not, I shall apologise to Carlyle for joining such Mummery. I only followed the example of my Betters." His apology was not written, however, for Carlyle's pub-lished response revealed that the tribute had pleased him. "But I must say," FitzGerald observed to Tennyson,

I thought the whole thing rather a cockney affair—*Address and Medal and White Satin Scroll*, which some dozen years ago, I think Carlyle would have been tempted to blow his nose upon, as the Sandwich Is-landers did with their playbills at the Theatre. Only I never did see

Carlyle use a handkerchief: and only once his fingers: which he did very adroitly without smearing them.[23]

Since his visit to the Isle of Wight in 1854, FitzGerald had maintained his friendship with Alfred Tennyson entirely by letter. He wrote at least twice a year, but rarely let the publication of a poem or volume by the poet laureate pass without writing to comment on it. His letters were always the same; warm affection and admiration were blended with a steady play of banter and a running fire of criticism, both favorable and unfavorable. "I bought your volume [the *Holy Grail*] at Lowestoft," he said in 1870,

and, when I returned here for Xmas, found a copy from your new publisher. . . . The whole myth of Arthur's Round Table Dynasty in Britain presents itself before me with a sort of cloudy, Stonehenge grandeur. I am not sure if the old knights' adventures do not tell upon me better, touched in some lyrical way (like your own "Lady of Shalott") than when elaborated into epic form. I never could care for Spenser, Tasso, or even Ariosto, whose epic has a ballad ring about it. . . . Anyhow, Alfred, while I feel how pure, noble and holy your work is, and whole phrases, lines and sentences of it will abide with me, and, I am sure, with men after me, I read on till the "Lincolnshire Farmer" [24] drew tears to my eyes. I was got back to the substantial rough-spun Nature I knew; and the old brute, invested by you with the solemn humour of Humanity, like Shakespeare's *Shallow*, became a more pathetic phenomenon than the knights who revisit the world in your other verse. There! I can't help it, and have made a clean breast; and you need only laugh at one more of "old Fitz's crotchets," which I daresay you anticipated.[25]

He wrote to Pollock in 1873, "I told A. T. of some miseries in his Gareth—among them

> Damsel, the Task
> To an abounding Pleasure

for one, which I told him was what a City Apprentice would say to his Partner at an East End Hop when she asked for a glass of Negus." [26]

In his letters to Tennyson FitzGerald gave full rein to his dislike for Browning. "I abuse Browning myself," he said, "and get others to abuse him; and write to you about it; for the sake of easing my own heart, not yours." After the publication of *The Inn Album*

23. MS. letter to Tennyson, Dec. 6, 1875.
24. "Northern Farmer: New Style," one of Tennyson's eminently successful dramatic monologues in Lincolnshire dialect, published in the *Holy Grail* volume.
25. Tennyson, *Memoir*, II, 95.
26. MS. letter to Pollock [1873].

in 1875, FitzGerald observed, "I see Browning has another of his uncouth works out: I call him the great Prophet of the Gargoyle School: in France they have a man equally disagreeable to me— Victor Hugo." [27] Tennyson defended Browning against these attacks but could not alter FitzGerald's views. "What do I mean by calling Browning *Cockney?*" the latter asked, replying to the poet.

Well; you know it's not easy to define; but I believe that by *Cockney* I mean the affected and over-strained style which men born and bred in a City like London are apt to use when they write upon subjects with which neither their Birth nor Breeding (both rather plebeian) has made them familiar. So Leigh Hunt's were the Cockney Pastoral: Bailey's Festus [28] (beg pardon!) Cockney Sublime: and I think Browning's Books Cockney Profound and Metaphysical. There is nearly always a smack of the *Theatre* in these writers. . . . Now a Tale I have read called "Maud"—deals with a Browning sort of subject in a very different way: and I venture to think that it will be found when B. is nowhere. I think you know I don't flatter you, Alfred; and *I* know you wouldn't care for it if I did. . . . But *you,* A. T., tell me he is grand; and I ought to hold my tongue; only I remember you wanted to cram Festus the Sublime down our throats—you magnanimous great Dog you! [29]

The Tennysons frequently urged FitzGerald to come to Farringford, but he could never be persuaded to repeat his visit to the Isle of Wight. "Thank old Alfred for his letter which was an unexpected Pleasure," he wrote to Mrs. Tennyson in 1860,

I like to hear of him and you once or twice in the year: but I know he is no dab at Literature in any Line, poor Fellow. "Paltry Poet"—let him believe it is any thing but want of Love for him that keeps me out of the Isle of Wight:—nor is it Indolence, neither. But to say *what it is,* would make me write too much about myself. Only let him believe what I *do* say.[30]

The Poet Laureate had sent FitzGerald a list of questions about sailors in 1862, while writing *Enoch Arden.* FitzGerald concluded his reply, sent to Mrs. Tennyson, with, "Some Summer—some Summer day send the old wretch here, where nobody scarce knows his name (don't be angry, Mrs. A. T.), though a duller place is not!" [31]

At Little Grange one day, about the middle of September, 1876,

27. MS. letter to Tennyson, Dec. 6, 1875.
28. Tennyson greatly admired the poem *Festus* by Philip J. Bailey (1816–1902), published in 1839.
29. MS. letter to Tennyson, May 6, 1869.
30. *Ibid.,* July 12, 1860.
31. Tennyson, *Memoir,* I, 516.

FitzGerald was handed a calling card on which had been written, "Dear Old Fitz—I am passing thro' and will call again." The last three words were crossed out and "am here" substituted. The card was Tennyson's. The poet and his son Hallam had been touring in Norfolk and stopped at Woodbridge on the return journey to London. Upon alighting from the train and asking for "Edward Fitz-Gerald," they had been directed to the home of the superintendent of the county police, who bore the same name. The officer had conducted them to FitzGerald's home. Little Grange was being painted within and without at the time; so the guests were lodged at the Bull.

"We fell at once into the old Humour," FitzGerald reported to Fanny Kemble, "as if we had only been parted twenty Days instead of so many Years." Tennyson was unchanged "except for his fallen Locks," but FitzGerald refused to compliment him on his looks because he had always noticed that men said, "How well you are looking!" when anyone was about to be sick.[32]

The Tennysons were at Woodbridge for two days. One of them was spent at Little Grange, where they strolled about the grounds or sat on an iron seat in the garden with pigeons fluttering about them. "We went over the same old grounds of Debate," the host related, "told some of the old Stories, and all was well." FitzGerald praised Crabbe's poetry and was so enthusiastic about *Don Quixote* that he believed he had almost inspired the poet to begin Spanish. When Tennyson complained of the multitude of poems which were sent to him, "Old FitzGerald," Hallam said, "recommended him to imitate Charles Lamb and throw them into his neighbour's cucumber frames." They talked of Tennyson's poetry, of course. "He (A. T.) has still some things on the Anvil," FitzGerald told Cowell. "I did not ask to hear anything of them—for indeed I think he might as well ship his Oars now. I was even impious enough to tell him so." [33] His defense for his "audacity" was that Tennyson had "so many Worshippers who tell him otherwise."

Hallam recorded that their host "was affectionate, genial, and humorous, declaring that the captain of his lugger was one of the greatest of men." FitzGerald was favorably impressed by the young man, whom he described as "a very nice Fellow, who took all care of 'Papa' as I was glad to hear him say, not 'Governor' as the Phrase now is." [34]

32. *Tennyson and His Friends*, p. 114.
33. MS. letter to Cowell, Oct. 5, 1876.
34. Tennyson, *Memoir*, II, 213–214.

During the visit Tennyson was irritated to read in a newspaper that he had forbidden Longfellow to quote from his poems. He wrote a denial to the American poet and sent Hallam to post the letter immediately. "So my House is so far become a Palace," Fitz-Gerald remarked to Norton, "being the Place of Despatch from one Poet to the other, all over that Atlantic!" On the second day of the visit FitzGerald took his guests by steamer down the Orwell from Ipswich, but the weather was not pleasant.

The two old friends enjoyed their reunion thoroughly, and Fitz-Gerald felt a pang of regret as they parted. "I suppose I may never see him again," he remarked to Mrs. Kemble, "and so I suppose we both thought as the Rail carried him off: and each returned to his ways as if scarcely diverted from them." Tennyson commemorated his visit to Little Grange in his lines "To E. FitzGerald," prefixed to "Tiresias," the title poem of a volume published in 1885, two years after FitzGerald's death. It is singularly ironic that the book was dedicated to Robert Browning.

Later FitzGerald told Grout, proprietor of the Bull, that Wood-bridge "should feel itself honoured by the visit." But Grout, who numbered European princes, to whom he sold horses, among his friends, had not been impressed by his lodger. "Pray, Sir," he asked, "what is the name of the Gentleman?" The innkeeper failed to catch FitzGerald's reply, so at his first opportunity he asked Archdeacon Groome who the gentleman was. "Mr. Tennyson," the clergyman answered, "the poet laureate." "Dissay," [35] John replied doubtfully, "anyhow he didn't fare [36] to know much about hosses when I showed him over my stables."

35. Suffolk for "daresay."
36. Suffolk for "seem."

XXVI

Greek Translations and Other Works

"He has not yet attained his true place in the honour of men
as poet."

CHARLES ELIOT NORTON

FITZGERALD had intended, when he printed his last two
translations from Calderon in 1865, to include a version
of *Agamemnon* by Aeschylus begun in 1857. However, he
was not then satisfied with it, and not until 1869 did he
have a hundred copies printed by Childs.[1] He sent one to Cowell in
April with the strict adjuration, *"Mind you don't leave* it about
. . . as well as not *say* a word of it." Cowell approved of the translation in the main, and FitzGerald bound it in the volume which he
sent to Trinity College Library that year thinking "it would slip
in unnoticed." Thompson, of course, discovered it.

Fanny Kemble was responsible for FitzGerald's completing the
play.[2] She had revived his interest in the work during the early
'sixties, and it was for her that he printed. Although he never did
so, he considered dedicating the play to her. She trumpeted the
book in the United States until Quaritch began receiving orders
for it and applied to the author for copies. FitzGerald's response
was characteristic. "You had the trouble to send before for 'Agamemnon' for some Gentleman from America," he wrote in November, 1875,

. . . He is very welcome to a Copy. . . . As this is not the first time
you have been asked for it, you may be asked again by one of your
Transatlantic Friends who are my Omar's best Friends also. So I will
send you half a dozen Copies in case you be asked again. . . . If not
asked, the Copies . . . won't take up much of your room, and if lost
won't cause stocks to fall.[3]

A few weeks later Thompson sent him a clipping from one of Quaritch's catalogues:

1. This edition was undated and Prideaux erroneously assigned it to 1865.
2. When FitzGerald began *Agamemnon*, he intended to translate Aeschylus' Ores-
teian trilogy. He wrote a draft of the *Choephori*, but never printed it.
3. *Letters to Bernard Quaritch*, p. 34.

Æschylus, *Agamemnon,* a tragedy (translated with English verse by FitzGerald) . . . 7s. 6d. (privately printed . . .). The universal interest which has been excited by the marvelous poem called "The Rubáiyát of Omar Khayyám" has created a strong desire on the part of the public to know more of Mr. FitzGerald and his works. The *Agamemnon* will help readers to a larger and no less sympathetic acquaintance with the Unknown Poet who has contrived to link, in the form of translation, the subtlest graces of poesy with the deep and strange imaginings of an unfamiliar philosophy.[4]

FitzGerald was astounded. "Surely you must have misunderstood me about those few *Agamemnons,*" he expostulated.

Surely I distinctly wrote along with them that they were to be *given* to any American who troubled himself to ask for them . . . And now a cutting from one of your Catalogues has [been] sent me announcing the Play for sale—at some terrible price for such a Scrap—and moreover *with my Name,* which I had always declined publishing—and such a Puff about me and my little works as I am really ashamed to read again. . . . But even then my Name should not have been added; and such praise, as (instead of doing me any good) will only make your Readers say "Who *is* this Mr. E. FG. so belauded etc.?" And I think it will hurt, rather than advance my cause—such as it is. However, it is done, and *I* cannot help it: but I think you should explain and exonerate me from any share in it, as far as you can.[5]

In December, 1875, FitzGerald sent the last copies of his play to Quaritch, but the dealer continued to receive orders. He therefore proposed publishing, to which FitzGerald agreed, but objected to having his name appear as author. "I always told you it would do both of us more harm than good by appearing on Title page or in Advertisement," he insisted.

Good, it could not; so many E. FG'S; no one of them celebrated but the Lord of that name. Why, there is one beside myself in this very Woodbridge, an Ex-policeman; there lately was another, a Parson, in a neighbouring village; you knew another to your Cost. In fact *one* of us was generally hanged in Ireland once a Year till the Law was altered. Shall all these dispute my Glory?

Quaritch's edition consisted of two hundred and fifty small quarto copies bound in half-Roxborough. The text filled only a small portion of the large pages and was enclosed in a decorative border. " 'Agamemnon' came safe and sound," FitzGerald wrote to Quaritch,

4. Enclosure in MS. letter to Mrs. Cowell [December, 1875].
5. *Letters to Bernard Quaritch,* pp. 36–37.

I am only ashamed at his looking so fine: but that is your doing, you know: and I only hope it won't lose you money, nor draw the "Evil Eye" on myself. If you advertise it in your Catalogue, please do so *without any encomium* till someone else offers you a Quotation. "By the Translator of Omar K." will be enough as to the Authorship.

Agamemnon by no means caused a sensation on the book market, but its reception was very different from that accorded FitzGerald's previous works. "Why haven't you sent us 'Agamemnon'?" the editor of *The Academy* demanded of Quaritch in February, 1877. "Here is Mr. Symonds waiting to review it along with Omar Khayyám."

The reviewer was John Addington Symonds, who wrote a favorable critique which appeared on July 7:

Those of us who for many years past have known Mr. FitzGerald's version of the *Rubáiyát* of Omar Khayyám by heart, and who have felt that in those quatrains, at once melodious and pointed, a real poet had revealed himself beneath the garb of a translator, received the announcement of his *Agamemnon* with no common interest. The command of language and metre displayed in the smaller work, its spontaneity of music, and its depth of thought and feeling, inclined us to expect much of the greater: . . . Nor was this expectation frustrated. Whatever deductions may have to be made by the student, who feels that in the *Agamemnon* Mr. FitzGerald has done less than a more sustained effort of his singular powers might have produced, it will be acknowledged by all competent judges that his translation separates itself at once from merely meritorious work, and takes a place apart among all English versions of Greek poetry. It is almost trivial to say that the diction of a modern author is Shakespearean. . . . Yet Mr. FitzGerald's style in the finest passages of this great torso has a weight, a compactness, and a picturesqueness, to find the proper parallel for which we must look back to Shakespeare's age. The strong sonorous verse has the richness and the elasticity of Marlowe's line; and for the first time, after so many attempts, the English reader catches in his translation a true echo of the pompous Æschylean manner. . . . The result is that, while the whole poem is profoundly penetrated with the Æschylean spirit, which it reproduces with wonderful vividness, and while certain portions are accurate transcripts from the original, the Greek student will find many of the most impressive passages suppressed, and some most carefully prepared effects omitted. . . . The language throughout the drama, even in the passages which may seem to have been injured by compression, is so grandiose, and the imagery is so Æschylean, that it is impossible not to regret the author's disinclination to grapple with the Greek more closely. Where he has adhered to the original most faithfully, as in Clytemnestra's description of the courier fire, and her reception of Agamemnon, the success has been so thorough as to make us feel that the whole drama might have been presented with equal force and splendour. Is it quite beyond hope that Mr. FitzGerald should reconsider his decision and complete the play upon the strictly Æschylean outlines? . . . In a word the most perfect portions of the tragedy are those which represent the Greek with most fidelity; the modern poet proving his ability to bear the whole Titanic weight if he had chosen, by the energy with which he has disposed of certain favoured passages. . . . In conclusion, it may be permitted to hope that this *Agamemnon* is only the first of a series; and that the poet who possesses such rare powers of reproductive and re-creative translation may trust them so far upon another trial as to render his original in all its fullness.

"I saw the Academy," FitzGerald told Aldis Wright. ". . . I wonder at so much favor from a University Scholar."

Mr. Symonds objected to FitzGerald's alterations in the dialogue between Cassandra and the chorus, but this very passage had been highly praised by a reviewer in *The Nation,* published in the United States the previous month. "There is no scene in Macbeth," the critic said, "of more tremendous power; and although all this . . . is rather a transfusion than a translation, yet it gives more of the real sense of the original than all previous translations put together." The reviewer did not approve the entire work. "It must be said," he admits, "that it is the stirring and dramatic passages in which Mr. FitzGerald is strongest, and that in the more delicate and tender descriptions his touch is not always gentle enough to satisfy." [6] FitzGerald saw the review and told Norton that it was "written by a superior hand, and, I think, quite discriminating in its distribution of Blame and Praise: though I will not say the Praise was not more than deserved; but it was where deserved, I think."

FitzGerald's practice of curtailing and altering a work to suit his purpose is already familiar to the reader. On the title page he described his play as being "taken from Æschylus," and in a prefatory note spoke of it as "This Version—or per-version." He stated in the introduction:

I suppose that a literal version . . . , if possible, would scarce be intelligible. Even were the dialogue always clear, the lyric Choruses, which make up so large a part, are so dark and abrupt in themselves, and therefore so much the more mangled and tormented by copyist and commentator, that the most conscientious translator must not only jump at a meaning, but must bridge over a chasm; especially if he

6. *The Nation,* No. 621 (May 24, 1877), 310.

determine to complete the antiphony of Strophe and Antistrophe in English verse.

He had long considered making a translation of the entire trilogy [7] but had been "frightened" by the choral passages. "So am I now," he had confessed to Cowell when he began his version in 1857.

. . . they are terribly maimed; and all such Lyrics require a better Poet than I am to set forth in English. But the better Poets won't do it; and I cannot find one readable translation. I shall (if I make one) make a very free one; not for Scholars, but for those who are ignorant of Greek, and who (so far as I have seen) have never been induced to learn it by any Translations yet made of these Plays.

His own choral passages never satisfied him. "The Dialogue is, I think, good," he told Donne in 1876, "and some of it very good: but the Choruses are doubly false to Æschylus as being utterly without his *dark Innuendo style,* and poor in any style. Their only merit is, that they carry on the story intelligibly to one who does not know the Original." [8]

FitzGerald followed the original rather closely to the point where Agamemnon enters the palace to meet his death; from there on, his alterations became more frequent and drastic. Although Cowell did not agree with him, he thought the latter half of the play the better done. He exercised his customary liberty of interpolation, and here and there are found passages which have no counterpart in the original. Some of them are distinct echoes of Omar. In the first choral passage, for example, FitzGerald gives the elders these lines:

> But thus it is; All bides the destined Hour;
> And Man, albeit with Justice at his side,
> Fights in the dark against a secret Power
> Not to be conquer'd—and how pacified?

Again, when Clytemnestra confronts the chorus after murdering Agamemnon, she exclaims:

> Call not on Death, old man, that, call'd or no,
> Comes quick; nor spend your ebbing breath on me,
> Nor Helena: who but as arrows be
> Shot by the hidden hand behind the bow.

FitzGerald assured his friends that *Agamemnon* would be the last of his translations. However, while working on the play, he

7. *Agamemnon, The Libation-bearers,* and *The Furies.*
8. *Donne and His Friends,* p. 318.

had made similar versions of the *Oedipus Tyrannus* and *Oedipus Coloneus* of Sophocles; and Norton urged him to complete them. Accordingly, he merged the two into a single drama, *The Downfall and Death of King Oedipus*. He sent the first half, which he called "Oedipus in Thebes" to Norton early in 1880, and the second, "Oedipus at Athens," in March, 1881.[9]

Again he insisted in his preface that his play "professes to be neither a Translation, nor a Paraphrase of Sophocles, but 'chiefly taken' from him: I need scarcely add, only intended for those who do not read the Greek." The alterations were made to simplify the action and to remove inconsistencies which appear in the originals. Ismene disappears from the second play as being *de trop* as far as the essential action is concerned. Creon's part in "Oedipus in Thebes" is considerably shortened to eliminate the inconsistency in his characterization which appears in the two original plays. Again, since Antigone is represented as a young woman in Sophocles' *Antigone,* FitzGerald does not present her father as a very old man in "Oedipus at Athens." Sophocles did not violate the tradition of his time in so doing; but combining the two actions in a single play demanded that Oedipus be presented throughout as a man in his prime. FitzGerald claimed that he achieved dramatic force by removing the catastrophe from "a time of life when death in some way or other is inevitable." Other inconsistencies were similarly removed. The choral passages again provided difficulties. "As I thought I should do no better with the Choruses than old Potter," [10] FitzGerald said in his preface, "I have left them, as you see, in his hands, though worthy of a better Interpreter than either of us."

A few lines of the dialogue between Theseus and Oedipus illustrate the verse in which FitzGerald's version is written.

Thes.   But Thebes and Athens, friendly powers of old,
          What quarrel should arise to make them foes?
Œd.   O son of Ægeus! to the Gods alone
          Belongs immunity from Change and Death:
          All else doth all controlling Time confound.
          Earth waxes old: and all that from her womb

9. Fifty copies of each were printed. "Only one copy was given to a friend in this country," Aldis Wright stated in the *Athenaeum* of June 23, 1883, "and that under bond of strictest secrecy." Mr. Wright, who had read the proof of the volume, no doubt was the recipient.

10. Robert Potter, 1721–1804. Four passages, however, FitzGerald himself translated: (1) Part I, the scene with Jocasta at the altar before the entrance of the Corinthian herald; (2) a few lines in Part II preceding the entrance of Theseus before the final catastrophe; and (3 and 4) the closing chorus of each play.

She brings to light upon her bosom dies,
And all is mutability between.
Ev'n so with Man, who never at one stay,
No less in mind than body changeable,
Likes what he liked not, loathes where once he loved,
And then perchance to liking turns again.
And as with man, with Nation none the less.
If now with Thebes and Athens all look fair,
Yet Time his furrow'd track of Night and Day
Pursues, wherein some grain of Discord dropt,
Perhaps no bigger than an idle word,
That shall infect his kindly Brotherhood,
And ripen'd Amity to rancour turn.

Critics, naturally, have been divided in their reception of the plays. "The power of his version," Norton told Aldis Wright in 1887, "never impressed me more than now. . . . He has not yet attained his true place in the honour of men as a poet." [11] However, A. C. Benson stated:

Half the charm, so to speak, of these ancient human documents is their authenticity. Not only the archaic form, the statuesque conventionality of the Greek stage, the traditions of a once-living art, are sacrificed; but, what is more important still, the very spirit of Greek Tragedy, the unshrinking gaze into the darkest horrors of life, the dreadful insistence of Fate, forcing men to tread unwillingly in rough and stony paths—these are thrown aside. And thus the force, the grim tension, which are of the essence of Greek tragedy are replaced by a species of gentle dignity, which leaves the stiffness of movement without the compensating strength, and the austere frigidity without the antique spirit. A kind of flowing and even Shakespearian diction takes the place of the gorgeousness of the original, but without any of the modern flexibility of handling.[12]

Late in 1878 the first American edition of the *Rubáiyát* was published in Boston by James Osgood.[13] "I wish that, at any rate, they would have let me know of their intention," FitzGerald told Quaritch, "as I have a few alterations and an additional note." The English publisher immediately suggested another edition, but FitzGerald replied, "There has been enough of him here, and now will be more in America. One day I may bring him out in better Company." He had long wished to republish *Salámán and Absál,* which he still regarded as his best work. When Quaritch continued to

11. Norton MS. letter, Nov. 28, 1887.
12. Benson, *FitzGerald,* pp. 119–120.
13. A reprint of the third (1872) edition.

press him for a new edition of Omar, FitzGerald finally gave his consent, with the provision that the allegory be included in the volume. "Of all this you must judge for yourself," he wrote on December 9, 1878, "and then let me [know] whether you wish to undertake the Book; for an Edition of how many Copies; and on what terms. If we do not agree, no harm done on either side." Quaritch offered £25 for the privilege of printing 1,000 copies. FitzGerald protested that the edition was too large; but, after further negotiations, the transaction was completed. The poet stipulated, however, that "my Name do not appear in any Advertisement, nor any notice of the Book added to any such Advertisement, unless quoted from some independent Review." In a later letter he stated, "Omar's *first three* Stanzas should contrive to go on his *first* page: they are the 'Lever de Rideau' as it were." [14]

The translator made few changes in the *Rubáiyát,* but shortened *Salámán and Absál* by about one third, thereby, he believed, much improving it. The book was placed on sale in August, 1879, and had "cleared expenses" by the following June.

The same year FitzGerald printed the results of his most ambitious editorial labors, an edition of Crabbe's *Tales of the Hall.* As early as 1865 he had asked Donne to query Murray about a volume of selections from Crabbe. The publisher, however, had lost money on the poet and "would not meddle." For more than a decade FitzGerald turned to Crabbe's works each autumn "reading and cutting out, with occasionally (for my own use only) a word or two to connect, which I do not feel to be so impious with so careless a Writer." During the seventies he edited the *Tales of the Hall* in this manner. He was anxious to call the attention of readers to the work, which revealed Crabbe's lighter vein. Both Horace Furness, the Shakespearean editor, and Norton were interested and approached American publishers, who proved to be as wary of the venture as Murray had been. Finally, in 1878, FitzGerald decided to print at his own expense. He prepared the volume during the winter, wrote a brief introduction, and had three hundred and fifty copies printed the following May. He expected to place the edition on sale but abandoned the plan when friends whose advice he sought counseled against it. In 1882, however, Quaritch agreed to sell a number of copies, and FitzGerald sent him forty-seven in February, 1883.[15] Leslie Stephen, to whom FitzGerald gave a copy,

14. *Letters to Bernard Quaritch,* pp. 58–62.

15. This small edition appeared in 1883, not in 1882 as bibliographers have heretofore stated.

later called his attention to a passage in praise of Crabbe in Newman's *Addresses to the Catholics of Dublin.* FitzGerald thereupon
incorporated this material in an enlarged preface and had two hundred copies printed in May. These were bound with the *Tales*
and were eventually disposed of by Quaritch.[16]

Tales of the Hall, the last of Crabbe's poems to be published
during his life,[17] consists of stories supposedly told by two brothers
as they sit over their wine after dinner.

"The scene," FitzGerald observed in his preface,

has also changed with Drama and Dramatic Personae: no longer now
the squalid purlieus of old, inhabited by paupers and ruffians with the
sea on one side, and as barren a heath on the other; in place of that,
a village with its tidy homesteads and well-to-do tenants, scattered
about an ancient Hall . . . "West of the waves, and just beyond the
sound."

The editor explained the purpose of his book and his method of
preparing it.

I must acknowledge that, while it shares with the poet's other works in
his characteristic disregard of form and diction—of all indeed that is
now called "Art"—it is yet more chargeable with diffuseness, and even
with some inconsistency of character and circumstance, for which the
large canvas he had taken to work on, and perhaps some weariness in
filling it up, may be in some measure accountable. So that, for one
reason or another, but very few of Crabbe's few readers care to encounter the book. And hence this attempt of mine to entice them to it by
an abstract, omitting some of the stories, retrenching others, either by
excision of some parts, or the reduction of others into as concise prose
as would comprehend the substance of much prosaic verse.

I have replaced in the text some readings from the Poet's original MS.
quoted in his son's standard edition, several of which appeared to me
fresher, terser, and (as so often the case) more apt than the second
thought afterward adopted.

Among other things, FitzGerald wished to disprove the popular
belief that Crabbe was merely "a Pope in worsted stockings" and
that he lacked humor. The book, it is to be feared, made few converts. Discussing a review of it in the *Atlantic Monthly,*[18] Fitz-
Gerald commented:

A very good paper . . . though too moderate in . . . praise to attract
others to him. The Critic, you will see, treats Crabbe's *Humour* as sum-

16. The preface was being printed when FitzGerald died in June, 1883.
17. *Tales of the Hall* was published in 1817–18. Crabbe died in 1832.
18. In May, 1880. The review was written by George Woodberry.

marily as Leslie Stephen did:—the very quality which makes me prefer those later Tales to any earlier ones. . . . But I really don't know if any of those I have bored about it in England see what I see.[19]

FitzGerald was engaged during his last years on three works which he left unfinished. The first, an edition of the prefaces to Dryden's works, he had suggested in a letter to *Notes and Queries* as early as 1861. "Why," he asked, "will no one reprint the whole, or a good abstract, of Dampier's fine Voyages?—and (now one is about it) all Dryden's Prefaces, which Johnson notices as things *sui generis* quite?" [20] No one acted on the suggestion, and in 1879 FitzGerald had completed a selection of his own; but he doubted his capacities as editor. He urged Aldis Wright to take the work which he had done, use as much or as little of it as he wished, and publish the book. "You are the man to do it," he insisted, *"not* yours, E. FG." At another time he pleaded, "But get Dryden done. I am rather hurt that no one ever will take my Advice on such points where I really feel some confidence in Yours always, E. F. G." His selection of "Glorious John's" [21] prefaces was never published.

The second work was a dictionary for "my dear Sévigné's" correspondence, one of his greatest reading pleasures during his last years. "Now I am at Madame de Sévigné's delightful Letters," he told Fanny Kemble in 1875. "I should like to send you a Bouquet of Extracts." He made a list of the dramatis personae as an aid against confusion in reading. Although the dictionary was made originally merely for his own use, he wrote to Charles Keene in 1880:

I was just finishing my Sévigné; I mean, reading it over. I have plenty of Notes for an Introductory Argument and List of Dramatis Personae, and a clue to the course of her Letters, so as to set a new reader off on the right tack, with some previous acquaintance with the People and Places she lives among. But I shrink from trying to put such Notes into shape; all writing . . . now very difficult, at seventy odd.

The task was completed for him by his grandniece, Miss Mary Eleanor FitzGerald Kerrich, in 1914.[22]

A third work which FitzGerald undoubtedly projected but never completed was a biography of Charles Lamb. He was an ardent ad-

19. MS. letter to Wright, 1880.
20. *Notes and Queries,* Second Series, XI (Jan. 26, 1861), 63.
21. FitzGerald's name for Dryden.
22. *Dictionary of Madame de Sévigné* (London, Macmillan & Co., 1914). 2 vols. Mary Eleanor FitzGerald Kerrich, ed.

mirer of the man as well as of his works and frequently mentioned
and criticized in his correspondence the various editions of Lamb's
letters. In 1881, when Alfred Ainger was preparing his edition of
the essayist's works, FitzGerald lent him a number of his books.
"He is welcome to them for as long as he pleases," he assured Aldis
Wright through whom he forwarded the volumes. "You," he told
Wright in 1883, ". . . must one day edit (as you won't) the Life,
with the help of such 'works' of Scissors and Paste as I shall commit
to you." After FitzGerald's death his library was found to contain
all the published editions of Lamb's letters, as well as various
biographical works. All contained numerous marginal corrections
and suggestions for the insertion of material. Annotated memoirs
of the essayist's friends, notebooks containing data on his life, and
numerous prints suitable for a biography were in the collection.

The meager harvest of all these labors, however, had been a brief
calendar dating the principal events in Lamb's life. Lamb's letters
had been published, not chronologically, but grouped according
to correspondents, so that it was difficult for a reader to keep ori-
ented in time while reading them. FitzGerald's calendar, therefore, was a convenient guide. In 1878, he had it printed and distributed copies among his friends.

His failure to complete the biography is to be keenly regretted.
He had remarkable skill as a biographer—a flair for catching the
significant trait or incident which exposed character, an easy narrative manner, and a pleasing, humorous touch. He fully revealed
his skill in his "Memoir of Bernard Barton," and proof that this
success was not accidental is found in another biographical sketch
published in *Temple Bar* in 1880 but to this day almost unknown.
The appearance of the article was the crowning of a life's ambition.

Since his first overwhelming triumph when, as a young man of
twenty-two, FitzGerald had placed "The Meadows in Spring," his
first contribution to magazines, in *two* periodicals, his offerings
had invariably been rejected. A review of the poems of Jean Inge-
low, written some time during the 'forties, "The Two Generals,"
Salámán and Absál, and the *Rubáiyát* had all been spurned by
editors. "As Lamb said of himself, so I say; that I never had any
Luck with printing," FitzGerald declared when *Macmillan* returned his manuscript of "The Two Generals." In 1880, however,
after a lifetime of desultory effort, he at last announced to Aldis
Wright, "I would have you know that . . . after several Trials,
I at last appear in a Magazine: Temple Bar for January: in the

shape of quite a pleasant little Paper on Percival Stockdale, which I turned up out of a Box and sent to Pollock, who got it in, and 'There you are!' "

The essay, which FitzGerald had written in 1857, describes a pilgrimage which he made in that year to Baldock in Hertfordshire to see the tavern and mill famed in the eighteenth century and commemorated in a popular ballad as the home of a maiden

> . . . so fair
> Of so pleasing a shape, and so winning an air
> That once on the ever-green bank as I stood,
> I could swear't had been Venus, just sprung from the flood.

Exactly one hundred years before FitzGerald's journey, Percival Stockdale, a soldier, hack-writer, and clergyman generously provided with self-esteem, had preceded him to Baldock on a wager that he could win a kiss from the rustic Venus. He won. Stockdale's description of this adventure forms the core of FitzGerald's essay. The sketch is written in his most delightful and entertaining prose. "In the year 1809," he begins,

Percival Stockdale published two octavo volumes of autobiography, in which he called on posterity to do him the justice that had been denied him by his contemporaries. These two volumes might be met with some thirty years ago upon the bookstalls, at the price of half a crown. And they were almost worth it; telling, as they did, the story of one among so many who mistake common talent for genius, and common feeling for rare sensibility. . . . written too when old age and infirmity, instead of abating vanity, simply made it more incapable of self-restraint.

The sketch is noteworthy as another illustration of FitzGerald's power to outline a man's life and clearly to portray a character within the confines of a few pages. A brief quotation illustrates his deftness:

. . . Stockdale gradually subsided into becoming "booksellers' hack," to supply them with any occasional verse or prose which they might want, or the writer need to subsist by. And "subsistence" with Stockdale was not so simple a concern; his bodily ambitions were not more easily satisfied than his mental: in the matter of eating and drinking, for instance, "though so early," he says, "a worshipper of Flora, of Vertumnus and Pomona"—(whatever all that may mean)—"yet was I also given to exalt and stimulate the olive of Minerva with the grape of Bacchus," which is quite intelligible. But, Minerva not being sufficiently stimulated to pay the cost of Bacchus, and no brighter prospect opening before her in London, poor Stockdale was half tempted to join the literati who were invited by the Empress Catherine to Russia.

FitzGerald was not accustomed to being paid for his writings. "I was really ashamed to take the £4.4. which Bentley sent me for such a thing . . . but Pollock told me to do as others did (Lady Pollock among others, I suppose) and there an end." Two years later he followed up this success by placing in the same magazine "Virgil's Garden," a poem in couplets which he had written twenty years previously.[23] For this he was paid, he confessed, "as I deserved— with a dozen copies."

FitzGerald's last work was a third edition of his first book, *Euphranor*. Again, a visit to Cambridge, made in the summer of 1881, revived his interest in the dialogue. A critical reading disclosed the work to be "disfigured by some confoundedly *smart* writing in parts." He revised it and had fifty copies printed the following May. Among other changes, he lengthened a passage which referred to Tennyson and added another.[24] "I really did, and do," he told the poet's son Hallam, "wish my first, which is also my last, little work to record, for a few years at least, my love and admiration of that dear old Fellow, my old Friend."

23. *Temple Bar*, LXIV, No. 257 (April, 1882), 597.
24. These passages may be found in the *Letters and Literary Remains* (1903 ed.), VI, 208–209 and 246–247. The former is the new passage.

XXVII

Last Years

For some we loved, the loveliest and the best
That from his Vintage rolling Time hath prest,
  Have drunk their Cup a Round or two before,
And one by one crept silently to rest.

. . .

And when like her, oh Sáki, you shall pass
Among the Guests Star-scatter'd on the Grass,
  And in your joyous errand reach the spot
Where I made One—turn down an empty Glass!

FITZGERALD'S Rubáiyát

WHEN FitzGerald was sixty-five years old, in 1874, he was confined within doors by illness for the first time since he had had measles as a boy. His ailment, bronchitis, became his "skeleton," which stalked from its closet each winter, with one exception, for the remainder of his life. The following year a physician told him that his heart had become affected. He was actually relieved by the information, for it gave him hope that he would escape what he most dreaded, a lingering final sickness. Later, hearing that an acquaintance also suffered from the ailment, FitzGerald congratulated him, saying that he was happy to be so afflicted, for when he came to die, he "didn't want a lot of women messing about." [1]

Except for the necessity of taking particular care of himself when suffering from bronchitis, FitzGerald's infirmities made very little change in his life. His friends visited him in the spring and autumn; his nieces stayed at Little Grange during the summer; and he visited Crabbe at Merton in May or June, made occasional trips to London, and each year passed several weeks on the coast.

The Edwardses spent their summers at Dunwich, and FitzGerald joined them in 1876, 1877, and 1878. There, in 1877, he met one of Edwards' friends, Charles Keene, the *Punch* artist. Keene described FitzGerald as "an old literate . . . a great friend of Tenny-

1. *Two Suffolk Friends,* p. 89.

son's and of poor Thackeray's, and quite a character—an Irishman, an author, and bookworm . . . who remembers Kean and the Kembles and Liston, and [is] full of talk about old times and 'dead and gone' people. We met every evening and talked belles lettres, Shakespeare, and the musical glasses till midnight." [2] Keene's attraction for FitzGerald is easily understood. He possessed a grave humor, was fond of old literature, and rarely read new books or newspapers. He became a frequent guest at Little Grange, usually taking with him his bagpipes, which he played as he walked the "Quarterdeck." "Keene has a theory that we open our mouths too much," FitzGerald told Archdeacon Groome, "but whether he bottles up his wind to play the bagpipes, or whether he plays the bagpipes to get rid of his bottled-up wind, I do not know." [3]

Edwards' health failed in 1878, and the following April Fitz-Gerald went to London to see him. It was still early evening when he left the invalid; so he stepped into the Lyceum Theater where Irving was playing *Hamlet*. "It was incomparably the worst I had ever witnessed from Covent Garden down to a Country Barn," he told Fanny Kemble. "When he got to 'Something too much of this,' I called out from the Pit door where I stood, 'A great deal too much,' and not long after returned to my solitary inn." [4] Of Aldis Wright he asked, "How could he have the impudence to lecture the players?" Again in October he spent four days in town, visiting Donne, who was in poor health, Mrs. Edwards, whose husband had died the previous month, and Fanny Kemble, whom he had not seen for twenty years. With the exception of 1881, when his eyes were very weak, he visited London during each of the last five years of his life.

Although he was active abroad, worked steadily at his desk at home when his eyes permitted, paced his "Quarterdeck" for exercise, or his upper hall when the weather was bad, and spent many hours each day reading or being read to; weakened sight, attacks of bronchitis, lumbago, rheumatism, and pains about the heart were unmistakable warnings that the end of his life was approaching. "My Family get on gaily enough till seventy," he told Thompson, "and then generally founder after turning the corner." He was then almost seventy-two. To Norton he wrote that the prospect of death "is no great regret to me."

Deaths of relatives and friends saddened his last years. His

2. Layard, George S., *Life and Letters of Charles Samuel Keene of "Punch"* (London, Sampson, Low, Marston & Company, 1892), p. 258.

3. *Two Suffolk Friends*, p. 92.

4. Letter to Fanny Kemble, April 25 [1879].

brother Peter, of whom he was very fond, died in 1875. His last words were Edward's name, thrice repeated. Four years later, in May, 1879, his eldest brother John died at Boulge after a lingering and painful illness. "We were very good friends," FitzGerald remarked, "of very different ways of thinking." In December his sister Andalusia died at Exeter.[5] "Now," he wrote to Fanny Kemble, "none but Jane Wilkinson and E. F. G. remain of the many more that you remember and always looked on with kindly regard." Mrs. Wilkinson returned to Boulge from her home in Italy in the autumn of 1881 and several times called at Little Grange. When younger, FitzGerald had apparently felt only a chill regard for her, but age and the deaths of the rest of the family had softened him. As they sat together, talking of old days, Mrs. Wilkinson said, his hand rested on hers. "We seemed," she told Aldis Wright, "as if we could not part, but he would not be persuaded to return with me to Italy."[6]

While in London in the autumn of 1880, FitzGerald was "all but tempted to jump into a Cab and just knock at Carlyle's door, and ask after him, and give my card, and—run away." *Almost*. Carlyle died the following February. FitzGerald asked the historian's niece for the bowl of a clay pipe such as the two had so often smoked together in the little Chelsea garden; but she sent, instead, a "handsome Meerschaum," a gift from Lady Ashburton, which the Scotsman had used when "from home." Carlyle was barely in his grave when Spedding was run over by a cab in London. FitzGerald had not seen him for twenty years but he could always rely on "Jem" for advice or aid, if need be, simply by writing a letter. "I cannot help thinking of him while I wake," FitzGerald confided to Pollock, "and when I do wake from Sleep, I have a feeling of something lost, as in a Dream, and it is J. S. . . . Dear old Jem! His Loss makes one's Life more dreary, and 'en revanche' the end of it less regretful."[7] Donne, who with Spedding shared FitzGerald's "oldest and deepest love," died a year later in June. "Of that Death I say nothing," he remarked to Fanny Kemble, "as you may expect of me."[8]

Deeply as he felt these losses, FitzGerald accepted them with

5. Peter was sixty-eight when he died; John, seventy-six; and Andalusia (Mrs. de Soyres), seventy-five.
6. MS. letter to Aldis Wright.
7. Letter to Pollock [1881].
8. Spedding died on March 9, 1881; Donne on June 20, 1882.

fatalistic resignation; but the dropping off of old friends was probably responsible for his reverting to old associations, his "premiers Amours," as he called them. "I can imagine how pleasant Cambridge now is and I should like to be there," he remarked in a letter to Wright in June, 1881. The following month, on his way to Merton, he stayed two days in the town, his first visit there in thirty years. In August he spent several days at Beccles and one morning drove to Geldestone. The Kerrich family was away at the time, but he wandered for several hours through the house and grounds. In 1880, 1881, 1882 he returned to Aldeburgh. It was there that he had gone as a boy. Mary Lynn, with whom he had then romped on the beach, was living in the village. His "old Dear," now gray and rheumatic "but with her fine Soul in her Face still," walked with him on the shingle where they had once played; and evenings FitzGerald called at Tiffany Cottage, where she lived, and she read to him. When at Little Grange, he sometimes walked out to his birthplace at Bredfield to sit alone on a bench in a corner of the garden—

> But all the sunshine of the year
> Could not make thine aspect glad
>   To one whose youth is buried here.
>
> In thine ancient rooms and gardens
>   Buried—and his own no more
> Than the youth of those old owners,
>   Dead two centuries before.
>
> Unto him the fields around thee
>   Darken with the days gone by:
> O'er the solemn woods that bound thee
>   Ancient sunsets seem to die.[9]

As "old Fitz" sat in the sun on the iron bench in his own garden at Little Grange, one wonders if he did not occasionally look back over the long years of his literary labor with keen and perhaps even bitter disappointment, for he had failed in almost all that he had attempted. *Euphranor* had awakened no one to the faults of English educational practice; *Polonius* had been shrugged off with as little ceremony as Hamlet had accorded Polonius himself. The reading of Aeschylus and Sophocles was still confined to the classroom, and Calderon and Crabbe were still read only by the curious

9. FitzGerald's "Bredfield Hall."

few. True, the *Rubáiyát* had won a hearing and its merits had been fully praised; but *Salámán and Absál,* which he considered his best translation, had been ignored.

There are artists in every field whose works are destined to be "caviare to the general." FitzGerald, with the exception of his *Rubáiyát,* is one of these. He wrote not what readers wanted to hear, but what he wanted to tell them. Nevertheless, he had succeeded while he had seemed to fail. He had succeeded in writing blank verse which is at once musical and vigorous. He had achieved lyric beauty by his skill in combining euphony with natural yet delicately modulated rhythms. Flowing rhythms also mark his prose. One need not turn, as FitzGerald thought, to Dryden or to the sermons of the seventeenth-century divines for prose models. One has but to turn to his own *Euphranor,* to "Percival Stockdale," to his prefaces, to discover the beauties of which English prose is capable.

Moreover, FitzGerald was to win immortality where he would have least expected it. Paradoxically, his letters, written for his most limited audience, have won for him his largest—the *Rubáiyát,* alone, being excepted. In the correspondence we find a distillation of all FitzGerald's qualities, personal as well as artistic. There we find his prose; and there, too, we find poetry, even though written in prose. There we find his criticism; there we find his enthusiasms and his prejudices; there we find his humor; there we find the man. And in his letters, too, we find the bulk of his literary work, for in writing of art, of his fellow men, of his friends, and of himself he created literature.

But if FitzGerald, sitting in his garden as his life drew to its close, may have felt regret for the small results which he had achieved, there was in his disappointment no tinge of envy that he had failed to win a fame comparable to that of Tennyson, Thackeray, or Carlyle. His maintenance of anonymity had been no pose. For personal recognition by the public at large FitzGerald simply did not care, even though he very humanly revealed modest gratification when it was offered. But he did earnestly desire that his friends recognize the merits of his works, and into his letters occasionally crept a note of disappointment at their apparent neglect. A dozen years after the publication of the first Calderon plays, Cowell asked him for a copy, which FitzGerald sent. "I have some others in a parcel upstairs, if you should ever want more," he wrote. "This I say because the Plays might interest some whom *you* know." And when Norton urged him to complete the Oedipus plays, FitzGerald replied, "I cannot say my attempt on Sophocles would please you and my American Patrons (in England I have none)." Donne, "good old Donne," to be sure, had never stinted his praise. In 1876 he had written, "I am so delighted at the glory E. F. G. has gained by his translation of the Rubáiyát of Omar Khayyám. The 'Contemporary Review' and the 'Spectator' newspaper! It is full time that Fitz should be disinterred, and exhibited to the world as one of the most gifted of Britons."

Although FitzGerald reflected much on the past, he was by no means gloomy or morose. He enjoyed having people about him and Keene, Archdeacon Groome, Aldis Wright, and others who came to visit him always received a hearty welcome. The guests found a host who, though he spoke wistfully of the past and caustically of the present, yet shook off these moods to provide entertainment. Perhaps he would play for them on his small organ; perhaps he would read a favorite passage from *The Spanish Tragedy* or some other old play, or repeat one of his few recitations, the thoughts of Hodge, an English laborer, as he worked in a ditch on a winter's day. The selection, written by a near-by clergyman, was, he said, "a piece of Shakespeare." And there were lighter moments. He enjoyed repeating anecdotes, one of his favorites being:

Scene—Country church on winter's evening. Congregation with the Old Hundredth ready for the Parson to give out some dismissal words.
Good Old Parson, not at all meaning to rhyme, "The light has grown so very dim, I scarce can see to read the hymn."
Congregation, taking it up to the first half of Old Hundredth—
        "The light has grown so very dim,
            I scarce can see to read the hymn."
Pause, as usual; Parson mildly impatient. "I did not mean to read a hymn; I only meant my eyes were dim."
Congregation, to second part of Old Hundredth:
        "I did not mean to read a hymn;
            I only meant my eyes were dim."
Parson, out of patience:
        "I didn't mean a hymn at all.
            I think the devil's in you all!"

Once, when Keene asked him if he minded his playing the bagpipes in the house, FitzGerald replied, "Not at all, providing you leave the drone off." This and similar remarks provided the cut lines for some of Keene's *Punch* drawings.

FitzGerald's sense of humor never deserted him. On trips to Beccles he visited with William Crowfoot, an old friend and a relative of Crabbe's. One member of the family recalled "how often the servants waiting at table when he dined with us found it impossible to repress an outburst of laughter and left the room to conceal [it]." [10] FitzGerald placed himself under the care of Dr. Richard Worthington of Lowestoft during the last years of his life but proved to be a refractory patient. When the physician's messenger appeared at his lodgings with medicine, FitzGerald would say, "What's that, Charley, another bottle? Well, put it there on the mantel; but before you go, take the one that's there and empty it in the garden." [11] He actually tried the potions, however. "I too am taking some medicine," he told Aldis Wright, "which, whatever effect it has on me, leaves an indelible mark on Mahogany: for (of course) I spilled a lot on my Landlady's Chiffonier, and found her this morning rubbing at the 'damned Spot' with Turpentine, and in vain." FitzGerald called in a cabinetmaker to restore the piece of furniture to "its 'sound and pristine health,' or such as I hope my Landlady will be satisfied with."

Nor did his mind ever lose its vigor nor his conversation its pith. In September, 1881, in company with Wright and Keene, he visited Crabbe at Merton. "The parson and Wright used to retire about ten o'clock," Keene related, "but FitzGerald and I sat and smoked in the greenhouse for a couple of hours more. He is a capital companion. His talk is of books and poetry. He's a great scholar; a slashing critic about pictures—his taste is for the old masters; and he knew all the literary men about town in Thackeray's early time." [12]

Although the two men had known each other for four years, and although their conversation often turned to literature, it appears that FitzGerald, with customary modesty, had summarily dismissed his own works. "I went to stay with my old friend FitzGerald, the old scholar at Woodbridge," Keene related after one of his visits.

I find since I've been back that he is a "great unknown" genius in some high critical circles. I was mentioning my visits to W. B. Scott, who is one of the Rossetti, Swinburne, etc., set and of my friend having translated some Persian poems and Calderon's plays, etc. He jumped off his chair! "Do you know him? Why, Ram Jam" (some wonderful Persian name he gave it) "is the most quite too exquisite work of the age, and Rossetti considers the translations from Calderon the finest—" etc. etc. So I shall tell the old man. I don't know whether he'll be pleased.[13]

10. MS. letter to Aldis Wright from Mary S. Crowfoot, Aug. 26, 1899.
11. Data furnished by Harry Goodwin, Esq., who in 1939 occupied FitzGerald's old lodgings in Marine Terrace. Mr. Goodwin was acquainted with Charles Hood, Dr. Worthington's messenger.
12. Layard, *Keene*, pp. 326–327.
13. *Ibid.*, p. 318.

The following June, again after returning from Woodbridge, Keene wrote to a friend, Joseph Crawhall,

He [FitzGerald] knows you from me and is much interested in your idea of a ballad opera. He believes it might be done with W. Scott's "Pirate," and I've persuaded him to draw up his plot, which he seems to have concocted. Two acts; only one girl, Minna or Brenda; the witch, a contralto; the men, a tenor and bass, and the pirates (chorus) not to appear till the second act. The scenery would be good too. That is, what I remember of his talk of it, but will send you his sketch, which he promises.[14]

FitzGerald's unfinished manuscript for this production is in Trinity College Library.

FitzGerald, moreover, retained his love for children until the end of his life. "This evening," he wrote a few years before his death, "the Children of St. John's Parish are coming to play in *My Grounds!* and I do wish the Cloud would pack away for the occasion. I have a large Barn cleared out, and a swing fixt on a Beam. . . ." He was unable to suppress his tenderness for children, even when angry with them. One autumn day he returned to Little Grange to find a boy filling his pockets with walnuts which he had knocked from one of the trees. FitzGerald seized him and administered a whipping. The boy started for home in tears but paused when the ogre called after him, "Why are you leaving these nuts to waste on the ground? Take them with you." After the culprit had filled his pockets, FitzGerald gave him half a crown and sent him on his way.[15]

FitzGerald survived the winter of 1882–83 without illness. In April he made his last will. Early the following month he was forced to journey to London on business, which he completed in time to go out to Chelsea before returning to Woodbridge. "I wanted to see the Statue [Carlyle's] on the Chelsea Embankment, which I had not yet seen," he told Norton, "and the old No. 5 of Cheyne Row, which I had not seen for five and twenty years. The Statue I thought very good, though looking somewhat small and ill set-off by its dingy surroundings. And No. 5 (now 24) . . . all neglected, unswept, ungarnished, uninhabited 'TO LET' ." [16]
While in London he invited Keene, who had been sick, to visit him. "Next week," he later wrote to Fanny Kemble, "I am expect-

14. *Ibid.*, p. 334.
15. Adams, *FitzGerald*, p. 42.
16. Letter to Norton, May 12, 1883.

ing my grave Friend Charles Keene, of Punch, to come here for a week—bringing with him his Bagpipes, and an ancient Viol, and a Book of Strathspeys and Madrigals; and our Archdeacon will come to meet him, and to talk over ancient Music and Books: and we shall all three drive out past the green hedges, and heaths with their furze in blossom."

Two of his nieces came in June to spend the summer at Little Grange, and on the thirteenth FitzGerald left for his annual visit to Merton. He did not feel well on his arrival, and Crabbe observed that he was not so animated as usual. He refused to eat but at nine o'clock asked for some brandy. An hour later he retired. Before the family arose the following morning, he was heard moving about his room; but he did not appear at breakfast. Crabbe tapped on his door at eight o'clock and, receiving no response, entered the room to find him "as if sleeping peacefully but quite dead."

On hearing of FitzGerald's death, Tennyson wrote to Pollock, "I had no truer friend: he was one of the kindliest of men, and I have never known one of so fine and delicate a wit. I had written a poem to him the last week, a dedication, which he will never see."

Tennyson's verses, a prologue to his poem "Tiresias," recalled his visit to Little Grange and paid tribute to FitzGerald's *Rubáiyát*. The closing lines read:

> And so I send a birthday line
>   Of greeting; and my son, who dipt
> In some forgotten book of mine
>   With sallow scraps of manuscript,
> And dating many a year ago,
>   Has hit on this, which you will take,
> My Fitz, and welcome, as I know,
>   Less for its own than for the sake
> Of one recalling gracious times,
>   When, in our younger London days,
> You found some merit in my rhymes,
>   And I more pleasure in your praise.

Before the publication of the poem, Tennyson added an epilogue. "One height and one far-shining fire!" he wrote, echoing the thought of the final line—

> And while I fancied that my friend
>   For this brief idyll would require
> A less diffuse and opulent end,
>   And would defend his judgment well,
>   If I should deem it over nice—

The tolling of his funeral bell
　Broke on my Pagan Paradise,
And mixt the dream of classic times
　And all the phantoms of the dream,
With present grief, and made the rhymes,
　That miss'd his living welcome, seem
Like would-be guests an hour too late,
　Who down the highway moving on
With easy laughter find the gate
　Is bolted, and the master gone.

Gone into darkness, that full light
　Of friendship! past, in sleep, away
By night, into the deeper night!
　The deeper night? A clearer day
Than our poor twilight dawn on earth—
　If night, what barren toil to be!
What life, so maim'd by night, were worth
　Our living out? Not mine to me
Remembering all the golden hours
　Now silent, and so many dead,
And him the last; and laying flowers,
　This wreath, above his honour'd head,
And praying that, when I from hence
　Shall fade with him into the unknown,
My close of earth's experience
　May prove as peaceful as his own.

On Tuesday, June 19, FitzGerald was buried in the little churchyard at Boulge. His grave is marked by a horizontal granite stone,
on one side of which is inscribed:

Edward FitzGerald, Born 31 March 1809, Died 14 June 1883.

This is balanced by a Biblical verse of FitzGerald's own choosing:

It is He that hath made us and not we ourselves.

TAMAM

APPENDIX A

Genealogical Table

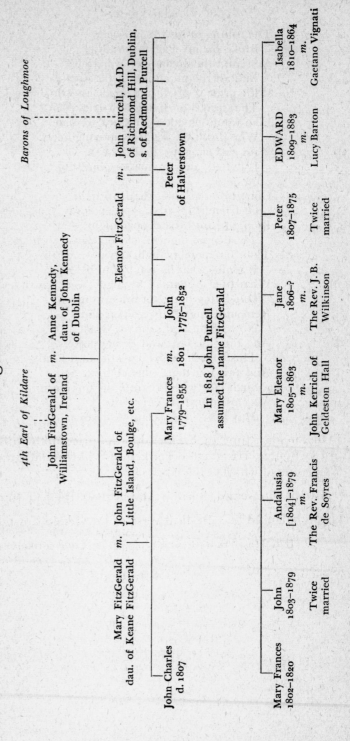

4th Earl of Kildare .... *Barons of Loughmoe*

Mary FitzGerald *m.* John FitzGerald of Little Island, Boulge, etc.
dau. of Keane FitzGerald

John FitzGerald of Williamstown, Ireland *m.* Anne Kennedy, dau. of John Kennedy of Dublin

Eleanor FitzGerald *m.* John Purcell, M.D., of Richmond Hill, Dublin, s. of Redmond Purcell

John Charles
d. 1807

Mary Frances
1779–1855

m.
1801

John
1775–1852

Peter
of Halverstown

In 1818 John Purcell assumed the name FitzGerald

Mary Frances
1802–1820

John
1803–1879

Twice married

Andalusia
[1804]–1879
m.
The Rev. Francis de Soyres

Mary Eleanor
1805–1863
m.
John Kerrich of Geldeston Hall

Jane
1806–?
m.
The Rev. J. B. Wilkinson

Peter
1807–1875

Twice married

EDWARD
1809–1883
m.
Lucy Barton

Isabella
1810–1864
m.
Gaetano Vignati

APPENDIX B

Translations from Béranger

As young men both FitzGerald and Thackeray tried their hands at translating lyrics by the French poet, Pierre Jean Béranger. In the spring of 1837 Thackeray returned to London from Paris where he had been serving as correspondent for *The Constitutional and Public Ledger.* One writer states that he was to become manager "and to apply artificial respiration" [1] to the faltering paper. On April 5 FitzGerald sent him five Béranger translations. "Do not feel bound to use them because I have sent them": he wrote, "indeed I think the Roi d'Yvetot is the only perfect one: . . . You and I know each other too well to need any ceremony about such matters as these: use them if you choose. . . . I will send your Roi d'Yvetot, if you wish: it is a paraphrase, and a very proper pendant to your Roger Bontemps. . . . P.S. Your Roi d'Yvetot has far more spirit than mine, but is not so literal." [2]

The five poems which FitzGerald translated are "Le Roi d'Yvetôt," "Le Grenier," "Le Convoi de David," "L'Ange gardien," and "Les Souvenirs du peuple." FitzGerald's note reads as though the poems were sent at Thackeray's request, and one wonders if the new editor proposed to vitalize the anemic journal by publishing a few lively lyrics. If so, the paper died in July before they were used.

Thackeray's *Paris Sketch Book,* published in 1840, contained four poems in imitation of Béranger. Two of these were translations of poems which FitzGerald had translated. They have always been considered Thackeray's work, and it is entirely possible that they are his versions of the two lyrics. On the other hand, they are so similar to FitzGerald's translations that it is possible that they are the same, revised and polished by Thackeray. With the exception of "Les Souvenirs," which is so rough as to have relatively little merit, FitzGerald's translations follow:

THE KING OF YVETÔT

There was a King of Yvetôt
    Of whom Renown hath little said:
He let all thoughts of glory go,
    And dawdled half his life abed.
And as every night came round
By Tessy with a nightcap crowned

---

1. Dodds, John, *Thackeray* (New York, Oxford University Press, 1939), pp. 16–17.
2. MS. letter to Thackeray. Owned by Mrs. Fuller.

                    Slept very sound—
Sing ha, ha, ha, and he, he, he,
That's the sort of King for me.

And every day it came to pass
    Four meals beneath his belt he stowed:
And step by step upon an ass
    Over his dominions rode.
And whenever he did stir
What think you was his escort, Sir?—
                    Why, an old cur—
Sing ha, ha, ha, and he, he, he,
That's the sort of King for me.

His charges ran to no excess
    Save from a somewhat lively thirst:
But he that would his people bless
    Odds fish!—must whet his whistle first.
So for himself a pot he drew
From every barrel opened new,
                    As Caesar's due.
Sing ha, ha, ha, and he, he, he,
That's the sort of King for me—

Firmly in all the ladies' hearts
    Was this sagacious prince installed:
And with strict justice on their parts,
    "The father of his people" called—
No other soldiers did he raise
But such as might at targets blaze
                    On holidays.[3]
Sing ha, ha, ha, and he, he, he,
That's the sort of King for me.

Neither by force, nor false pretence,
    He sought to make his kingdom great:
And made, oh princes learn from hence,
    "Live and let live" his rule of state.
'Twas only when he came to die
    That the people, who stood by,
                    Were known to cry.
Sing ha, ha, ha, and he, he, he,
That's the sort of King for me.

3. FitzGerald told Thackeray that he had difficulty with the last portion of this stanza and asked him to "set it right" if necessary.

The portrait of this best of Kings
  Still does the duty of a sign,
And o'er a village tavern swings
  Famed in that country for its wine—
The people in their Sunday trim
Filling their glasses to the brim
         Look up to him:
Singing ha, ha, ha, and he, he, he,
That's the King, the King for me.

THE GARRET

With pensive eyes the garret I review
  Where in my youth I weathered it so long:
With a wild mistress, a staunch friend or two,
  And a light heart that trebbled into song.
Making a mock of life and all its cares,
  Rich in the glory of my rising sun,
Lightly I bounded up four pair of stairs
  In the brave days when I was twenty-one.

It is a garret—let him know't who will:
  There stood my bed—how hard it was and small:
My table there: and I decypher still
  A half-made couplet charcoaled on the wall.
Ye joys, that Time hath swept with him away,
  Rise up—ye royal dreams of love and fun:
For you my watch I pawned how many a day
  In the brave days when I was twenty-one.

And thou, my little Nellie, first of all—
  Fresh, and fresh drest as daisies, in she flies:
Her little hands already pin the shawl
  Across the narrow window curtainwise—
Along the bed she spreads her flowing gown
  For coverlet, where coverlet was none—
I have heard since who paid for many a gown
  In the brave days when I was twenty-one.

One noble evening, when my friends and I
  [Sang] in full chorus round the little board,
A shout of triumph mounted up thus high,
  And the deep cannon through the city roared:
We rise: we join in the triumphant strain:
  "Napoleon conquers! Austerlitz is won!
Tyrants shall never tread us down again!"—
  Oh the brave days when I was twenty-one.

Let us be gone—the place is sad and strange—
   How far, far back these happy times appear!
All that I have to live I'd gladly change
   For one such month as I have wasted here.
To dwell in one long dream of love and power
* $\left\{ \begin{array}{l} \text{By founts of} \\ \text{Quaffing of} \end{array} \right\}$ hopes that never would outrun
And concentrate life's essence in an hour
   Give me the days when I was twenty-one.

* Which of these is best?—[FitzGerald's note.]

THE FUNERAL MARCH OF DAVID [4]

"Hold back!—you go no further here."
   They heard the frontier sentry call
Who the dead painter on his bier
   Were bearing to his native Gaul.
"Soldier," they answered in their gloom,
   "Does France proscribe his memory too?
And you deny his ashes room
   Who left eternal fame to you?"

Chorus
Exiled, unfriended and forlorn
   He pined beneath a despot's eye:
Thrice happy those who lived and die
   In the dear land where they were born.

"Hold back—you cannot pass, I say"—
   The soldier still in fury cries.
"Soldier, as even in death he lay
   Toward France he turned his dying eyes.
For her alone and all in all
   He wrought in exile and in woe:
And made from many a palace wall
   The genius of her people glow."
Chorus

"No, no—hold back—you cannot pass,"
   The soldier somewhat touched returned.

4. Jacques Louis David (1748–1825), painter to Louis XVI and later to Napoleon. In spite of the king's patronage David became an ardent revolutionist and, as a member of the Convention, voted for Louis' death. Upon the return of the Bourbons, he was exiled as a regicide and lived the remainder of his life in Brussels. His friends actually were stopped at the border when they attempted to return with his body for burial in Paris.

"The man that drew Leonidas
  With equal love of freedom burned—
With him began the bright array
  Of conquest and of art, when France,
Spurning the bonds of Kings away,
  Rose like a giant from her trance."
                              Chorus

"No, no—I cannot let you on,"
  More gently said the soldier then.
"Soldier, 'twas he that could alone
  Portray the greatest of great men.
While Homer raised his soul above,
  And round the imperial eagle flew,
He seemed elect to picture Love,
  But 'twas Prometheus whom he drew."
                              Chorus

"No, no—you cannot pass the walls,"
  The soldier said in accent mild.
"Soldier, at last the hero falls,
  And the great painter is exiled.
Death reaches him in foreign lands,
  Death—a sad and bitter one—
Oh France, hold forth a mother's hands
  To the great ashes of thy son."
                              Chorus

"No, no. I dare not yield to you,"
  The soldier all in tears replied.
"Well, let us turn—Sweet France, adieu,
  Land of our birth, our love, our pride!
Quenched is the glory from whose birth
  The blaze of Roman art decayed.
We go to beg six feet of earth
  Where these great ashes may be laid."
                              Chorus

THE GUARDIAN ANGEL

A beggar drawing near his end
  Saw his good angel at the door:
And said to him—"Now my good friend,
  Trouble yourself for me no more."
Good angels bring one little joy
But never mind—good bye, my boy.

"Am I what people call God's heir
  Born on a strawheap in a loft?"
"Yes," said the Angel, "I took care
  That the straw was fresh and soft."
Good angels bring one little joy
But never mind—good bye, my boy.

"What had I left me, but a face
  And tongue, of brass, to take folks in with?"
"What!" said the Angel—"Of my grace
  An old friar's wallet to begin with."
Good angels bring one little joy
But never mind—good bye, my boy.

"Then, 'listing, to the wars I went,
  And lost a leg ere I got out."
"Well," said the Angel, "be content,
  That leg would soon have had the gout."
Good angels bring one little joy
But never mind—good bye, my boy.

"Then with a pocket I made free,
  And the law got me by the ears."
"Yes," said the Angel, " 'twas through me
  You only were in gaol three years."
Good angels bring one little joy
But never mind—good bye, my boy.

"Then I must needs make Love my game,
  And from the chase retreated sore."
"Yes," said the Angel, "but through shame,
  I always left you at the door."
Good angels bring one little joy
But never mind—good bye, my boy.

"Next a wife I took in tow,
  And never was a worse miscarriage."
"Yes," said the Angel, "but you know
  We angels never meddle with marriage."
Good angels bring one little joy
But never mind—good bye, my boy.

"Is this the peaceful end that ought
  To crown a life of pain and toil?"
"Yes," said the Angel, "and I've brought
  A priest with rag and holy oil."

Good angels bring one little joy
But never mind—good bye, my boy.

"Shall I then to hell go pat,
  Or fly away to happier spots?"
"Why," said the Angel, "as to that,
  You may—or may not—let's draw lots."
Good angels bring one little joy
But never mind—good bye, my boy.

So this poor soul with faltering tongue
  Made the folks merry round his bed:
He sneezed—the Angel as he sprung
  Upward for Heaven "God bless you" said—
Good Angels bring us little joy
But never mind—good bye, my boy.

APPENDIX C

Writings Ascribed to FitzGerald

Two writers on FitzGerald have attributed to him poetry which is beyond doubt the work of others. Thomas Wright, in his *Life of Edward FitzGerald,* published "The Old Beau" and "The Merchant and His Daughter," poems which had appeared in an annual, *The Keepsake,* in 1834 over the name of Edward Fitzgerald. The *g* in lower case type should be noted. In a letter sent to the *Athenaeum* after the appearance of the biography in 1904, Aldis Wright denied that the verses were FitzGerald's and suggested that they were by Edward Marlborough Fitzgerald, "a writer of occasional verse, with whom Edward FitzGerald had no wish to be identified, and who caused him to avoid using his own surname." [1] Subsequent evidence has verified the assumption.

In 1933 Charles Ganz, editor of *A FitzGerald Medley,* a volume of miscellanea, credited FitzGerald with a book of verse by "E.-F.," published in Paris in 1829. This volume, entitled *Translations into Verse from Comedies of Molière and Casimir Delavigne, to Which Are Added Original Poems, Imitations, School Exercises, and The Magic Lantern, a Satire,* was first mentioned by the late T. J. Wise, who possessed a copy. His *Ashley Library Catalogue* states, "This little book with leaves measuring $7\frac{1}{8}$ x $4\frac{7}{16}$ inches, appears to have been only too successfully suppressed, as it now ranks among the rarissima of nineteenth century poetry." [2] Two other copies have been found, Mr. Ganz states, one in the British Museum, and another in the *Bibliothèque Nationale* in Paris.

Mr. Ganz says that Mr. Wise bought his copy from Aldis Wright and "was told by him that it was the only one in existence." [3] This statement, the use of the initials "E.-F.," and passages in the poems for which Mr. Ganz finds parallels in FitzGerald's writings are the grounds on which authorship is attributed to him.

I cannot believe that the poems are by FitzGerald. Aldis Wright definitely stated in 1902 that "The Meadows in Spring" (1831) was the earliest verse "which has yet been discovered," and he never announced any subsequent discoveries. Mr. Wright was a meticulous scholar and a man of strictest integrity. It is impossible to conceive of his selling any material entrusted to him as FitzGerald's editor. Furthermore, it would be a strange act, indeed, for the librarian of Trinity to sell the only copy

1. Letter to the *Athenaeum*, No. 3980 (Feb. 6, 1904), 178.
2. *Ashley Library Catalogue*, II, 118.
3. Ganz, *FitzGerald Medley*, p. 207.

of a work by a Trinity writer rather than to place it in the college library. Messrs. Carter and Pollard, in their *Enquiry into the Nature of Certain Nineteenth Century Pamphlets,* have revealed that part, at least, of Mr. Wise's "rarissima" is not above suspicion. Mr. Wise's amazing career as a discoverer of lost manuscripts and rare first editions has been revealed more recently in *Forging Ahead,* a biography by Wilfred Partington.[4]

FitzGerald frequently used the signature, E. F. G. or E. FG., but in the two thousand or more letters, published and unpublished, of which I have copies, he never signed the initials, E. F.; and there was no reason whatever for writing "E.-F." Mr. Ganz's parallels are not conclusive. The Paris volume contains a poem entitled "The Arms of Cupid," and Mr. Ganz implies that this is a parallel to FitzGerald's "Of All the Shafts of Cupid's Bow" by reprinting the second poem as a footnote. The only similarity in the two, however, is that both mention Cupid, his shaft, and his bow.

On the other hand, there is considerable evidence to indicate that FitzGerald was not the author of the volume. He was not in Paris in 1829 when the volume was published, although he was there during the spring of 1830. Mr. Ganz disposes of this discrepancy by assuming that FitzGerald had antedated his manuscript. The explanation would be plausible were there other evidence to indicate that FitzGerald was the author. The introduction, however, which speaks familiarly of "the close of a long war," "the lessons which that war has inculcated," and "the benign influence of a peace, which it is to be hoped may remain uninterrupted," suggests that the author was an older man. FitzGerald was only six years old when the Napoleonic wars ended in 1815.

Internal evidence presents an even stronger case. There is not the slightest similarity in the Paris volume, which is dominated by the conventions of eighteenth-century poetry, to any of FitzGerald's known writings. It contains a preponderance of rhymed couplets, a wealth of personification, numerous classical allusions, and the characteristic artificial eighteenth-century phraseology. For example:

> While yet a boy, I used to rove
> Thro' flowery mead, and verdant grove,
> Nor like my fellows loved to hurl
> The flying ball; and less adroit
> With strength and sinewy arm to twirl
> Straight to the mark the heavy coit.

The writer speaks, too, of "the finny race" and the "sportive ramblers of the tide." In all FitzGerald's writing there is nothing like this. The verse in the book is as ornate and diffuse as FitzGerald's is simple and concise. The poems could hardly have been acceptable in 1829 to the man who,

4. Published by G. P. Putnam's Sons, New York, 1939.

in 1831, wrote "The Meadows in Spring" and who, in 1833, criticized Tennyson's early work by saying, "It is fine to see how in each succeeding poem the smaller ornaments and fancies drop away, and leave the grand ideas single."

Further evidence against FitzGerald's authorship is the fact that the book contains a poem called "The Amusements of a Fisherman," which reveals a knowledge of angling and an enthusiasm for the sport which FitzGerald did not possess. It was not until after he met W. K. Browne in 1833 that he became interested in fishing, and then its chief attraction was Browne's companionship. He dropped the sport before his friend's death. Mr. Ganz actually contradicts himself by quoting a letter written by Donne in 1837—the date should be noted. "I heard from Edward FitzGerald," he said, ". . . Some time since, not being an angler himself, and not particularly affecting the company of rivers and standing pools, he nevertheless struck up an acquaintance with one who occupies himself by such waters." [5]

Thomas Wright also ascribed to FitzGerald brief character analyses of eight of his friends and of his sister, Mrs. Kerrich.[6] The "Word Portraits," as Wright called them, are not altogether flattering; and Aldis Wright denied that FitzGerald had written them. He contended that they were by "a person in London who professed to describe character from handwriting." [7] The explanation is very likely correct. In 1849 FitzGerald was intrigued by an analysis of his own character made from his handwriting by one "Warren." [8] It would appear that he also submitted samples of his friends' handwriting to Warren.

5. *FitzGerald Medley*, pp. 293–294.
6. Wright, *FitzGerald*, II, 225–226.
7. *Athenaeum*, No. 3980, 178.
8. Letter to George Crabbe, Oct. 22, 1849.

References

The following list contains Edward FitzGerald's major publications and sources of information bearing upon his life and work.

In addition to published sources, I have examined more than a thousand unpublished FitzGerald letters as well as manuscript letters and notes by members of the FitzGerald family, Alfred Lord Tennyson, Lady Tennyson, Frederick Tennyson, William Makepeace Thackeray, Anne Thackeray Ritchie, John Ruskin, James Spedding, Bernard Barton, Mr. and Mrs. E. B. Cowell, Sir Frederick Pollock, Archbishop R. C. Trench, James Russell Lowell, Charles Eliot Norton, H. Horace Furness, W. Aldis Wright, Charles S. Keene, George Crabbe of Merton, Robert Stephenson, John Loder, John Charlesworth, and a number of others. Other unpublished material includes the diaries of John Allen and Frederick Spalding and twelve scrapbooks compiled by FitzGerald.

FITZGERALD'S MAJOR WORKS

The meadows in spring. *Athenaeum, 193,* 442, 1831.

Memoir of Bernard Barton. Published in Poems and letters of Bernard Barton. London, Hall, Virtue & Co., 1849.

Euphranor, a dialogue on youth. London, William Pickering, 1851.

Polonius, a collection of wise saws and modern instances. London, William Pickering, 1852.

Six dramas of Calderon, freely translated. London, William Pickering, 1853.

Euphranor, second edition. London, John W. Parker & Son, 1855.

Salámán and Absál, an allegory translated from the Persian of Jámí. London, John W. Parker & Son, 1856.

Rubáiyát of Omar Khayyám. London, Bernard Quaritch, 1859.

The mighty magician. Such stuff as dreams are made of. Distributed privately, 1865.

Rubáiyát, second edition. London, Bernard Quaritch, 1868.

The two generals. Distributed privately [1868].

Salámán and Absál, second edition. Distributed privately, 1871.

Rubáiyát, third edition. London, Bernard Quaritch, 1872.

Agamemnon. London, Bernard Quaritch, 1876.
    This translation had first been privately distributed in 1869.

Rubáiyát of Omar Khayyám and Salámán and Absál. London, Bernard Quaritch, 1879.
    The fourth edition of the Rubáiyát and the third of Salámán.

The downfall and death of king Œdipus. Distributed privately, Part I, 1880; Part II, 1881.

Readings in Crabbe, tales of the hall. London, Bernard Quaritch, 1882.
　First printed and distributed privately in 1879.
Euphranor, third edition. Distributed privately, 1882.
　Fifty copies only of this edition were printed by Billing & Sons of
　London and Guildford.
Readings in Crabbe. London, Bernard Quaritch, 1883.
　This edition consists of the remainder of three hundred and fifty
　copies which FitzGerald had printed in 1879 and for which he
　wrote a new introduction.
Dictionary of Madame de Sévigné. London, Macmillan & Co., 1914.
　Mary Eleanor FitzGerald Kerrich, ed.

COLLECTED WORKS

Aldis Wright Editions

Letters and literary remains of Edward FitzGerald. London and New
　York, Macmillan & Co., 1889. 3 vols.
Letters of Edward FitzGerald. London and New York, Macmillan &
　Co., 1894. 2 vols.
　The correspondence in the 1889 edition plus forty-three new let-
　ters. Published in Macmillan's Eversley Series.
Letters of Edward FitzGerald to Fanny Kemble. London and New
　York, Macmillan & Co., 1895.
Miscellanies. London and New York, Macmillan & Co., 1900.
More letters of Edward FitzGerald. London and New York, Mac-
　millan & Co., 1901.
Letters and literary remains of Edward FitzGerald. London and New
　York, Macmillan & Co., 1902–3. 7 vols.
　Wright's final edition; a compilation of all that he had published.

Quaritch Edition

Works of Edward FitzGerald. London, Bernard Quaritch, New York
　and Boston, Houghton, Mifflin & Co., 1887. 2 vols.
　This edition contains "Polonius" and "Sea Words and Phrases,"
　which were not published by Wright.

Variorium Edition

Variorium and definitive edition of the poetical and prose writings
　of Edward FitzGerald. New York, Doubleday, Page & Co., 1903.
　7 vols. George Bentham, ed.
　This edition does not contain the correspondence but includes
　"Percival Stockdale and Baldock Black Horse," "Polonius," and
　"Sea Words and Phrases," not published by Wright. The pagina-
　tion of FitzGerald's original editions is noted in the margins.

INDIVIDUAL LETTER COLLECTIONS

Some new letters of Edward FitzGerald to Bernard Barton. London, Williams & Norgate, 1923. F. R. Barton, ed.

This volume is an entertaining introduction to FitzGerald as a letter writer.

Edward FitzGerald's letters to Bernard Quaritch. London, Bernard Quaritch, 1926, C. Quaritch Wrentmore, ed.

A FitzGerald friendship, letters to W. B. Donne. New York, William Rudge, 1932. Mrs. Catharine Bodham Johnson and N. C. Hannay, eds.

See also James Blyth's book listed immediately below.

BIOGRAPHICAL SOURCES

Adams, Morley. Omar's interpreter. London, Priory Press, 1911.

In the footsteps of Borrow and FitzGerald, London, Jarrold & Sons, n.d.

Benson, A. C. Edward FitzGerald. London, Macmillan & Co., 1905.

The volume appears in the English Men of Letters Series. Benson drew chiefly upon Thomas Wright's *Life* for his biographical data.

Blyth, James. Edward FitzGerald and "Posh." London, John Long, 1908.

Glyde, John. Life of Edward FitzGerald. London, C. Arthur Pearson, 1900.

Groome, Francis Hindes. Two Suffolk friends. Edinburgh and London, William Blackwood & Sons, 1895.

Intimate sketches of FitzGerald and his friend, Robert H. Groome, by the latter's son.

Wright, Thomas. The life of Edward FitzGerald. London, Grant Richards, 1904. 2 vols.

REMINISCENCES OF MARY ELEANOR FITZGERALD KERRICH

Homes and haunts of Edward FitzGerald. *Blackwood's Magazine, 174,* 439-452, 1903.

Edward FitzGerald, a personal reminiscence. *Nineteenth Century Magazine,* LXV, 461-469, 1909.

Memories of Edward FitzGerald. *The East Anglian Magazine,* August, 1935, 83-87.

More memories of Edward FitzGerald. *The East Anglian Magazine,* November, 1935, 159-165.

GENERAL

Brookfield, F. M. The Cambridge apostles. London, Sir Isaac Pitman & Sons, 1906.

Browne, E. G. A literary history of Persia. London, T. Fisher Unwin, 1902–6. 2 vols.

Bury St. Edmunds, record of the tercentenary of the foundation of the King Edward VI school, commemoration volume. London, B. Fellowes, 1850.

Carter, John, and Pollard, Graham. An enquiry into the nature of certain nineteenth century pamphlets. London, Constable & Co., 1934.

Clodd, Edward. Memories. New York, G. Putnam's Sons, 1916.

Colvin, Sir Sidney. Memories and notes of persons and places. London, Edward Arnold & Co., 1921.

Cowell, George. Life and letters of Edward Byles Cowell. London, Macmillan & Co., 1904.

de Tassy, Garcin. Note sur les rubá'iyát de 'Omar Khaïyám. *Asiatique Journal*. Paris, Imprimerie Impériale, 1857.

Dodds, John W. Thackeray. New York and London, Oxford University Press, 1941.

Dole, Nathan H. Rubáiyát of Omar Khayyám, variorium edition. Boston, L. C. Page & Co., 1898. 2 vols.

Dutt, W. A. Some literary associations of East Anglia. London, Methuen & Co., 1907.

Grier, R. M. John Allen, a memoir. London, Rivington's, 1899.

Heron-Allen, Edward. Some sidelights upon Edward FitzGerald's poem, the rubá'iyát of Omar Khayyám. London, H. S. Nichols, 1898.
    Contains a facsimile of the Ouseley ms. of Omar's quatrains.
Edward FitzGerald's rubâ'iyât of Omar Khayyâm. London, Bernard Quaritch, 1899.
    Collates FitzGerald's quatrains with their Persian sources.
The second edition of Edward FitzGerald's rubá'iyyát of 'Umar Khayyám. London, Duckworth & Co., 1908.

Huber, V. A. English Universities. London, William Pickering, 1843.

Johnson, Catharine B., ed. William Bodham Donne and his friends. London, Methuen & Co., 1905.

Kemble, Frances Ann. Record of a girlhood. London, Richard Bentley & Son, 1878. 3 vols.
    Records of later life. London, Richard Bentley & Son. 1882.
    Further records. London, Richard Bentley & Son, 1890. 2 vols.

Layard, George S. Life and letters of Charles Samuel Keene. London, Sampson, Low, Marston & Co., 1892.

Lounsbury, T. R. The life and times of Tennyson. New Haven, Yale University Press, 1915.

Lowell, James Russell, letters of. New York, Harper & Bros., 1894. C. E. Norton, ed.
    New letters of. New York, Harper & Bros., 1932. M. A. deWolfe Howe, ed.

Lucas, E. V. Bernard Barton and his friends. London, Edward V. Hicks, Jr., 1892.

Lucas, F. L. The decline and fall of the romantic ideal. London, Cambridge University Press, 1937.

Ten victorian poets. London, Cambridge University Press, 1940.

M'Carthy, Denis F. Calderon's dramas. London, Henry S. King & Co., 1873.

McCarthy, Justin H. Rubáiyát of Omar Khayyám. London, David Nutt, 1889.

Maurice, Frederick. The life of Frederick Denison Maurice. London, Macmillan & Co., 1884.

Melville, Lewis. William Makepeace Thackeray. London, Ernest Benn, Ltd., 1927.

Some aspects of Thackeray. Boston, Little, Brown & Co., 1911.

Merivale, Charles. Autobiography. London, Edward Arnold & Co., 1899. J. A. Merivale, ed.

Neff, Emery E. Carlyle. New York, W. W. Norton, 1932.

Nicolas, J. B. Les quatrains de Khèyam. Paris, Imprimerie Impériale, 1867.

Norton, Charles E., letters of. London, Constable & Co., 1913. 2 vols. Sara Norton and M. A. deWolfe Howe, eds.

O'Hart, John. Irish pedigrees. Dublin, McGlashan & Gill, 1876.

Payne, John. The Quatrains of Omar Kheyyam of Nishapour. London, Villon Society, 1898.

Pollock, Sir W. Frederick. Personal remembrances of. London, Macmillan & Co., 1887. 2 vols.

Prideaux, W. F. Notes for a bibliography of Edward FitzGerald. London, Frank Hollings, 1901.

Reid, T. Wemyss. The life, letters, and friendships of Richard Monckton Milnes, first Lord Houghton. London, Cassell & Co., 1890.

Ritchie, Hester Thackeray. Letters of Anne Thackeray Ritchie. London, John Murray, 1924.

Published in New York by Harper & Bros. the same year under the title, Thackeray and his daughter.

Ryland, Richard. The history, topography, and antiquities of the county and city of Waterford. London, John Murray, 1824.

Scudder, H. E. James Russell Lowell. Boston and New York, Houghton, Mifflin & Co., 1901.

Shirazi, J. K. M. Life of Omar al-Khayyámi. Edinburgh and London, T. N. Foulis, 1905.

Shorter, Clement. William Makepeace Thackeray and Edward FitzGerald. Privately printed, 1916.

Smyth, George Lewis. Ireland, historical and statistical. London, Whittaker & Co., 1844.

Suffolk, history of. London, Constable & Co., 1902. 2 vols. William Page, ed.

Teichman, Oskar. The Cambridge undergraduate one hundred years ago. Cambridge, W. Heffer & Sons., 1926.

Tennyson, Frederick, letters to. London, Hogarth Press, 1930. Hugh J. Schonfield, ed.

Tennyson, Hallam. Alfred Lord Tennyson, a memoir. London and New York, Macmillan & Co., 1897.

Tennyson and his friends. London, Macmillan & Co., 1911. Lord Hallam Tennyson, ed.

Thackeray, William Makepeace, the works of, biographical edition. London, Smith, Elder & Co., 1899. 13 vols.

  Collection of letters of, 1847–1855. New York, Charles Scribner's Sons, 1887. Mrs. J. O. Brookfield, ed.

  Some family letters of Boston and New York, Houghton, Mifflin & Co., 1911. Blanche Cornish, ed.

Trench, R. C. Calderon's life's a dream. London, John W. Parker & Son, 1856.

Tutin, J. R. A. A concordance to FitzGerald's translation of the rubáiyát of Omar Khayyám. London, Macmillan & Co., 1900.

Walker, Hugh. The literature of the victorian era. Cambridge, University Press, 1921.

Whewell, William. On the principles of English university education. London, John W. Parker & Son, 1837.

  Of a liberal education in general and with special reference to the University of Cambridge. London, John W. Parker & Son, 1850.

Wilson, D. A. Life of Thomas Carlyle. New York, E. P. Dutton & Co., 1923–34. 6 vols.

Young, G. M., ed. Early victorian England. London, Oxford University Press, 1934.

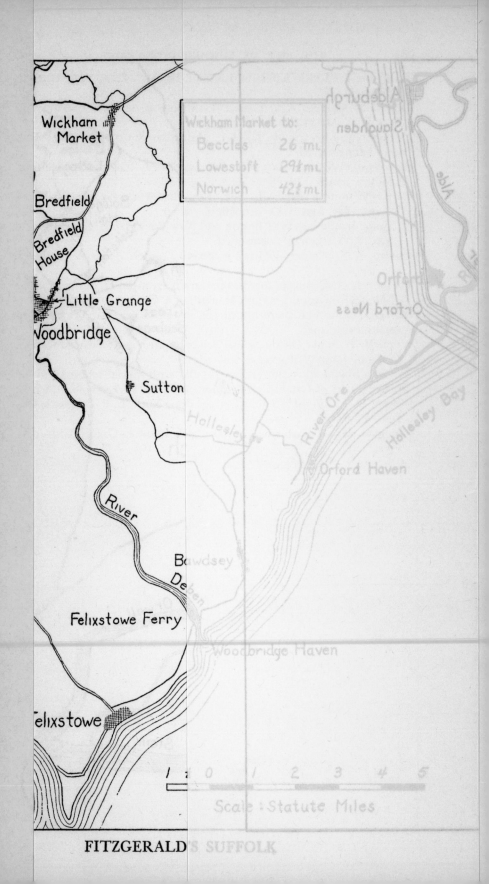

Wickham
Market

Wickham Market to:
Beccles   26 mi.
Lowestoft   29½ mi.
Norwich   42½ mi.

Bredfield

Bredfield
House

Little Grange

Woodbridge

Sutton

River

Bawdsey

Deben

Felixstowe Ferry

Felixstowe

1 0 1 2 3 4 5

Scale: Statute Miles

FITZGERALD'S SUFFOLK

Claydon to:
Bury St. Edmunds 20 mi.
Cambridge 47 mi.
Bedford 75 mi.

Boulge
Cottage

Boulge
Hall

Hasketon

Grundisburgh

Claydon

Great
Bealings

Farlingay Hall

Playford

Bramford

Ipswich

Wherstead Lodge

River

Orwell

River Stour

Index

291; stimulates EFG to Spanish reading and translation, 141–142, 145, 163, 165, 282–283, 283–284, 340; from Bramford to Oxford, 142–144; review of *Euphranor*, 158 n.; appointment to Calcutta, 174, 189–190; at Ipswich with EFG, 190, 204; and EFG's marriage, 197–198, 199–200; repays loan from EFG, 242; return from India, and EFG's shyness, 263–264; appointment to chair of Sanskrit at Cambridge, with EFG's help, 264–266; and EFG's translation of *Agamemnon*, 323, 327

Cowell, Mrs. Edward Byles (Elizabeth Charlesworth), 47, 248, 263, 316; EFG's romantic attachment to, 136–141, 174, 197–198, 199–200, 205, 264; marries Edward Cowell, 138–139; controversy with EFG over Cowell's going to Oxford, 142–144; friend of Mrs. Tennyson, 182; departure for Calcutta, 189–190; letter to, from EFG, on Cowell's appointment to Cambridge, 265–266

Cowper, William, 16, 69
Crabbe, Caroline, 138 n.
Crabbe, George, the poet, 64 n., 233, 289, 321, 339–340; *Tales of the Hall*, edited by EFG, 257, 330–332
Crabbe, George, vicar of Bredfield, 64, 102, 104–106, 154, 186, 188, 202, 233, 234, 264
Crabbe, George, Jr. ("Young Crabbe"), rector of Merton, 64, 88, 152 n., 189, 193 n., 194, 202, 248, 309, 336, 342, 344
Criterion, yacht, 244
Cromwell, Oliver, 63. See also Naseby, battlefield of
Crowfoot, William, 341–342
Crystal Palace, 234

DAMPIER, WILLIAM, *Voyages*, 332
Dante, 249
Darwin, Charles, 24–25
Deben, river, 1, 134, 238, 240, 242, 243, 245, 299, 304, 306
Delavigne, Casimir, 354
De Quincey, Thomas, 306
de Soyres, Andalusia FitzGerald, sister of EFG, 8, 44, 185, 338, 346
de Soyres, Julian, 302
de Soyres, Leopold, 301–302
De Vere, Aubrey, 117, 119
De Ville, phrenologist, 45
Dickens, Charles, 111, 148, 309
Diderot, Denis, 69

Digby, Kenelm, 156, 157
Disraeli, Benjamin, *Lothair*, 306
D'Israeli, Isaac, *Mejnoun and Leila*, 171, 171 n.
Don Quixote, 170, 321
Donne, William Bodham, 65, 166 n., 182, 184, 199, 330; at Bury St. Edmunds, 16–17, 19, 142; EFG's regard for, 17, 185, 314, 338; at Cambridge, 20, 26, 27; his comments on EFG, 44, 89, 91, 95–96, 101, 189, 191, 200, 201, 295; his visits to EFG, 91, 238, 248, 305; EFG's visits to Mattishall, 92, 96, 100; opposes Cowell's going to Oxford, 142–144; and EFG's Calderon translation, 163; Examiner of Plays, 163 n.; librarian of London Library, 185; visits from EFG in London, 185, 233, 306, 318, 337; and the *Rubáiyát*, 207, 210, 291, 341; his death, 338
Dove, William, builder, 262, 263, 294
Dryden, John, 332, 340
Duncan, Francis, 30, 37, 111
Dunwich, Suffolk, 305, 336

"E.–F.," *Translations into Verse . . .*, 354–356
East Anglian, The, 289, 290
Edgeworth, Francis Beaufort, 31, 99, 122
Edgeworth, Maria, 99–100
Edinburgh, 243, 317
Edwards, Mr. and Mrs. Edwin, 308–309, 336, 337
"Effigy," EFG signature, 290
Eliot, George, 258
Emerson, Ralph Waldo, 312
Etty, William, 252
Euphranor, A Dialogue on Youth, by EFG, 20, 63, 230, 339, 340; 1st ed. (1851), 154–159; 2d ed. (1855), 159, 173; 3d ed. (1882), 335

FARLINGAY, SUFFOLK, 185, 186–188, 234, 235, 239, 316
Farringford, Isle of Wight, Tennyson's home, 185–186, 307, 319, 320
Fielding, Henry, 257
Fields, James T., 309
Firdusí, Abul Kasím Mansur, 172
FitzGerald, Andalusia. See de Soyres, Andalusia FitzGerald
Fitzgerald, Lord Edward, 71, 71 n.
FitzGerald, Edward: birth, 1; name at birth, Edward Purcell, 2; parentage and family background, 2–8, 346; early years at Bredfield, 8–10; list of broth-